ANCIENT OLIVE PRESSES AND OIL PRODUCTION

British Institute for Libyan and Northern African Studies Open Access Monograph 3

ANCIENT OLIVE PRESSES AND OIL PRODUCTION

IN CYRENAICA (NORTH-EAST LIBYA)

Ahmed M. A. Buzaian

BILNAS
BRITISH INSTITUTE FOR LIBYAN
& NORTHERN AFRICAN STUDIES

British Institute for Libyan and Northern African Studies Open Access Monograph 3

Published in 2022 by
The British Institute for Libyan and Northern African Studies
c/o The British Academy
10–11 Carlton House Terrace
London SW1Y 5AH
www.bilnas.org

ISBN: 978-1-915808-00-4

Cover and interior design by Chris Bell, cbdesign

TABLE OF CONTENTS

These Appendices are available as a pdf on the British Institute for Libyan and Northern African Studies website, with the Open Access version of the book.
References to figures in the Appendices are referred to as AI or AII followed by the figure number.

LIST OF TABLES

Chapter 6

Chapter 7

Chapter 8

LIST OF FIGURES

Chapter 4

Chapter 5

Chapter 6

ACKNOWLEDGMENTS

The research for this book was undertaken as part of a PhD thesis at University of Leicester, completed in 2019. I wish to acknowledge and express my wholehearted gratitude for the immeasurable support and encouragement shown to me by my PhD supervisor, Prof. David Mattingly. His insight, subtle guidance, feedback and patience, along with his genuine and enthusiastic engagement in academic research, has been a continual inspiration to me.

I am grateful to the British Institute for Libyan and Northern African Studies for supporting the publication of this book. A special thanks goes to the reviewers that took part in this work, Andrew Wilson and Martin Sterry, who, having read the entire text, added numerous valuable and helpful comments. Thanks also to Jean-Pierre Brun for additional helpful information.

I would also like to express my deep appreciation to the following: Mohammed al-Twati and Moammer Ghoma. Without their tireless assistance the fieldwork would not have been completed. I thank Fath-Allah Khalifa, Abdulslam al-Kwash, Fraj Abdulkarim, Dr Ahmad Emrage, Prof. Hwaidi el-Rrisshi, Ibrahim al-Mismari and Salem Bujnnat for their assistance and invaluable guidance during fieldwork. Special thanks must go to the late Abdulgader al-Mzeni, the former controller of Shahat who, with his wide knowledge on Cyrenaican sites in the Gebel Akhdar, was the perfect guide during fieldwork. I also thank Dr Mohamed Abdrbba for providing me with photos and information on a recent discovery of an olive press at Shahat.

Thanks are also due to Dr Matthew Hobson for offering valuable assistance in QGIS, and to Prof. Fuaad Bentaher and Abdullah al-Rhebi for their invaluable support in general. Special thanks must indeed be extended to the Libyan Department of Antiquities, through its two Offices at Benghazi and Shahat, for allowing me the unique opportunity to conduct all my fieldwork.

I would very much like to thank Dr Paul Bennett, to whom I owe a great debt of gratitude beyond measure for being a constant source of encouragement and support, together with Nicholas Brown for his ad hoc linguistic editing support and neighbourly friendship. I would further like to thank Drs Julia Nikolaus, Nichole Sheldrick, Louise Rayne and Victoria Leitch for their academic and technical support.

This acknowledgement could never be complete if I omitted to express my sincere gratitude to my entire family – my wife Muna Abdelhamed and my sons Mustafa, Kamal and Zakaria – for their unconditional love, patience and understanding and for all the sacrifices they have tirelessly made in supporting me throughout my studies.

My parents are among those departed, their absence significantly impacted my life and served as the main incentive that encouraged me to continue to completion this study. I therefore dedicate this work to their souls and to the remembrance of all that they did for me while they were on this earth.

PART ONE

chapter one

INTRODUCTION

Previous works on ancient olive oil and wine production in the ancient Mediterranean (Frankel 1999; Brun 2003b, 2004) and North Africa (Mattingly 1985; 1988a-d; 1993; 1994; 1995; 2009; Mattingly and Hitchner 1993) have broadened our knowledge on specifications, techniques and scale of production of Roman presses. These works discuss how this significantly contributed to the success of the Roman economy and long-distance trade. They also provided important information for larger debates about the overall Roman economy and the most dynamic exporting areas in the ancient Mediterranean. The scale of production and the export of olive oil in the Mediterranean was accompanied by technological developments and regionalised technologies.

Cyrenaica is a critical zone linking the Eastern Mediterranean to the Western Mediterranean and North Africa to the Greek world. An important point of debate concerns the extent to which Cyrenaican data can contribute to our understanding of Mediterranean trade networks and the role it played within these wider trade patterns.

Although a great deal of information is now available on ancient olive oil production in North Africa, Cyrenaican press technology is poorly represented in the literature and has not been fully integrated into our understanding of the pressing technologies employed in Roman Africa. This book examines ancient olive oil production in Cyrenaica during the mid- to late Roman periods. It investigates, for the first time, the archaeological evidence for olive oil production in Cyrenaica in terms of typology, technology and capacity, with an attempt to establish the importance of the industry to the regions economy. The study examines archaeological evidence that was collected during recent fieldwork, with data gathered from some 104 rural sites across a wide geographical area covering about 30,000 km^2. A further important aim of the research was the attempt to identify typology and characteristics of Cyrenaican pressing elements, and to establish a site typology. In addition, the scale of production is assessed with reference to local production of amphorae, to address the role Cyrenaican olive oil production played in the economy of North Africa and the Mediterranean.

This book is divided into two parts, with Part I organised into nine chapters. Chapter 1 provides a brief geographical and historical background of the research case study (Cyrenaica). The chapter additionally reviews the most relevant previous studies of the Roman olive oil/wine production in Cyrenaica, starting from early travellers to the most recent studies on the subject. Chapter 2 starts with the main research issues and introduces the research questions and the methods employed in my archaeological field survey. Chapters 3 and 4 investigate the press element typology and distribution patterns of milling and pressing equipment in Cyrenaica. Chapter 5 contains information about characteristics of milling and pressing equipment in Cyrenaica. Chapter 6 outlines the typology of the archaeological sites in Cyrenaica and their distributional patterns. Chapter 7 investigates oil production and provides an estimation of the region's population for assessing the scale of demand for olive oil within Cyrenaica. This examination provides the basis for comparison of Cyrenaician oil production with Tripolitania and other Mediterranean regions. Chapter 8 deals with the evidence of local amphora production (containers for transporting olive oil) and long-distance trade. This chapter identifies the already known local fabrics and types of Cyrenaican amphorae and their intra- and interregional distributions, along with the imported transport vessels. Finally, Chapter 9 presents the most important results with a number of suggestions for further research into the rural economy and settlement in Cyrenaica.

Part II of this book is organised into two appendices: Appendix I contains additional supplementary tables on the different types and measurements of pressing elements gathered during the survey and collected during the field survey. Appendix II presents a gazetteer of the sites visited during my survey. These are available as a pdf on the BILNAS (formerly Society for Libyan Studies) website, with the Open Access version of the book. Geographical reference to each site and a description of visible remains within it are given, illustrated with figures and plans.

1.1 General Setting

1.1.1 Location

The ancient region of Cyrenaica is located in the north-east region of modern Libya (Figure 1.1). A grasp of the present morphology of the study area is essential to understanding and reconstructing the region's ancient landscape. It is important to first consider the climate geography and geology of the area.

1.1.2 Climate

The majority of the Mediterranean, including Cyrenaica, has relatively mild winters and very warm summers. The Libyan climate in general is dominated by the hot arid Sahara, but it is moderated along the coast where it is damper and cooler. The Sahara plays an important role in the Cyrenaican climate and in Libya in general. Its influence is stronger in summer and the desert climate reaches along the coast to the southern fringes of the Gulf of Syrtes. The region suffers from periodic drought, which often recurs every four or five years (Fisher 1952: 148). Annual rainfall in Tripolitania to the north-west is also extremely erratic in its distribution and it has been shown that the Gebel Tarhuna is affected by drought in two out of every seven years. In the pre-desert zone beyond, this pattern of variation is even more serious and droughts of four to seven years have been recorded (Brehony 1960: 60–9).

Along the coast, the Mediterranean climate is characterised by a cool, rainy winter season and a hot, dry summer. The warmest months are July and August and the temperatures in Benghazi (ancient Berenice) range between 21.4°C and 32.3°C while in Shahat they can vary from 19.5° to 29.9°. The coolest months are January and February and in the winter months temperatures in Benghazi range from 18.3°C to 9.1°C, while those in Shahat (ancient Cyrene) range from 13.8°C to 7.8°C (Figure 1.2). The weather is cooler in the highlands of the Gebel Akhdar than in the lowland areas.

Most rain falls during the winter months between October and March. Shahat has an average January rainfall of 55 mm, while Benghazi receives an average of 48 mm (Figure 1.3) with an average annual precipitation of 400 to 650 mm and less than 400 mm, respectively (Figure 1.4). There is also the possibility of snowfall at high elevations (Fantoli 1952; Laronde 1987: 257; Raju 1980)[1]. The same figures apply to the area stretching from Cyrene to Messa. Annual rainfall is relatively high with an average of 541.5 mm at al-Gubba and Ain Mara, to 501 mm at Slonta, Maraua, Taknis and al-Merj. Farther inland annual precipitation declines and its variability increases. The dry climate is exacerbated by the ghibli, a hot, arid wind that blows from the south over the entire country several times a year. The wind carries large quantities of sand and dust and can seriously affect crops.

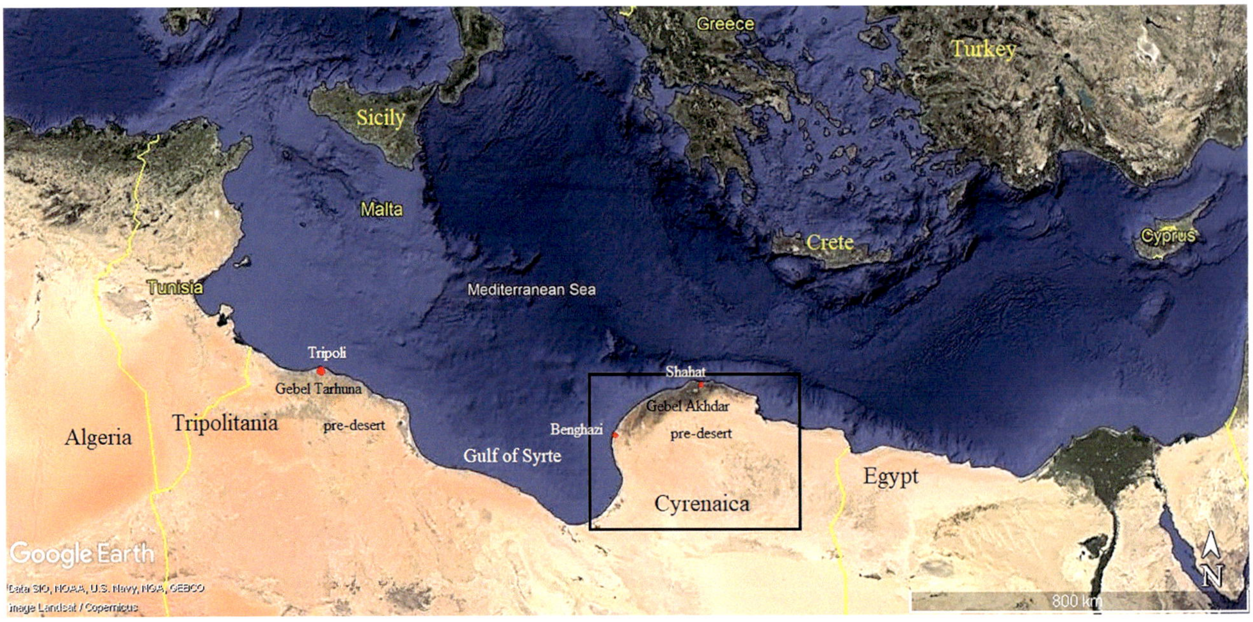

Figure 1.1: Location map of Cyrenaica *(Source: Google Earth, Data SIO, NOAA, US Navy, NGA, GEBCO, Landsat/Copernicus © 2021).*

[1] Some 28 meteorological stations cover the area from Suluq in the west to Shahat in the east. Some of these have records going back to 1915. Regular records are only available from 1954.

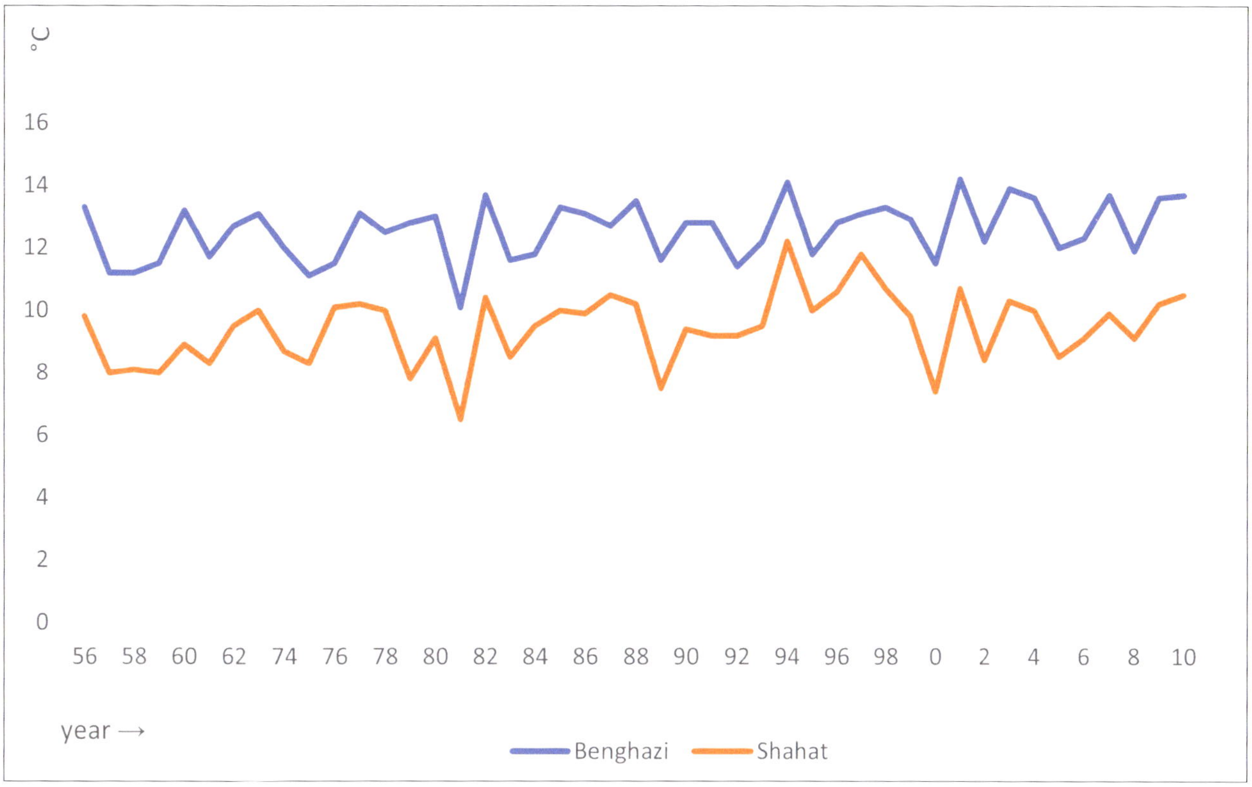

Figure 1.2: Benghazi and Shahat: average January temperatures, 1956–2010
(Source: Benina and Shahat Meteorological Station).

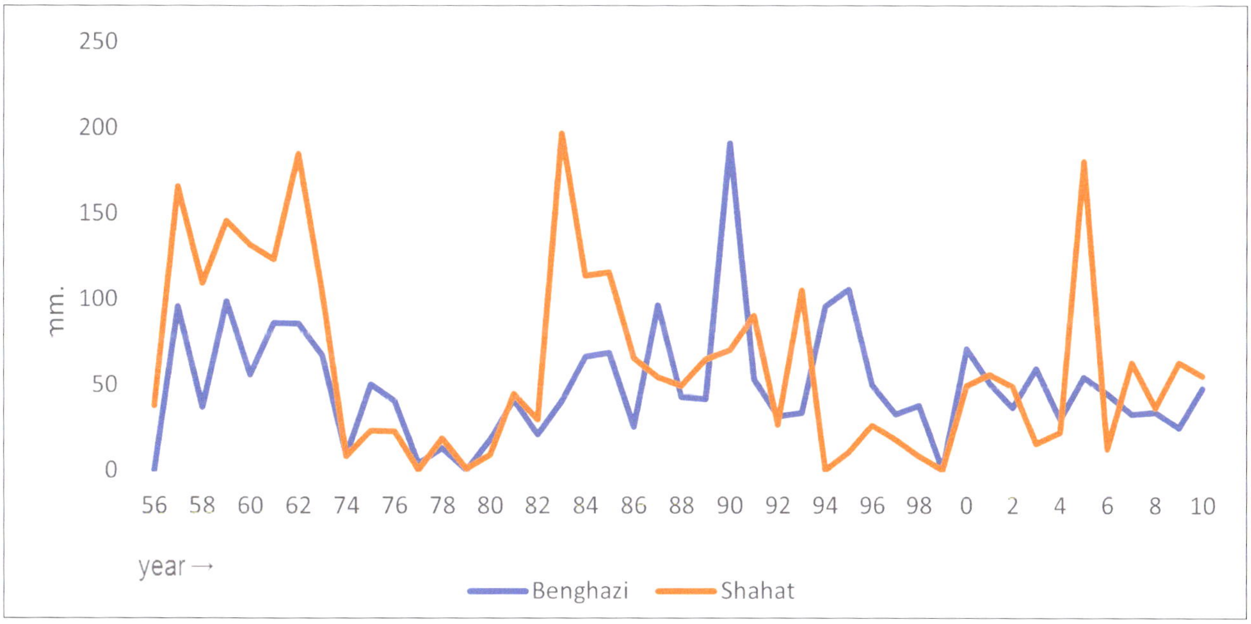

Figure 1.3: Benghazi and Shahat precipitation in January, 1956–2010
(Source: Benina and Shahat Meteorological Station).

The low rainfall is reflected in the absence of permanent rivers or streams and most of the perennial lakes are brackish or salty. The main water source instead comes from numerous springs of fresh water which go back to the Pleistocene Age (Little 1954). The bottoms of the Cyrene and Faidia formations have an important impermeable marl stratum which traps ground water. Once these layers emerge at the surface, subsurface water is forced off laterally in the form of springs. There are over 300 springs in the north-eastern part of the Gebel Akhdar, which mostly occur along the scarp faces in different geological zones. As Bukechiem (1993) writes it is clear that the most plentiful springs are located between al-Beida in the west and Derna in the east and that they

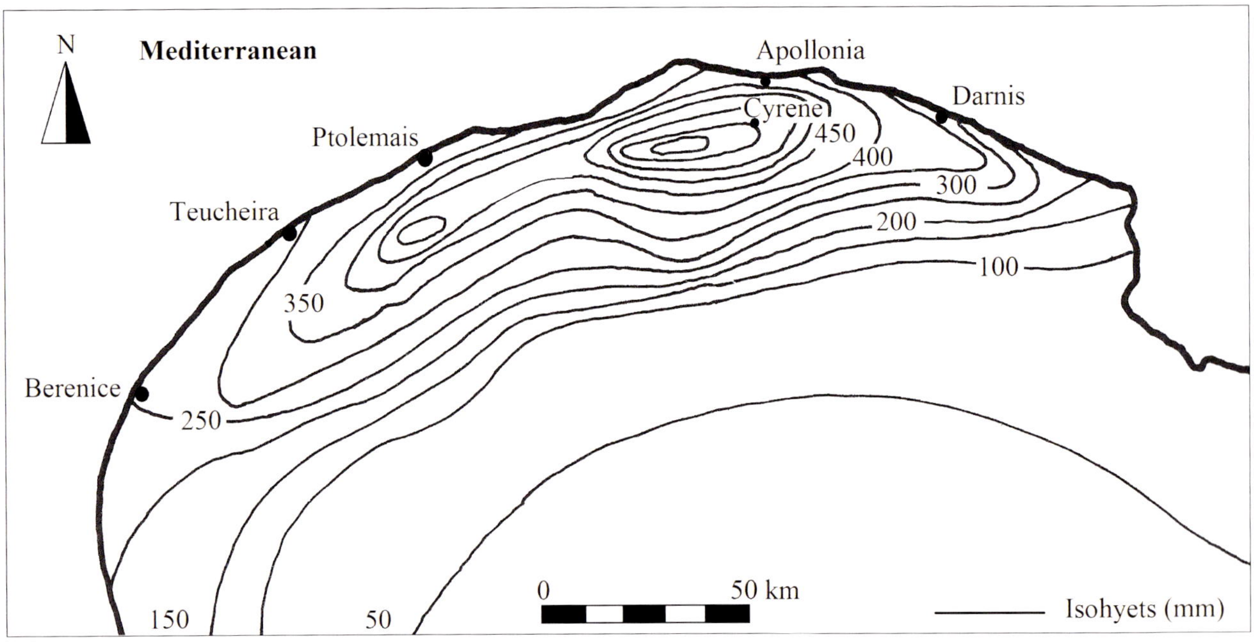

Figure 1.4: Rainfall Isohyets in Cyrenaica (in mm).

have an output in the winter months of over 10 litres per second (1993: Table 11). These springs along with the rainfall were main factors influencing the primary Greek settlements around Cyrenaica and the more habitable areas (Applebaum 1979: 80).

Spring	Rate of flow 1/sec.
Ayn Dabussiah	200
Ayn Marrah	40–80
Ayn Stewah (Ras-al-Hilal)	15
Ayn Kersah	30
Ayn Bumansur (Derna)	195–230
Ayn Blanaj (al-Beida)	10

Table 1.1: North-east Gebel Akhdar springs with a flow of more than 10 litres/second *(Bukeshiem 1993).*

1.1.3 Geology and morphology

Cyrenaican geology consists of outcroppings of rock, all sedimentary in origin and mainly marine limestone in nature. The oldest beds dated to the Upper Cretaceous Age and occupied the crest of the Gebel and part of the north coast. Much larger areas are covered by Eocene and Oligocene beds and restrained in and around the Gebel. Rocks from the Miocene Age are the most widespread and covered the greater part of the region, with a very limited number of Pleistocene beds (McBurney and Hey 1955: 10).

The morphology consists of three main features: a coastal plain, a high limestone plateau named the Gebel Akhdar (Green Mountain, so called because of its leafy cover of pine, juniper, cypress and wild olives) and a further high plateau farther inland. From the Gebel, Cyrenaica extends southward across a barren grazing belt that gives way to the Great Sahara.

Part of the coastal plain is known as the 'Plain of Benghazi'. This is roughly triangular in shape with the the north-eastern end near Tocra, where it is only 4 km wide, extending west 120 towards Benghazi by which point it is 25 km wide before widening rapidly and fading out towards the south in the Syrtic desert. Generally speaking the Benghazi plain is almost flat terrain, with a gradual incline to the east where some rugged slopes occur near the scarps of the Gebel Akhdar. Many large isolated marshlands are spread along the coast, including the marshes of Bersis and Bojrar.

There are a number of *karst* phenomena, known as *dolinas* or sink holes, which consist of several large depressions in the limestone floor. A group of small lakes is located just to the east of Benghazi, the largest of which are the lagoons of Bodzerah and Ayen Zaianah. The coastal plain continues east of Ptolemais, but narrows considerably and even disappearing in a few places, particularly in the area from Ras al-Hilal to Latrun near Derna. It rarely exceeds one kilometre in width between Apollonia and Derna. The Gebel Akhdar forms the main geographical feature in Cyrenaica. In extent, it is a limestone plateau about 250 km wide east to west by 80 km long north to south. Generally, the dip-slope is gentle and descends gradually into the interior until it merges with the semi-desert zone. To the west, the Gebel drops abruptly to the shores of the Syrtic Gulf, and to the east, it falls gently toward the Gulf of Bomba and the Marmarica. Its northern parts descend abruptly towards the coast and end by sharp scarps overlooking the coastal plain and the sea.

The northern line of the Gebel Akhdar is marked by long successive terraces, which vary in width and stretch from west to east in line with the Mediterranean Sea. It is possible to distinguish three main terraces separated by escarpments, which vary in height and the degree of their descent.

The first and longest escarpment has an average height of 250-300 m above sea level and increases in height between Apollonia and Ras al-Hilal. The escarpment is intercut by a range of short and deep valleys. The first terrace beyond varies in width and reaches around 20 km at al-Merj basin, which is structurally a giant sinkhole. It then begins to narrow gradually eastward, where it is characterised by a large network of deep valleys cut off from the slopes toward the north.

The second escarpment is a gentle dip-slope and is not as high, with an average height of 120 m away from the first and is intercut by a number of valleys. The second terrace ranges in height from 420 to 600 m and appears in the form of simple low hills separated by a series of valleys.

The third escarpment rises along the slope and is smaller than the two previously mentioned, with an average height of 60 m. It is followed by the third terrace, which comes in the form of elevated ground in the case of Sidi al-Homry, which rises up to 880 m above sea level.

Of the main Cyrenaican cites founded by the Greek settlers, only Cyrene and Barca were located on the plateau. The former was established on the edge of the second escarpment, while the latter was founded in the heart of the first terrace beyond the first escarpment. The other cities, Apollonia, Teucheira, Ptolemais and Euesperides, were located in the coastal plain bordering the Mediterranean as the Greeks preferred to live near to the sea (Applebaum 1979: 2).

1.1.3.1 Soil

Very little research has been devoted to the soil in Cyrenaica. There are different types of soils and they can vary from place to place depending on the source material, as well as climatic factors and biological conditions. Cyrenaican soils can be classified into two main groups:

1. Soils of the sub-humid and sub-arid zones. These are the best agricultural soils and are concentrated in the region of Gebel Akhdar and the coastal strip.
2. Soils of arid zones.

In general, very little of the total area of the country is suitable for agriculture and fertile lands exist in pockets distributed between the Gebel Akhdar and the coastal plain. The alluvial soils of the inland regions are fertile. These were formed by the deposition of sediments carried by water from the northern mountains, which formed fans before being deposited in the wadis.

It is possible to distinguish between different classes of soils. Red soil rich in iron silicate known as Terra Rossa is considered to be one of the most important soils in the region. It is a deep depositional sediment, found mainly in the al-Merj and al-Ftaieh areas east of Derna. Structurally it is of good quality and the use of fertilisers such as nitrogen and organic manures would tend to increase its phosphorus content and thus the soil fertility. There is also a type of reddish-brown dry calcareous soil found in south-western Benghazi, Taknis and Marawa. Shallow limestone soils rich in calcium carbonate and nitrogen but poor in phosphorous are also available at al-Beida, Labraq and al-Gubba (Johnson 1973: 8–10).

The modern agricultural land of the Gebel Akhdar can be divided into several categories in terms of agricultural potential. The first type is considered the richest agricultural resource in Cyrenaica and is estimated at around 16,251 hectares, being used for cultivation of various crops. The next type covers 51,688 hectares and is of lesser quality with abundant trees. The third category is suitable for cereal and occupies approximately 41,291 hectares of clay of medium to shallow depth with notable limestone outcrops. The remaining soils today are generally poor and very thin. They are unsuitable for agricultural activity and cover limestone terraces and sloping terrain that can be exploited for trees (Benkhaial 1995: 549-627).

1.1.4 Cultivation and transhumance

In the last 100 years pastoralism and agriculture have been the two main activities for most people. The staple foods consisted of barley, wheat, olives and grapes, which were grown in northern areas (Applebaum 1979: 82-3, 91). Historically, pastoralism has also been important (Laronde 1984: 5). The majority of the nomadic and semi-nomadic inhabitants sow their fields with barley and wheat during the rainy season in winter. Herds of goats remain throughout the year in the north part of the Gebel and the more rugged parts of the country (Johnson 1973: 27). After the December rains, some herds of goats and sheep will move with their shepherds due south in search of better pasture and, at the same time, camel herds will shift farther south across the inland plateau (Barker 1979: 7). With the beginning of summer and lack of pasture and water, the goat and sheep herds will return to the north and be replaced by camels. Cattle on the other hand seem to have played an insignificant role in the nomadic system. They were never grazed over substantial distances, were often herded in small numbers and were confined to the northern areas of the Gebel (Johnson 1973: 39–66).

With few exceptions, there was no dividing line between arable farming and animal husbandry. During these transhumance movements, nomadic people based in the northern regions planted their fields with crops when the rains came in late September and early October. The staple crop was barley which was mainly grown for local consumption, although surpluses could be sold overseas (Barker 1979: 7). At the beginning of October and during their journey to the south with their herds they would also cultivate a second crop. The second crop would be harvested and the stubble would support the camel herds in the summer. After they return to the north, the first crop would be harvested between April and May (Barker 1979: 7).

Clearly, pastoralism and agriculture are the primary components in the economy of ancient and modern Cyrenaica and a large part of arable agriculture appears to have been used for cereal cropping. Based on the relatively recent historical past it seems that olive cultivation, otherwise, was not a widespread traditional occupation.

1.2 Historical Outline

Before the Greeks, Cyrenaica was occupied by different tribal groups conventionally known as Libyans. Archaeological evidence for these natives is rather ambiguous and there is scarce information on them, which often derives grasped from ancient Egyptian sources that dated back to the Old Kingdom (Carter 1963: 18).

Greek colonisation of Cyrenaica began only in the second half of the seventh century BC. when they first founded the mother city, Cyrene (modern Shahat) in 631 BC on the upper plateau, some 18 km from the coast. Battos I was the first Greek king of the city and his family ruled for eight generations, alternately named Battos and Arkesilaos (Herodotus 4.159-205). With no complete control of the hinterland, four more Greek cities were established along the coast: Teucheira (modern Tocra), the port of Cyrene, Apollonia (modern Susa), Barce (modern Al-Merj) and Euesperides (later Berenice, modern Benghazi). By this time, Cyrenaica grew rich from grain, stockbreeding and silphium and Cyrene became one of the famous intellectual centres of the Greek world.

When the Persians occupied Egypt, the Cyreneans sent a diplomatic mission to the Persian king announcing their subordination to the new rulers. In 440 BC, the Battid monarchy came to an end when Arkesilaos IV was killed in Euesperides. Subsequently, the region suffered from political unrest caused by bitter competition between aristocratic and popular parties and increased risk of attacks by the Libyan tribes. The Republic that followed (440–322 BC) was also characterised by a political schism which eventually enabled the protagonists to set up a mixed constitution (Diodorus 14.34). After Alexander the Great conquered Egypt in 331 BC, Cyrenaica willingly submitted at once to him (Diodorus 17.49.3). Soon after his death the region went to one of his Macedonian generals, Ptolemy, who ruled it with Egypt. The Ptolemies enacted a new constitution (SEG IX, 1–4) to Cyrene which became customarily governed by a king appointed by the Ptolemaic dynasty. However, the region suffered from political unrest and increased risk of attacks by the Libyan tribes until it was finally suppressed by Magas, who had re-established the monarchy again by claiming himself as the new king of Cyrenaica and declaring independence from the Ptolemaic rule. After the death of Magas, Cyrenaica was involved in a civil war that resulted in its return to Ptolemaic control until its last king, Ptolemy Apion, bequeathed it to Rome in 96 BC (SEG IX, 7).

At first, Rome did not show any interest in the region when it became under indirect control of the Roman Senate. The five main cities of the province were collectively known as Pentapolis (Pliny NH 5.5.5) and were united with Crete into a single province sometime in the middle or second half of the first century BC (Chevrollier 2016: 23). Chaos prevailed once again and it was not until the reign of Augustus (27 BC–14 AD) that the region was returned to relative order and prosperity. About a century later, by the reign of Trajan, the region was heavily devastated by the major events of the Jewish Revolt in AD 115–117. The turmoil, which spread across Egypt and extended to Palestine (Fuks 1961: 98–104), had conspicuously shattered Cyrenaica, Cyrene being sacked and resulting in huge loss of life (Romanelli 1943: 115; Applebaum 1979: 269–84). An ambitious program was launched by Hadrian in an attempt to revive the Greek legacy and bring back the region to prosperity (Fraser 1950). A new ill-fated coastal city, Hadrianopolis (named after Hadrian), was established between Berenice and Teucheira and later the region was temporarily called Hexapolis (Goodchild 1967a).

Cyrene had been severely devastated by a localised earthquake in AD 262 (Goodchild 1967a). A few years later the province suffered a serious calamity caused by an invasion from the Marmaric tribesmen, during which Cyrene seems to have been sacked. In AD 268 the prefect Probus defeated these tribes and Cyrene, at this time, was renamed Claudiopolis (SEG IX, 9). In AD 365 the Cyrenaica was affected by a major earth tremor that occurred in the central and eastern Mediterranean regions (Ammianus Marcellinus XXXVI, 10, 15–18; Libanius 'Oratio XVIII, 291–3'). These natural and man-made disasters depopulated the region considerably.

As mentioned above, the province combined with Crete as a single province. This was continued until the reforms of Emperor Diocletian at the end of the third century or at the beginning of the fourth century AD. After that, Cyrenaica was divided it into two provinces. The first is Libya Superior or the Pentapolis with its capital Ptolemais. The second is Libya Inferior, or Sicca, that covered the area between Darnis (modern Derna) and Alexandria, which was at the beginning administrated from Paraetonium (modern Marsa Matruh) and then Darnis (Roques 1987: 74–5).

By the fifth century raids of the native Libyan tribes became more frequent and formidable and was greatly exacerbated by inefficient and corrupt military governors. The correspondences of Syensius, the Bishop of Cyrenaica, depicts a grim picture of the political situation of the region and difficulties at that time.

Early reference to Christianity in Cyrenaica was from the records of the first Bishop of Ammonas of Berenice in AD 260 (Kenrick 2013: 7). Toward the first quarter of the fourth century, we hear of bishops in Teucheira, Ptolemais, Barca and Boreum in the Libya Superior, Antiburgos (modern Tobruk) and Ammonium (modern Siwa) in the Libya Inferior (Goodchild 1981: 22–24).

By the time of Anastasius I (AD 491–518) the provincial capital was relocated from Ptolemais to Apollonia-Sozousa (Pedley 1976: 20–21). This step with a new military command structure (dux Libyae Pentapoleos) was perhaps taken as one of the measures against the successful Vandal conquest of the western half of North Africa (Barthel 2017). Although the Byzantine Empire regained the region in the sixth century AD under the reign of Emperor Justinian, it still suffered from frequent tribal attacks. By the middle of the seventh century AD, the Islamic troops had advanced to Cyrenaica and westwards across the whole of North Africa to put an end to the Byzantine rule.

The following section presents the available information on olive oil and wine production provided by early travellers and previous archaeological works (Figure 1.5).

1.3 The Literary and Archaeological Evidence for the Olive Tree and Oil Press in Cyrenaica

1.3.1 Ancient literature

The richest area of Cyrenaica in terms of soil fertility and high rainfall is located on the second escarpment of Gebel Akhdar, which is where the city of Cyrene is situated. Indeed, the Greeks settled this part of Cyrenaica primarily for agricultural reasons. Olive trees thrive in zones which receive 400–600 mm rainfall per year, but it is possible for olives to grow even in areas where rainfall does not exceed 200 mm per annum (Pansiot and Rebour 1961: 42). The tree can survive temperatures in excess of 40° C, but unless hardy cannot survive temperatures below 7° C (Pansiot and Rebour 1961: 40). Clearly, these growth and development factors make the olive tree suitable for the climate of Cyrenaica.

Theophrastus (*c*.371–287 BC) (HP, IV, 3, 1) was fascinated by the enormous number of olive trees around Cyrene and the region's high levels of production. Diodorus Siculus (*c*.90–30 BC) (*Bibliotheca historica*, III, 50, 1) tells us that the land near Cyrene had a deep fertile soil that provided wheat, vast vineyards, olive groves and natural forests. Pliny (AD 23–79) (*NH.* V.5) included Cyrene within the most fertile part of a tree-rich habitat known as the *arboribus fertilis*. This division of the Cyrenaican landscape in the first century AD is strikingly similar to the current topography of Gebel Akhdar and reflects the region's soil fertility and agricultural potential.

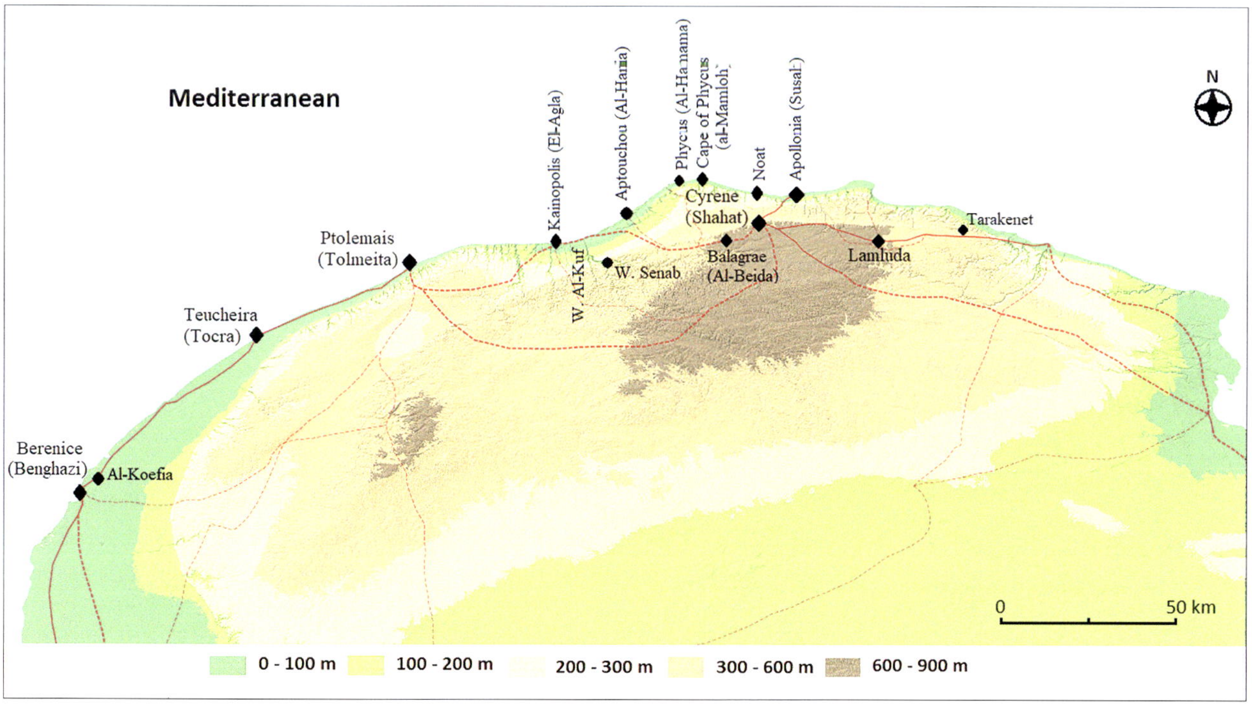

Figure 1.5: The Cyrenaican sites mentioned in early travellers' accounts and previous archaeological works conducted in different parts of the region *(Source: 2012 Ancient World Mapping Center).*

The Roman jurist Scaevola wrote towards the end of the second century AD (Digesta 19.2.61.1) that a cargo of at least 250 tonnes (which included 3,000 *metretae* of oil = at least 200 tons and 8,000 *modii* of grain = *c.*55 tons) was shipped from Cyrenaica province to Aquileia, northern Italy, for a fixed price.

In the early fifth century AD, Synesius, the celebrated bishop of the five cities, wrote letters to his brother and friends containing references to the lives of several contemporary inhabitants of the region. He talked about their crops, livestock and farming, as well as the production of olive oil. He highly praised the local heavy olive oil and its utility as a lighting fuel, in addition to its use as a massage oil for athletes (letter 148). In the same letter, he also mentioned that the region was rich in olive trees and told his brother Euoptius that when he prepares himself to face an enemy, he should use clubs made of hard wood taken from wild olive trees. On another occasion in letter 134, Synesius talks of a cargo sent to a friend with a load of wine. He adds that another shipment, presumably of local origin, containing olive, saffron, ostriches and silphium, had been unable to reach its destination due to tribal raids. Synesius, however, was evidently personally partial to Cypriot wines (letters 146 and 264). Agricultural vandalism in the early fifth century was recorded in considerable detail (letters 125 and 130).

Palynological investigation of deposits in the wadis al-Rejel, Murgus and al-Athrun in the Gebel Akhdar show evidence of ancient forest clearance and cultivation (Hunt *et al.* 2002). A conventional pollen and palynofacies analysis of three samples taken from about 1m below the current wadi floor indicated the presence of human activity in the landscape in the form of olive and cereal cultivation, as well as land reclamation and animal grazing. The samples are no older than the Archaic period, which marked the transition from semi-nomadic pastoralism to agricultural urbanism in Cyrenaica. It is likely that the Cyrenaican landscape was affected by the extensive and intensive farming operations which began in the early first century AD as a result of growing demand for agricultural products in imperial Rome, particularly olive oil. This proposed date corresponds somewhat with the ubiquitous olive oil and wine presses distributed across the region. However, without wider excavation and accompanying systematic soil sampling, especially in the rural sites, one can hardly say more.

1.3.2 Early European exploration

When Cyrenaica was annexed by the Ottoman Empire in 1638, travel in the region became safer. Throughout the eighteenth century, European travellers entered the country not only as tourists but also to investigate archaeological sites. Most of these travellers were not trained scholars, but were rather treasure hunters interested in retrieving artefacts for a growing number of European collectors and museums. They nonetheless produced invaluable information regarding the condition of the ancient sites they visited.

Ever since the Banu Hilal and Banu Sulaym invaded North Africa in the mid-eleventh century, a shroud of mystery has been cast over the area west of the Nile. Despite its proximity to Egypt, Cyrenaica was apparently unable to escape Maghrebi influence. The narratives by the Muslim geographer Al Idrisi (1099-1165) on Cyrenaica have no archaeological or antiquarian interest. The year 1706 marked the journey of Lemaire, the region's first European explorer and the French consul in Tripoli, who visited a number of ancient sites in country's inhospitable region. In 1730 another attempt was made by the French surgeon Granger, who was followed by the British traveller Bruce in 1766. Both of these visitors, like their predecessors, displayed great concern for the ancient cities but paid little attention to the rural sites and the surrounding landscape.

The Italian physician Paolo della Cella crossed Cyrenaica in 1817 as a medical officer accompanying a punitive military campaign sent from Tripoli. He was struck by the fertility of the land and the number of wild olive trees which throve throughout the country. Della Cella remarked that the local inhabitants used no sauce other than butter, did not understand the significance of the tree or its fruits and made no oil (Della Cella 1822: 118).

The British traveller James Hamilton pushed inland in 1852 as far east as the port of Derna before returning to Benghazi. During his passage in the area between Wadi al-Kuf and Balagrae (modern al-Beida), he found groves of domesticated olive trees almost everywhere. However, these trees were neglected and their fruits used only to feed sheep and cattle. He believed that olive trees had played an important economic role in antiquity and that the local people could potentially make great profits from their cultivation (Hamilton 1856: 80). In al-Merj, Hamilton reported that there were many ambitious government-funded development schemes. Among these new constructions was an olive oil press project, as the governor planned to benefit from the abundant olive trees found across the region. Although he recorded a useful account his travels, Hamilton misinterpreted the round flat stones hollowed on one side with a square hole in the centre, which were found in great numbers at Lamluda, as the cap stones of cisterns (Hamilton 1856: 106–7). As we shall see later (section 6.3.3.1), this was, in fact, important evidence for ancient olive oil and wine installations.

In 1881 the Società di Esplorazione Commerciale e Scientifica di Milano organised two exploratory expeditions to Cyrenaica. The first was conducted by Manfredo Camperio, who visited the region to assess its economic, commercial and agricultural potential. He reported that the Ottoman census in Derna and its environs contained upwards of 111,000 olive trees (Camperio 1881: 70). Giuseppe Haimann (1882) led the second scientific and cultural mission, which estimated that there were 200,000 wild olive trees between Benghazi and Derna. A concurrent journey led by Giacomo De Martino (1912: 26) found a 'spectacular' number of olive trees growing on the upper plateau in al-Guba and around Ain Mara.

Less than two decades later Gregory led an expedition to explore Cyrenaica as the head of an ITO scientific mission assessing the area for possible Jewish colonisation. He reported the presence of many plants, trees and shrubs. Among the trees were cedars, cypresses, palms, lentisks (*Pistacia leatiscus*), carobs (*Ceratonia siliqua*), apples, figs, pomegranates and oranges. He mentioned the presence of large numbers of olive trees and noticed a lack of commercial production (Leake 2011: 34, 125–7).

Enrico Corradini visited Cyrenaica in 1911 and was particularly impressed by the number of wild olive trees growing almost continuously along the road from Cyrene to al-Merj and which were almost everywhere in the region's forests and valleys (Wright 2005: 233–4). Corradini saw the immense agricultural potential of this resource and believed that the olive had become naturalised in the region. He considered it to be a favoured and prolific tree.

The narratives of nineteenth and early twentieth century travellers make it clear that olive trees were mainly grown along the greater part of the coastal plain from Ghemines to Derna and from the first escarpment of the Gebel Akdar to the fringe of al-Faidia, some 13 km south of Shahat.

It has been aptly pointed out by both ancient and modern writers that the lands of Cyrenaica were of great agricultural potential. Silphium, the legendary plant, cereals and many other agricultural products thrived in the region and much of them found their way in external markets, but time has shown that this situation of plenty could not be sustained for a long period. After the Islamic conquest of Cyrenaica in the mid seventh century AD, the population seems to have had less interest in olive cult and the production of olive oil and eventually shifted to stock-breeding and pastoralism. This led to gradual abandonment of the intensive land exploitation and consequently urban and rural centres went into decline. Life, however, continued though in a slow pace at least until the arrival of the Banu Hilali in AD 1046, which marks the decisive move to exclusively nomadic life (Goodchild 1967b; 1976: 226; Laronde 1987: 260). It was not an abandonment of crops but a disappearance of the sedentary lifestyle. This may be seen as an oversimplified and straightforward explanation but future fieldwork and excavation, of course, are desperately needed. At a relatively recent date a similar picture had been depicted when the Italian farmers fled from Cyrenaica in 1943. The Arabs returned and took their previously confiscated lands. The British Military Administration failed to revive the agricultural potential of the Gebel Akhdar and the locals were even reluctant to cultivate the land and in fact ignored the already planted fruit trees and pitched their tents in the shade of the farmhouses (Foot 1964: 82).

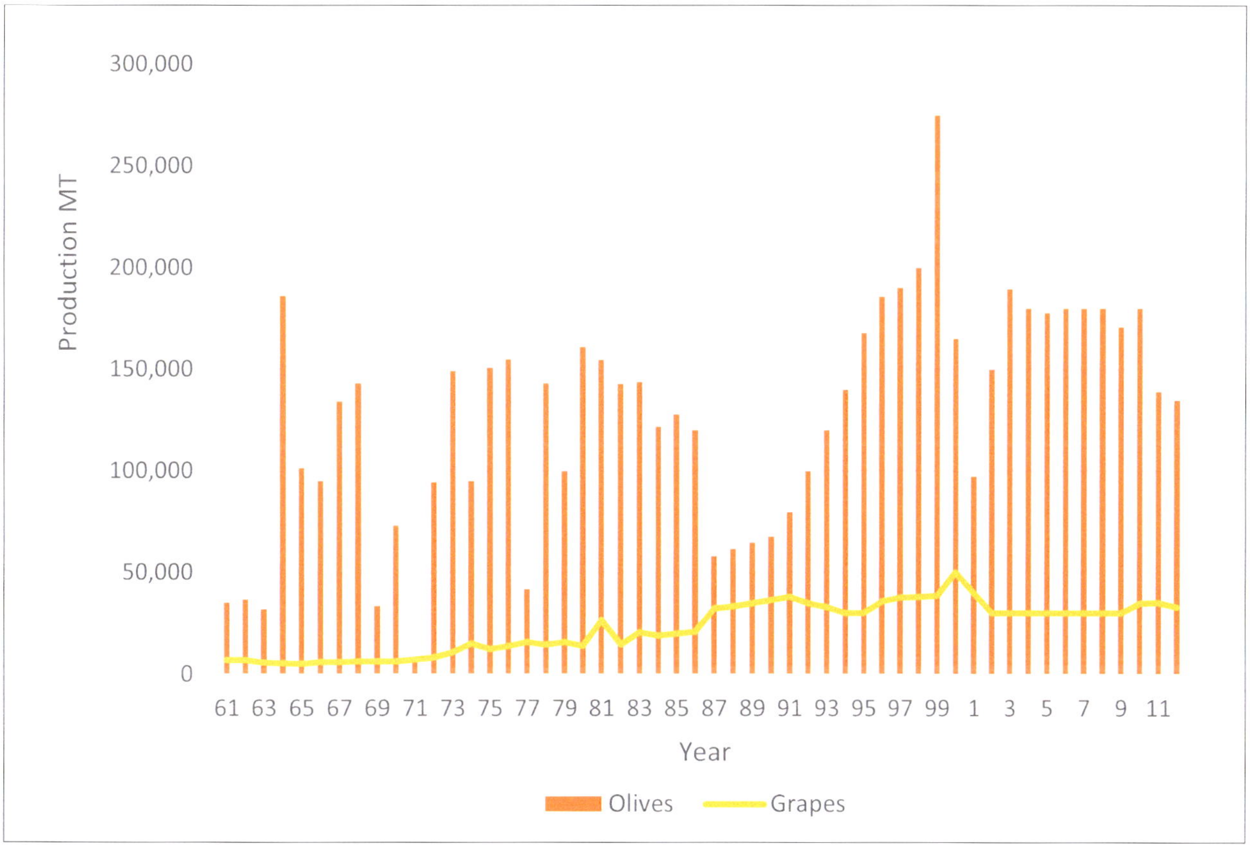

Figure 1.6: Olives and grapes production in Libya from 1961 to 2011 in metric tonnes *(FAOSTAT data)*.

When Libya was granted independence in 1951, agriculture and livestock-breading were the two main activities that employed most of the local working population. In 1958 agriculture absorbed 72% of the labour force (McLachlan 1982: 14). At the same year, oil was discovered in Libya (Hallett 2002: 20) and ever since then the Libyan economy has become heavily reliant on the export of hydrocarbons, now the major contributor to the national income at 93% of the total revenues (Edwik 2007: 12).

In 2002 these trees produced about 150,000 metric tons of olives. Figure 1.6 shows the average annual olive oil and grape production from 1961 to 2012. Obviously, grapes have had only a modest production while the output of olives has oscillated, generally due to the combination of the biannual bearing nature of the tree and the degree of fluctuation in annual rainfall that normally occurs, i.e. one good year in two to five years. The year 2012 indicates there being a marked reduction, perhaps due to the increasing number of unproductive trees and unstable security. In addition, olives may be attributable to a lack of investment in the agricultural sector, both in arboriculture and dryland farming.

According to a study published by the FAO in 1969, the grape was the most cultivated tree in the Gebel Akhdar, particularly in the territory of Messa and al-Beida which enjoys more than 600 mm of rainfall. Unsurprisingly, it is the same geographical area that was heavily populated and farmed in ancient times. The report added that the most important horticulture were almond and olive trees (1969a: 53). After independence in 1951, as a part of tree cultivation initiative, the Ministry of Agriculture supplied the private farmers with young olive trees free of charge. However, due to inadequate maintenance and irrigation their productivity was negligible. The farmers were in fact reluctant to harvest the olive trees even for their home consumption. For example, the Government from 1963 to 1965 was forced to shut down the olive presses in Messa because of shortage of supply (General Report 1969a: 167). This also indicates that there were no presses owned by the private sector. A mixed agricultural regime was adopted and because of deficiency soil moisture companion planting grapes and olive together has proved to be an unsuccessful practice (1969b: 42).

1.3.3 Iconographic and epigraphic evidence

Pharaonic Egyptian documents may provide us with the oldest archaeological evidence for olive trees in Cyrenaica. The Libyan or *Teheno* stele is a relief sculpture found in Abydos, Egypt, which bears three scenes depicting the booty taken from a defeated tribe by the Egyptians and included possible depictions of olive trees (Gardiner 1972: 394). If the identification is correct, this is the first evidence we have which demonstrates the value of the tree to the region.

Epigraphical evidence from the late Classical and early Hellenistic periods indicates that there were a number of notable agricultural products. The most important evidence comes from the stelai of the *Demiourgoi*, which were part of a series initiated in the fifth century BC and that continued until the second century BC (Applebaum 1979: 33; Laronde 1987: 325). These inscriptions listed Cyrenaican crops and provided approved prices and weights for each commodity.

The revenue generated by many estates and groves in Cyrene was dedicated to the maintenance of several cults (Applebaum 1979: 87–8). An inscription dating from the first century BC (SEG IX, 4) tells us that Barkaios son of Theochrestos bequeathed his olive grove and its oil to the gymnasium of Cyrene (SEG IX, 4, 43–6). This inscription implies the value of the gift and that these trees were fruitful and produced a good harvest. At the same time, Claudia Venusta, whose wealth was probably derived from agriculture, funded several religious construction works in Cyrene (SEG IX, 163–164).

An inscription, probably from the mid-fourth century AD, records that Demetria, daughter of Gaios and her son Theodoulo died, possibly in an earthquake, and were buried by their family in a substantial tomb found in the northern necropolis of Cyrene:

> (Chi-Rho)) Διμιτρία θυγάτηρ
> Γάϊου τοῦ ὠνηcαμένου
> τὸ μνημῖο<ν> το̣ῦτο ἔνθαδε κῖτε
> μετὰ τοῦ υἱοῦ αὐτῆc Θεω-
> δούλου· οὗτοι ἐτελεύτηcαν
> ἐπὶ [ἀ]γροῦ Μυροπ̣ῶλα cιcμοῦ
> γενομένου· τέθικαν αὐτὸc
> Κάλλιππος ὁ {υ} ἀνὴρ αὐτῆc κὲ
> {κὲ} υἱὸ̣c̣ αὐτοῦ Γάϊοc κὲ γαμ-
> βρεὸ̣́[c] αὐτοῦ Πο̣λύβουλοc
> Κ(ύρι)ε μνηcθήτω τὸν ἐντὸ[c] cπελέ-
> ου τούτου.
>
> Translation:
> Dimitria daughter of Gaius, who bought the tombs, lies here with her son Theodoulos; they died on the farme Myropylas, in an earthquake. Kallippos himself, her husband buried them and his son Gaius and his brother-in-law Polyboulos, Lord, remember those within this cave.
>
> Reynolds, Ward-Perkins and Goodchild, 2003

This inscription is somewhat curious as it indicates the possibility that the victims were members of a farm named Μυροπ̣ῶλα, which onomastic lexicons suggest that it was not used as a personal name. Therefore, the farm belonged to an *unguentarius*, a perfumer or dealer in unguents and acquired the name Myropylas which could easily have also been chosen as a result of him growing unguent-bearing plants (Bacchielli *et al.* 1992:

22). The inscription may also hint at the possibility that there had been a scent-sellers' quarter, or market, within the city. The region was renowned for its roses and *unguentum rosaceum* (Pliny NH 21. 10.19). Therefore, it is difficult to resist the idea that there were workshops around Cyrene for producing very high quality olive oil or unguents, tasks for which wedge or direct screw presses would have been better suited (Mattingly 1990; 1996). Fine olive oil was used as a key base for ancient perfume. The presses of these types were probably usually completely fabricated of wood and therefore rarely survive within the archaeological record.

1.3.4 Archaeological evidence of presses and mills

The first secure archaeological evidence of ancient olive oil production was found in al-Koefia area, 13 km north-east of Benghazi and about 2 km south of the Central Prison of al-Koefia. The site was reported by Narducci (1934: 84) and is consisting of two separate buildings which were less than 40 m apart (Figures AII.48–50). The west building was rectangular in shape, consisting of seven rooms and housing four mill mortars. The east building was also rectangular but smaller in size with five rooms of different dimensions and seems to form an ancillary unit to the western building. At about 200 m to the east are the remains of an ancient settlement situated in a modern cemetery. It now is overgrown with vegetation and largely obliterated by modern graves.

The two landmark studies by Brun in 2003a and 2004 on the production of olive oil and wine in the ancient Mediterranean, from prehistory down through the Late Roman period, provide an indispensable background to this subject. In his first work Brun investigated the early primitive attempts of prehistoric societies to produce these two valuable liquids, which were among the most important commodities in the ancient world market. With the dawn of history, more advanced techniques began to emerge as a response to the increasing alimentary demand for these goods. It is unsurprising to see Cyrenaica included in the chapter devoted to Greece (Chapter III, 73–90). Cyrene was founded by the Greeks around 631 BC and soon became the core of the cultural, economic and political life of the region, which was known as Cyrenaica. Consequently, as Fitzgerald (1926: 16) inferred from Synesius' letters, the Cyrenaican people still regarded themselves as Greeks, despite the Roman domination of the region for over five centuries.

In a succinct section on Cyrenaica, Brun (2003a: 156–7) summarises the sparse textual and archaeological data, the latter compounded by the absence of related excavations and field survey studies. Archaeological data on olive oil, wine and perfume production in Cyrenaica during the Greek and Hellenistic periods remain dubious, despite the relatively vivid literary narratives that evidently held the agricultural potential of the region in high esteem (Aristotle, Hist. Anim. V, 30; Diodorus III, 50, 1; IV, 17, 4; Herodotus IV, 199; Scylax Periplus, 108, 109). This eerie silence from the early archaeological evidence is largely the influence of the colonial archaeology in Libya, when Italy tried to revive the glory of ancient Rome and reconstructed the ancient cities in an idealised Roman model (Munzi 2012: 81). Otherwise, Brun (2004: 86–9) gives a wider perspective on the region during the Roman period. He provides a full description of the industrial installations found in the Wadi Senab area, as well as those discovered at the site of Siret Qasrin el-Giamel in the centre of the city of al-Beida. Surprisingly, he did not mention the vats discovered in Berenice (Lloyd 1977: 214), Teucheira (Buzaian 2000: 67-8) and Apollonia (Pedley 1979; Rebuffat *et al.* 1978: 269, n. 5). Moreover, little effort was paid to considering the issue of the function of the underground chamber discovered in Siret Qasrin el-Giamel. While the above-ground evidence strongly suggests wine production, the underground elements are still ambiguous in this regard. However, it is probably not far from the truth to envisage that the press was used for wine making.

1.3.5 Archaeological excavations of pressing installations in Cyrenaica

Since scientific excavations in the field of archaeology started in Libya over a century ago, no systematic field survey of Cyrenaica has taken place and urban excavations have continued to be predominant. There are few excavated presses in the hinterland of Cyrenaica and most of them involved clearance of the site with little attention to obtaining a detailed record of the archaeological material.

The first reference to an excavated olive oil press came from Tarakenet, some 12 km east of the modern village of al-Gubah and about 0.6 km north-east of the main road to Derna on the edge of the upper plateau (Figures AII.153–154). This was an underground chamber and excavated by the Department of Antiquities under Goddchild's supervision between 1959 and 1960 (Goodchild and Reynolds 1962). Stucchi (1975: 345) suggests that the chamber was originally intended for burials and that the chamber was later converted to industrial use. Similar arrangements of the tanks with drains have been noted in almost every underground press visited in Cyrenaica. The rock-cut chamber contained Greek inscriptions, stylistically datable to the sixth century AD, in its south, west and north walls[2]. A reference in one of three inscriptions that was carved in the south wall of the chamber may support

[2] For further details on these inscriptions see Goodchild and Reynolds, 1962.

the interpretation that the installation was used solely as an underground olive-press. The word ἐρlαλίον in the inscription has been interpreted by Robert (1964, no. 586) to refer to an oil-press. Goodchild apparently missed a counterweight which was laid opposite the eastern end of the north wall. A parallel counterweight was presumably located along the south wall, but stone rubble prevented this from being confirmed.

Similar arrangements of the tanks with drains have been noted in almost every underground workshop visited in Cyrenaica. Inscriptions found within a workshop are unusual, but in this case having been found, it would suggest different phases and an alternative use of the chamber. Despite this there is no conclusive evidence to indicate that the rock-cut chamber was initially established as a tomb and then converted into an olive-press. A reference in one of three inscriptions that was carved in the south wall of the chamber may support the interpretation that the installation was used solely as an underground olive-press. The word ἐρlαλίον in the inscription has been interpreted by Robert (1964, no. 586) to refer to an oil-press.

The second press was found at the site of Lamluda, 28 km east of Cyrene. It was excavated by Goodchild in 1950s, but nothing close to a final report ever appeared. It should be noted that many pressing facilities in North Africa were initially identified as oil installations, but there is increasing demand for many of them to be re-examined. Some presses discovered in these regions were certainly wineries; for example, we now know now that Meunier's (1941) identification of the site of Khirbet Agoub in the region of Constantine Algeria as an olive oil facility was incorrect. Numerous presses in previous surveys and excavations were identified as olive oil installations, but it now appears that a number of these were actually used for wine production (Brun 2004: 196; Decker 2001: 79–80). My recent study (Buzaian 2009) on the press found at Lamluda was thus an attempt to re-examine the available archaeological evidence and reignite discussion on this controversial issue. Although the results are not conclusive, they may help to promote our standards and validate archaeological interpretation. Goodchild (1968) briefly made mention to this press and saw it as connected to olive oil production. However, the absence of a crushing basin in the pressing room proper was taken as the first clue, suggesting that the facility was used for wine production rather than olive oil. In addition, there was a treading tank with a channel leading directly into a deep vat and a lever-press to extract more juice. Other supporting evidence includes a group of sunken *dolia* found adjacent to the pressing room to the north, which suggests that production was geared beyond immediate family needs. Brun (2004: 6) has claimed that wine production was only conducted systematically in *dolia* in southern Europe. This appears to be a possible African exception.

Farther west is the third olive press which located at the southern limit of the Northern Necroplois, about 1 km north-east of Cyrene. It was found during building works in 2014, parts of it were then cleared by the Department of Antiquities at Shahat (Cherstich *et al.* 2018: 145–50). There is evidence suggesting that this was originally a rock-cut tomb, probably dating to the Hellenistic period with several transformations for subsequent Roman burials. At some later date the tomb was converted to an olive-pressing room. One of the interesting features found in the press was a rectangular tank lined internally with *opus signinum*. Its base a channel was cut along the entire length to breach the northern wall to end into an adjacent square rock-cut collecting vat. Therefore, it is reasonable to assume that the same installation served also for wine production. This interpretation is based on similar feature found associated with presses found in Lamluda, Balagrae and Wadi Senab and was thought to have been used for wine production.

The fourth site is Siret Qasrin el-Giamel at modern al-Beida, on the main road across Cyrenaica, a few kilometres east of the ancient site of Balagrae. The excavations brought to light two complexes dating back to the end of the fifth century AD and which continued to be occupied until the seventh century (Catani 1976; 1978; 1998; Stucchi 1975: 423, 523, 531, 547). The two complexes (Figure AII.108) include a monastery to the east, with domestic buildings of simple construction which housed a wine press, and a fortified agricultural villa to the west. The latter was associated with three press facilities, one underground and two above ground. The latter were certainly connected with wine making.

More intriguing industrial evidence dating back to the early Roman period evidence came to light during the recent excavations at Balagrae, modern al-Beida (Bentaher and Buzaian 2006; 2010; Buzaian and Bentaher 2002; 2006). The project is part of a training programme conducted under the auspices of Omar al-Mokhtar University and indeed a turning point in Cyrenaican archaeology given the prevalence of the urban excavation over the rural. As might be expected, the Balagrae excavations explicitly demonstrate that the countryside is a promising mine of economic information and suggests that most industrial activities were probably non-urban. The evidence almost exclusively relates to wine making and was discovered at the north-eastern edge of the settlement approximately 100 m east of the Roman temple of Asclepius. The excavations discovered a variety of shapes of pressing facilities, which were no doubt used for the production of wine.

These presses excavated in Balagrae can be divided into two types by their design features. The first type consisted of a sloped treading floor connected to a deep vat. The juice was conveyed directly to the vat through a channel with no means of housing a collecting receptacle. The second type consisted of a built-up tank coated with impermeable mortar. Its floor had a shallow channel which extended along almost its entire length, and which turned sharply to end in a small settling tank. Further excavations have brought to light a press room furnished with a raised circular press bed in the middle of the treading floor, which is direct evidence of the use of the lever technique for wine making. It is impossible to elaborate further on the subject of these installations as the details have not yet been fully published.

Further evidence of industry comes from the coastal city of Ptolemais (modern Tolmeita), which became the regional capital at the beginning of the fourth century AD as a consequence of Diocletian reforms. A counterweight made from a reused frieze block was found in House G and was considered to be an upright for an olive press (Ward-Perkins *et al.* 1986). It was later reinterpreted as a screw press type (Mattingly 1996: no. 44). Based on parallel examples from the region, Buzaian (2009, no. 2) states that this block is a typical Cyrenaican counterweight stone with two holes and grooves cut on the underside for mounting the windlass. The press seems to be installed within the house after a short abandonment, possibly caused by a natural disaster. Further industrial features possibly involved in olive oil production were found in the so-called North-East Quadrant house, located just across the road opposite Building G (Ward-Perkins *et al.* 1986: 123–6).

A little farther east of the Colonnaded Palace, recent excavations carried out by the Polish archaeological mission have unearthed a luxurious urban villa which boasted lavish mosaics and painted wall-plasters that could be dated to the late second or early third century AD (Łajtar 2012: 257). The villa was ruined as a result of an earthquake in the middle of the third century AD and as a consequence the possession of part of it passed to a new owner named Leukaktios (Łajtar 2012: 258). Seven vats with rebated mouths were discovered in various rooms of the villa, with openings which varied in diameter from 0.86m to 1.06m and which were 0.95m to 3.00m deep. A ledge was noticed in the shaft of each of these vats, which was interpreted as a division between the upper and lower parts of the vat, or as having held some kind of framed mesh (Żelazowski *et al.* 2010: 17). Similar phenomena have been detected in the excavated vats at Tocra (Buzaian 2000: 67–8) and were likely seen as marking the level at which the bedrock started and the digging became difficult. Corresponding examples found elsewhere in Cyrenaica led them to be identified as receptacles for liquids with wine probably the most likely candidate (Żelazowski 2012: 141). This was suggested by the absence of a crushing facility. In archaeological survey, the presence of the crushing mill is taken for granted as constituting evidence for oil production; however, this criterion was also applied in the excavation in a straightforward manner, without consideration of the other archaeological finds. Other similar vats were found in the northern part of the Roman villa (Kraeling 1962: 136) and the southern end of the Colonnaded Palace (Pesce 1950: 64–5). The evidence therefore suggests that urban centres were also engaged in olive oil/wine production and other industrial operations.

Furthermore, a number of vats have been discovered at Teucheira (modern Tocra). A group of three were discovered in the so-called Roman villa (Buzaian 2000) and a group of eight were found within building VII, which was excavated by Benghazi University (Bentaher 1994; Buzaian 2000: 67–8). A rebated groove around the mouths of most of the vats seems to have provided a seating for a lid. While only two of the latter group of eight have been fully excavated, these provided a large quantity of coarse pottery. The most distinctive of these sherds belong to cooking wares of a corrugated body type made in Berenice from the late second to the early third century AD (Riley 1979: 263–4, fig. 104, D515). Another group of four vats was recently discovered due north of the excavated area and could be dated to the mid third century AD.

At Berenice (modern Benghazi), a series of 18 vats installed in two rooms of Building PI have been dated to the third century AD (Lloyd 1977: 214, fig. 41). These vats were clearly designed for the storage of liquids, implying a connection with olive oil or wine. On the basis of these comparable examples, it seems logical to assume that by the mid second century such wine making installations had become commonplace across the entirety of Cyrenaica. It would appear that wine production was in full swing in the region by the beginning of the first century AD. This date seems to be fairly consistent with a gradual growth of trade between Cyrenaica and Italy following the establishment of the Roman administration in the early first century BC (Lloyd 2002; Riley 1979: 410).

1.3.6 Archaeological surveys

Only a few detailed studies of rural sites have been carried out, due to the fact that Cyrenaican archaeology has long been marked by the traditional focus of urban over rural sites and so landscape surveys thus played no part in the archaeological work. In 1974, S. Stucchi and his team published the first detailed account on the survey of Wadi Senab. The site is a very curious, as it composed of troglodyte units dedicated to agricultural production (section 6.7; Appendix II: site no. 86). It included several industrial installations for olive oil and wine production, in addition to two large caves. All these rock-cut features were obviously used for agricultural processing and there is no clear evidence of habitation. Remains of a small bath complex were found immediately at the southern end of one of the large caves located on the west bank of the wadi. The later modification of part of the baths into an olive press room may indicate a change in the function of the site during the late antique period, when such a luxurious facility gave way to industrial activities. seems to have been continually occupied from the Hellenistic era down to the Byzantine period. The close proximity of the site to the hilltop settlement of *qasr* Wadi al-Sanab (just 350 m to the east) suggests that it was linked to the *qasr*, which also encompassed a number of agricultural and industrial feature indicating that the whole area extensively exploited the fertile soil on wadi bottoms through a series of retaining walls constructed across the course of the nearby wadis.

The Italian mission was also able to carry out a brief survey in Ghot Giaras, which is *c.*2 km north of Wadi Senab (Bacchielli 1974–1975: 260-1). Rock-cut tombs pitting the cliff were reported along with many other archaeological features, including rock-cut oil and wine presses perched on a spur overlooking the fertile fields of Ghot Giaras.

One of the weaknesses of the Italian publication is that there were no detailed measurements. However, a visit to the site in 2010 has enhanced knowledge by providing more detailed measurements, which have been included and properly recorded as part of this research (Appendix II: site no. 27).

In the early 1980s the Department of Antiquities in Shahat conducted an archaeological survey of the area around Wadi al-Kuf, west of al-Beida (Abdussaid *et al.* 1984). The project covered an area of difficult mountainous terrain interspersed with arable tracts and endowed with adequate rainfall for sustained cultivation. The deep gorges of Wadi al-Kuf formed a natural barrier in antiquity between Apollonia and Cyrene in the east and the other major cities in the west. Both sides of the wadi are dotted with ancient settlements, farms, fortified buildings and field systems, which testify to its vitality and potent strategic position. The survey recorded about 34 sites and was a simple catalogue of sites with no attempt to offer information on site types or intra-regional relationships. In general, the study was descriptive, and interpretation of some features was ambiguous, especially those related to industrial aspects. For example, it was mentioned (p. 71) that the site of Bartamido has 11 tanks, but there is no description of their shapes or dimensions. Based on the attached plan (not numbered), it appears that they were circular in shape and arranged together in three rows, meaning they were more likely to be seen as vats. The presence of olive oil and wine production is inferred from the general description given to certain pieces of evidence. Terms such as 'press', 'pressing element' and 'rock cut chamber press' were frequently used with no regard to their definite function. However only one photo was published and this shows a crushing basin to give a clear indication of its use. Despite its shortfalls, the study remains an important site record of an area that may now be almost destroyed as a result of the region's accelerated agricultural expansion and looting activities.

In 2003 S. Akab carried out an archaeological survey in the environs of Cyrene and identified 20 sites with olive presses. Part of his work was published in 2010 in the proceedings of the conference held in Urbino in 2006. While the work is an invaluable record of the many archaeological sites located around Cyrene, there were a number of misinterpretations made relating to the function of some of the industrial elements involved in oil production. He pointed out that there were three sites in the surveyed area, not mentioned by name, which employed stone piers erected in pairs (*orthostats* = *arbores*). In fact, there is no evidence so far for the use of *arbores* in the region. Cyrenaican oil presses are of a different kind, with the pressing beam anchored in a free-standing stone or in the wall of the press room in a purpose-made niche or socket. Additionally, a counterweight block was interpreted as an upright (Akab 2010: fig. 3). The work reflects the desperate need for further survey projects in light of the accelerating destruction of the region's archaeological sites since the 2011 revolution and consequent political troubles.

The Archaeological Mission of Chieti's survey project under the direction of Oliva Menozzi is a step in the right direction, as it will allow us to flesh out our information about rural Cyrenaica (Menozzi and Antonelli 2014). The preliminary results illustrate that the countryside prospered between the fourth and seventh centuries AD, with surplus revenues accrued from specialised industry in olive oil and wine production invested in fortified and ecclesiastical buildings. This view seems to support Roques (1987) of a late antique economic boom, but contradicts Wilson (2001: 28) who suggested there was economic recession.

Nevertheless, production of olive oil and wine production did not exclude the importation of these commodities from abroad, as evidenced by the frequency of the LR1 amphora. The LR1 amphora type enjoyed a wide distribution throughout the Mediterranean (Empereur and Picon 1989). Its occurrence in Lamluda (Menozzi and Antonelli 2014: 75–6) as well as Berenice (Riley 1979: 212–5) and Tocra (Reynolds 1995: 389) indicates a lively commercial exchange between Cyrenaica and the eastern Mediterranean. Menozzi and Antonelli (2014: 76) connected the presence of the LR1 amphora at Lamluda with the *milita annona* supply of the military garrisons based in Cyrenaica. This hypothesis is in line with Wilson (2001: 39), who is sceptical about the role of Late Roman Cyrenaica in Mediterranean trade. He assumes that if the exchange pattern was one-traffic trade heavily reliant on imports, then some of the imported items may have been confined to the provisions for military garrisons.

However, the contents of LR1 amphorae could have either been imported directly to the local markets or exchanged between the locals and the mobilised soldiers (Karagiorgou 2001: 153; Poulter 1999: 43). Nevertheless, we must not underestimate the LR1 amphorae which were found in association with the vats discovered at Berenice, as the type was probably reused again for the same purpose (Lloyd 1977: 148) at least on the interregional level.

Nonetheless, much work needs to be done to clarify the context in which the LR1 amphora arrived in Cyrenaica. Similarly, there is a desperate need to evaluate the processing capacity of the Cyrenaican presses. At the same time, without quantifiable data this type of imported amphora and these retrieved finds would remain negligible and their economic implications are limited.

More recently, three doctoral research projects were launched in different areas of the region. The first was carried out by A. Emrage (2015) who adopted a combination of extensive and intensive archaeological, topographical and landscape surveys in the Wadi al-Kuf region. He recorded during this Archaeological Survey (KAS), which covered *c.*1,350 km^2, the remains of 55 sites and found a range of new evidence regarding the function of the recorded buildings in an undulating terrain. The recorded sites could generally be divided into two main types. The first comprises sites that are most likely of military character and the second relates to fortified buildings (*qsur*) and *qasr*-like buildings of civilian function associated with industrial features. These included olive presses and wine production elements.

The second survey was conducted by M. Hesein and aimed to assess the harbours along the Cyrenaican coastline. An area of 50 km long has been chosen from outside of the surveyed area for more in-depth investigation. This area extends from the ancient site of Kainopolis (El- Agla) to the area of Noat, about 17 km to the west of Apollonia. The new evidence has greatly increased our knowledge about productive activity along the coast of Cyrenaica. The sites of Noat 1 and 2 are perhaps one of the interesting sites that were engaged in industrial activity. The first site, Noat 1, is located 16 km to the west of Apollonia and it has been suggested that wine was produce here as the site contained at least 23 dolia and 15 rock-cut vats, along with pressing elements, such as counterweight blocks and a millstone (Hesein 2015: 218). In fact, evidence of a crushing facility may indicate that the site may also have been involved in oil production. Farther west at a distance of 200 m is the second site, Noat 2, which consists of a set of parallel circular vats that might have also been involved in wine making, rather than tanning for tanning processes (Hesein 2015: 219). Hesein published in 2014 a further analysis of vats, that were documented during his PhD fieldwork, found in six coastal sites distributed within the same strip. Initial estimates of the capacity of the vats recorded suggest that these coastal sites were involved in large-scale manufacturing. He concludes that some of these vats are more likely to be associated with the production of fish-related goods (Hesein 2014: 140). However, this hypothesis is based on an analogy of similar vats found along the coast of North Africa and their location by the sea. Only evidence from excavation and chemical analysis can provide conclusive proof as to what these features were used for.

The third project was carried out by M. Abdrbba (2019) who addressed the nature of the Cyrene's suburban zone and its relationship to the core site. The study revealed that most fortified farms around the city were associated with oil presses and it has been suggested that this could have been due to the relative lack of space within the city. In addition, proximity to the city was for reasons of protection, while the middle location, that between the city and the orchards, would have played a crucial role in facilitating the transfer and marketing of various crops (Abdrbba 2019: 169–70). The work recorded a plethora of archaeological sites around the ancient city. Most of the presses found around Cyrene were commonly open air and more likely related to wine making. These were exclusively rock-cut and consisted of a sloping floor connected to a lower sunken collecting vat, while others were established within rock-cut chambers. The latter were originally tombs and evidence of mill mortars found in most of these installations indicating that they were oil presses.

In sum, these previous works demonstrate that up to now little attempt has been made to investigate Cyrenaican production and trade in relation to both local and overseas markets. The survey projects have on the other hand revealed the high potential of the Cyrenaican countryside and the need for interdisciplinary work at both urban and rural sites, along with collaborative synthetic research and analysis.

chapter two

METHODOLOGY

This chapter deals with the research questions that underpin this study and addresses the mechanics and facilities needed for olive oil and wine production. The methodology used in the field survey is described, including the recording methods, the numbering system given to the visited sites and the terminology used in the recorded press elements. The chapter also explains how the data were gathered through opportunistic fieldwalking and collection of datable pottery to understand the archaeology and distribution of olive oil presses. The methodologies adopted to assess the load capacity of Cyrenaican olive oil presses, along with the estimation of the ancient population of Cyrenaica, are also discussed. In addition, the approach followed to address the evidence of local olive oil/wine amphora production is also elucidated. Finally, challenges and limitations encountered during my survey are explained.

2.1 Research Questions

- What were the technical characteristics of ancient olive mills and presses in Cyrenaica?
- How far is it possible to discriminate oil and wine production from the archaeological evidence?
- Was the form of the olive oil press similar to the lever and windlass technique used in Roman Africa or did it follow instead the indirect or direct screw system and how did Cyrenaican pressing technology differ from that used elsewhere in North Africa and the Greek world?
- Was Cyrenaican olive oil production orientated towards local consumption or, due to high surplus production, was it also exported? And, how does the research on Cyrenaican olive oil production relate to the broader study of Cyrenaican trade and exchange?

2.2 Aims

A great deal of information is now available on the ancient olive oil production technology used across most of North Africa. However, Cyrenaican press technology has been missing from our understanding of the pressing technology employed in Roman Africa. This is important because Cyrenaica was linked geographically, culturally and perhaps technologically, with the East Mediterranean. Therefore, the main aim is to identify and characterise Cyrenaican presses and identify the role of Cyrenaican olive oil production in the Roman economy of North Africa and the Mediterranean, during the mid- to late Roman periods.

The principal objectives of this research focus on the following:

- Recording the archaeological evidence for pressing elements along the coastal plain, the upper plateau and farther south across the inland plateau.
- Re-examining the scale of olive oil and wine production carried out at some urban and rural sites.
- Investigating the function of the surveyed sites and establishing a typology of the settlement patterns in Cyrenaica.
- Analysing the archaeological evidence of olive oil and wine trade between Cyrenaica and other parts of the Mediterranean basin.

2.3 Research Context

Integrating the collected data into the wider debate concerning ancient olive oil and wine pressing technology and its efficiency will provide a better understanding of ancient mechanical technology and the conflict between efficiency and satisfaction. Mattingly (1996) presented the most significant of current discussions of Romano-African press technology. The lever and windlass type of press was predominant throughout North African ancient history, with limited evidence for the adoption of screw technology as well (Ahmed 2019; Hitchner and Mattingly 1991; Mattingly 1996: 588, fig. 3). This picture (Table 2.1) does not match the eastern Mediterranean situation, which apart from the Methana region of Greece seems to have embraced screw technology on a larger scale (Callot 1984; Frankel 1997; Hadjisavvas 1992). Screw technology may have been invented by the first century BC and frequently occurred in different kinds of press mechanisms towards the middle of the first century AD (Brun 1993: 543–9). In terms of press-technology, while the deployment of the lever and screw press is more effective in terms of pressure per unit area than that of the lever and windlass, its operation is more labour-intensive. However, framing choice of press simply in terms of efficency is problematic, as an active interest in a certain technique does not necessarily mean a state of being backward (Mattingly 1996: 590).

Cyrenaican literary sources and epigraphic evidence explicitly identify silphium (Applebaum 1979: 84; Coster 1969: 116), grain (Applebaum 1979: 22, 85) and horses (Rostovtzeff 1941, I: 293) as major exports. It has been suggested that in the first two centuries AD that the Cyrenaican economy experienced a revival and underwent a period of relative prosperity (Lloyd 1985; Kenrick 1985; Riley 1979). However, there is a great deal of scepticism concerning the region's economic performance from the third century AD onwards (Wilson 2001a: 28; 2002: 265; 2004: 152).

Region	ER press type	LR press type
Africa/ Numidia/ Tripolitania	Lever and windlass	Lever and windlass
Mauritania Tingitana	Lever and windlass	Lever and screw
Istria/ Dalmatia	Lever and windlass	Lever and windlass
France	Lever and windlass	Lever and screw
Italy	Lever and windlass	Lever and screw
Spain	Lever and windlass	Lever and screw
Mithana	Lever and windlass	Lever and windlass
Cilicia	?	Lever and screw
Cyprus	Lever and weights	Lever and screw
North Syria	Lever and weights	Lever and screw
Palestine	Lever and weights	Lever and screw
Crete	? Lever and windlass	?

Table 2.1: Comparison of olive press technology from several Mediterranean regions in early and late Roman periods *(adapted from Mattingly 1996, table 2).*

It is generally believed that the Jewish revolt in AD 115–117 led to a great loss in the region's population and wreaked havoc on its infrastructure. Several ambitious imperial initiatives were launched in order to restore and repopulate the region (Fraser 1950; Walker 2002). In addition to the increasing danger posed by tribal incursions and a localised earthquake in the mid-third century AD, the region's worst blow was dealt in the summer of AD 365. At this time a second major earthquake shook the entire central and eastern Mediterranean basin, causing mass casualties and a tremendous amount of damage (Goodchild 1976: 234–7). These successive disasters have led many modern scholars (Alston 2001: 130; Wilson 2001a: 150–2; 2001b: 41) to believe that the entire region was completely devastated and subsequently failed to experience the kind of economic growth similar to that attested to in other eastern Mediterranean regions such as Egypt (Banaji 2001), Palestine (Bar 2002; Dar 1999; 2003; Kingsley 2001) and North Syria (Callot 1984; Decker 2001; Tate 1993; Tchalenko 1958). Similarly, there is clear evidence of late Roman prosperity in Asia Minor (Baird 2004; Foss 1994; Vanhaverbeke *et al.* 2004). Some intensification of settlement from the fourth to sixth centuries was also reported from Crete (Bintliff 1997) and an increase in the number of rural sites was, likewise, revealed in Cyprus during the fifth to sixth centuries (Rautman 2000).

Generally, records on the Cyrenaican economy are rare and we cannot rely on Synesius' narratives alone (Wilson 2001a: 150). Archaeological evidence is thus the prime source of data for reconstructing the Cyrenaican economy. Accordingly, this research investigates the archaeological evidence of olive oil production that has largely been neglected thus far by the literature on the Cyrenaican economy.

Recent excavations at Euesperides (modern Benghazi) have noted an absence of olive stones in the archaeobotanical samples retrieved from the excavated archaeological deposits, which spanned from the early sixth to the middle third centuries BC (Pelling and Al Hassy 1997). However, olive wood has been identified in charcoal from fourth century BC contexts (Wilson *et al.* 2005). Elsewhere, olives, grapes, figs and date palms comprise the oldest group of cultivated fruit trees in the Mediterranean (Zohary and Spiegal-Roy 1975). Although it is impossible to tell apart wild olive stones, wood and pollen from cultivated varieties, their presence here suggests that olives were at least known if not utilised at an early stage. This was confirmed by palynological studies conducted in two wadis in the area of Ras al-Hilal, east of Apollonia (Hunt *et al.* 2002). Pollen analysis here has shown that olive cultivation was known in Cyrenaica since at least the beginning of the Greek period, which marks the transition from semi-nomadic pastoralism to agriculture and urbanism. Therefore, it is probable that oleoculture was introduced by the Greeks sometime after 631 BC (Hunt 2002: 5, 7).

The Roman period saw the spread of oleoculture across Cyrenaica (Laronde 1984). It is thus no surprise to see the countryside dotted with olive and wine presses, most of which are thought to belong to the Roman period. There is a contradiction between these abundant vestiges of agricultural development and the views that the region's economy was stagnant and lacking in population growth.

2.4 Olive Oil versus Wine

The early evidence for food processing in the ancient Mediterranean is scarce and ancient sources are unhelpful in this regard. Archaeological evidence is therefore of prime importance in determining the ancient technology connected with food and nutrition. Ancient Greek oil presses are almost absent in comparison to the well-known and impressive Roman ones. Scholars have taken this as an indication that the Greeks produced olive oil solely for self-consumption (Foxhall 2007: 26), which can be achieved using a simple device on the household level. These primitive pressing devices were affordable and easily manageable, but unfortunately are rarely found in the archaeological record (Foxhall 1993: 193–4).

The tools needed for this purpose were a large flat boulder and a stone roller. Olives were spread on the flat surface, and the roller was moved back and forth to reduce the substance into pulp. A piece of cloth was used to contain the paste, which was in turn placed on a flat surface and topped by a heavy stone. The resulting fluid was drained into a collecting receptacle, and the oil could then be ladled out. The same method can be used to process smaller amounts of olives. This requires a flat stone with an inscribed circular channel on its upper surface which ends in an outlet then opens into a conjoined small hollow pit. The olives were either crushed in this pit with a pestle, or on the flat surface with a stone roller. The paste is treated using the same method outlined above, and the liquid extracted is then drained through a channel which ends in a depression (Foxhall 1993: 193–4; Frankel 1994: 28–9). Variants of this method continued to be used well into the early twentieth century AD, with a production that was intended to outstrip domestic consumption (Amouretti 1986: 158–62; Brun 1986: 45, 68-9, 81). Although they lacked the conjoined depression, several late Roman examples were found by the Benghazi University excavation at Tocra, and further evidence comes from Wadi Senab in Wadi al-Kuf and from Tansoluk, which is 15 km west of Tocra. Driven by increased demand, the olive oil industry experienced a substantial amount of technical development. This resulted in the introduction of mechanical equipment used in crushing and compressing operations.

A crushing stage is necessary in the production of oil to crush the olives into a uniform paste ready for pressing. In contrast to the rudimentary method referred to above, specialised mills were developed to produce greater amounts of olive pomace in a shorter time. These had upright millstones that revolved around their own axes and turned around a central pole inside a circular mill basin (powered by either humans or animals) Two main types of crushing basins have been identified: the *trapetum* (Cato XX–XXII) and *mola olearia* (Columella 12.52: 6). The former is concave in shape and operated with a lens-shaped millstone, while the latter is cylindrical in form with a wheel-shaped millstone. There are literary references that had suggested that the olives were bruised without breaking the stones, but archaeological and ethnographic evidence is equivocal. Brun (1986: 163) argued that in the *trapetum* type the space between the millstone and the floor surface of the basin could be adjusted to prevent the stones being crushed. Foxhall (2007: 133) meanwhile believes that olives would have been fully crushed even in the *trapetum* type. Ethnographical evidence suggests that olives were crushed alongside the kernels, which would give the resulting oil a bitter flavour (Frankel 1994: 34). However, modern oil production crushes kernels into sharp fragments, which have been shown to be beneficial to the flow of oil from the paste. Traditional Libyan cultivators claim that a number of factors affect the bitterness of the oil, such as twigs (from the olive tree), whether the olives were cleaned, the ripeness of the fruit and the storage conditions of the oil – rather than the crushing of the kernels.

The next step was the use of the lever and weight technique (Figure 2.1). A beam made of a large tree trunk was fixed into a socket hole cut into a standing architectural feature. Force was applied to the free end of the beam to exert downforce pressure on the olive mash heap, which was placed on a pressing bed carved with circular or square grooves. Soon the stacked heap would start to release the fluid under its own weight and by the extra pressure exerted by the beam. Consequently, the liquid runs through the channel and drains into a settling tank set either under the pressing bed or adjacent to it. The floating oil is skimmed off with a ladle, or eventually moves into a second tank under the influence of gravity. The lever and weight mechanism continued to develop over time, so that the older technique did not become obsolete but remained in use alongside the new one (Frankel 1994: 28). White (1984: 32 cited in Mattingly 1996: 586) suggested a straightforward sequence for the evolution of pressing techniques (Figure 2.2), as follows:

1. Simple lever press
2. Lever press with hanging stone.
3. Lever press with fixed windlass.
4. Lever and screw press with a mobile windlass attached to a counterweight block.
5. Lever press with improved screw and counterweight.
6. Direct screw press.

Figure 2.1 (top right): Lever and windlass press and its main components *(after Frankel 1994: fig. 14).*

Figure 2.2 (bottom right): A linear model for the development of olive pressing technology *(Mattingly 1996: fig. 4, after Brun 1986).*

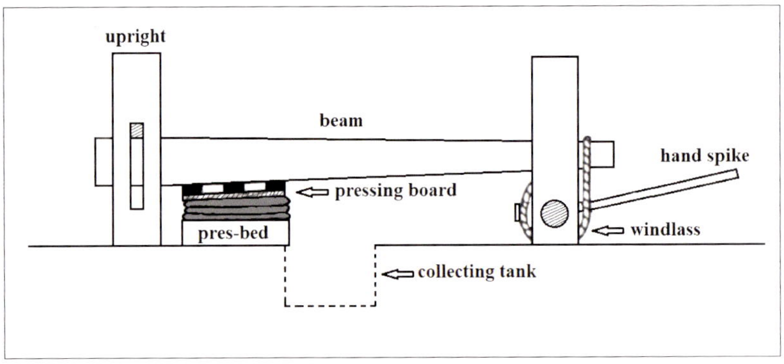

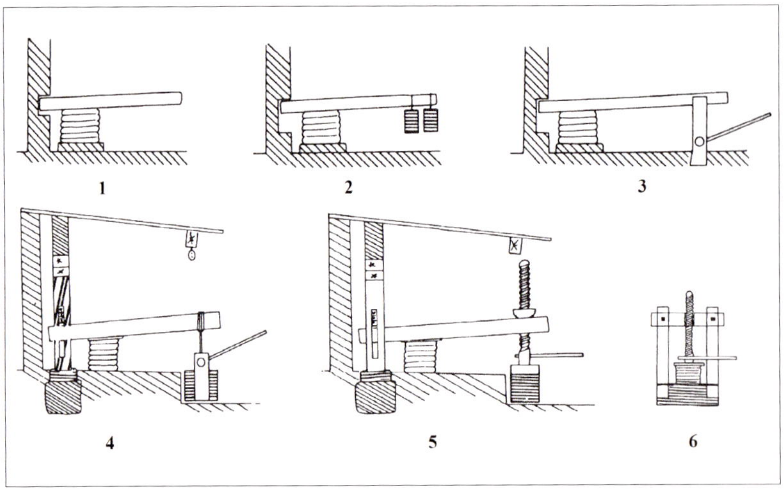

Brun (1986: 81-132; 1987: 86, fig. 28) proposed a more acceptable progressive process with different types remaining in operation alongside each other. Mattingly (1996: 592, fig. 5) proposed a 'technological shelf' model for the technology used in North African presses. Ancient technology developed at a slow pace with improved techniques evolving in an extremely slow version of the industrial revolution. In antiquity, the technological potential of a new invention could easily have been overestimated, but as long as the old instrument could accomplish a given task efficiently, there would have been no reason to change to a newer technology. Instead of being made redundant, the old technique was retained and so avoided becoming obsolete (Greene 1990; 1992: 101–2, cited in Mattingly 1996: 583). Specifications for certain pressing tasks with adequate wood sources and the existence of competent carpenters were important factors in the change in technology and its subsequent diffusion. It is worth mentioning that technological change is a sign rather than a cause of socio-political transition (Foxhall 2007: 186). In summary, the introduction of beam presses can be taken as a strong indication of capital investment and the presence of a specialised industry for surplus production (Mattingly 1988b: 157).

The lever type of oil press was the most predominant form across Roman Africa and throughout the Mediterranean (Mattingly and Hitchner 1993). Its basic elements were:

1. A large press timber beam or tree trunk firmly fixed at one end to a wall, between pair of ashlar uprights (sometimes wooden posts), or a vertical monolithic stone.
2. A horizontally-bedded slab of stone, usually with circular or square grooves, on which the stacks of olive mash baskets were placed beneath the beam.
3. A device attached to the free end of the beam to increase the pressure on the stacked baskets. This can be divided into three types:

   a. Suspended weights
   b. A windlass device made from timber and either placed in a recess in the ground or mounted on a rectangular stone counterweight block.
   c. A screw mechanism which was usually attached to a cylindrical counterweight block provided with mortices and which may be confined only to the screw technique (Mattingly 1988b: 158).

Unfortunately, wooden objects are rarely found in the archaeological record, but the sockets and different shapes of mortices cut into the different types of counterweights are of great assistance in reconstructing how these devices were used and the way they worked.

2.5 Approaches to Olive Oil Presses in Cyrenaica

The primary dataset of this project comes from my own field survey of sites likely to be linked to olive oil production conducted between 2007 and 2010. Most of these sites were previously unknown and were recorded for the first time. Additional data were gained from the training excavations conducted by Omar al-Mokhtar University at Balagrae (modern al-Beida) that I directed between 2001 to 2006. Further information was obtained from the training excavations of the Benghazi University conducted at the ancient site of Teucheira (modern Tocra) that was also under my direction between 1994 to 2012.

There are also supplementary data from the re-examination of some poorly documented early excavations. More recent work and some previous surveys (e.g., *The Archaeological Survey of the Wadi al-Kuf National Park* 1984 (in Arabic) and *Christian Monuments of Cyrenaica* 2003) have proved an important source of information about settlement locations and knowledge that has not been previously documented.

The primary goal of my fieldwork was to collect data relevant to the issue of olive oil production in Cyrenaica during the Roman period. Particular attention was paid to locations of archaeological significance associated with olive oil and wine installations and recording the dimensions of different pressing elements. An additional goal was to collect data that might provide initial information about the typology and functions of the Cyrenaican sites in which the press elements were found. My survey used methods designed to assess the agricultural potential of Cyrenaica by investigating archaeological evidence of olive oil production, however the vast terrain and difficult communications of the study area inevitably played an important role in restricting the survey to certain regions. The dataset was thus gathered by a vehicle-based reconnaissance of the widely distributed visible remains scattered across the area from Benghazi, and which extend to the east as far as Ras al-Teen, 50 km east of Derna. The north-south axis stretches from the coast to the limits of the pre-desert zone to a maximum depth of around 80 km (Figure 2.3). Time limitations and lack of resources did not permit this study to cover the whole region, but 876 milling and pressing elements across 111 sites were identified. This is an enormous increase in the archaeological evidence relating to olive oil production and pressing establishments in Cyrenaica (Figure 2.4; Appendix I).

My investigation includes as many sites as possible across the region to enable a better understanding of the geographical distribution of Cyrenaican olive oil presses. During the early stages of my research, I started by collecting all the available existing information on the study area. Detailed 1/50,000 American Army series maps (1941), which have plotted a large amount of ancient remains, were of great significance for the exploration of archaeological sites. Available satellite images (via Google Earth imagery) were also used to locate and identify sites and information compared to what was then already found on the ground. Furthermore, some brief reports of visits by inspectors found deposited in the Departments of Antiquities in Benghazi and Shahat provided useful information on the location of archaeological sites and their remains. Valuable knowledge on the location of archaeological sites within the periphery of Shahat was kindly made available by the late Abdulgader al-Mzeni. In addition, the locals have proved to be of great help in reporting the whereabouts of these sites as well as my students, especially those based in these rural areas. For example, the region along the Benghazi coastal strip, which covers the area from Benghazi to Ptolemais (modern Tolmeita), has received little attention from scholars and archaeologists. Nonetheless, a combination of information obtained from a survey conducted south of Driana (ancient Hadrianopolis) by Jones and Little in 1971, together with my previous knowledge, has allowed me to identify many archaeological sites in this area.

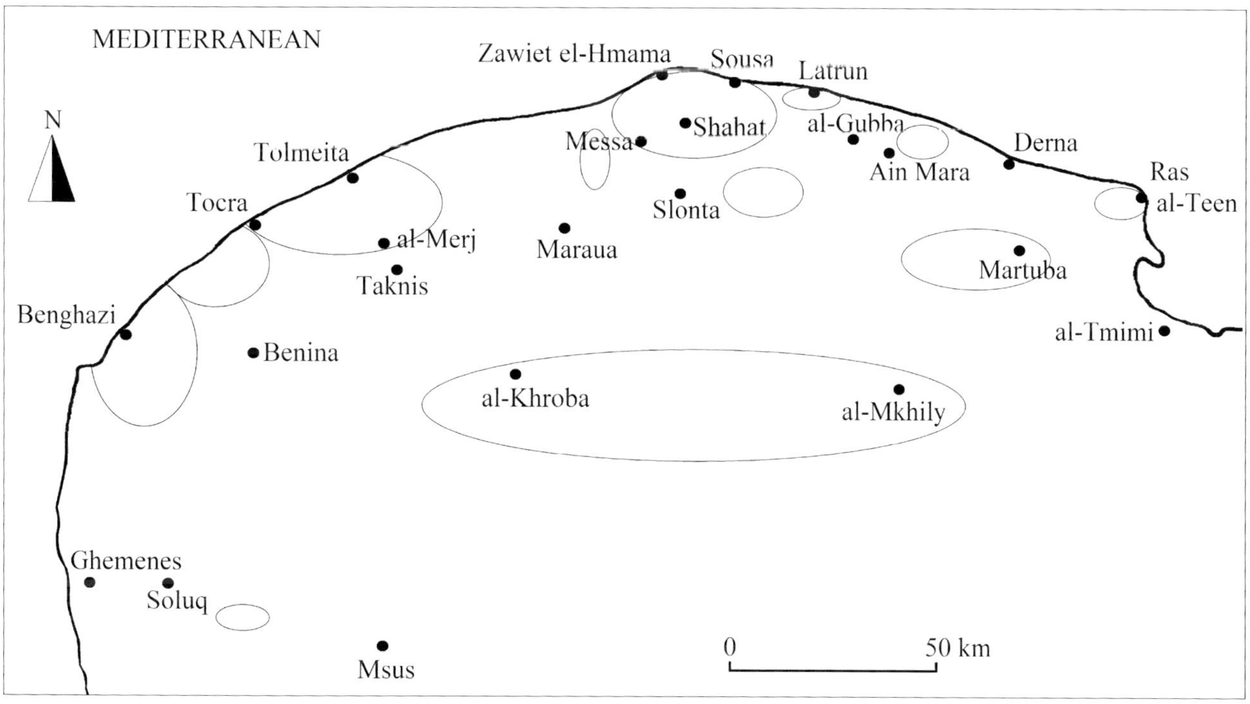

Figure 2.3: Encircled areas show approximate surveyed locations. Shaded areas associated with presses. Other marked areas show the complete absence of pressing installations.

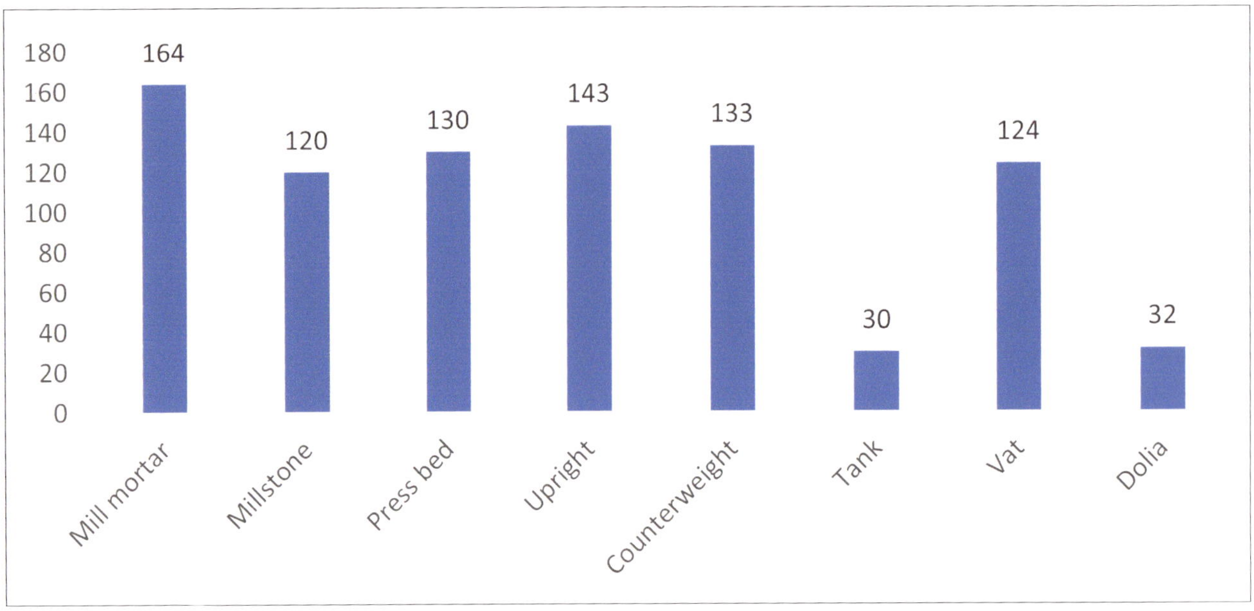

Figure 2.4: The number of milling elements found and recorded at 111 sites.

Although it was not possible to survey the entire region in detail, coverage was extended by sampling different areas across a series of different topographical zones. The upper plateau provided a particular challenge with its rugged terrain and undulating hills restricting access to some areas. This was one of the reasons why the region between Slonta to the east and al-Abiar in the west was not investigated. For similar reasons the areas farther east and west of Cyrenaica were not examined as thoroughly. The fieldwork was principally conducted by me, frequently accompanied by an archaeologist, and there was often a member of the local community present. Data was collected in notebooks and included: a unique code for the site, the name of the site (ancient when known), the date of the visit, spatial coordinates (collected by a Garmin Geko 201 handheld GPS), a general description of the site's condition and visible remains, measurements, photographs and drawings of all mill and press elements, additional comments and finally a general photographic record. Written descriptions were, whenever possible, accompanied by drawn plans. These varied from paced sketches that were then compared with Google Earth imagery and measured drawings made at a variety of scales.

Except where otherwise stated all, photos and drawings are my own. Photographic scale is used, and size is mentioned; in addition, direction, if appropriate, refers to the photographer's point of view when shooting a scene. Some site plans were produced from high resolution satellite images.

The survey did not implement systematic field-walking or any artefact collection. I walked at random around the site to collect diagnostic pottery sherds. The date of a site and press installations found in it were recorded when possible. This was mainly based on a brief observation of diagnostic surface pot sherds. This approach is suitable for broad and rapid coverage of large areas (Ben Baaziz 1992: 13); however, there is considerable debate regarding the extent to which one can rely on surface finds and whether they really provide a trustworthy overall picture of the past (Renfrew and Bahn 1991: 74). At present, secure dating evidence of these archaeological sites is lacking and yet brief observations of some diagnostic fineware found during surface investigations make it possible to give a broad dating. Of these sherds, Campanian Black Glazed sherds dating from the third to first centuries BC were noted. A number of sherds of first-century AD Italian Sigillata were observed. In later periods, it was possible to identify African Red-Slip Ware, Form 27, dating from the second half of the second century to the first half of the third century AD; Form 76, dating to the fifth century AD; and Form 104, dating from the early sixth to the first quarter of the seventh century AD. Sherds of Phocaean Red-Slip Ware (Late Roman C – Form 10) from the sixth and seventh centuries AD were also observed.

The methods used to record the different pressing elements were largely based on the landmark survey of the Kasserine region in west-central Tunisia (Mattingly and Hitchner 1993). However, certain recording forms were modified to fit with the nature of a number of architectural characteristics which appeared to be unique to Cyrenaican archaeology. For example, as illustrated below, the counterweight element had two identical sockets that were completely cut through at both ends of the block, whilst another had two narrow and shallow grooves in the lower edges of either the short or long sides of the block (used to secure the wooden posts) which usually extended across the two socket holes. Apparently, this counterweight block differs from the 'Semana' variant, which was the most frequently used weight in the ancient world (Frankel 1999: 102).

Almost all the recorded crushing basins were in an excellent state of preservation. Thus, dimensions and profile drawings for each crushing basin found were undertaken, and a scale of 1:10 was chosen as an appropriate measure for the drawing (Figure AI.1). In doing this, I was able to create a mill mortar typology by looking at the section of the internal surface of the crushing basin. It was also possible to draw some comparisons between the crushing basins found in my survey region with those previously published from various other regions of Roman Africa, especially in Tripolitania and Tunisia. Nothing was previously known about the typology of Cyrenaican press elements, as data regarding their typology are, to date, unrecorded. The data now available from my survey enabled me to produce an initial typology of the different elements of presses in the region. Since most of the Cyrenaican mill mortars are variants of the *mola olearia* type, the typological work of Mattingly and Hitchner (1993) on crushing basins from the Kasserine region served as a general guide for my typology, but due to the diversity and the unique design of many Cyrenaican mills further categories clearly need to be added; indeed, this is also true for the other Cyrenaican press elements. For the counterweight block types, although the general typology proposed by Brun (1986: fig. 59), especially types 10 and 40, was adopted, other new types were added. Nevertheless, the types of uprights are to be considered as entirely regional. Many pressing elements were still partially buried, making it impossible to take their full measurements as no attempt has been made to dig around them. Nonetheless, the recorded visible elements helped to reconstruct similar character. The + symbol indicates the maximum observed dimension in cases where the full measurement of a buried or broken element proved impossible. All measurements of different pressing elements are in centimetres and recorded as follows:

2.5.1 Recording mill mortars

Key to headings as shown in Table 2.2 and Figure 2.5:

- Dims = overall external dimensions.
- Lip = width and internal depth of outer lip of mortar.
- Basin = lower and upper width of the milling area between lip and central pivot multiplied by depth of milling area. If the wall was stepped, additional readings were taken at each breaking point whilst if the wall was curved the reading was then recorded, if possible, at the point where the wall met the base.
- Skt. H. = dimensions of socket.
- The '+' and '–' signs indicate that the lip width was uncertain (it might be narrower or wider).
- Integ. col. = dimension of the integral column that may sometimes be left projecting from the centre of the basin in which the pivot rotates (height from the crushing surface × thick).
- sq. = square, cir. = circle, rec. = rectangular, pi = pierced.

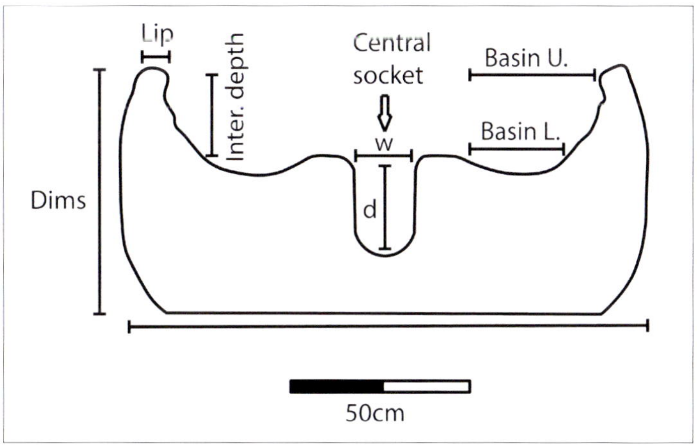

Figure 2.5: Illustration of mill mortar showing the relevant dimensions.

Site name	Element code	Type	Dims	Lip	Basin	Skt. H.	Integ. col.
Al-Asseda (ASD)	ASD-B1	2	140 × 70	10 × 20	25/37 × 35	Sq. 16 × 16 × 27	8 × 12

Table 2.2: Example of recording a mill mortar.

2.5.2 Recording counterweight blocks

Key to headings as shown in Table 2 3 and Figure 2 6:

- Dims = overall external dimensions.
- Sq. H1 – Sq. H2 = size of the two square holes.
- Interval Sq. H1 – Sq. H2 = distance between the two holes. Under-side grooves 1 and 2 correspond Sq. H1 or Sq. H 2, respectively. Lateral – Longitudinal (underline the appropriate description).
- A measurement in italics denotes that the overall dimension was estimated as based on a symmetric base (e.g., *180 cm*).

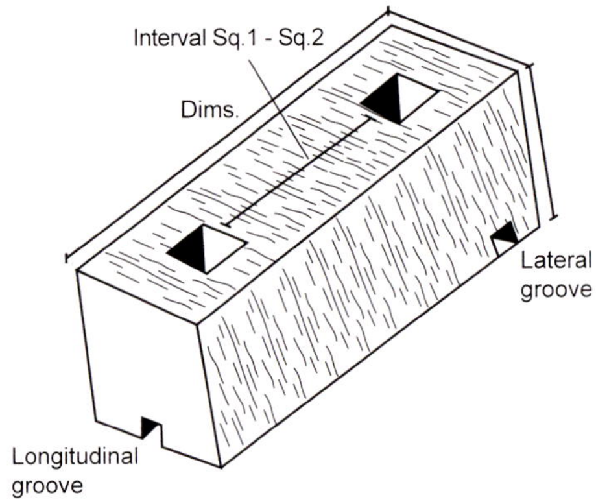

Figure 2.6: Illustration of counterweight block showing the relevant dimensions.

Site name	Element code	Type	Dims	Sq. H 1	Sq. H 2	Interval Sq1 – Sq2	Under-side groove	
							groove 1	groove 2
Qasr al-Hmeira (HMR)	HMR-C2	1	L. 192 W. 92 T. 60	25 × 25	25 × 25	80	L. 75 W. 10 D. 10 Lateral	75 10 10 Longitudinal

Table 2.3: Example of recording a counterweight block.

2.5.3 Recording uprights

Key to headings as shown in Table 2.4 and Figure 2.7:

- Holes = number, shape and size of fixing holes; H1-H2 = height difference between lower edge top hole H1 and lower edge second hole H2 in upright.
- H1/H2-b = height of lower edge of top or bottom hole above base of upright. Sometimes, the fixed end of the beam was anchored in a wall niche; in such instances, only the height between the socket hole and the pressing area was recorded.

Figure 2.7: Illustration of upright showing the relevant dimensions.

Site name	Element code	Type	Dims	Hole(s)	H1 H2	H1-b	H2-b	Note
Lamluda (LAM)	LAM-U1	1	215 × 120 × 75	Shape: 1 circular H. 40 W. 44 D. 25	-	90+	-	A second block measuring 160 × 75 × 30 capped the upright.

Table 2.4: Example of recording an upright.

2.5.4 Recording press-beds

Key to headings as shown Table 2.5 and Figure 2.8:

- Dims = overall dimensions of press bed (overall diameter, or L × B); Channel = dimensions of circular channel defining area where baskets were stacked; Diam. Int. = interior diameter of circle defined by channel.

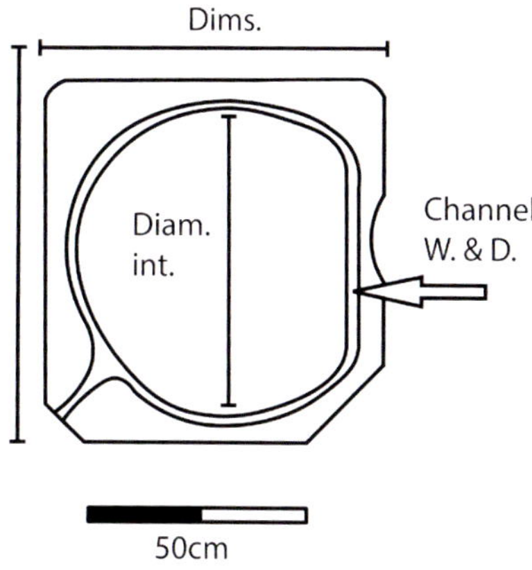

Figure 2.8: Illustration of press-bed showing the relevant dimensions.

Site name	Element code	Type	Dims	Channel	Diam. int.
Al-Assedah (ASD)	ASD-P1	2	85 × 80 × 30	W. 3 - 5 D. 3	irregular 75–65

Table 2.5: Example of recording a press-bed.

The weight of the press counterweight and upright blocks is defined by applying the following formula:

> Weight = L[ength] × W[idth] × T[hickness] × 2.67 g/cm^3 [approximate limestone density]. For example, the weight of the counterweight block from the Tarakent chamber press (TRK-C1) may be calculated as follows:
>
> 140 × 80 × 45 × 2.67 = 1.345 tonnes. However, in the above equation, it is necessary to deduct the volumes of the two vertical holes, which can be calculated using the same formula (34 × 25 × 45 × 2.67 = 0.102 tonnes) which can then be subtracted from the total weight (1.345 – 0.204 = 1.141 tonnes).

The calculation of basin capacity is estimated as shown by the following:

1. The total volume = V = $\pi r^2 h$. For example, the mill mortar Tarakent chamber press can be estimated as: $\pi \times (0.67)^2 \times 0.30 = 0.4231$ m^3.
2. Excluding the pivot volume = $(0.15)^2 \times 0.23 = 0.0163$ m^3.
3. Gross volume (capacity) = 0.4231 – 0.0163 = 0.4068 m^3.

Estimates of the upright weight will be calculated when appropriate, since some are not represented by a large free-standing stone but rather appeared in a simple niche carved in one of the sides of an underground rock chamber. In the case of the above-ground presses, the walls do not often survive to leave any evidence regarding the method by which the beam was anchored.

Each site was given a three-letter code for its name. For example, the code **LAM** stands for the site of Lamluda, followed by the first letter of the press elements. Thus **LAM-B1** designates crushing **B**asin number **1** in the site of **Lamluda**; **LAM-S1** designates crushing **S**tone number **1** at the site of **Lamluda**; **LAM-P1** designates **P**ress-bed number **1** at the site of **Lamluda**; **LAM-U1** designates **U**pright number **1** at the site of **Lamluda**; and **LAM-C1** designates **C**ounterweight block number **1** in the site of **Lamluda**. All the information on the press elements found at the site was separately tabulated in relation to their categories and then entered into a spatial database for further distributional analysis using QGIS 2.18 an open-source GIS program.

Another issue is the fact that while some pressing elements were made of wood, stone was normally preferred for making the pressing tools. Objects made from stone would last much longer than other more perishable equipment, meaning it is possible that some of these tools have experienced more than one period of use, and indeed may have been subject to later modifications for other functions. Nevertheless, the majority of the recorded presses are associated with standing buildings that have been broadly dated to the late Roman and Byzantine periods, from the fourth to the seventh centuries AD. Furthermore, unless reused as building material spolia, these apparatuses were mostly visible on the surface in situ with very little evidence of later disturbance or encroachment.

2.6 Distribution Patterns of Site Types

A total of 104 rural sites and 7 site within urban contexts have been visited in the surveyed area (*c.*30,000 km^2). The chronology of most of the surveyed sites extended from the third century BC to the seventh century AD, with an increase in occupation in Late Antiquity and the Byzantine period (although later pottery is usually more visible on the surface). While the Hellenistic evidence has been largely obliterated by later occupation, it may yet be judged from the remaining ceramic material (Emrage 2015: 193; Jones and Little 1971a; Menozzi 2014: 67; Stucchi 1975: 439–40; Reynolds 2002; Abdussaid *et al.* 1981: 16–9). It does not appear that there is any evidence for a hiatus or the wholesale abandonment of the surveyed sites from the Hellenistic through to the Byzantine periods.

The diffusion of structural elements and pottery scatters allowed a close estimate of the size of many sites. Although the exact surface areas of the sites were not recorded, approximate dimensions were given based on paced measurements which were then refined by measuring imagery in Google Earth. Although only limited and tentative conclusions may be drawn, high resolution satellite imagery of the region has proven particularly useful in this regard.

The overall distribution of surveyed sites represents only a small fraction those that must exist across the region and blank areas should not be considered as areas lacking archaeological sites. However, in general, it may be noted that the ancient sites were mostly located along the coastal zone and on the upper plateau of the survey area and were sparse in the southern steppe where the rainfall barely reaches 100 mm per year. The minimum amount of annual rainfall needed to maintain successful dryland farming is between 300 and 600 mm, which is clearly reflected in the density of the sites recorded in the survey.

The pressing elements recorded meticulously during the survey were arranged in a database which allows one to discern any possible regional variations that may appear in the overall press design and arrangements. In other words, did the geographical location have an impact on the design and arrangement of the press?

2.7 Olive Oil or Wine Press?

Oil and wine are liquids extracted from crushed olives and grapes, respectively. The similarities between these two commodities are reflected in the ways in which they are produced as Frankel (1999: 41) has outlined (Figure 2.9). Nonetheless, the distinct physical characteristics of grapes and olives led to the employment of different crushing strategies. While the former can be easily trampled with bare feet, the latter needs effective mechanical tools to guarantee maximum output. Accordingly, the presence of a crushing basin facility is considered as conclusive evidence for industrial olive oil production (Brun 1993: 518; Foxhall 1993: 183, 186; 2007: 147; Matijasić 1993: 252; Vismara 2007: 457). However, interpretations of oil presses that rely on the presence of an associated crushing facility can be confounded in regions where oil mills were removed and reused for other purposes. This results in poor surface visibility and a misinterpretation of a press for wine rather than oil.

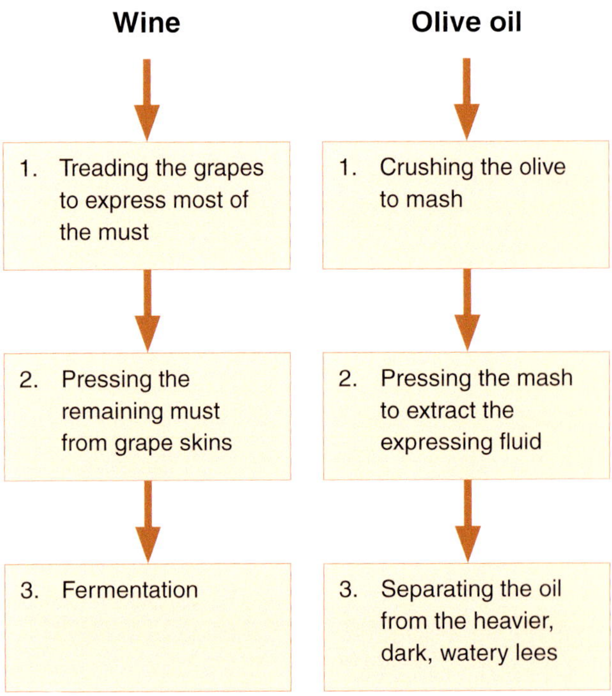

Figure 2.9: Flow diagram depicting the wine and olive oil extraction processes *(based on Frankel 1999: 41).*

Archaeological excavation can provide firmer identification from archaeobotanical sampling, residue analysis as well as the opportunity to conduct a close investigation of the milling pressing evidence. For example, Mattingly (1984), despite the absence of a crushing basin within the excavated site, concluded from the overall evidence that the Lm4 farm installation discovered in the Wadi el-Amud was used for olive, and perhaps also wine, production. It is possible that a crushing facility was made available in an adjacent (unexcavated) building or that the pulping of the olives was simply carried out in a trough or by using a roller-and-bed (Mattingly 1985: 31). Crude crushing apparatus was attested in the pre-desert settlement of Ghirza (Brogan and Smith 1984: 63–4), in the recent past of Tripolitania (Franchetti 1914) and has also been noted in the medieval settlement of Methana, in Greece (Foxhall 1993: 193). Nonetheless, one can be less certain about the use of such time-consuming equipment for crushing olives (usually used for domestic consumption) at Lm4. Logically, the expenses inherent in building a large-scale olive oil pressing establishment (used for surplus production) would imply investment in a rotary crusher to make the installation profitable. The fact that not a single olive mill was found amongst the 62 presses recorded during the Libyan Valleys Survey Project (Mattingly 1985: 39) suggested that the Lm4 press, with many other installations, could be used to produce liquids other than olive oil and/or wine. In fact, the sediments within the press building contained no olive stones at all, however there was an abundance of pips from grapes (van der Veen *et. al.* 1996: 245), leading Brun (2004: 196) to see it rather as a wine press. Similarly, Vismara's excavations at the site of Uchi Maius in northern Tunisia yielded no evidence of crushing elements but were interpreted, nonetheless, as being for olive oil production. However, Mattingly (2009: 717) suggested that some of these installations were employed for wine production although he does not exclude the idea that some installations were multifunctional (Mattingly 2009: 719, see also: Boardman 1976: 188; Forbes and Foxhall 1978: 42; Vismarra 2007: 458). Concomitantly, Frankel (1999: 57) states that this latter possibility is acceptable in theory, but it appears to be quite complicated and unmanageable in practice. Opponents to the theory of dual-purpose equipment argue that the product of one would affect the process of the other (Eitam 1980: 26, cited in Frankel 1999: 57).

Fortunately, the excellent state of preservation of the Cyrenaican rural sites meant that crushing basins were ubiquitous in my survey area, and I found 164 mill mortars across 64 sites. By contrast, the scarcity of the same element was noted in many archaeological surveys of known olive oil-producing areas (section 3.3.2; Table 3.2).

To address the distinction between wine and oil presses, it is first necessary to consider the issue from the perspective of archaeological surveyors and excavators. The former deals with open areas and is primarily concerned with understanding only what is apparent on the surface. In this sense, there is a consensus that the presence of a crushing basin or rectangular trough alongside other pressing elements is strong evidence in support of olive oil production. This is equally valid from the excavator's point of view. Other archaeological evidence, such as multiple small settling tanks, is considered further supportive evidence. However, such tanks could have been employed in pressing both olives *and* grapes or involved in other industrial activities (Foxhall 2007: 146–7; Mattingly and Dore 1996: 140). Usually, settling tanks in olive oil production were much smaller in comparison to those used for wine processing (Frankel 1999: 57; Mattingly 2009: 719), but again this is not a rule, and can be implemented in both facilities.

Wine presses in Cyrenaica mainly consist of a sloping shallow rock-cut or built-up tank connected to a slightly lower collecting tank or vat. Most of the time, both rock-cut and built-up tanks, and floors and walls were lined with hydraulic mortar. Lever and counterweight presses were also used for wine production in Cyrenaica, where both grape skins and stalks were packed into frails or loaded into wooden boxes then placed on a press bed and under the beam, and their employment provide evidence for production on a commercial scale. No examples of identical stone press beds with inscribed surface channels were found, which suggests that this was only used in oil installations. Instead, the pressing area was always represented by a platform covered with an impermeable layer of strong mortar, which went around all sides of the pressing floor (e.g., as at Lamluda: Buzaian 2009). The treading floor was often built on a higher level than the pressing room floor (*cf.* Palladius, On Agriculture 1.18 cited in Humphrey *et al.* 1998: 155). Sometimes a raised circular press bed made of small stones and bricks and combined with lime mortar was centred on the pressing mortar floor (Wadi Senab and Balagrae: personal observation). Wherever mortar floors are found, mill mortars and stone pressing beds are absent, and vice versa. The *Geoponika* (6.1 cited in Decker 2008: 82) mentions that for clean produce, the pressing area in the wine press must be plastered with waterproof mortar. Another piece of evidence in favour of wine production was the use of storage jars; however, these were also present in oil installations (Cato Agr. 10, 4). Fermentation is an essential stage in wine production, and it is unlikely that oil would be stored for longer than two years since beyond this point it goes rancid (Mattingly 1988b: 22). Brun (2004: 6) stated that in Europe *dolia* (large storage vessels), and in some case wooden casks, were widely used in wine-making for climatic reasons. However, buried *dolia* associated with pressing installations were also found in North Africa. For example, Goodchild's excavations in the 1950s at the site of Lamluda to the east of Cyrene brought to light a pressing room associated with a group of sunken *dolia* (Buzaian 2009: 47, 52; Menozzi and Antonelli 2014: 72). Further similar examples were recorded during my survey and I suggest that their presence, in combination the complete absence of crushing apparatus, can be taken as a likely indication of wine production.

A recent archaeological survey carried out along the coastal landscape west of Lepcis Magna used oleic acid erosion on a press bed as a diagnostic feature of oil production (Schörle *et al.* 2012: 151). A very small number of African press beds show obvious signs of this type of acid erosion. However, Sehili (2009: 156) refutes that surface notches are unequivocally caused by acid erosion.

In conclusion, as Brun states (1993: 533), there are no absolute criteria by which to discriminate olive oil and wine presses, though the presence of olive mills is a sure indicator of oil production. A better understanding of regional pressing elements and manufacturing techniques would be of great benefit in improving the quality of our interpretation in this regard.

2.8 Assessing the Capacity of Cyrenaican Olive Oil Presses

Another aspect of the research which has been strongly connected to olive oil production is the assessment of the loading capacity of the presses. With the near-total lack of adequate quantitative studies on Roman amphorae, combined with the paucity of literary evidence, Roman historians cannot assess whether Cyrenaica was an exporter region. Nevertheless, I would support Mattingly's statement that 'The involvement of a press is generally an indicator of a higher form of social or economic organisation' (1988c: 157). Its mere existence is therefore a clear indicator of production whose intention goes beyond that of the needs of simple subsistence. Based on this hypothesis, the possibility of an export market, even at the intra-regional level, will be assessed. To address this issue, I first evaluated the capacity of Cyrenaican olive oil presses by adapting the equation used by Mattingly (1988a) in his attempt to describe the scale of production of the installations found in Tripolitania and Tunisia. Quantitative estimates of olive oil production were calculated as follows. Firstly, by measuring the exact height between the press-bed and beam socket where the fixed end of the lever was anchored. This equated with the maximum height to which olive mash baskets could be stacked. Secondly, by recording the internal diameter of the circular or square channel cut on the pressing surface, it was possible to calculate the maximum diameter of the baskets used to contain pulped olives. These two measurements allowed the maximum of the pile of the stacked baskets to be estimated. However, some examples of the pressing areas in Cyrenaican presses were made of mortar floors or were merely represented by a plain slab block with no sign of the defined groove.

Since there are no figures on the yield per tree in Cyrenaica, I accept the figure proposed by Mattingly (1988b) and assume a minimum of 20 kg of olives per productive tree. There is also no reliable evidence relating to the planting density (trees per hectare) system practised in either ancient or modern Cyrenaica. Therefore, special effort will be made to identify the ancient olive tree orchards reported by early European travellers and match them with the current situation, using high resolution satellite images from Google Earth.

2.9 Estimating the Population of Roman Cyrenaica

An estimation of the population of Roman Cyrenaica was made to determine whether the likely total annual olive oil production met the needs of the regional population and whether surplus could have been achieved. Many scholars have endeavoured to estimate the ancient demography across the Mediterranean through the seating capacities of theatres or amphitheatres, or through the excavation of cemeteries, or on the daily delivery volumes of aqueducts. However, these approaches are most likely underestimates and are believed to be invalid (Wilson 2011: 170). Other, different techniques have recently emerged for estimating ancient populations during the Roman period based on extrapolation from city areas (Wilson 2011) and on population density for rural sites, per square kilometre (Fentress 2009 and Mattingly 2011). The population was divided into two groups: those who lived in cities (urban) and those who lived in the hinterlands (rural). Thus, it was inevitable that each needs to be tackled separately and then brought together to form one entity. However, previous studies have tended to concentrate their research only on one of the two. As far as the current study is concerned, no attempt has been made to estimate the entire population of Roman Cyrenaica. A starting point are the figures suggested by Wilson (2011) for the total population in Cyrenaican cities around the second century AD. However, Wilson does not give figures for urban centres that were reasonably small, such as Apollonia, Barce and Hadrianopolis. These were added to the overall urban demography, which must have had, on average, no more than a few thousand inhabitants. Regarding the rural population, no attempt has yet been made to estimate the rural population of Roman Cyrenaica. Based on the narratives of early travellers, the mapping work of R. G. Goodchild and the important works of Ward-Perkins and Goodchild (Reynolds 2003) and Stucchi (1975), in addition to the data collected during my survey, the countryside appears to have been densely populated. To explore the rural population, two case-studies were selected to record the number and the type of settlements located within them, and thus estimate their populations. The first target area of this investigation was chosen in the area located on the coastal plain stretching between the major cities of Cyrenaica, Berenice and Teucheira. This area has received very little archaeological investigation and is considered as one of the most fertile areas in the region, even today producing cereals, and seeing use as grazing land for animals. The second area is in the Wadi-al-Kuf region, farther east on the middle plateau of the Gebel Akhdar. Previous surveys carried out in this area uncovered a great deal of archaeological evidence that indicated vibrant occupation that could be traced back to the Hellenistic period, or even earlier (Abdussaid *et. al.* 1984; Attiya 1974–75; Emrage 2015; Goddchild and Ward-Perkins 2003). The survey conducted by Abdussaid and his team from the Department of Shahat in an area of 100 km^2 was used as the second case-study. The figure gained from this study was added to that gained from the first area, to give an average population within an area of around 100 km^2. An effort was made to provide a rough estimate of rural Roman Cyrenaica's population using the hypothetical population numbers for different types of site applied by Mattingly for some of the site types recorded in the Kasserine survey (2011, Table 4.2). In addition, population estimates based on households recorded in the village of Philino was applied to a similar category found in both case studies. Consequently, the average number of people extracted from the two case studies was applied to half the area of Cyrenaica to generate the overall population of the region. It is expected that half of the area was only partially habitable since it is either covered with a rugged terrain or indeed located beyond the 100 mm rainfall isohyet within a territory of low agricultural potential. Finally, the resulting figure for the overall population was compared with the total annual output of the olive oil presses recorded during the survey.

2.10 Local Amphorae and Trade

The oil that was produced in Cyrenaica generated a need for transport vessels, in order to be marketed overseas. We know that Cyrenaican amphorae were produced, and hitherto 13 amphora types have been identified. However, our knowledge with respect to the scale of amphora production and the extent of their distribution is still limited.

The presence of kilns for local production of amphorae is directly connected with the agricultural production with which these were filled and transported. Information about provenance and contents that remains in these large vessels is of great help in identifying their origins and the commodities they contained. In Cyrenaica, there is a lack of fabric and form analyses, except for a few sites with locally produced amphorae (Göransson 2007; Mazou and Capelli 2011; Riley 1976; 1979a; 1979b; 1983) and more effort needs to be devoted to such studies to provide a comprehensive study of transport amphorae in Cyrenaica from the Greek period through to the late Roman period. The study of amphorae is mainly based on the stamp they may depict (frequently on handles) or the painted markings, *tituli picti*, on the amphora, the vessel form and the petrographical analysis of the clay fabric. Since a very low proportion of the amphorae were either stamped or depicted painted writings, a combination of both morphological and petrological analyses should be applied in identifying the origin of these transporting vessels and tracing their distribution across the ancient world. Distinguishing the amphora based on the form alone is entirely misleading. To get an idea of the level of intra- and inter-trade in essential commodities like olive oil and wine, we need to know if there was surplus production for export, merely self-sufficiency, or indeed even shortages and thus the need for import. The available evidence of industrial installations alone may not be sufficient to imply abundance and thus infer export. My attempt to assess trade was based on the identifying local amphora types. This task relied largely on the information available through the published material retrieved from excavations conducted at Euesperides, Berenice, Tocra and Lathrun. I briefly described the Cyrenaican fabrics and then give the outline characteristics of the recognised local amphora forms. This was aimed at looking for local evidence of amphora manufacturing established across the region, and to gain further information about their distribution in the region and beyond.

2.11 Limitations of the Survey

All my fieldwork was conducted on holidays and weekends across several years. It was clear from the very beginning of my survey that the region had great archaeological potential, but that investigating in detail a large area (over 30,000 km^2) was far beyond the scope of available time and resources. The insecurity of the country in the aftermath of the Libyan revolution at the beginning of 2011 until my arrival in the UK in 2013 brought my survey to an end was also a significant factor. In many cases, during the survey, local people were very helpful in finding items of interest to my research. But, access to some archaeological sites was not possible because neighbouring landowners refused access as they considered them as part of their property and privacy.

I initially planned to process a small quantity of diagnostic pottery sherds collected from the visited sites, but unfortunately the abrupt war in Benghazi in 2015 prevented me from gaining any access to this material. My house in which the material was stored was fired upon, which forced my family to flee and seek safe refuge in another part of the city. The house was partially destroyed and eventually ransacked, and most of the material was lost.

Nevertheless, the data collected from the survey provides a new baseline of information about the olive and wine presses in Cyrenaica. Although time and resources did not allow the coverage of the whole region, the collected data are sufficient for me to create a press element typology and to expand knowledge of the rural settlement hierarchy.

chapter three

TYPES AND DISTRIBUTION PATTERNS OF CYRENAICAN MILLING ELEMENTS

3.1 Introduction

The interpretation of mechanical instruments made of stone and wood is always controversial. Organic matter such as timber tends to decay over time due to the natural decomposition process, while the stone parts nearly always survive. This of course depends on the nature of the environment and climate in which such material is buried or exposed. The diverse local environments and semi-arid conditions of northern Africa do not seem to preserve most kinds of organic materials. Accordingly, when a worked stone is found which displays differently-shaped holes and cut-outs, it needs to be interpreted carefully. This can be accomplished by referring to different sources of knowledge. Frankel (2009: 1) provided a useful summary of the four main sources of knowledge: literary, pictorial, pre-industrial and archaeological evidence.

Literary sources are not always promising since there are many issues the literature does not fully address, and some which are never even mentioned. This obvious shortcoming is perhaps attributed to the general lack of interest on the part of the writers. Wall depictions, ceramic paintings and other artworks are always imaginative, and the interpretation of imagery is often problematic. On the other hand, the potential of archaeological remains organic materials are usually absent in the archaeological record. Nonetheless, they remain a great mine of data that helps us to follow technical developments across the ancient world, define distribution patterns and possible regional variations. With respect to pre-industrial evidence, technological changes across time mean it seems impossible to find out exact parallels across long spans of time. Frankel (2009: 1) rightly emphasised that in order to gain a better understanding of the evidence, integration of all these four sources is the best possible approach. This is of course dependent on the availability of data from these different categories.

3.2 Categorisation

The typology of olive press elements has been divided into two main categories: (a) milling elements (millstone and mill mortar) and (b) press elements (upright, press-bed and counterweight). This chapter focusses on the milling elements and their spatial distribution within Cyrenaica. The following chapter does the same for the press elements.

3.3 Types of Cyrenaican Milling Elements

3.3.1 Millstones

A total of 120 millstones was recorded in over 100 visited sites (Table AI.1). Almost all were found in a complete state and had clear wear marks around the central hole and working surface due to long use. In general, the number of mill mortars and millstones found in many previous surveys has been remarkably low, perhaps suggesting that most of the installations, such as in the UNESCO Libyan Valleys Survey (Mattingly and Dore 1996: 135–40), were wine presses. However, Mattingly (1993: 443) argues that their general lack in most archaeological surveys was more likely because they had been removed and reworked. For example, Ahmed (2019: 100, Table 4.4) found only five stone crushers in 64 sites. By contrast, the Cyrenaican survey produced comparatively high numbers. Concomitantly, it is reasonable to suppose that crushing stones found at sites which have not produced crushing basins can still provide strong evidence for the operation of a rotary crushing mill (Anderson-Stojanović 2007: 92). There is thus a reason to propose that evidence of millstones alone can equally be used as an alternative way to identify a press that was used for olive oil production. These stones did not need to be heavy like a mill mortar or counterweight block, and their relatively low weight tends to mean that they move far and are not

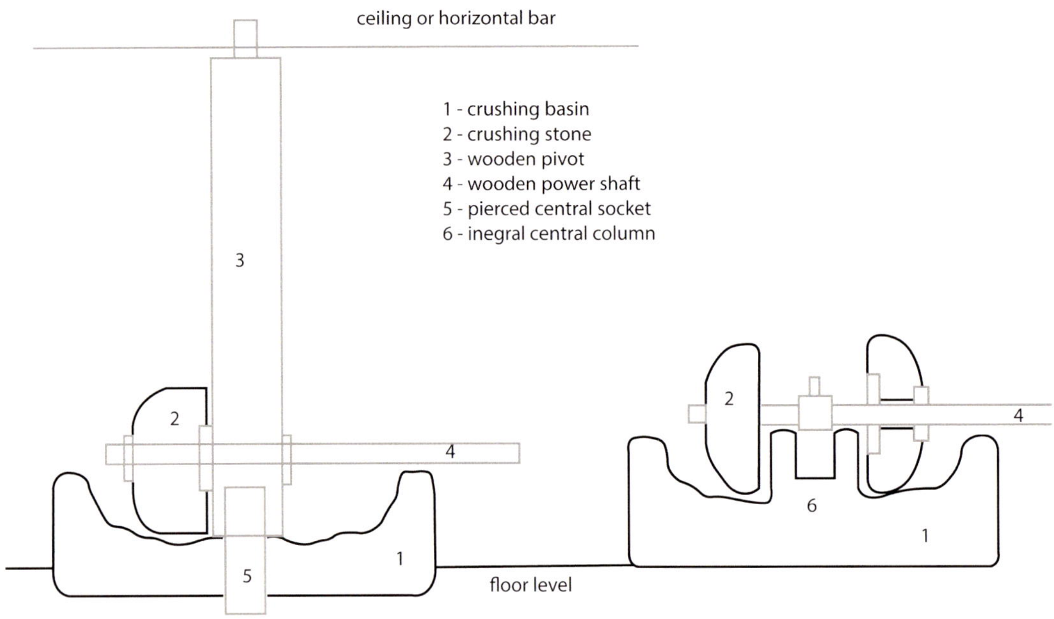

Figure 3.1: Reconstruction of mill mortar and millstone from Qasr Silu (left) and Siret Etbia (right).

often found *in situ*. Their presence is thus less concrete but no less suggestive.

The form of the examined crushing stone suggests that they were designed to match the profile of the opposing mill mortars. A supportive example of this is the clear match between the mill mortar (SIL-B1 '*Type 1c*') and millstone (SIL-S2 '*Type 3a*') found beside each other at the site of Qasr Silu (Figure 3.1). The discovery of flat and concave mill mortars is an indication in favour of this suggestion. All but two of the examined crushing stones have a central perforation, which is square on the outside and round in the middle.

Although, as stated above, the relatively small size of the millstones in comparison to the other pressing equipment could have facilitated their removal from ancient sites and subsequent reuse elsewhere, in fact *c*.70% of the stone crushers recorded during the field survey were found adjacent to crushing basins and other pressing elements strongly connected with oil production. It can therefore be argued that their architectural context is defined and largely reliable. Table 3.1 below shows the correlation between the main types of millstone and a number of mill mortar types.

Type A: The type is generally cylindrical in shape with quite clearly defined edges and a flat working surface. The diameter ranges from 0.50 m to 1.05 m, with the majority falling into the 0.60–0.65 m span. The thickness is in the range of 0.20 m and 0.48 m, with an average of 0.35 m. The salient point to be mentioned is that the larger the diameter, the lesser the thickness. Three sub-types (Figure 3.2) are noted and can be described as following.

Sub-type A1: The type has a central square depression and a round hole in the middle. The outside central square is generally well defined, but usually shows marks of wear and weathering. Its dimensions range from 0.38 × 0.38 m to 0.15 × 0.20 m and 0.05 m to 0.10 m in depth. The average diameter of the middle perforation is 0.15 m, and the range varies from 0.10 m to 0.20 m.

Sub-type A2: The type has a similar crushing surface to type A1 but lacks the central square depression which was replaced by two channels extending downwards about half the length of the central perforation.

Sub-type A3: This has a square central hole with an outside rounded depression. How this crushing stone was mounted is unclear. It is conceivable that a pipe of wood, square on the outside and round in the centre, was placed in the square hole in which the axle wooden shaft passed to operate the stone and prevent it from being in direct contact with the wood.

Millstone type	A	B	C	D	E
Mill mortar Type	1a–1c, 3, 3a–3b, 2, 2a, 3b,I, 4b	1d, 1e, 1f, 2b, 3a, 3b, I, 3b, iii, 4a–b	1e, 2, 4a	1e, 2a–b, 3a, 4b	1g, 2a, 3, 3a, 3b, ii, 4, 4b

Table 3.1: The correlation between each millstone type and its mortar type.

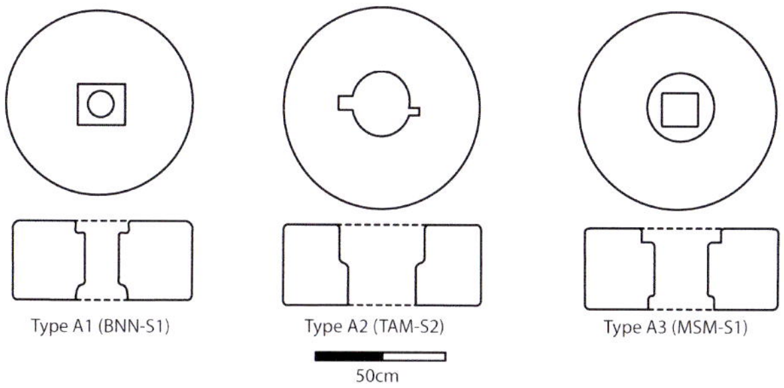

Figure 3.2: Millstone. *Type A*.

Type B: Aside from having clear round corners in its working surface, this wheel-shaped type crusher (Figure 3.3) is nearly identical to Type A. Its average diameter is 0.65 m, while the range varies from 0.50 m to 0.80 m. The thickness in this type ranges from 0.20 m to 0.45 m, with an average of 0.35 m. The dimensions of the square depression and middle perforation are very similar to those noticed in the previous type.

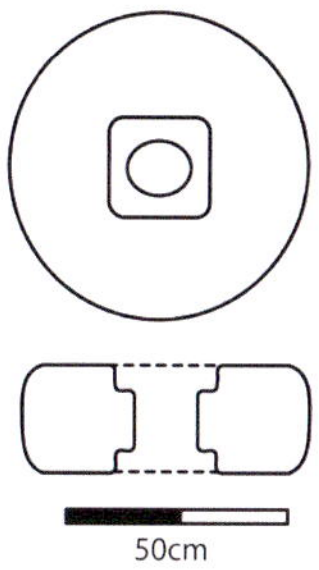

Figure 3.3: *Type B* (HRR-S1).

Type C: Lens-shaped profile (Figure 3.4). Only two examples were found. The first (MES-S1) has a diameter ranging between 0.30 and 0.70 m and a maximum thickness of 0.27 m. The second (YRA-S3) is much smaller and is between 0.32 m and 0.50 m in diameter and 0.35 m thick. Both have a central square perforation measuring 0.20 × 0.20 × 0.06 m and 0.24 × 0.30 × 0.05 m respectively. The middle hole in the former is square and measures 0.15 m a side, while the hole in the latter is round and measures 0.13 m across. The presence of this particular shape of millstone implies the use of the *trapetum* type of mill mortar with its distinctive cup-shaped section.

Type D: Its profile is less curved and its working surface is broader, and bears a closer resemblance to *Types A* and *B*. The crushing stone WKR-S4 (Figure 3.5) has a wide shallow channel across its flat side. This is probably evidence of modification or repair as damage has occurred to the square depression. SHG-S1 is another example, as it has a 'V' shaped groove across its curvature. Its purpose was perhaps to house a rope that was fastened around the stone to hold a square block of wood in the square hole, and through which a wooden pole would have been placed to rotate the crushing stone.

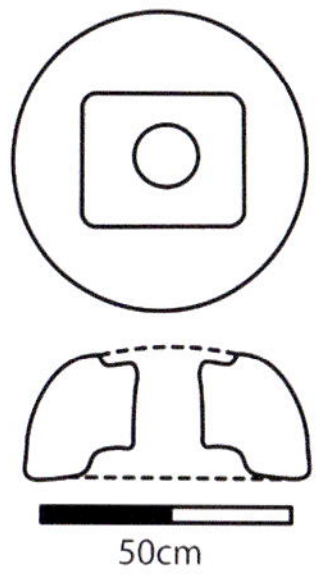

Figure 3.4: *Type C* (YRA-S3).

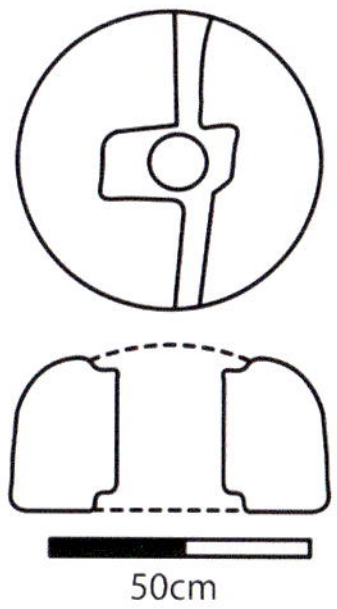

Figure 3.5: *Type D* (WKR-S4).

Type E: (Figure 3.6). Slightly conical millstone ended on both sides by a clear edge with a working surface which varies in width from 0.35 m to 0.4 m. The two sides range in diameter from 0.45 m to 0.62 m. The outside central square does not exceed 0.20 m in length and 0.05 m in depth. The middle hole ranges from 0.10 m to 0.13 m.

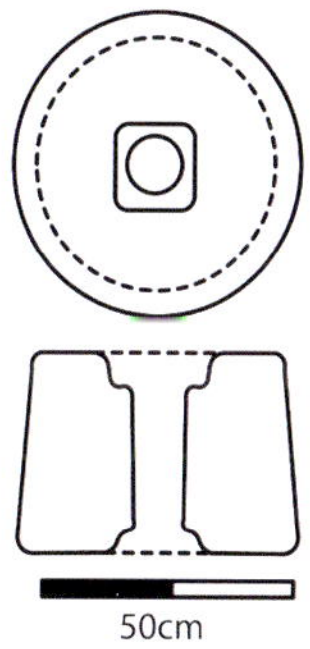

Figure 3.6: *Type E* (WKR-S3).

Type E1: Similar to *Type E*, except the working surface is cut by elongated striations to help the crushing process (Figure 3 7).

Figure 3.7: E1 (LAM-S5).

In two cases, a crushing basin was found associated with twin crushing stones, one at Qasr Silu and another in a site north of Labraq. The latter shows unequivocal evidence that the mill was operated by two millstones. This perhaps demonstrates that the crushing process was of a relatively short duration. The simultaneous use of two millstones would have been more efficient than the use of just a single stone. In such cases, it is possible to envisage two or more presses being supplied from a single crushing basin.

3.3.2 Mill mortar

During the survey over 160 mill mortars (also known as crushing basins) were recorded across 92 sites (Table AI.2). This is a significantly high figure when compared with the extraordinary low number of mill basins found in archaeological surveys conducted in different Mediterranean regions (Table 3.2). The recorded crushing basins were either found fashioned from a single solid limestone boulder or were hewn into the living rock despite the importation of grain mill-stones of marble and volcanic rock elsewhere in Cyrenaica. The former type was often associated with above-ground installations, while the latter was predominantly noted in underground facilities. Most of these mills were in a good state of preservation, including a group that were found *in situ*, and particularly those cut into the natural rock. Several other crushing basins were recorded, but due to their fragmentary condition it was not possible to assign them to a particular type with certainty. However, their presence remains the most reliable evidence for olive oil production.

As already noted there is consensus among scholars (see for example: Brun 1993: 518; Foxhall 2007: 147) that evidence of a crushing basin is sufficient to identify an establishment as an olive oil press. The interpretation of installations connected with olive oil production in Cyrenaica is thus valid, and the level of certainty is high in comparison with other survey projects in which, for many different reasons, the absence of crushing apparatus was a common phenomenon.

The mill mortars found in the Cyrenaica survey have been classified here on the basis of their internal profile (Figure AI.1). Attention focused specifically on the central area of the working surface with variant types based around the shape of the base of the mill and the central pivot structure. The centre usually possessed a pivot-socket either cut directly into the base or hewn in an integral column, which may also be described as a low ridge around the socket. Alternatively, this appeared in the form of a solid protrusion, was represented in a shallow depression, or was even left plain with neither socket nor protrusion. Hence, the socket shape was not given any weight in the typology. Nevertheless, it was defined and considered to be an indication of the method used to secure a lost wooden pivot. Flat bottomed mills had a cylindrical millstone (*mola olearia*), while sloping bases may indicate the use of convex millstones (*trapeta*).

Type 1: Generally, a large flat-bottomed shallow/deep basin with pierced central area similar of the Kasserine type 2 (Mattingly and Hitchner 1993: 444, fig. 3), which was also found just to the north in Thala, Kasr Tlili and the Jebel Semmama (Hobson 2015: 94). Seven sub-types were identified:

1a: (11 examples). A flat crushing surface with sunken perforation through the central area (Figure 3.8) The outer wall meets the crushing area at a sharp point, and either stands almost at a right angle on the crushing surface or is gently diverted away from it.

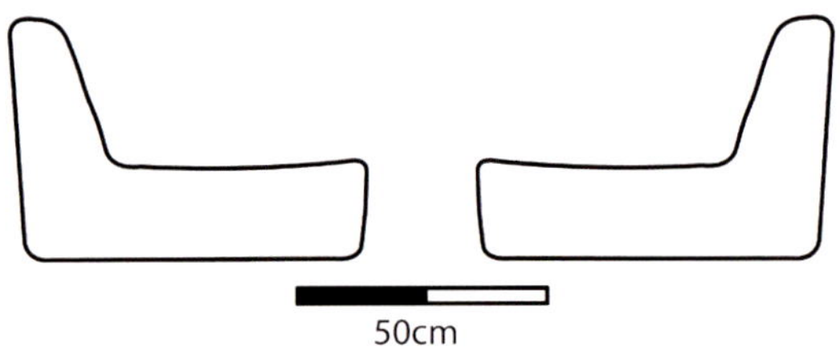

Figure 3.8: *1a* (MAK-B1).

Survey	No. of mill mortars	No. of sites	Mortar/site	Reference
Cyrenaica	160	92	1.74	This volume
Gebel Tarhuna, north-west of Libya	11	64	0.17	Ahmed 2019: 99
L'oued el-Htab, central Tunisia	9	97	0.09	Ben Baaziz 1985: 209–15
Kasserine, west-central Tunisia	7	18	0.39	Hitchner 1990
Dougga, northern Tunisia	4	95	0.04	Lanfranchi 2009: 274
Caesarea – Cherchell, west of Algeria	3	55	0.05	Leveau 1984
Istria – Eastern coast of the Adriatic	8	70	0.11	Matijasi 1993: 252
Provence, south-east France	8	105	0.08	Brun 1986: 223

Table 3.2: Mill mortars recorded in various archaeological surveys.

1b: (3 examples). Similar to *1a* except that this type shows either a pronounced or gentle stepped wall (Figure 3.9) The advantage of the stepped wall is perhaps that more space was available to add more olives in during the crushing process. However, the same can be said of a basin with a curved wall (*type 1c*).

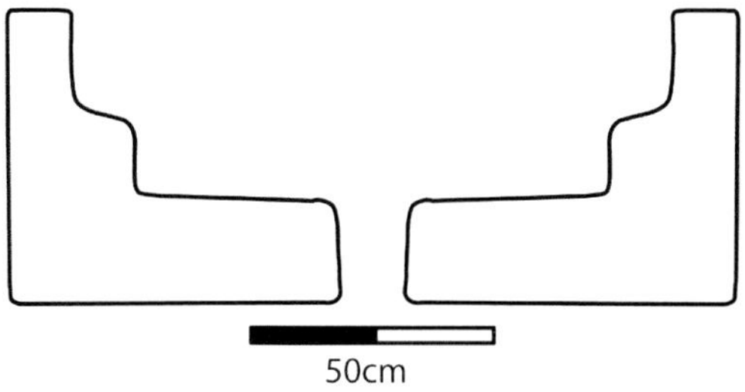

Figure 3.9: *1b* (BSN-B1).

Of the 14 identified pierced sockets in these two groups, nine are circular and range in diameter from 0.10 m to 0.30 m. Another four had square-shaped perforations, two of which were not cut through vertically. In basin JEB-B1 the socket is square at the top then circular all the way down. Basin LAT-B2 was square with a round shape in its lower part. BTR-B2 was the only basin missing a pivoting zone, and while the central hole was undoubtedly pierced it could not be identified with certainty. The shape of these perforated pivot sockets varied, which suggests that several different methods were used to adjust the vertical axis of the wooden pivot where its lower end revolved in the pivot-socket or was firmly fixed and immobile.

1c: (8 examples). The area where the outer wall meets the crushing surface is somewhat curved in profile (Figure 3.10). Some examples having a working surface which dips slightly towards the central pierced hole. Four of the sockets ranges in diameter from 0.10 m to 0.24 m. A square socket is also recorded in three basins with sides between 0.13 m to 0.20 m in length.

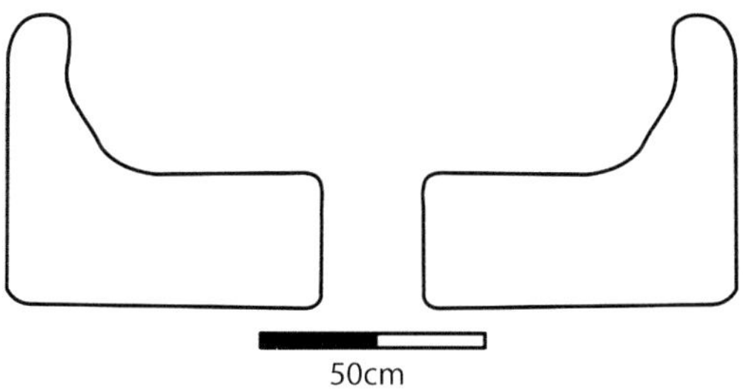

Figure 3.10: *1c* (SKH-B1).

1d: (7 examples). The crushing basin (Figure 3.11) resembles *Type 1c*, but is provided with a slightly deeper convex crushing bed and the pivot socket is surrounded by a fairly low raised protrusion (GBR-B2). All the perforated central holes are round and range in diameter from 0.10 m to 0.30 m.

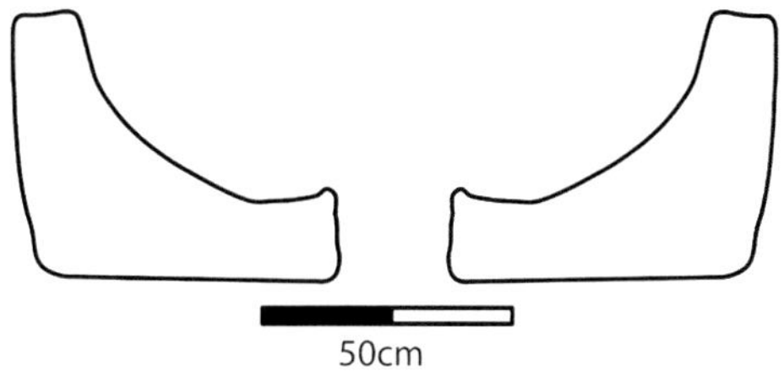

Figure 3.11: *1d* (GBR-B2).

1e: (1 example) Similar to *Type 1d*, but the crushing area is more curved and has a pierced socket cut into a projecting stone cylinder at the centre (Figure 3.12). Only one example (ZHR-B1) found in Cyprus is recorded to have possessed an integral central perforated column identical to *Type 2b* (Hadjisavvas 1992: 14, fig. 19d). This mill is represented by one basin, and is therefore included here within the same group, since future surveys may record further examples. The socket is square and measured 0.20 m a side.

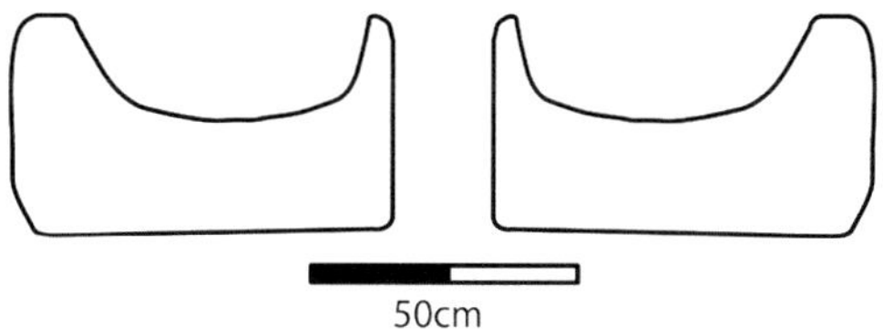

Figure 3.12: *1e* (ZHR-B1).

1f: (6 examples). The crushing basin (Figure 3.13) resembles *1d* but has a sunken pivot socket cut directly into the crushing stone. Among the 6 basins in which central perforated sockets are recorded, 5 were found to have round sockets ranging in width from 0.10 m to 0.24 m, and only one is provided with a square socket (LAM B6) measuring 0.20 m on each side. However, this pivot-socket is peculiar, and it seems likely that the socket was originally not pierced and subsequently worn so badly a perforated hole was left as the result of constant contact between the wooden pivot and the stone socket. However, this deformation did not affect the efficiency of the crushing operation as the device was modified to allow the wooden pivot to be secured in place. Accordingly, this mill mortar is treated here as part of this pierced socket group.

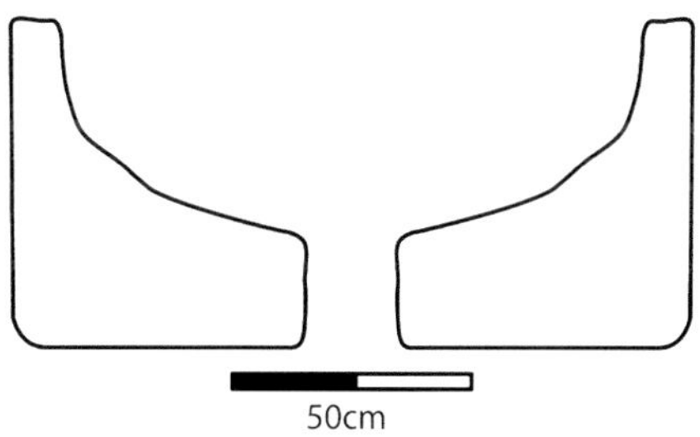

Figure 3.13: *1f* (WAS-B1).

1g: (3 examples). A large concave basin with a deep internal base Figure 3.14), generally similar to *1f* but with an uneven crushing space and a central perforation surrounded by either a very low protrusion or a sunken pierced hole encompassed by a shallow circular recess. These sockets were all round and ranged in diameter from 0.10 m to 0.22 m. The undulated crushing surface may have been caused by use of different millstones at different times.

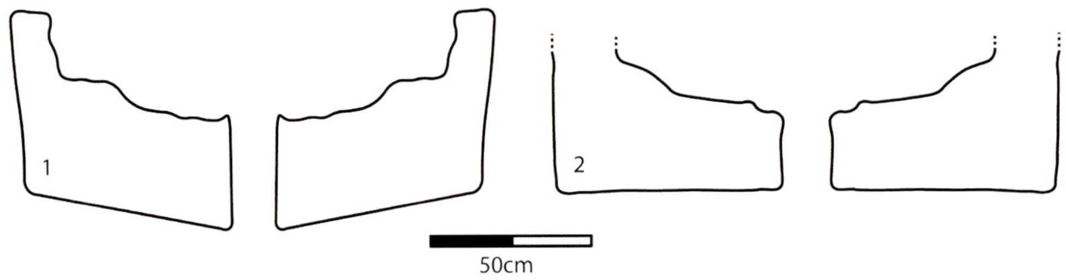

Figure 3.14: *1g:* 1 (HRR-B2), 2 (FWA-B4).

Amongst *Type 1*, the thickness of the outer rim is on average 0.14 m, while the range of the internal diameter varied between 0.85 m and 1.55 m with an average of 1.29 m (Table 3.3).

	External	Internal
Average diameter	1.54 m	1.29 m
Maximum diameter	1.90 m	1.55 m
Minimum diameter	1.00 m	0.85 m

Table 3.3: Overall diameters of *Type 1*.

Type 2: (11 examples). The outer wall slopes gently towards a slightly convex deep inner face (Figure 3.15). The crushing basin has a square, rectangle or round pivot socket cut into a very low protrusion at the centre. The pivot socket comes in three common shapes. Almost half of them were round with a diameter ranging from 0.16 m to 0.22 m and 0.13 m to 0.24 m deep. Three sockets were oblong, and these ranged in width from 0.10 m to 0.30 m, 0.10 m to 0.3 m in length and 0.05 m to 0.23 m in depth. Two sockets were square with sides 0.15 m long and a significant difference in depth of between 0.13 and 0.27 m.

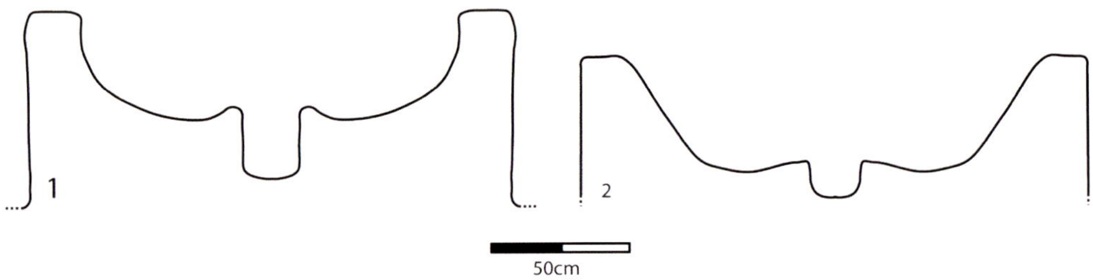

Figure 3.15: *Type 2:* 1 (DJJ-B1), 2 (MRK-B1).

Type 2a: (11 examples). Similar to *Type 2*, but has a fairly flat working surface and a vertical sidewall dipping into a deep or shallow base (Figure 3.16). Circular and rectangular sockets are equally represented, with one example being square shaped. Their depth ranged from 0.10 m to 0.23 m, and the diameter of the circular type was 0.10 m to 0.16 m. Meanwhile, the width and length of the rectangular type varied from 0.15 to 0.25 m. The only square socket measured 0.12 m a side and 0.10 m deep.

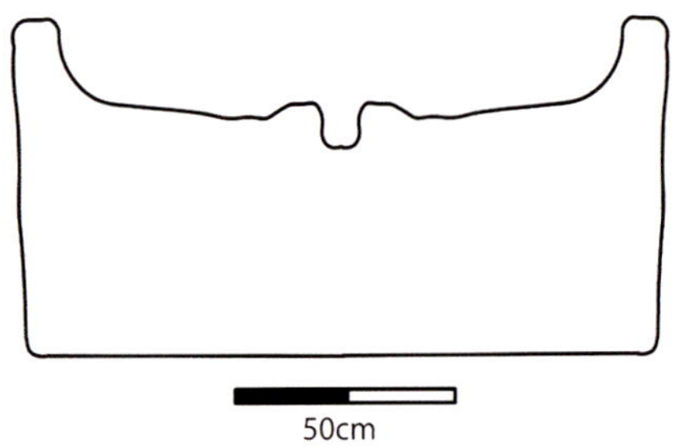

Figure 3.16: *2a* (BTH-B1).

Type 2b: (6 examples). Large concave basin similar to *Type 2*, but the base is provided with a sunken socket (Figure 3.17). The round shape is numerically predominant and varies between broad to narrow and from vertical to oblique sides. Their outside diameter ranged from 0.15 m to 0.35 m and from 0.10 m to 0.34 m deep. One is represented in a slightly tapering rectangular hole, measuring 0.20 × 0.23 m at the top to 0.13 × 0.10 m with a total depth of 0.25 m.

The average internal diameter of basins in Type 2 is 1.35 m, and ranged from 1.52 m to 1.1 m. The average thickness of the rim is 0.15 m and ranged from 0.08 m to 0.22 m (Table 3.4).

	External	Internal
Average diameter	1.60 m	1.35 m
Maximum diameter	1.85 m	1.52 m
Minimum diameter	1.30 m	1.10 m

Table 3.4: Overall diameters of *Type 2*.

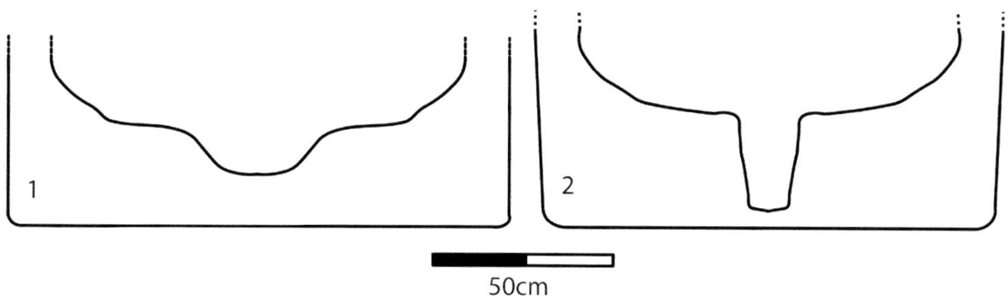

Figure 3.17: *2b:* 1 (BED-B1), 2 (MAS-B6).

Type 3: (27 examples). The mill mortars are generally flat in section, which corresponds to the profile of *Type 1*, sometimes with a deep and sometimes with a shallow profile (Figure 3.18). The main difference here is that the centre of the basin bears a sunken pivot socket cut directly into the crushing floor. The shape of this sunken pivot socket varies. Almost equal numbers of circular and square shapes were found, and one example was found with a rectangular socket. The circular sockets range from 0.16 m to 0.20 m in diameter, and their average depth is 0.22 m. In the square sockets, the length of the sides ranges from 0.12 to 0.24 m, with clear differences in depth from 0.05 m to 0.25 m. The only rectangular socket is 0.20 m deep and varies in dimensions from 0.15 × 0.20 m at the top and 0.15 × 0.20 m nearly at the bottom. The socket in JEB-B4 is round through its upper part and 0.14 m across, with a square hole at the bottom which was 0.12 m on each side.

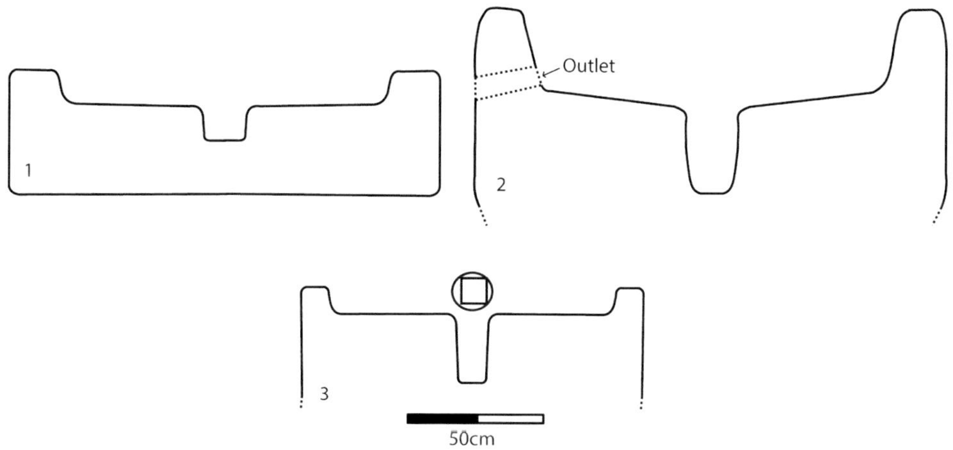

Figure 3.18: *Type 3:* 1 (BSF-B2), 2 (LAM-B4), 3 (JEB-B4).

An example of this type is the crushing basin which was found with an outlet hole cut into the sidewall (LAM-B4). Mill mortars with outlet channels are rarely found in the Levantine and North African sites (Frankel 1999: 73; Mattingly and Hitchner 1993: 456). While the purpose of this outlet hole is uncertain, Ayalon (2009: 163) argued that the hole was used to drain off rainwater based on a similar crushing basin found in the open air. This idea relies on the fact that the manufacturing process takes place in the rainy season, but strikingly neglects the fact that leaving the crushing area unsheltered would not only make the work messy but would also spoil the olive paste. It is more likely that the hole was used as an expedient way to evacuate the watery liquid (Mattingly and Hitchner 1993: 456), presumably during routine cleaning.

Type 3a: (10 examples). The type is similar to *Type 3*, but the centre of the basin bears a pivot socket cut into a central low sleeve that protrudes from the working surface, which is either flat at the top or bears a round edge (Figure 3.19). The socket is generally circular, 0.10 m to 0.20 m across and 0.07 m to 0.39 m deep. The square hole measured between 0.17 m and 0.3 m on each side and between 0.10 m and 0.23 m deep. In one example the socket is rectangular, measuring 0.08 m × 0.12 m and 0.06 m deep. In another case the square socket is widened in the upper part to become smaller all the way down. In one case, a socket was represented by a round pivot socket that is kinked to narrow toward the bottom (LAT-B1). Another similar socket was found in basin (BTR-B1), but it had been ground down into tapered sections.

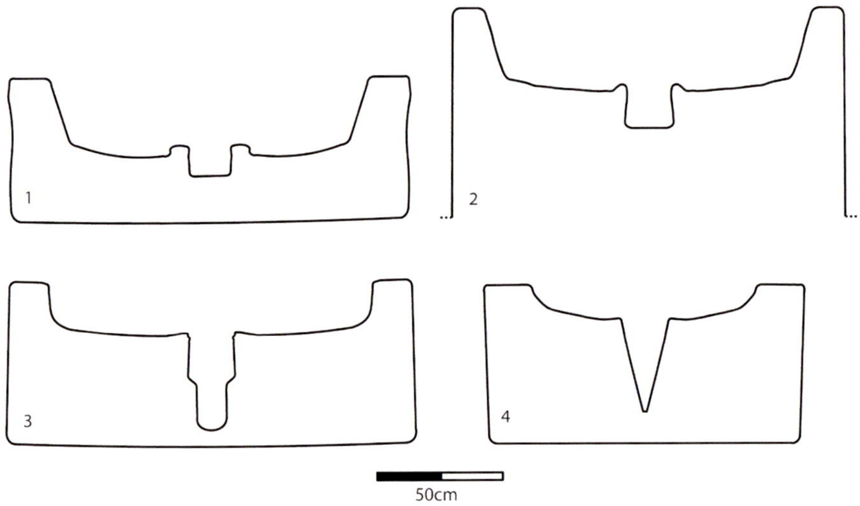

Figure 3.19: *3a*: 1 (FWA-B5), 2 (SNB-B4), 3 (LAT-B1), 4 (BTR-B1).

Type 3b: (9 examples). Similar *Type 3* with a flat crushing surface, but it lacks both a socket and an integral central column. Three sub-types of this type were found (Figure 3.20).

3b, i: Possesses a very shallow depression from round to square, which ranges in width from 0.10 m to 0.20 m and has an average depth of 0.03 m. Only two examples (LAM-B9 and TOC-B1) are provided with an outlet cut through the side wall in the base of the mill (see above *Type 3*).

3b, ii: This is closely akin to the sub-type *3b, i*, but the crushing surface shows a gentle slope towards a central low depression (BIA-B1 and BNN-B1).

3b, iii: Possesses a slight projection instead of a central shallow pivot socket (MAS-B5). In this basin, the slight solid protrusion in the centre of the floor may indicate that this element is closer to the shape of the pressing bed (compare the press-bed *Type 5* 'SHB-P1'). However, the diameter of the basin was 1.50 m, and a similar though not identical example was found at Khirbet Zabadi in Upper Galilee (Frankel *et al.* 1994: fig. 24A). This suggests that this element more likely corresponds to the shape of the mill mortar. As this type lacks a socket to hold a vertical pivot for mounting a crushing stone, then there must have been two millstones on one axle which supported each other in position (Frankel 1999: 72).

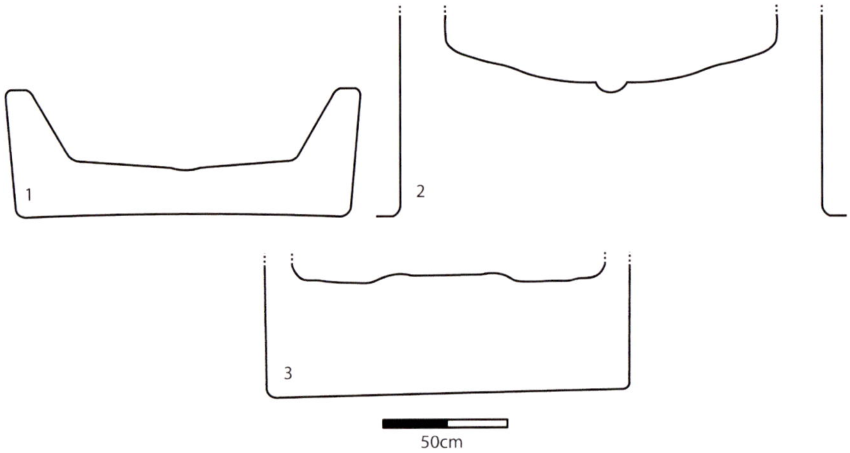

Figure 3.20: *1: 3b, i* (ZET-B1), 2: *3b, ii* (BIA-B1), 3: *3b, iii* (MAS-B5).

While the inside diameters of the basins are quite similar to those noted in Type 1 (Table 3.5), the thickness of the rims varies significantly from 0.07 m to 0.25 m, with an average of 0.14 m.

	External	Internal
Average diameter	1.57 m	1.29 m
Maximum diameter	1.90 m	1.60 m
Minimum diameter	1.00 m	0.85 m

Table 3.5: Overall diameters of *Type 3*.

Type 4: (18 examples). Mill mortars of this type include a shallow and deep bowl-shaped profile, with a stepped sidewall and a sunken central hole (Figure 3.21). Sometimes the stepping appears on the crushing surface, and the central socket is represented by a sizable (SAG-B6) or simple shallow central notch (SRH-B3). In the 11 basins with sunken sockets, 5 were found to be circular, 3 had square holes, 2 had rectangular sockets, and one was deformed. The round sockets were between 0.12 m and 0.2 m in diameter, with one exceptional case measuring 0.4 m. In the square sockets, the length of the sides ranged from 0.15 m to 0.25 m. The rectangular socket's sides varied from 0.12 m to 0.18 m in length, apart from one example which possessed a socket only 0.03 m deep. Two fell into the 0.11 m to 0.22 m span, and one had neither socket nor protrusions.

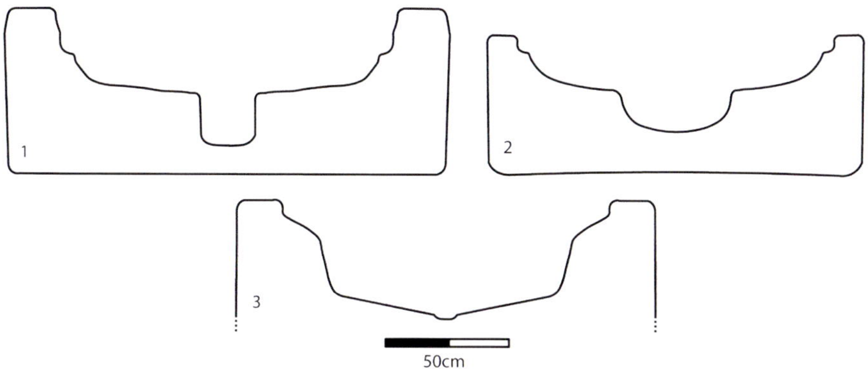

Figure 3.21: *Type 4:* 1: (TRT-B1), 2: (SAG-B6), 3: (SRH-B3).

Type 4a: (6 examples). This sub-type (Figure 3.22) follows *Type 4* in again having a stepped side wall, but it also has a pivot socket cut into a projecting stone cylinder at the centre which varies in height from 0.04 m to 0.35 m as in the mill mortar (ETB-B1) which is almost identical to a crushing basin (*Type 5*) published by Ben Baaziz (1991: 44, planche 2, no. 5). The sockets are 0.10 m to 0.30 m deep, with an insignificant difference in shape between the types mentioned above. Among the same group is a crushing basin (HRR-B4) which has slightly spiral striations on the working surface to help the crushing process.

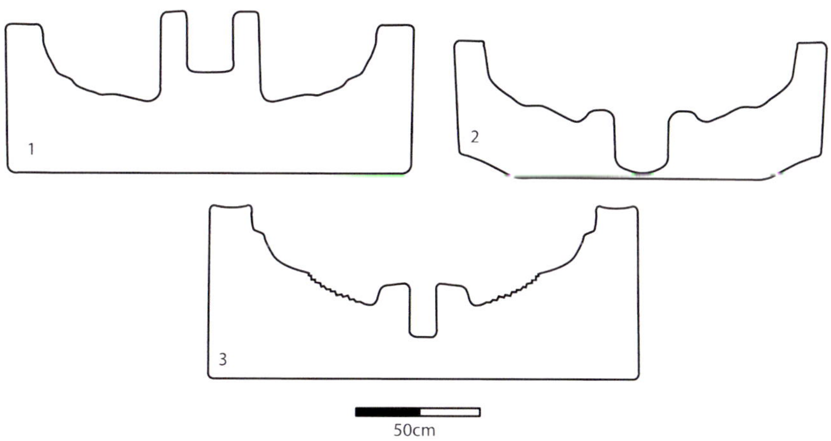

Figure 3.22: *4a*: 1: (ETB-B1), 2: (ZHR-B4), 3: (HRR-B4. Striated crushing surface).

Type 4b: (5 examples). The raised socket which protruded from the centre of the working surface is more or less resembling that of *Type 4a*, except that the base is generally shallow with a slightly concave base and straight side wall (Figure 3.23). The height of the integral column here is far shorter than that recorded in *Type 4a*, with an average of 0.12 m. Although the socket does appear in its three common shapes there is less difference in its depth, which ranges from 0.12 m to 0.20 m.

The inner diameters vary between 1.55 m to 1.05 m with an average of 1.33 m. The thickness of the rim ranges from 0.06 m to 0.20 m with an average of 0.14 m (Table 3.6).

	External	Internal
Average diameter	1.60 m	1.33 m
Maximum diameter	1.95 m	1.55 m
Minimum diameter	1.30 m	1.05 m

Table 3.6: Overall diameters of *Type 4*.

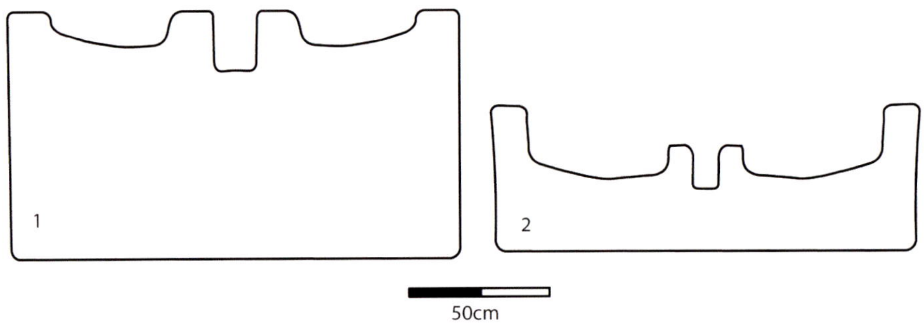

Figure 3.23: *4b:* 1: (HND-B1), 2: (NOL-B1).

Table 3.7 below shows the summary dimensions for the external and internal diameters and the rim thicknesses of the crushing basins recorded during the field survey in Cyrenaica. In all of the four main identified types, the external and internal diameters vary from between 1.00 m to 1.95 m and 0.58 m to 1.60 m respectively. The average inner diameter is 1.28 m, with a maximum basin diameter of no more than 1.60 m.

However, some of these mills can be classified with the first three groups of the largest known Roman mills (Table 3.8), as listed by Brun (1986: 77). The inside diameter of Cyrenaican mills is quite similar to that recorded in both eastern Algeria and Slougia and Dakhlet Zmit in the Tunisian high steppe, where their inner diameter ranges from 1.00 m to 1.53 m (Lanfranchi 2009: 273) and 0.70 m to 1.55 m (Hermassi 2004) respectively. Of the eleven recorded basins in the Tarhuna plateau, only one measures 1.85 m in diameter (Ahmed 2019: Table 4.2, DUN128), while the rest seems to have approximately the same inner diameter as the Cyrenaican mills. The thickness of the outer rims of Cyrenaican basins ranges from between 0.06 m to 0.32 m, and averages 0.15 m.

Type	Diameter	Ext. dia.	Int. dia.	Thickness	Rim
1	Av.	1.54 m	1.29 m	Av.	0.14 m
	Max.	1.90 m	1.55 m	Max.	0.32 m
	Min.	1.00 m	0.85 m	Min.	0.08 m
2	Av.	1.60 m	1.35 m	Av.	0.15 m
	Max.	1.85 m	1.52 m	Max.	0.22 m
	Min.	1.30 m	1.10 m	Min.	0.08 m
3	Av.	1.57 m	1.29 m	Av.	0.14 m
	Max.	1.90 m	1.60 m	Max.	0.25 m
	Min.	1.00 m	0.85 m	Min.	0.07 m
4	Av.	1.60 m	1.33 m	Av.	0.14 m
	Max.	1.95 m	1.55 m	Max.	0.20 m
	Min.	1.30 m	1.05 m	Min.	0.06 m
All types	Overall Av. Dia.	1.54 m	1.28 m	Overall Av. Th.	0.15 m

Table 3.7: All types. Overall external and internal diameter and rim thickness of basins.

Mill location	External diameter (m)	Reference
Sbeitla (Tunisia)	1.50	Duval and Baratte 1973
Wadi Sebt (Algeria)	1.50	Leveau 1979
Slougia and Dakhlet Zmit (Tunisia)	1.55	Hermassi 2004
Kafr Nabo 1 (Syria)	1.60	Callot 1979
Taqle (Syria)	1.65	Callot 1979
El Arba (Algeria)	1.70	Leveau 1979
Khorazin (Palestine)	1.80	Yeivin 1966
Aghrem (Algeria)	1.90	Leveau 1979
Tirat Yehuda (Palestine)	1.90	Yeivin 1966
Khirbet Yajuz (Palestine)	2.00	Thomson 1979
El Kfeir (Syria)	2.05	Callot 1979
Kafr Nabo 2 (Syria)	2.10	Callot 1979
Amman (Jordan)	2.10	Zayadine 1977-8
Gebel Tarhuna (Libya)	2.10	Ahmed 2019

Table 3.8: The large olive mills recorded from different Mediterranean sites *(after Brun 1986: 77).*

Among the 129 basins in which the shape of the central pivot is discernible, 39 (30%) are pierced (Table 3.9). Basins with circular holes are found to comprise 58% of the total, followed by square sockets which comprise 31%, while only 11% have been found to have rectangular holes.

Type	circle	square	rectangle	total
1a	7	3	0	10
1b	2	0	0	2
1c	4	3	0	7
1d	7	1	0	8
1e	5	1	0	6
1f	3	0	0	3
2	5	1	3	9
2a	7	0	2	9
2b	2	1	1	4
3	11	13	3	27
3a	6	3	1	10
3b	6	2	0	8
4	8	5	3	16
4a	1	3	2	6
4b	1	2	1	4
Total	75	38	16	129

Table 3.9: Shape of the central socket in all types.

The depth of the milling area varied from 0.03 m to 0.55 m with an average of 0.27 m. As opposed to the flat-bottomed mills which are predominant in most of North Africa (Ben Baaziz 1985; Mattingly 1996: 578), the Cyrenaican basins had sloping or convex working surfaces. Consequently, the lower and upper spaces of the milling areas between the outer wall and the central socket are considerably different. In general, the width of the crushing space varied from 0.20 m at the bottom to 0.70 m at rim level.

Many basins have a convex profile, which demonstrates the use of the *trapetum* type of mill stones. Others had a flat-bottomed crushing surface, indicating the use of the *mola olearia*. The bowl-shaped mill mortar is abundant in Cyrenaica. The region saw a wide variation in the shape of the basins. Thus, the processing capacity of the mill mortar varied considerably (Table 3.10). Among the 138 basins in which the internal profile was discernible, 71 possessed a convex or gently round profile while 67 had a flat crushing surface. It is surprising that this is rarely recorded in the Mediterranean world (Frankel 1993: 478; 1999: 73). This is a strong indication that their use was part of a tradition entrenched in Cyrenaica's main cultural stream.

	Element no.	Type	Capacity (litre)
Min.	MSM-B1	3a	16.6
Max.	SNB-B1	3	829.0
Av.			326.7

Table 3.10: Estimation of processing capacity for some of the recorded mills. The capacity is estimated without subtracting the volume of the stone crushers and it is unclear whether the mills in Cyrenaica were single or twin millstones, but the latter was more likely.

3.3.2.1 Distribution patterns of mill mortar types

The distribution maps of the four main types of mill mortars generally appear to show an equal distribution across the region from the upper escarpments of the Gebel to the coastal strip (Figure 3.24). However, this distribution looks slightly different if we also consider sub-types as shown in figures 3.25–3.28.

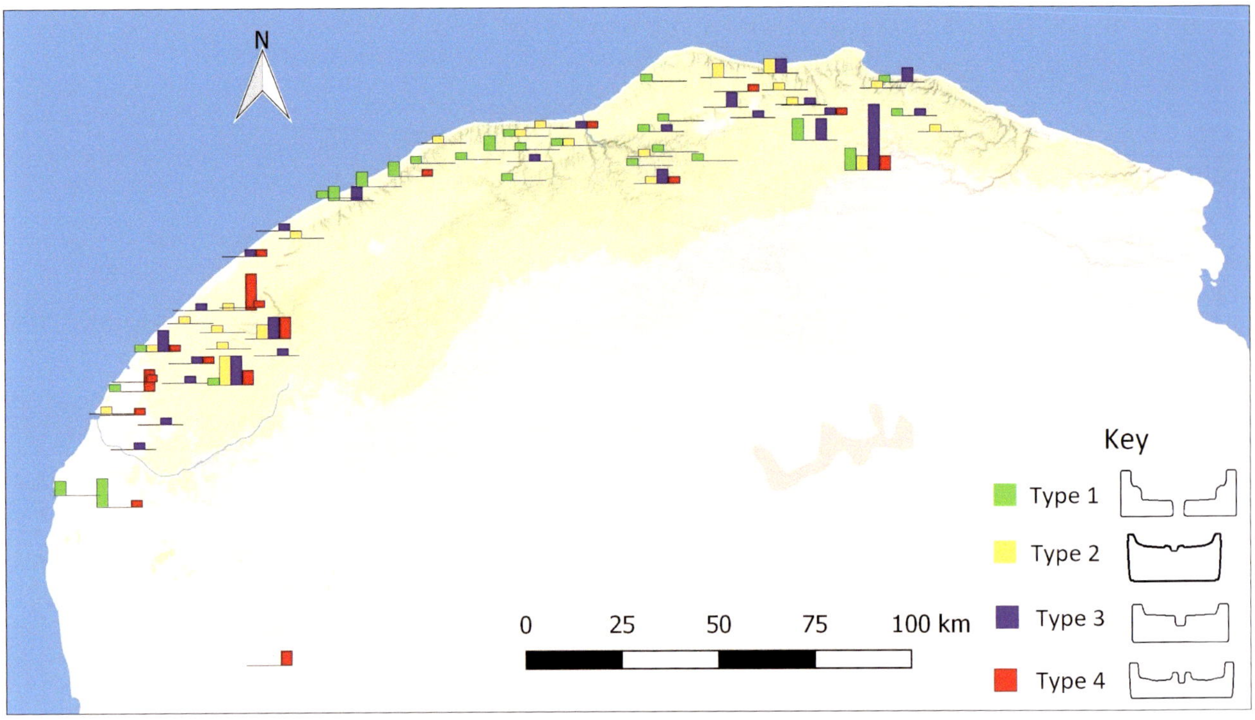

Figure 3.24: Distribution map of the four main mill mortars, types 1–4.

One of the key differences between these four main types is that the crushing basin, *Type 1*, has a pierced central socket. Ben Baaziz sees this type, which was found in Tunisia, as being used for milling grain, but Mattingly and Hitchner (1993: 444) and Sehili (2009: 144–145) regard the type as more likely used for milling olives. The latter interpretation is confirmed by ample evidence of *Type 1* originating from Cyrenaica and being strongly connected to oil production. This was the most numerous type (49 examples) and its distribution is clearly defined in the central area, while variants were found in eastern and western Cyrenaica (Figure 3.25). This type of mill mortar would work well with millstones of *Types A* to *D*. The predominance of the *Type 1* mill in the central area was perhaps a result of greater conservatism in this region. However, one should not ignore the obvious lower weight of this type in comparison to other mill types, thus its carting and ease of its manufacture were possibly the reasons for its widespread geographical distribution. Of the seven variants *Type 1a* was common across the region, though more concentrated in the upper plateau. *Type 1b* was less common and only found in the upper plateau, east of Wadi al-Kuf. *Type 1c* had a clear concentration in the central area and seems, with *Type 1e*, to be predominant in the Benghazi coastal area with a clear absence of the other *Type 1* sub-types. These two sub-types were totally absent in the upper plateau, east of Cyrene. *Type 1d* has a similar distribution to *1c* but it was very rare in the Benghazi region. *Type 1f* was concentrated in the central area and frequent in the upper plateau but very rare in the Benghazi region. *Type 1g* was absent in the area east of Wadi al-Kuf and rare in the central area, but was frequently found westwards, especially in the area west of Teucheira.

The second most numerous mill mortar is *Type 3* (Figure 3.26) which would work well with millstones of types A, B, D and E. It is spread across most parts of the eastern Gebel, mainly in Lamluda, but also commonly found throughout the western region in the Benghazi coastal plain. It is less commonly found in the central area. Two further sub-types and three variants are recognised in this group. *Type 3a*, was common in both eastern and western areas but was not found in the central region. *Type 3b, i* was only found in the upper plateau east of Cyrene and the Benghazi coastal plain, being completely absent in the central region. *Type 3b, ii* was very rare, only being found in the Benghazi coastal plain. *Type 3b, iii* was not common, and only one example was found in the Benghazi coastal plain.

Meanwhile, *Types 2* and *4* are represented in almost equal numbers (Figure 3.27 and Figure 3.28). These two types show similar distribution patterns with a clear concentration in the eastern and western areas, but whose presence was extremely rare in the intermediate area between Ptolemais and Qasr Libya. *Type 2* was present in both the upper plateau and the Benghazi area but very rare in the central region. *Type 2a* had a distribution similar to that of *Type 2*, though less common and *Type 2b* was frequently observed in the central region but was very rare in both the upper plateau and the Benghazi coastal area. *Type 4* would work well with millstones of types A to D and was found at many sites in the eastern upper plateau but poorly

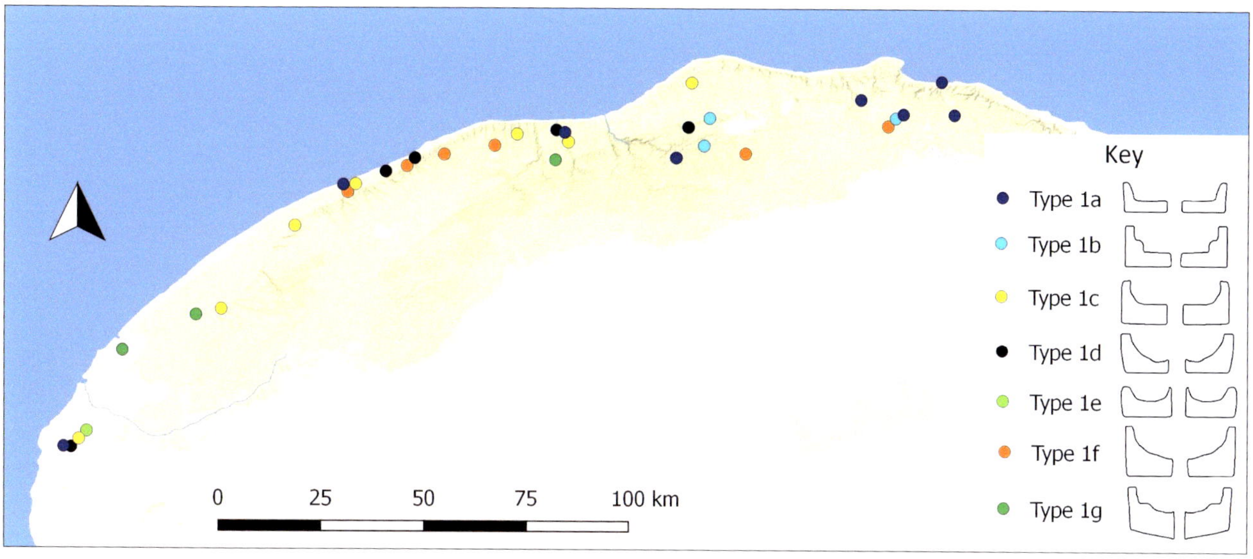

Figure 3.25: Distribution map of sub-types of mill mortar type 1.

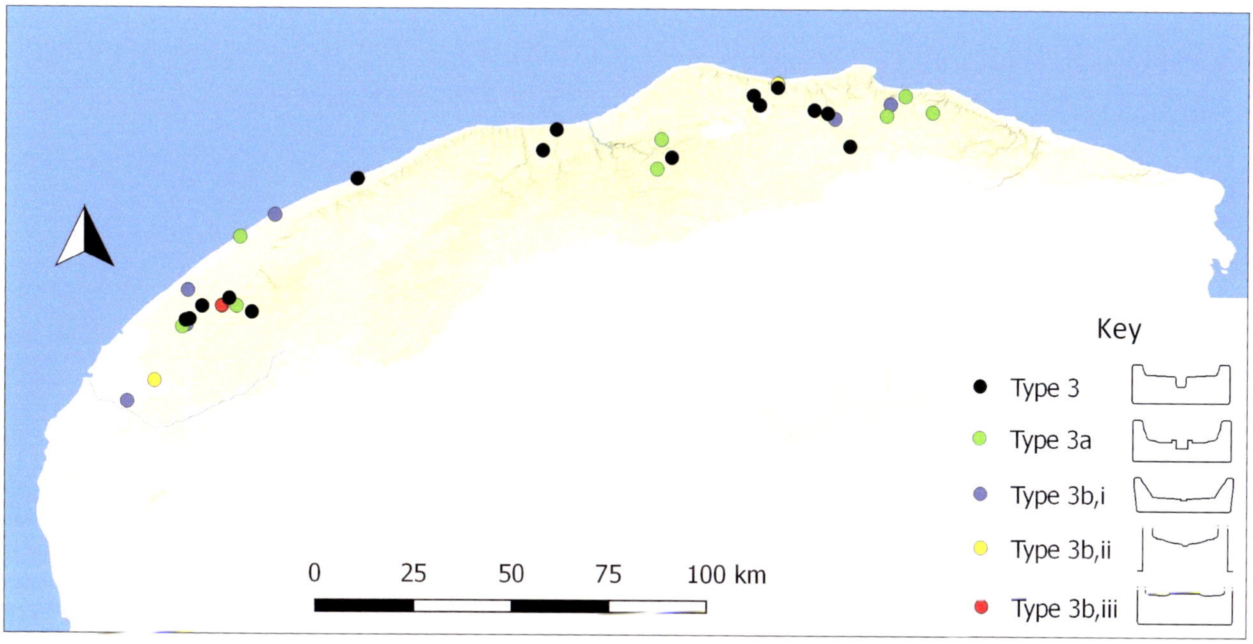

Figure 3.26: Distribution map of sub-types of mill mortar type 3.

represented in the central area. It was commonly found in the Benghazi coastal plain but there was only one example found in south-eastern Berenice, which can be seen as representing the western limit of the Cyrenaican distribution. *Type 4a* resembles Ben Bazziz's *Type 5* found in Tunisia and considered by him to belong to the *trapetum* type (Ben Bazziz 1991: 44). These two sub-types would work well with millstones of types C and D. This convex basin was only common in the area west of Tocra and only two examples in the upper plateau have so far been recorded *Type 4b* was also common in the Benghazi coastal plain area, but very poorly represented in the central region and with a complete absence in the eastern upper plateau.

In general, the flat-surfaced crushing basin, *mola olearia*, represented by *Types 1–3*, was the predominant type in Cyrenaica. It should be noted that the lens-shaped crushing stones found in Cyrenaica were thicker than those found in Olynthus, the latter being thought to belong to the *trapetum*-type mill with its cup-shaped profile (Foxhall 1993: 190, fig. 5 a and b). Concomitantly, the shape of most crushing basins in Cyrenaica does not take the distinctive convex profile that appears in the *trapetum* type, but rather that of a gentle sloping working edge which most likely represents the wear process after long periods of use. However, three examples that have been noted in Cyrenaica can be included in the *trapetum* category. The first is a

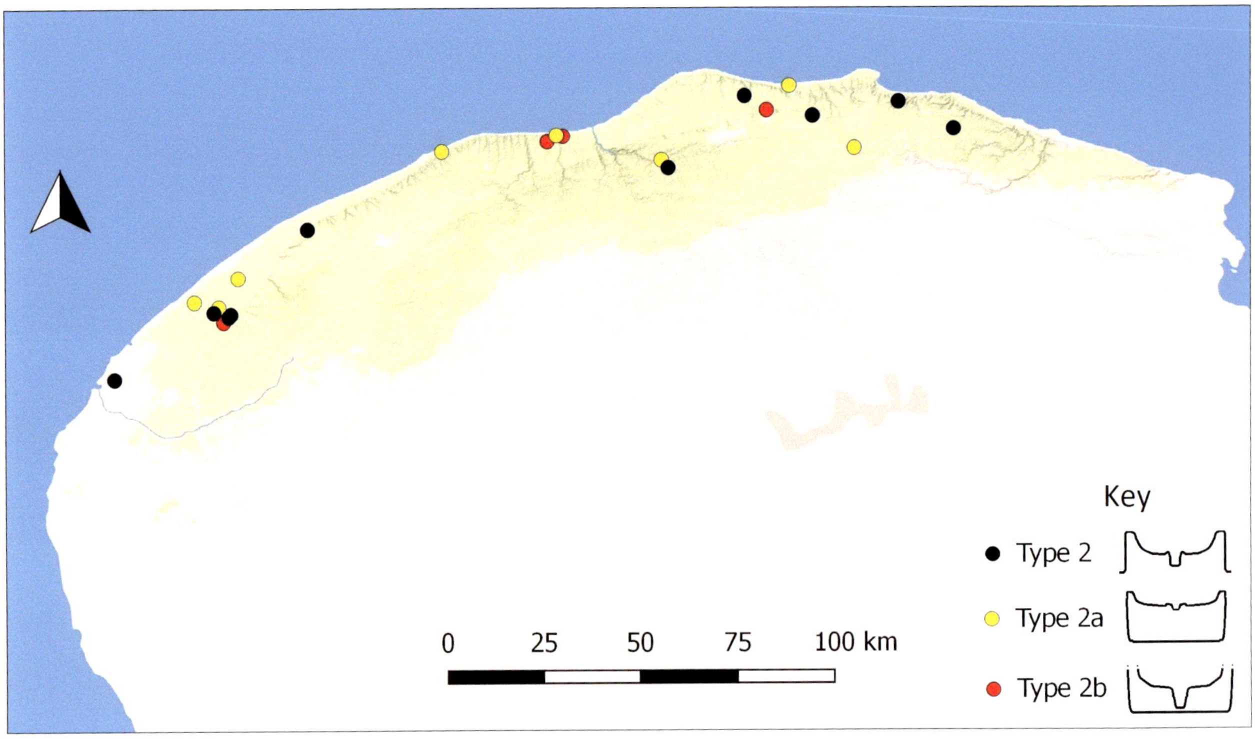

Figure 3.27: Distribution map of sub-types of mill mortar type 2.

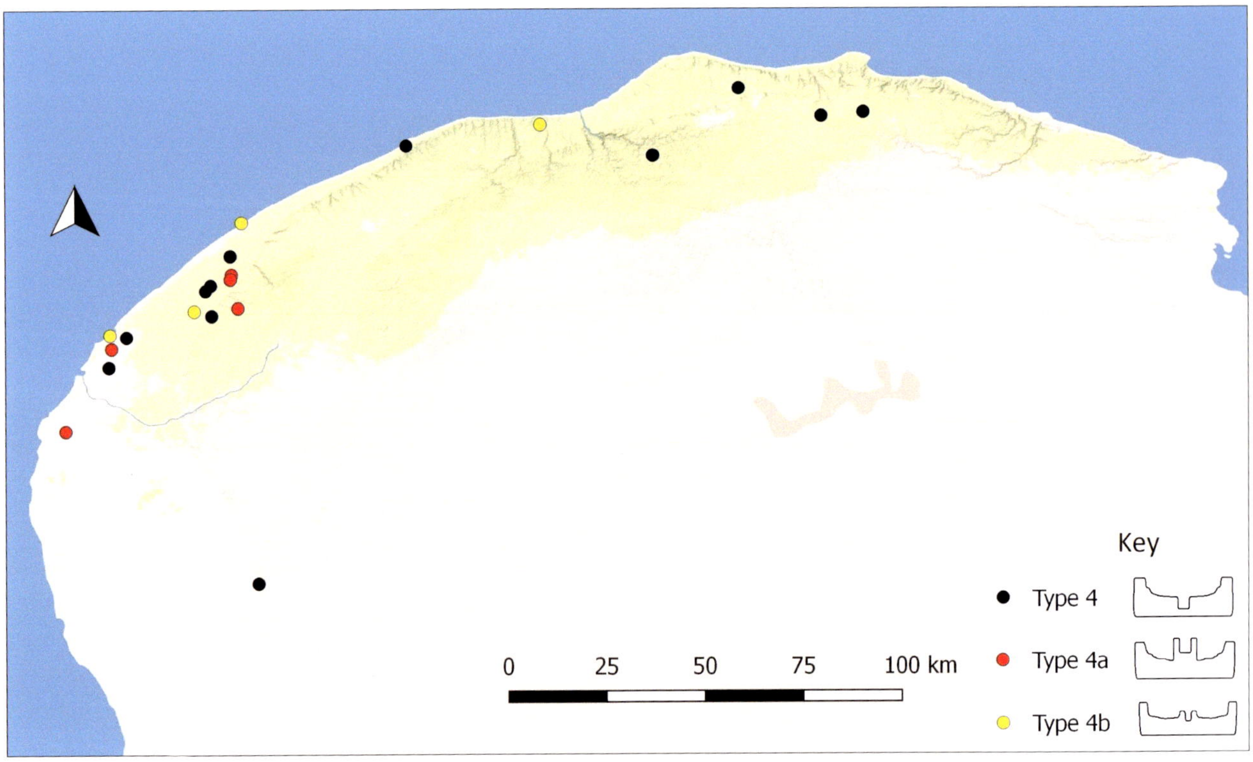

Figure 3.28: Distribution map of sub-types of mill mortar type 4.

crushing basin (ETB-B1), classified as *Type 4a*. The second is represented by a *Type 4c* lens-like crushing stone (YRA-S3). The final example (not included in the database) came from a site recently bulldozed just north of the village of Labraq (Figure 5.2). A similar picture for the distribution pattern of the *trapetum* type was also observed in North Africa (Mattingly 1996: 578: fig. 1), where it seems more likely to have a localised distribution with a concentration around Cap Bon (Ben Baaziz 1991: 43) and the Gulf of Gabès (Hobson 2015: 69). The concave basin was also found in Greece, Malta, southern Italy, and Spain (Frankel 1999: 73).

Archaeological evidence from the various regions of the Mediterranean basin indicates that the *mola olearia* millstone type is the most prevalent, both in the western and eastern Mediterranean, including amongst the major producers. Hobson (2015: 70) rightly pointed out that the widespread distribution of this type of mill crusher was likely since its manufacture was easier than that of the *trapetum* type, which required skilled workmen to produce. If we accept that there is no evidence that crushing olive stones tints the flavour of oil, then the type of mill used will not have affected the quality of the oil. There are many factors that would have affected the quality such as the ripeness of the fruit and the storage conditions before it ended up in the mill (see section 3.4.1). Understandably, the producers were aware of the fact that well crushed olives would have a much greater yield of oil than those that were only bruised (Foxhall 2007: 134).

chapter four

TYPES AND DISTRIBUTION PATTERNS OF CYRENAICAN PRESSING ELEMENTS

4.1 Introduction

This chapter focuses on the large number and remarkable diversity of pressing elements that are evident across Cyrenaica. The early days of archaeological exploration were marked by ambiguous identification of some pressing elements. For example, upright monoliths found by nineteenth-century travellers in the south-west of Cyprus (Cesnola 1877: 198) and north-west of Libya (Cowper 1897: 131) were initially imaginatively interpreted as religious artefacts with mysterious properties. By contrast, similar standing features in the upper plateaus of Cyrenaica, particularly at Lamluda, were overlooked by these early travellers. The Cyrenaican type was clearly less impressive in height when compared with those cited above, which may explain why they went unmentioned.

4.2 Types of Cyrenaican Pressing Elements

4.2.1 Uprights

A total of 143 different upright artefacts was investigated (Table AI.3). These evidently varied, probably due to the range of natural resources available for exploitation and the quarrying potential. The uprights recorded during the survey have been classified into three types regardless on whether the beam socket or fulcrum was rectangular, square, circular or was a 'T' shaped niche carved from the rock or built into a wall. A very few uprights also had two beam sockets.

Type 1: A monolithic free-standing large stone with a beam socket cut in its face almost in the middle (Figure 4.1). A large block stone is sometimes transversely laid on top of the standing upright, made of either single or twin blocks. Presumably the installation was roofed, and the upright was incorporated into the wall fabric of the pressing room.

Figure 4.1: *Type 1*: LAM-U1.

Type 1a: similar to the main Type 1 but made of two stones standing side by side (Figure 4.2). One example (USM-U1) bears a butterfly tenon at the edge of the two joined stones for further stability. Type 1 and Type 1a are both associated with the press bed Types 7 and 9.

Figure 4.2: *Type 1a*: JEB-U1.

Figure 4.3: *Type 2,* left: CNS-U2; right: two beam sockets: DJJ-Us 2 and 3, scale 0.5 m.

Type 2: A niche carved into the face of the living rock in either a surface or subterranean press room (Figure 4.3). Only associated with press bed *Types* 6 and *8*.

Type 3: In this type, the pressing beam is anchored in the wall of the press room in a purpose-made niche or socket (Figure 4.4). These press room walls rarely survive, unlike the large free-standing stones. In most cases the walls have collapsed, and the presence of oil presses can only be attested by the presence of the press bed. Taking measurements is not possible. The best surviving example was found in Jebra.

Figure 4.4: *Type* 3, left: JEB-U2; right: YRA-U1, scale 0.5 m.

Miscellaneous: A monolithic upright with oval shaped niches (Figure 4.5) was made of two stones standing side by side (only half of this existed). Two holes at the upper corners were 15 cm in diameter and 10 cm deep. Another elongated hole (10 × 5 × 5 cm) was cut some 30 cm off the niche. The half niche indicates that the upright was composed of two joined stones. Similar holes were noted in uprights from Cyprus provided with perforated pierced niches (see Hadjisavvas 1992: figs 187, 194 and 212i).

Figure 4.5: Miscellaneous, LAM-U39, scale 0.5 m.

4.2.1.1 Distribution patterns of upright types

As with other parts of North Africa, the predominant type of ancient press in Cyrenaica was the lever press with the three main types of uprights. Similar methods of securing the fixed end of the pressing beam were found in many parts of the Classical, and even later

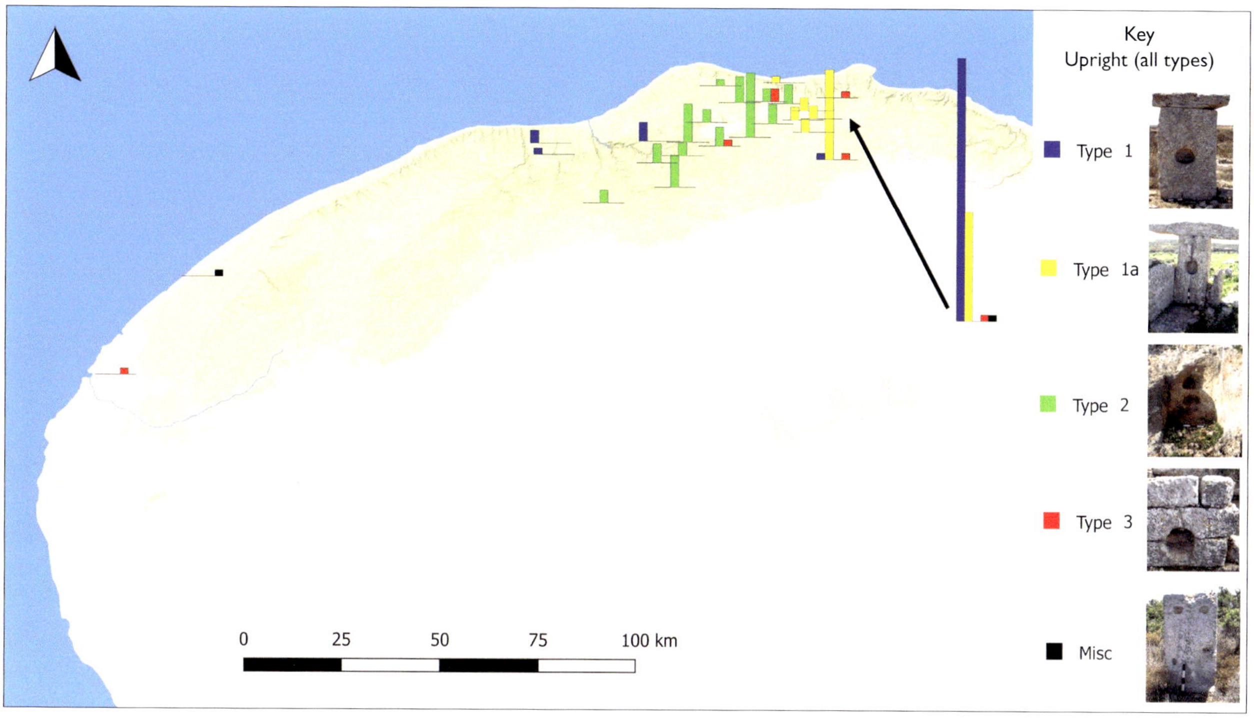

Figure 4.6: Distribution map for upright types.

in Hellenistic and Roman Greece (Foxhall 2007: 137), Cyprus (Hadjisavvas 1992; 1993) and southern Palestine (Frankel *et al.* 1994: 40–1). Evidently, the use of a pair of limestone uprights (*arbores*) with a range of different combinations of holes, slots and grooves that was the most obvious archaeological feature in Tripolitanian and central Tunisian pressing sites was not encountered in Cyrenaica. Cyrenaican presses were all operated by a weight suspended from the beam. Figure 4.6 shows the distribution of the different means of securing the fixed end of the press beam to the fabric of the press room.

In the region east of the Wadi al-Kuf the presses are characterised by free-standing uprights (*Type 1*) or rock-cut niches (*Type 2*). Farther to the west, the fixed end of the beam seems exclusively to have been anchored via a socket built into the fabric of a standing wall (*Type 3*); this, therefore, explains the absence of any other types of uprights in these archaeological sites.

4.2.2 Press beds

Nine types of pressing-bed element found during the work are identified here. Most of these press beds were made of a single monolithic block, and some were carved into available outcrops or the living rock (Table AI.4). Small examples were also noted in flat mortar floors, which were sometimes provided with further raised constructed circular *ara*. The *opus signinum* pavement seems to have been related to winery rather than oilery installations. All these stone pressing beds possessed a circular channel cut on the press bed surface, except for those found with flanked standing slabs.

The first two types were made from a single rectangular or square base stone, which can be of varying thickness and usually sports a run-off channel of internal diameter ranging from 0.32 m to 0.85 m in diameter. However, a few examples have been found which probably had run-off grooves carved through the outcrops. The moveable ones range in weight from 133–1021 kg. Nevertheless, the overall size and absolute movability of the stone is not helpful in differentiating between these two types. Instead, the internal diameter of the circular grooves can be used to delineate *Type 1* and *2*. This criterium indicates that different sizes of baskets of pulp were employed, and thus helps to estimate the capacity of the olive oil press.

Type 1: A small square or rectangular press-bed with a circular to oblong run-off groove ranging in diameter from 0.30 m to 0.55 m (Table 4.1). Sometimes a further channel running across the surface to divide the defined pressing area into two halves is also noted (Figure 4.7).

Block weight (kg)			Channel int. diameter (m)		
Average	Minimum	Maximum	Average	Minimum	Maximum
245	133	455	0.40	0.30	0.55

Table 4.1: Different measurements of *Type 1*.

Figure 4.7: *Type 1*, left: TSK-P1; right: SIL-P1, scale 0.5 m.

Type 2: Square or rectangular, with a circular run-off groove made of either a monolithic large slab or cut into an available outcrop (Figure 4.8 and Table 4.2). This type is similar to *Type 1*, but its circular channel is over 0.55 m in diameter and has large dimensions in the overall size. The channel is usually ended by a simple outlet, and sometimes a two-channelled mouth. Variations of this type were found with a slight defined circular depression and direct outlet (SRH-P1).

Block weight (kg)			Channel int. diameter (m)		
Average	Minimum	Maximum	Average	Minimum	Maximum
534	273	1021	0.67	0.57	0.85

Table 4.2: Different measurements of *Type 2.*

Figure 4.8: *Type 2* examples, left: SAG-P4 made of a single stone; right: FWA-P3 cut into the outcrop. Scale 0.5 m.

Type 3: A circular press-bed with a circumferential run-off groove and an outlet opening (Figure 4.9). A variation of this type (Table 4.3) is encompassed by a broad ridge and a channel with a short projection (WKR-P1).

Block weight (kg)			Channel diameter (m)		
Average	Minimum	Maximum	Average	Minimum	Maximum
832	170	1321	0.72	0.60	0.85

Table 4.3: Different measurements of *Type 3.*

Figure 4.9: *Type 3* examples, left: LAT-Ps 1 and 2; right: WKR-P1 plan and section. Scale 0.5 m.

Type 4 (twin press bed): A rectangular press-bed with two circular run-off grooves (sometimes of different size). It is always provided with an outlet opening at one of the circular channels (Figure 4.10 and Table 4.4). One or even two branching channels are usually cut to connect the two circles, but sometimes they merely merged to share one border or open into each other. One example (NOL-P2) was found to have three circular channels but were carved clustered and not in a line on the long surface like those found at the site of Mari-Kopetra in Cyprus (Hadjisavvas 1992: 36, figs. 61–62, 65).

Block weight (kg)			Channel int. diameter (m)		
Average	Minimum	Maximum	Average	Minimum	Maximum
1024	288	3039	0.65	0.50	0.88

Table 4.4: Different measurements of *Type 4*.

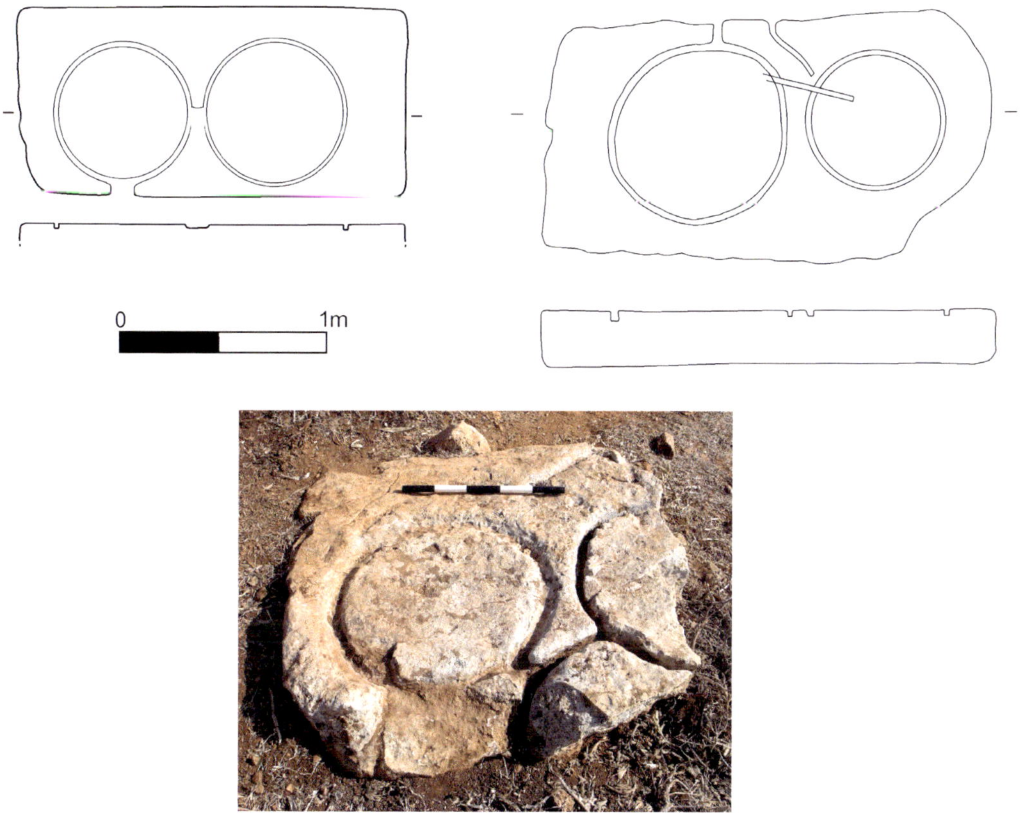

Figure 4.10: *Type 4* examples, top-left: FWA-P1; top-right: HGR-P1; bottom: NOL-P2, scale 0.5 m.

Type 5: A shallow round press-bed with a slightly raised pressing surface surrounded by a low wall. A circular channel is cut along the wall and ends in an open spout. A variation of this type was found with an outlet hole in the base of the pressing area (Figure 4.11 and Table 4.5).

Block weight (kg)			Channel int. diameter (m)		
Average	Minimum	Maximum	Average	Minimum	Maximum
1108	339	3025	0.79	0.63	1.05

Table 4.5: Different measurements of *Type 5*.

Figure 4.11: *Type 5* SHB-P1 with plan and section. Scale 0.5 m.

Type 6: A box-like compartment cut into the living rock (Figure 4.12 and Table 4.6). The inner face was either rectangular, square or circular in shape. A stub of rock-cut walls sometimes projects from either side of the opening, and there are often two vertical grooves cut opposite each other close to the entrance of the pressing area. In some instances, the pressing area is circumscribed by a shallow wide groove to open into a sunken adjacent collecting tank. In others the surface is left plain with slight sloping to the outside. This type is associated with the upright *Type 2*.

Min. dims.	Max. dims.
0.40 × 0.60 (0.24 m^2)	1.10 × 1.10 (1.2 m^2)

Table 4.6: Min. and Max. dimensions *Type 6* press-bed.

Figure 4.12: *Type 6* examples, top-left: MDS-P4 vertical grooves and plain sloping surface, scale 0.5 m; top-right: DJJ-P1 circumferential groove and a stub of walls in the opening; bottom: SHA-P4 a circumscribed circular channel on the pressing surface, scale 0.8 m. Photo: M. Abdrbba.

Figure 4.13: *Type 7:* JEP-P4 and plan. Scale 0.5 m.

Type 7: A box-like press-bed built of two stone slabs set on edge parallel to each other on a right angle from the standing upright (Figure 4.13). One or two and occasionally three grooves were cut vertically into the internal face of the two flanking screen walls. These grooves were set opposite each other with unequal intervals. Based on the number of uncovered examples, the stone floor seems to have generally been left plain without any marks of a carved channel or similar. This pressing bed type is only found in association with the free-standing uprights *Types 1* and *1a*.

Type 8: This type, rather than being formed from a stone removed from a quarry, is carved into the edge of a cliff, or cave. Two examples have been observed, subdivided here into *Type 8a* and *Type 8b*. In each case one or more socketed recesses are visible into which the fixed end of the press beam would have been placed (Figure 4.14).

Type 8a: In this case, the press-bed was formed by a circular recess carved into the rock. This recess was in a raised position, creating a platform upon which the stack of olive sacks would have been placed. This elevated position allowed the olive oil to run-off into a channel and then into a collection tank below. In contrast to other press-beds, no carved circular groove was visible on the floor of the press-bed.

Type 8b: In this example, a number of presses were positioned side-by-side and the remains of carved circular channels on the floor of the press-beds could be seen. Different methods of fixing the press beam into the carved rockface had also been used.

Figure 4.14: Left: *Type 8a* SNB-P5 plain raised press bed, scale 0.5 m; right: *Type 8b* SHA-Ps1-3. Photo: M. Abdrbba.

Figure 4.15: *Type 9* examples, left: MDS-P3 raised press bed above the rock floor level; right: SGG-P6 cemented press bed above mortar floor, scale 0.5 m.

Type 9: A bare or coated flat floor without a circular groove (Figure 4.15). In some cases a raised circular press-bed is built in front of a beam socket niche, and is probably connected with wine production. Nevertheless, a decisive conclusion from the cited examples cannot be made until further investigations are carried out accompanied by selective excavations across the region.

4.2.2.1 *Distribution patterns of press bed types*

A typology of the nine types of press-bed found during the survey was identified. Attributes and distributions (Figure 4.16) of each type can be described as follows:

Type 1: A small square or rectangular press-bed with a circular to oblong channel, its small size suggests that it was intended for household and self-sufficient production Its frequent observation in urban sites such as Tocra confirms this hypothesis. It is worth noting that large-scale olive oil installations were absent in an urban context. This is an indication that the urban elite possibly preferred to invest their capital in rural exploitation, although some light industry was also practiced within urban centres. There was widespread use of this type east of the central region and the western area of the Benghazi coastal strip.

Type 2: A circular channel carved into either a large monolithic round or square slab or cut into an available outcrop. The type is poorly represented in the eastern Gebel and the central area, but fairly common in the western region.

Type 3: A circular press-bed with a round channel with an outlet opening. A variant of this type has a channel bordered by a ridge and with a short projecting spout. The type was poorly represented in the upper plateau and very rare in the Benghazi coastal plain.

Type 4: A rectangular press-bed with double or triple circular channels, often with one outlet opening. The type was characteristic of the Benghazi coastal plain area but less common in the central region and quite rare in the upper plateau.

Type 5: A cylindrical press-bed with a slightly raised pressing surface surrounded by a low wall that ended in an open spout or an outlet hole in the base of the pressing area. The type is generally rare, where only a few examples were found in the Benghazi coastal region and was very poorly represented in the central area. It was completely absent in the upper plateau.

Type 6: A rectangular, square or circular box-like compartment hewn into the natural rock. A stub of rock-cut walls sometimes projects from either side of the opening, and there are often two vertical grooves cut opposite each other close to the entrance of the pressing area and whose purpose is to support the olive baskets and cross-pieces, which can also be placed at the top to raise the beam when it is not in use. A similar press-bed, circular in shape, was found in a traditional olive press in Yefren in the Western Gebel of Tripolitania. This type was only

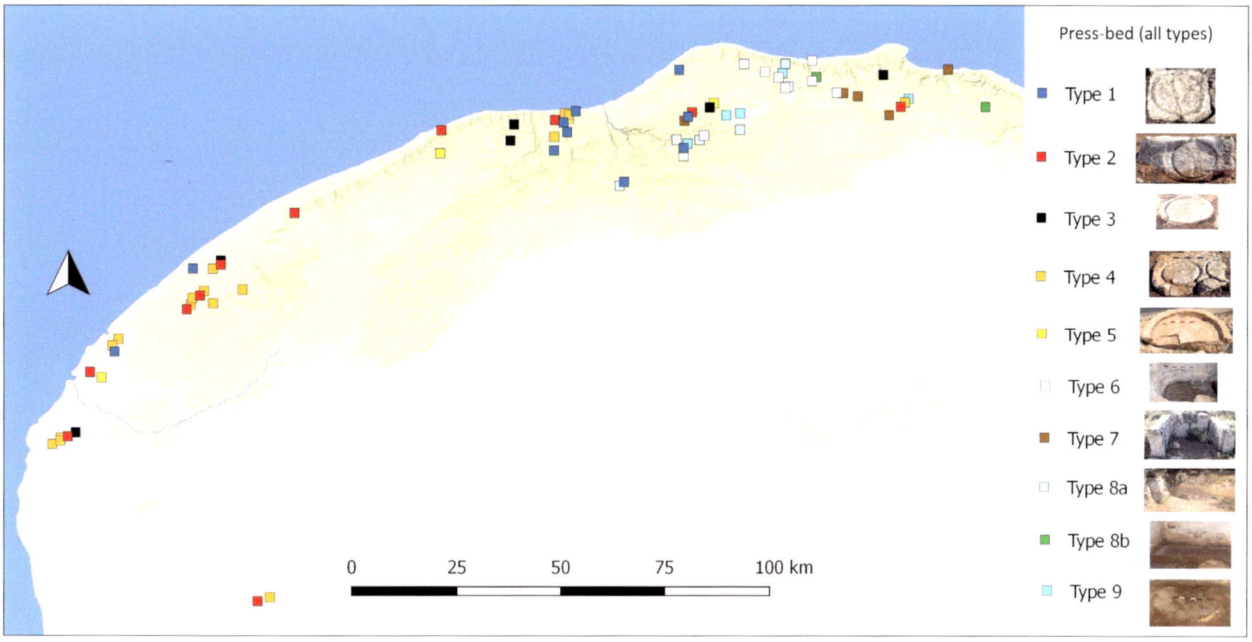

Figure 4.16: Distribution map of press-bed types.

associated with the upright *Type 2* and was restricted to the sites in the upper plateau east of Wad al-Kuf.

Type 7: A built-up, box-like pressing bed usually made of two stone slabs set on edge parallel to each other and at a right angle from the standing upright. One or two, and occasionally three, vertical grooves were cut into the anterior faces of the two flanking screen walls. The type is only found in association with the free-standing uprights *Types 1* and *1a*, which were limited to the upper plateau east of Wadi al-Kuf.

Type 8: Without the typical carved circular groove, but rather consisting of a raised platform cut against the wall in which the socket niche was cut. It was very rare and once again only found in the region around Cyrene.

Two further variants were observed:

Type 8a: The surface is either plain with a slight inclination or provided with a shallow circular depression.

Type 8b: A press floor defined by a circular channel.

Type 9: A raised round flat floor without a circular groove usually built against the beam fulcrum. The type was limited to the upper plateau region and usually found in association with a wine installation.

The most interesting question that remains is without doubt the origin of the box-like press bed built of two stone slabs (*Type 7*). The reason for the preference for this type in the north-eastern region, especially in Lamluda and Jebra, is not clear. Press beds similar to this type have been reported in Henchir Ouled Moussa in Kettana, south of Gabès in Tunisia (Mrabet, A. 2000: 50, Cliché 43993). The two flanking stones are much taller than those in Cyrenaica, though the pressing area itself seems smaller.

4.2.3 Counterweights (Table AI.5)

The free end of the press beam was mainly operated by means of a windlass or winch, mounted on top of a counterweight block. When found in situ, the distance such a counterweight from the beam socket can give an indication of the length of the pressing beam. As is the case elsewhere in North Africa, counterweights of the screw type are almost unknown. Seven main types have been found, with variation in the method of fixing the windlass.

Type 1: A rectangular block with two identical sockets cut through. Another two narrow and shallow grooves run along the lower edge of either the short or long sides of the block, usually extending across the two socket holes (Figure 4.17). This type is characterised as Brun Type 40.

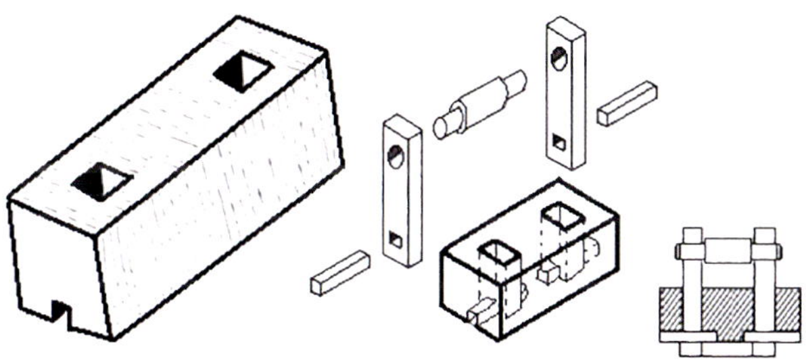

Figure 4.17: *Type 1*, the windlass device (=Brun Type 40: 1986, fig. 59).

Figure 4.18: *Type 2*, left: MAS-C2 with two open mortices; right: SRH-C2 with one closed and other opened mortices, scale 0.5 m.

Type 2: A rectangular block with two dovetail open mortices which either extend the full height of the block or are just cut halfway of vertical short side. A combination of both open and closed mortices used in the same block (Figure 4.18), so both are classified under one type for the sake of convenience and to avoid any possible confusion.

Type 3: Parallelepiped block with fairly long narrow open or wide closed mortices, with two shallower cuts in the long sides (Figure 4.19). The mortice does not extend the full height of the block, and two rather shallower recesses are cut opposite each other almost halfway along the long side. A similar mortice found cut into the outcrop with no indication of its counterpart suggests that a single wooden post may have been used to secure some kind of mechanical apparatus.

Figure 4.19: *Type 3*, top left: MAS-C7 with two open mortices; top right: SRH-C3 with two closed mortices, scale 0.5 m; bottom: HGR-C1 with one mortice cut into the outcrop, scale 0.25 m.

Figure 4.20: *Type 4*, HRR-C1, scale 0.5 m, and details of 'T' shaped mortice, scale 0.25 m.

Type 4: Rectangular block with two closed 'T' shaped mortices cut into the upper face of the stone (Figure 4.20). Their vertical walls make it difficult to identify the method used to secure the windlass and how it was mechanically effective in exerting huge pressure over the stacked pile of mash baskets.

Type 5: Rectilinear block with dovetail cut-outs of its short sides and not extending to the full height of the block (Figure 4.21). No longitudinal groove on the upper surface.

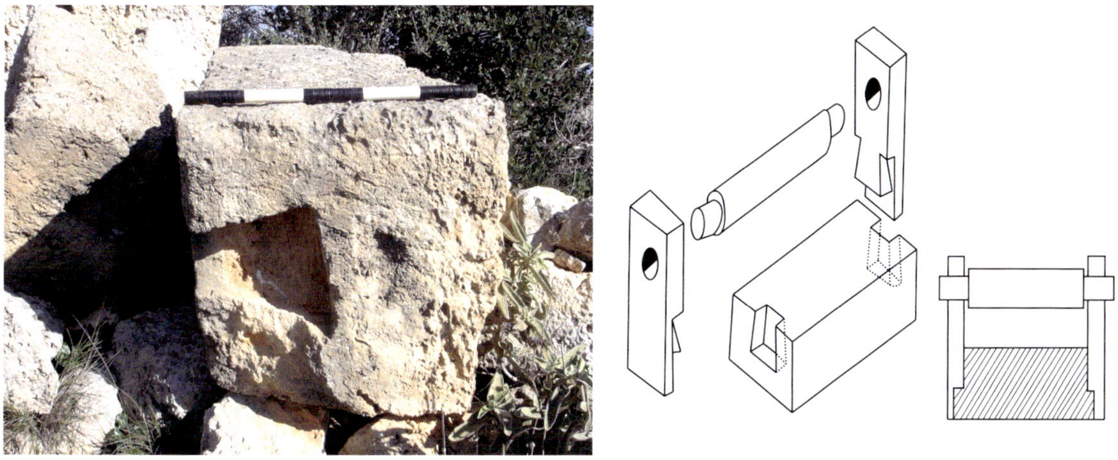

Figure 4.21: *Type 5*, SLT-C1, scale 0.5 m, and the windlass device (= Brun Type 10, 1986: fig. 59).

Type 6: A pit hewn into the exposed bedrock floor (Figure 4.22). Variants of this type have been noted, although how they functioned remains a mystery. Their association with cement floors and adjacent large vats suggests that they were probably connected to wine presses.

Figure 4.22: *Type 6*: Rock cut counterweight, left: SGG-C2; right: SIH-C1. Scale 0.5 m.

Type 7: Rectangular suspended weight stone with a diagonal suspension hole (Figure 4.23). The perforation is near the edge of one of the upper corner areas.

Figure 4.23: *Type 7:* Suspended weight stone WKR-C5. Scale 0.25 m.

Miscellaneous: Two counterweight blocks were noted that fall outside the typology. These were of the dominant rectangular type but possessed a different arrangement of sockets for mounting mechanical pressure devices. The first, ESH-C1 possessed mortices in the shape of parallel line grooves, which extended the full height of both of its short sides (Figure 4.24). A crude wide and shallow groove was cut along both the upper and lower surfaces of the block to connect the two vertical grooves. This counterweight may be compared to Hadjisavvas' Type 3 (1992: 70, fig. 137), with the reservation that the latter had mortices widening downwards and lacked elongated grooves across the top and underside of the block.

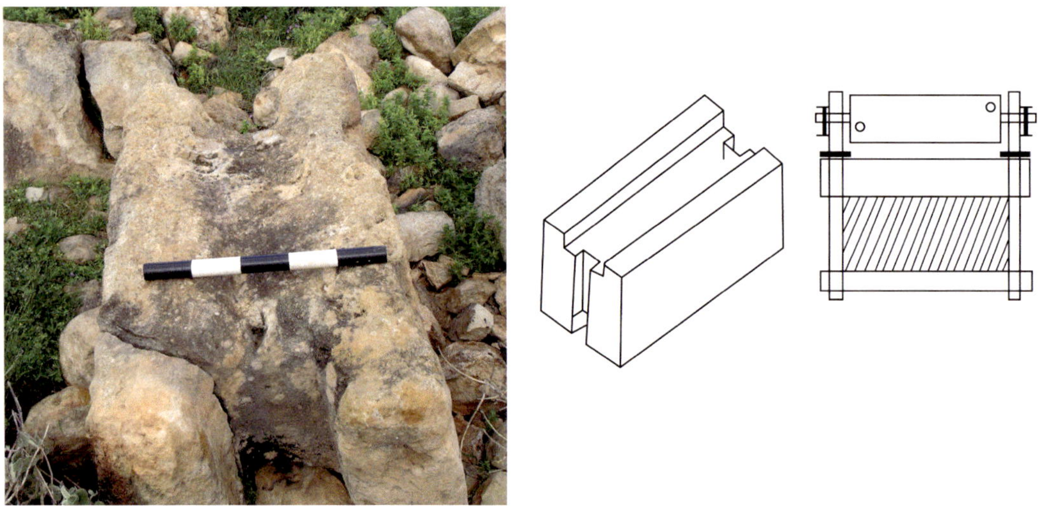

Figure 4.24: Miscellaneous 1, ESH-C1, scale 0.5 m. Reconstruction of the windlass device.

The second, HMR-C1 is rather unique, and likely represents a counterweight that employed a screw device (Figure 4.25). It is similar to ESH-C1, but has a central socket without external channel cut-outs. This counterweight block is a variant of Brun's Type 51 but lacks the small holes for metal clamps in its upper surface.

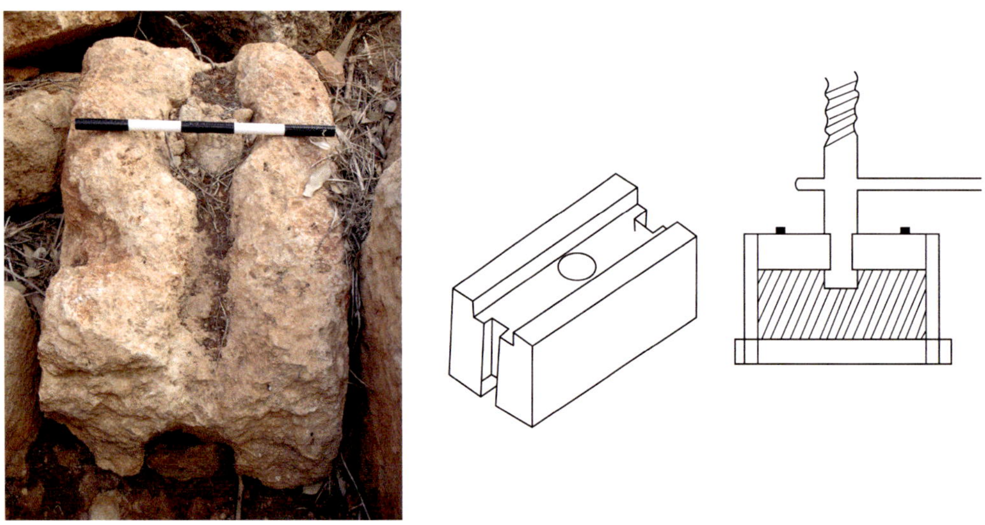

Figure 4.25: Miscellaneous 2, HMR-C1, scale 0.5 m. Reconstruction the windlass device.

The vast majority of the counterweights recorded in Cyrenaica are *Type 1* rectangular blocks whose approximate weight may have been as high as 4 tonnes (Table 4.7). By way of comparison, the maximum weight of a counterweight in Kasserine was just over 1 tonne (Mattingly and Hitchner 1993: Table 8), while those from the Tarhuna plateau exceeded 7 tonnes (Ahmed 2019: Table 4.9) and those found in the pre-desert zone barely reached 2 tonnes (Mattingly 1993: 458). Consequently, Cyrenaican counterweights (Table 4.8) are amongst the largest known counterweights in the ancient North Africa in terms of size and weight.

Type 1	Type 2	Type 3	Type 4	Type 5	Type 7
1.5	1.2	2.2	1.7	0.400	0.045

Table 4.7: The average weight of Cyrenaican counterweights (tonne), apart from *Type 6* which was hewn into the living rock. *Type 7* was only represented by one example.

4.2.3.1 Distribution patterns of counterweight types

There are seven main types of counterweight which show different distribution patterns (Figure 4.26 and Figure 4.27). *Type 1* was the most common, and most widely distributed, in Cyrenaica. It remained the dominant counterweight block in the eastern country and the intermediate region but frequently occurred with other types of weights in the Benghazi coastal plain. Two examples, one of a rectangular shape and the other with a T-shaped section, have been reported in the literature as originating from the Methana in modern Greece (Foxhall 2007: figs. 6.29 'b' and 6.31 respectively) to which *Type 1* is perhaps directly connected (Frankel 1999: 105). *Type 2* was found only in the Benghazi coastal plain. It is probable that the type developed from other weights with similar dovetailed sockets found in this region. *Type 3* was only found in the area west of Tocra. *Type 4* was very rare, and as for the two previous types was only found in the Benghazi coastal plain. The reason for the preference for this type of counterweight in this particular area is unclear. The degree of variation in the provision of mortices shown on the counterweight blocks found in the Benghazi coastal plain (*Types 2–4*), indicates that there were multiple ways to attach a windlass securely. Another aspect of typology of Cyrenaican presses is the absence of screw counterweights. The spread of screw technology will be considered further below (section 9.6). *Type 5* is reminiscent of the Semana type weight and was very rare in Cyrenaica. Only two examples were found in Cyrenaica, one in the Ras al-Hilal area and another in Qasr Shibna in the environs of Benghazi. The block has two dovetail mortices and is categorised as a Brun Type 10. A similar type was noted in Sidi Haddouch, Tigzirt in Algeria, Oued el-Htab in Tunisia, as well as in various other sites in southern France (Frankel 1999: T5512). Generally, the type is related to the standard Semana type, which was the most common weight stone in Tripolitania (Ahmed 2019: 104) and Tunisia (Mattingly and Hitchner 1993: 454). It was also widespread across the western Roman Mediterranean, particularly in southern France and Spain (Frankel 1997: 77). The Semana weight was also found in

Site	Element number	Type	Length (m)	Width (m)	Thick (m)	Weight (tonnes)
BLG	C1	1	1.88	0.85	0.63	2.16
DJJ	C1	1	1.90	0.90	0.50	2.183
LAM	C5	1	1.75	0.92	0.70	2.822
BSF	C1	1	2.35	1.25	0.55	4.13
HUG	C1	1	2.00	0.68	0.51	1.716
SRY	C1	1	1.80	0.90	0.45	1.766
SSH	C1	1	1.35	0.73	0.40	0.983
WKR	C2	1	1.68	0.75	0.70	2.071
MAS	C1	2	1.25	0.75	0.75	1.829
SRH	C6	2	1.58	0.85	0.20+	0.621
ZBD	C1	3	1.80	1.05	0.45	2.181
MAS	C2	4	1.90	1.05	0.45	2.325
SHB	C1	5	0.50+	0.70	0.45	0.404+
WKR	C5	7	0.45	0.25	0.15	0.045
ESH	C1	Misc.1	1.20	0.65	0.45	0.817
HMR	C1	Misc.2	1.20	0.50	0.50	0.694

Table 4.8: Selected Cyrenaican counterweight blocks recorded during the field survey.

the eastern Mediterranean where it possibly originated from (Frankel 199: 103), although it was not found in large numbers. It was also reported from other east Mediterranean sites in Hendek Kale in the Marmara region, north-east of Turkey (Bennett and Coockson 2009: 319), Cyprus, and other variants have been found in Crimea and Delos (Frankel 1999: 103). *Type 6* was limited to north-eastern Cyrenaica. *Type 7* is a small weight, rectangular in shape with a diagonal hole in one of the upper corners. It was suspended under the free end of the press beam with ropes. The suspended weight stone (*Type 7*) was very rare, and only one example of such was found in the upper plateau. This element was possibly of widespread use, but its rarity in the archaeological record can perhaps be attributed to the high possibility of removal and reworking. Examples from the Levant and Greek world tend to be chronologically early. Technologically, suspending weights on the beam is a simpler solution, which was likely to be employed at an early point of time. For Cyrenaica, this may be either an indication of early production or for more domestic focus production. Presumably the

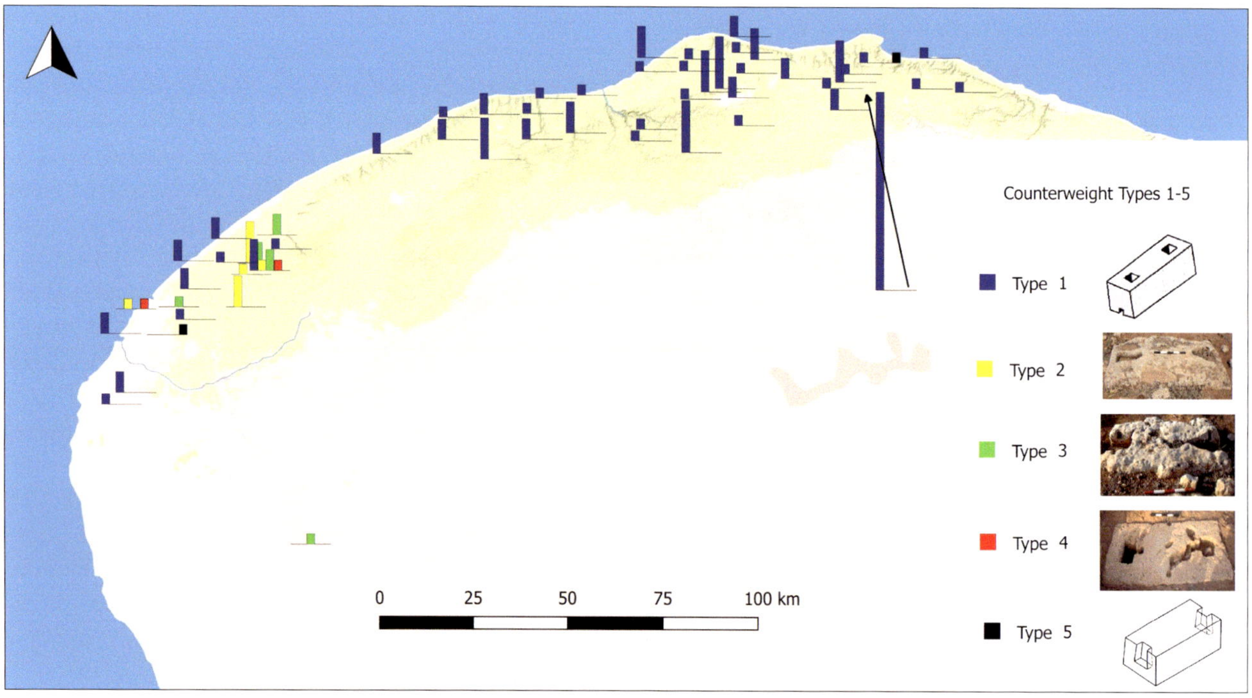

Figure 4.26: Distribution map of counterweight *Types 1–5*.

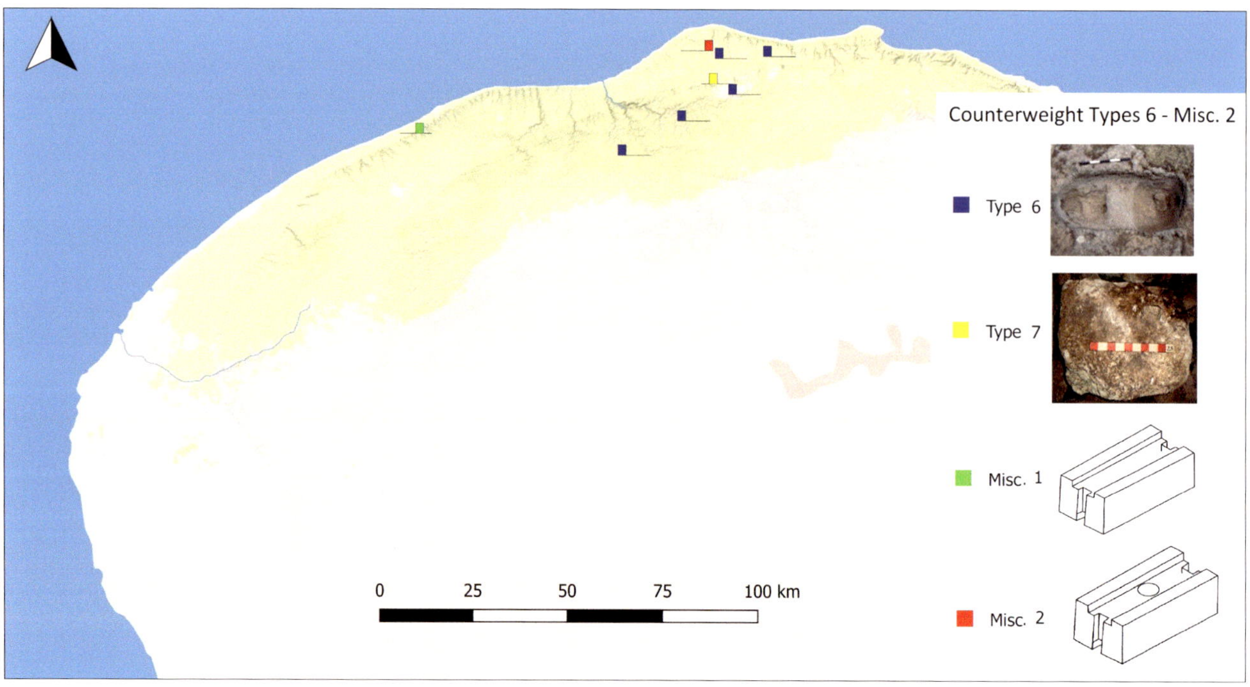

Figure 4.27: Distribution map of counterweight *Types* 6 and 7 and Misc. 1 and 2.

most sophisticated end of production had developed more advanced weights. The technological level of this particular type of weight was different from that of the other weight stones, which were all attached with a windlass device.

Stone weights with suspension holes were known in Greece (Foxhall 2007: 136) and Cyprus (Hadjisavvas 1992: 21), probably dating to the late Bronze Age (*c.*1400–1200 BC). Similar examples of suspended beam weights were reported from the Iron Age (*c.*1200–568 BC) in Palestine (Frankel 1994: 39–40; 1999: 106). Simple beam weights have not yet been found elsewhere in North Africa and Italy, where this absence is probably due to the late introduction of the olive-pressing technique in these regions (Frankel 1999: 105). WKR-C5 is the only example recorded in Cyrenaica and was found in a Roman tomb that was converted during the Byzantine period into an olive press. Although in Cyrenaica this type of weight belonged to a very late period compared to the early versions found in the Levant and Greece, it might be a hint at the presence of an early history related to the olive oil industry in the region. The *Demiourgoi* inscriptions (SEG 9.11–15, 18, 23, 26, 30) attest to the fact that by the fourth century BC, olive oil was being locally produced.

There are two further weight blocks, both rectangular in shape, that were classified as miscellaneous. Both possessed different arrangements of mortices for attaching mechanical device. One has joints in the shape of a parallel line cut full height in both short sides with a wide and shallow channel hewn along both the upper and lower surfaces of the block to link the two vertical grooves. The weight is similar to that found in Cyprus, but the latter used dovetail mortices without the elongated grooves across the top and underside of the block (*cf.* Hadjisavvas 1992: 70, fig. 137, 'Type 3'). It was found in the Benghazi coastal plain, west of Ptolemais. The other lacked external mortices but had elongated channels across both sides of the block and a central round socket in the top side that can be distinguished as employing a screw device. It was found in the upper plateau, north of al-Beida.

4.3 Conclusion

Analysis of millstones and mill mortars in Chapters 3 and 4 demonstrates a wide variability in mill element types, which indicates that Cyrenaican milling equipment had distinctive characteristics when compared to those found in North Africa. This gave us a new view on the characteristics of Cyrenaican milling, which were different to those found in other Mediterranean regions. The same is true with the pressing elements, which also show a great deal of regional variation in terms of size and shape. An interesting aspect, with particular bearing on the subject of calculating the pressure exerted by Cyrenaican presses, is the regional diversity of mortices used to fix windlass mechanisms to the counterweight blocks, which varied in shape from cross-form to 'T', either closed or open. The archaeological evidence shows these types of counterweight blocks to be located only in the Benghazi coastal plain. One exceptional example of a weight, which is different from those found in the region, consists of a single cross-form mortice cut directly into an outcrop. Again, this type appears to have been confined to the Benghazi coastal plain. Overall, the counterweight blocks are amongst the largest in the Mediterranean, whereas the sizes of press beds are comparatively small. The implication is that Cyrenaican presses exerted high pressure in comparison to the apparent small size of the pressing bed; consequently, the processing time is drastically reduced and two loads per day can easily be processed. The basic lever and windlass press was found predominantly across Cyrenaica, with examples of a screw mechanism rare in the region. This situation is similar to what is found in North Africa, where lever and windlasss technology also prevailed.

chapter five

CHARACTERISTICS OF CYRENAICAN MILLING AND PRESSING ELEMENTS

5.1 Introduction

The large number of milling and pressing elements recorded during my survey merit further analysis. They were discovered during survey and not archaeological excavations, which makes it difficult to date them and define their chronological development. However, the other indicators suggest that the presses broadly date from the mid-to-late Roman periods. All the pressing elements were produced locally using limestone, with no marble or other imported stones.

The most notable characteristic of the presses found in Cyrenaica so far is that they rarely used screw technology, whether for direct screw or lever and screw presses. The only indirect screw mechanism seen so far was found in Qasr al-Hmeira to the south of Balagrae and was discovered beside a typical Cyrenaican counterweight (*Type 1*) that employed a windlass device. Questions arise here as to whether these two techniques were contemporary, and, if so, why would two such different techniques be together at the same time. These questions will be addressed below, with further analysis regarding the implications of the presence of this example of the screw technique and its use in Cyrenaican presses. According to the archaeological data collected during the survey, the direct screw press was completely absent. Nonetheless, there is a possibility that some equipment may have been partly or completely made of wood, which has long since disappeared. In archaeological terms, disentangling this kind of evidence is therefore a significant challenge.

The olive oil presses found in Cyrenaica are of the lever press type, which was the predominant form used throughout the Roman world. This local type operated on the same general principles as other lever presses:

- force was applied by means of a wooden beam attached to a windlass mechanism mounted on a counterweight block;
- the pulped olives were stacked on a press bed for pressing;
- decanting tanks were used to collect the extracted liquid.

However, their characteristics vary considerably at both the inter- and intra-regional levels, probably as a response to socio-economic and geographic factors (Mattingly 1996: 582–4).

The presses found in Cyrenaica generally belong to Brun's class A2. These are lever and windlass presses, with one end of the beam anchored into a niche cut either into the face of the living rock, a free-standing upright, or built into the press building's masonry. The free end was attached to a windlass mechanism, which was often mounted on a rectangular counterweight block placed parallel to the long axis of the press beam. This counterweight block alignment differs from the normal arrangement found in other North African olive presses and was evidently an important regional variation.

5.2 Characteristics of Cyrenaican Milling Elements

5.2.1 Millstone

Two main millstone types are known to have been used in the ancient world: crushing stones with typical half-moon sections, and cylindrical or conically-shaped stones with flat crushing surfaces. The first type is commonly believed to have been specifically designed to operate in the crushing basin of a concave crushing area known as a *trapetum* (Drachmann 1932: 7–14; Brun 1986: 71–3). Conversely, the shape of the second type implies the use of a flat crushing basin, which is now known as a *mola olearia* (Brøndsted 1928: 111–2; Brun 1986: 73–8; Drachmann 1932: 42–5; White 1975). The shape of the millstone thus dictates the shape of the mill mortar, and vice versa. Basins used with the second type of millstone were likely easier to manufacture, which may be attributed to their widespread geographical distribution across the ancient world (Hobson 2015: 70). Except for the two examples classified under sub-types A2 and A3, all the recorded crushing stones were provided on both sides with a shallow square depression cut around the central round hole. The crushing stone turned both on its own axis and around the mill mortar, and it is it possible that the mills in Cyrenaica were operated by twin millstones. However, it is unclear whether the crushing stone was adjusted to leave a small gap between the working area and the surface of the mill mortar, or whether it rested directly on the crushing surface. The former method is thought to prevent the olive stones from being crushed, produces a high-quality oil and is generally accepted to fit with the *trapetum* described by Cato (*De Agricultura* 23: 1–2). Without giving any specific reason for doing so, Cato provided detailed information on how to adjust the space between the millstone and the convex crushing surface.

Deposits of uncrushed carbonised olive pits were found in two furnaces at an excavated site at Saint-Michel à la Garde, south-eastern France, along with a lens-like millstone. The site was initially for producing wine, but this production was later abandoned and replaced with equipment for producing olive oil for local consumption (Brun forthcoming). These later artefacts led Brun (1986: 163) to conclude that the excavated oil press used an adjustable mill mortar of the *trapetum* type to bruise the flesh from the olives without crushing the pits. Evidence of uncrushed olives has also been found in excavations at the site of the Arbaia pottery kiln in Tripolitania (where no evidence of mill mortars of the *trapetum* type has been found, Ahmed 2019: 149) and at Tria Platania in Pieria, southern Macedonia (Margaritis and Jones 2008).

Furthermore, a small quantity of uncrushed carbonised olive kernels was found at Leptiminus (Mattingly and Hitchner 1995) and at the site of Uchi Maius, northern Tunisia (Vismara 2007: 190–93). Mattingly (1988c: 156) argues that we should not necessarily assume these charred uncrushed pits were first lightly pulped, and after being compressed were used as fuel – even if light bruising was carried out it is still difficult to tell how many stones were left uncrushed. There is no compelling reason to believe that these intact olive stones unequivocally came from the pressing process. Equally, carbonised olive stones could have resulted from small branches that still had some over-ripe fruit after the pruning season. The period of olive oil production coincides with a period when the demand for fuel increased significantly due to cooler seasonal temperatures (Russo *et al.* 2008: 4). Pompeiians used vine and olive cuttings as kindling; however, the latter has an oily character and leaves nothing but ash which is unidentifiable in the archaeological record (Veal and Thompson 2008: 294). Similarly, these olive stones might be the remains of pickled olives that were to be used as solid fuel. Another possibility is that stored olives harvested in the bumper years and awaiting processing became rotten and ended up as fuel (Ahmed 2019: 149).

Although no pressing equipment was reported from Tria Platania, Greece (Margaritis and Jones 2008) the botanical remains found at the site most likely relate to olive oil production with clear evidence that the olive kernels had been crushed during the milling process. However, the site dated to the Hellenistic period, so crushing appliances used there would differ from the later *trapetum* version referred to by Cato. Consequently, our interpretation remains biased to the Roman sources, and the plant remains could be misleading if it is accepted that there were slight differences in technique between the Roman *trapetum* and the Classical and Hellenistic equipment.

As discussed above the flat crushing surface of the *mola olearia* is thought to allow for the possibility of adjusting its millstone in the same manner as the concave mill (Columella 12.52. 6; Drachmann 1932: 42). However, there is no way to trace this archaeologically, and fully-crushed olives produced larger yields of oil with no appreciable effect on its flavour. This is in striking contrast with the argument that crushed stones cause the oil to turn sour (Amouretti 1986; Douzougli 2003; Forbes 1993; Frankel 1993). Indeed, either fully-crushed or gently-bruised olives would have similar chemical characteristics (Vaughan 1970). However, the matter of whether olive stones were completely crushed or merely bruised during the milling process is controversial and remains unresolved.

We should not take the statements of the ancient agricultural writers too literally and view them as scientific authorities (e.g., Cato, *De Agricultura* 66.1 and Columella, *Rust.* 12.52.6). Many factors can affect the quality of oil that the Roman elites had no idea about. Presumably, they were not fully aware of the harvesting issues and production process, and modern scholars have expressed concern as their accounts are often based on anecdotal evidence rather than personal experience. Recent studies of modern olive milling technology have suggested that crushing stones does not have a significant impact on the taste (Tyree and Stefanoudaki 1996: 176; White 1984: 71). The taste of oil is affected by a combination of factors, primarily the time of picking, as unripe and mature olives will produce different oils. In addition, inconvenient storage conditions before milling can seriously affect oil flavour. Crushing the olive pits is only a minor factor (Tyree and Stefanoudaki 1996: 177).

Above all, partially crushing olives would be time consuming and uneconomic, and would be a thoroughly impractical decision. Fully crushing the olives adversely affects the flow of oil in the paste and would have yielded more oil than if they were lightly crushed (Foxhall 2007:

134). Therefore, it can be concluded that in the production of oil in large quantities, no attempt was made to avoid crushing the olive stone, and this issue was perhaps only considered when a limited amount of high-quality oil was being produced.

Generally, the millstones recorded during the survey show significant differences in diameter from those found elsewhere in the Mediterranean. For instance, the crushers found on the Tarhuna plateau were mainly of a wheel-shaped type similar to my *Type A1*, varying in diameter from 0.45 m to 0.55 m with a grinding surface around 0.45 m wide and a constant central hole 0.15 m across. On the other hand, Cyrenaican millstones range in diameter from 0.55 m to 1.05 m and 0.20 m to 0.48 m in thickness. The depth of the central perforation varies in the same type from 0.10 m to 0.20 m, but in other different types it was recorded as 0.29 m, and in one case the central hole was square in shape. Along with some other different types that lacked a square depression on both sides, this indicates different local modes in mounting the millstone, and may possibly have chronological implications. It is interesting to note that the only striated surface of a Cyrenaican millstone belongs to the conical type but has a slightly round surface (Figure 3.7). Similar striations on a flat crusher were reported in Tripolitania (Ahmed 2019: 100, site TUT18), Volubilis and Madauros, and a type of conical striated crushing stones was also found in southern France (Frankel 1999: figs. T383 and T389). Though evidence is sparse, the fact that Cyrenaica marks the eastern limit of this type of striated millstone combined with the fact that it did not spread far to the East Mediterranean more widely strongly suggests that it originated in the west.

5.2.2 Mill mortar

Archaeological surveys have always found mill mortars in relatively small numbers compared with other pressing elements. This is largely attributable to the absence of archaeological excavations, as well as the fact that they were often carried off or reworked (Mattingly and Hitchner 1993). However, the remarkable paucity of mill mortars in many archaeological surveys is in stark contrast with the number recorded in the Cyrenaican survey, where crushing basins made up the largest proportion of the elements found. Human and natural factors, which vary from region to region, thus appear to have played a crucial role in both the high frequency of crushing basins in Cyrenaica and their paucity in the other Mediterranean regions. The relative lack of post-Roman olive cultivation could be a factor in Cyrenaica. In the western Libya and Tunisia olive cultivation continued to some extent, thus favouring reuse of mill basins.

However, even in the surveys where crushing basins were relatively rare, their presence sometimes has important implications for olive oil production. Mattingly (1993) reliably predicted that the more mill mortars found in a site, the more likely it is that a high number of presses will also be found. In almost all the surveyed areas it is quite common to find that every two presses were equipped with at least one mill mortar. This arrangement indicates that the pressing process took longer than the crushing and that one crushing basin could serve more than one press (Brun 1986: 279; 1993: 518; Kloner 2009: 373; Porath 2009: 100; Yeivin and Finkielsztejn 2009: 107).

It has been suggested that the frequency of the various pressing elements found at a site can be used to estimate the minimum number of presses (MNP) at that site (Hobson 2015: 80; Mattingly 1985: 34). For example, two recorded counterweight blocks would indicate the presence of two presses. In Cyrenaica, the operating height of the press beam, and the volume of the stacked baskets of pulped olives during the pressing process, were both much smaller than those in the rest of North Africa. However, Cyrenaican mill-mortars show similar dimensions to their counterparts. By contrast, almost all the recorded Cyrenaican rock-cut presses were provided with at least two beam sockets, or even more. In addition, a number of built-up presses employed a double press-bed operated by a single beam. Nevertheless, both types only had one mill mortar. Accordingly, I would suggest that the single mill mortar – at least in a rock-cut press or installation employing a double press-bed operated by one beam socket – indicates the presence of two presses, or perhaps even more. In installations other than these two categories, a mill mortar represents just one press unless it is associated with two uprights, counterweights, or separate pressing beds, in which case it represents two presses. In addition, two millstones would represent one press. In this case, one press is considered if no mill mortar was present. This is based on what has already been suggested, that the mill mortar in Cyrenaica could have been operated with twin millstones. Of course, at least one crushing stone still counts as one press. Lamluda stands as an exceptional site with 60 uprights, but an estimation of the number of presses here is based on the existence of 18 crushing basins, each of them serving two presses. This would indicate that at least 36 presses were engaged in oil production. Taking all this into consideration, gives a minimum estimate of 265 presses from the 111 surveyed sites over an area of 30,000 km^2 (indeed, subsequent to my survey further presses have been identified). It must be borne in mind, however, that all these presses were by no means contemporaneous.

A large number of presses were recorded during the survey work. In total, the survey detected 876 milling and pressing elements, the largest number (164) comprising olive mills. Economically, it is not necessary to use mills to meet subsistence consumption needs, where other cheap, small-scale methods of crushing may be applied. Conversely, the use of a mill in its own right is a conclusive indicator of commercial production.

The internal diameters of the mill basins range from 0.85 m to 1.60 m, and average 1.3 m. The thickness of the outer rim is on average 0.17 m, and ranges from 0.06 m to 0.32 m. A track or space only about 0.50 m wide was left around both rock-cut and free-standing basins, suggesting the millstones were rotated by human rather than animal power.

For 40 of the basins the walls were approximately 0.10 m thick, while 20 had walls about 0.20 m thick and 50 had walls 0.30 m thick. The depth of the milling area varied from 0.03 m to 0.55 m, with an average of 0.27 m. Unlike the flat-bottomed mills predominant in most of North Africa (Ben Baaziz 1985; Mattingly 1996: 578), the Cyrenaican basins generally had sloping or convex work surfaces. Consequently, the lower and upper spaces of the milling areas between the outer wall and the central socket were considerably different. In general, the width of the crushing space varied from 0.20 m at the bottom to 0.70 m at the rim level.

The depth of the milling area in Cyrenaican basins varied considerably within each group and across different types (Figure 5.1). The deepest basin was recorded in *Type 3* at 0.55 m, which also featured the shallowest of all the investigated basins at 3 cm. This type was characterised by a flat surface area. Nevertheless, the same difference was also noticed in the convex basins *Types 1f*, *2* and *4*, whose depths varied from 0.06 m to 0.44 m. This depth seems to match the height recorded in the millstones, which varied broadly from 0.50 m to 1.05 m.

The different shapes of the central socket hole suggest that the crushing stones could be mounted in a number of different ways. Among the recorded crushing basins in which the internal pivot socket was preserved, 88 were found to have round shapes. Only 8 sockets were pierced right through the base, while 60 were rectangular and 10 were square. Basins with round central pivot holes were found mainly in the north-eastern part of the Gebel, while those with square holes were found in the littoral region and in the area east of Cyrene at the sites of Lamluda and Jebra. In the survey, 15 basins were found to have sunken sockets and only 8 had integral columns that projected upwards from the centre of the crushing surface. These were found only in Benghazi's coastal plains.

The round socket varies in diameter from 0.20 m to 0.25 m. In the square sockets, the length of the sides ranges from 0.10 m to 0.25 m; in 20 of these sockets, representing some 25% of the amassed data, the length of the sides is 0.15 m to 0.20 m. The sockets are 0.10 m to 0.35 m deep, with no significant differences in the depth dimensions between the two types. Five round sockets were found at upper plateau sites with bottom ends which had been hewn into conical shapes. At Siret al-Algili a round socket was found with a horizontal square cut in its upper part, suggesting that the lower vertical wooden pivot was fixed with an upper rotary element.

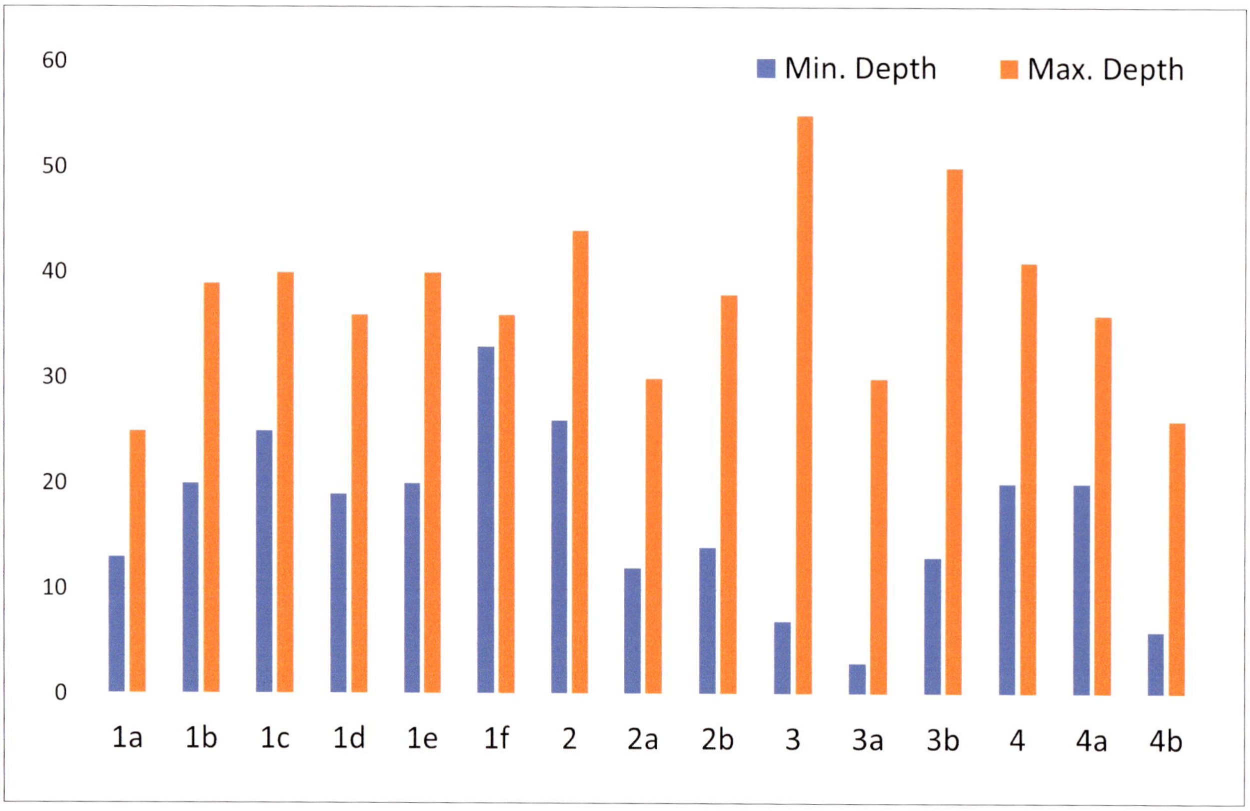

Figure 5.1: Maximum and minimum depth of the crushing basins in all types (depth in cm).

5.3 Characteristics of Cyrenaican Pressing Elements

5.3.1 Beam-anchoring

The technique by which the fixed end of the beam was anchored in place may have been largely influenced by topographical and geological factors where the landscape was characterised by steep cliffs and rugged terrain. However, local and regional preferences and traditions may also play an additional role in the beam fixing. In Cyrenaica, the most widespread evidence attests to the use of stone niches in which the fixed end of the wooden press beam was pinned (Figure 5.2). The niche in Cyrenaica was normally represented in three forms:

1. Cut into the face of a monolithic stone (arbor) or twin blocks which either stood side-by-side or backing onto one another. A good example from the site of Jebra suggests that almost all the upright blocks were incorporated in the press wall and were not free-standing. The upright JEB-U10 from the site of Jebra constitutes the tallest arbor recorded by the survey, reaching 1.75 m in height and incorporated into a wall fabric built of ashlar blocks that rises to more than 3.20 m in height.
2. Carved into the natural rock face.
3. A recess built into the wall of the press room.

Stone pier bases used to secure a single or two wooden uprights were not encountered during the survey. However, considering that the gathered data derive solely from standing features and that wood as a perishable material is rarely present in Cyrenaica's archaeological record, the absence of wooden uprights cannot be assumed. Throughout the eastern Mediterranean, the most common method used in almost all periods was apparently to anchor the fixed end of the beam in a stone niche (Frankel 1999: 170).

There is general agreement that the set of holes cut in various positions in the uprights was designed to adjust the centre height of the press beam. Mechanically, as the constant pressure of the beam press on the load of pulped olives compresses the stacked pile, the process becomes less efficient. By readjusting the end beam into a lower niche, efficient pressure can be regained and the pressing process can continue to extract more liquid. For example, two niches cut above each other were found at a Hellenistic press at Praesos and are thought to have been used for beam adjustment (Frankel 1999: 90). The distance between the lower base of the top hole and the lower base of the bottom hole was normally in the range of 0.30 m to 0.85 m. In both categories, the top niche was frequently 0.80 m. This technique was not widely applied in Cyrenaica, and only 5% of the total recorded installations were found to have two beam sockets one below the other. Given the low operating heights of Cyrenaican presses in comparison to their North African counterparts (Table 5.1), this may indicate that the extra holes in Cyrenaican examples were not considered necessary. The low stack-heights of small baskets is implied by the low height of the beam socket (see section 5.3.4).

The inconsistency of the shape of the niches used to anchor the press beam is significant. Six different types of beam sockets can be distinguished (Figure 5.3).

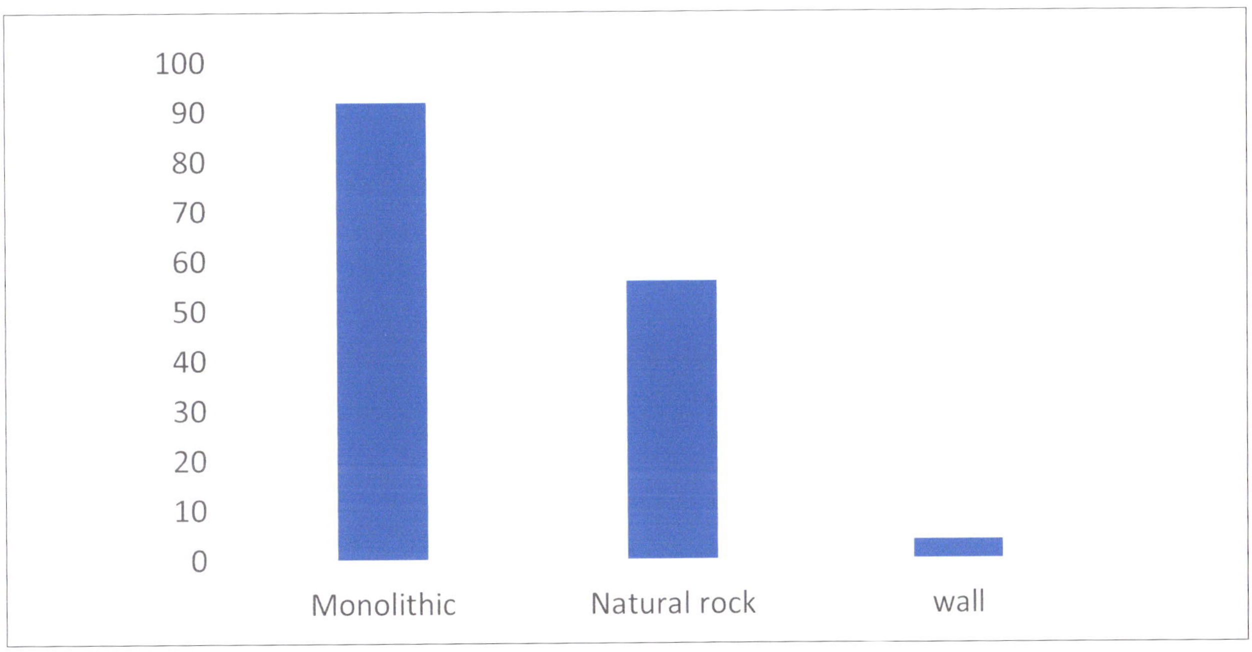

Figure 5.2: Numbers of different types of beam niches in Cyrenaica. Bear in mind that walls often do not survive, unlike the monolithic stones.

Region	Maximum height of the top hole base	Minimum height of the top hole base	Average height of the top hole base
Tripolitania	2.10 m	1.45 m	1.65 m
Kasserine (central Tunisia)	1.85 m	1.10 m	1.4 m
Cyrenaica	1.25 m	0.40 m	0.80 m

Table 5.1: Maximum and minimum operating heights of selected presses from Tripolitania, the Kasserine region (*based on Mattingly 1993: table 2*) and Cyrenaica.

The 'T' shaped hole is by far the most common type of beam socket, and ranges in height from 0.25 m to 0.8 m and varies in depth from 0.20 m to 0.55 m. The slots were carved into the sides of the niche and are all positioned at the upper end of the niche, with one exception which was cut at the base. The full length of these slots, including the width of the niche (Figure 5.4), ranges from 0.37 m to 1.25 m.

The most likely interpretation for the presence of this horizontal cut, which extends on both sides of the socket hole, is that it was used to align the beam above the loaded frails on the pressing stone and prevent it from swinging. This can be achieved by placing a piece of wood in the cut across the beam to maintain it at a right angle in relation to the piled loaded baskets. In some examples where the height of these niches reaches

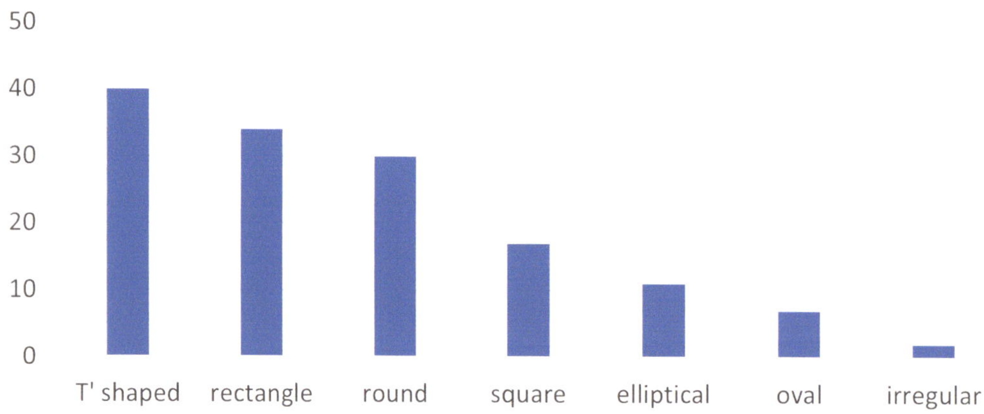

Figure 5.3: Numbers of beam sockets by shape.

Figure 5.4: 'T' shaped beam socket JNN-U1 with slot carved at the upper end of the niche. Scale 0.5 m.

0.80 m, it is possible that the beam was first fixed in these upper extending cuts and then later lowered during the pressing process. Similar niches were found in Maresha, east of Ashkelon in Palestine. Although dimensions were not given, they seem to have been somewhat larger than the Cyrenaican examples. The existence of the pair of extending slots on either side of the socket hole has been interpreted as a second phase of use intended to stabilise and adjust the beam after a long period of operation that caused disfiguration of the niche's shape (Kloner and Sagiv 1993: 127, fig. 7). Given the high proportion and possible relatively small size of the Cyrenaican examples it is more likely that these extending cuts were original rather than a later alteration.

In the second type, the niche is a roughly-cut rectangular-shaped recess. It ranges in height from 0.18 m to 0.62 m, in width from 0.25 m to 0.42 m and in depth from 0.20 m to 0.40 m. The round hole is the third most common type, with a diameter of 0.25 m to 0.65 m. Its depth is frequently 0.20 m, and generally ranges from 0.13 m to 0.35 m. In the fourth type the hole is of a regular quadrilateral shape, while the length of the sides ranges from 0.23 m to 0.45 m with the same depth noted in the rectangular hole. In the fifth type the hole most likely resembles an elongated circle stretched into an oval shape and varies in width and height from 0.30 m to 0.70 m and 0.35 m to 0.55 m respectively. The depth shows no significant difference from the other types.

5.3.2 Beam length

It is clear the Romans understood that the longer the lever between the counterweight and the fulcrum, the greater the force exerted on the load (Landels 2000: 195), although one could argue that a short beam could also generate greater force on the load if the material to be pressed is placed closer to the fulcrum (Frankel *et al.* 1994: 35). The beam length in Cyrenaican presses ranges from 5 to 6.5 m. In this case the press size is smaller in terms of beam length than used in Roman Tripolitania and some other regions in the Adriatic Sea, the Aegean Sea and Levantine (Figure 5.5). In the meantime, quite similar beam lengths have been detected in other regions in Palestine, Cyprus and the Tripolitanian pre-desert zone. However, beam length in Cyrenaica seems to be longer than many other examples from Palestine and Greece.

With such a beam length being used in Cyrenaica, the pressing-bed was placed closer to the fulcrum point (usually 0.5 m from the centre of the press-bed) than in the Tripolitanian presses which used a longer beam (*c.*9.5 m) and the pressing area was moved some distance from the arbores (between 2.5 to 3.5 m). Evidently, the length of the beam dictates the position of the loading point, so high pressure could be generated. Although the Tripolitanian long beam had an advantage, as it allows large baskets to be used, the shorter beam length used in Cyrenaica (perhaps due to the limited length of available

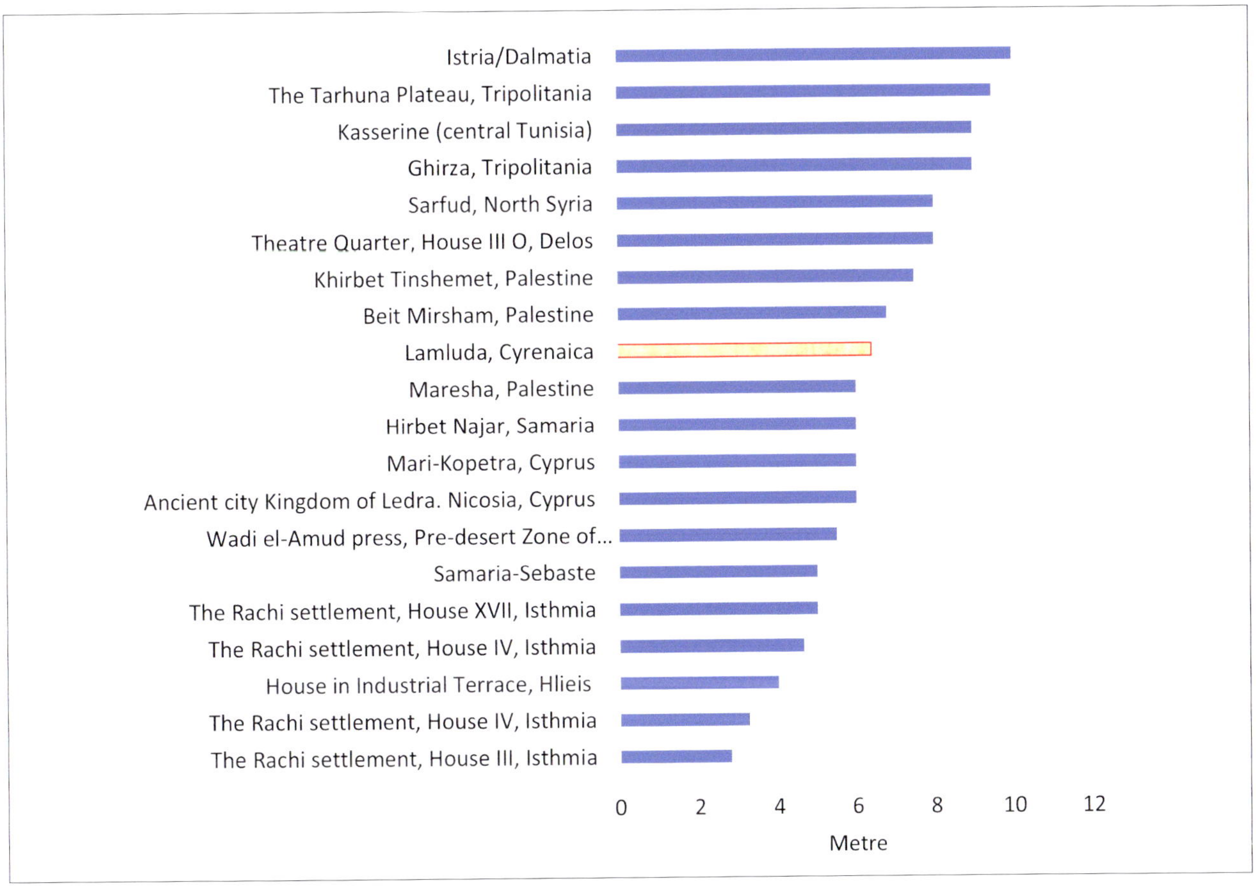

Figure 5.5: Beam lengths recorded in Cyrenaica and other Mediterranean sites.

timber) meant the pressing-bed was moved closer to the upright and the basket size was smaller to attain the maximum possible pressure.

5.3.3 Pressing-bed

An interesting device used in presses from Cyrenaica is the twin press bed, *Type 4*. Two similar examples were reported from Dehes in Syria and Pola in western Croatia (Frankel 1999: 91, T4266), while a rather different type with triple circular channels was found at Mari-Kopetra, Cyprus (Hadjisavvas 1990: 40, figs. 62, 65). These examples have been interpreted as most likely extra channels within which frails were placed after pressing in order to extract more oil by pouring boiling water on the stacked baskets. A further, early example came from a press found in House III west in the Theatre Quarter, Delos, which dated back to the first century BC (Blackman 1998: 105). Here two press beds were constructed on a paved platform but operated by two beams. Based on the apparent difference in length between the two beams and the existence of small and large receptacles it has been suggested that both were operated simultaneously to produce a virgin oil. This would then be followed by a second product of rather low-quality oil (Brun and Brunet 1997: 598, cited in Foxhall 2007: 162–3). While the latter interpretation seems to broadly fit with the Cyrenaican examples, the conclusive evidence of only a single outlet and settling tank located next to the pressing bed in Cyrenaica suggests that the two circular channels were operated concurrently using one beam to produce a homogenous grade of oil in one pressing, and possibly a lesser quality product in a second pressing. One should bear in mind that the pressure exerted on a double press-bed if operated by single beam would be decreased by half, and consequently the processing time for each pressing is extended but the carrying capacity of the press is not reduced.

There are two other types of pressing beds that are of special interest. Two of my types took the form of a box-like pressing bed found either carved into the living rock inside a cave or installed in a building, *Types 6* and *7* respectively. They belong to the lever and windlass press type which, while varying somewhat in the character of the pressing area, were uniform in the other apparatus, the beam anchoring and the windlass attachment. Although the way they functioned is still in dispute, the olive paste was probably wrapped in a sheet of coarse cloth or loaded into a wooden box.

The *Type 6* rock-cut *ara* was rectangular or square in plan, though one circular case was found cut into the rock just against the wall where the beam was anchored. The pressing surface was usually plain and inclined slightly away from the centre. In some cases, a peripheral groove had been cut at the point where the surface met the walls, plus radial shallow channels had been cut which directed the expressed liquid into adjacent collecting vats. The pressing areas varied in size from 0.35 m × 0.65 m to 1.10 m × 1.10 m. The walls stood at variable heights, but usually did not extend higher than the beam socket position (max. 0.80 m). Both open ends of the pressing area had vertical grooves cut opposite each other. These were presumably slots in which to insert timber planks to secure the *factus* or load firmly within the pressing area. As the load decreased and went down during the pressing process, the timber slats could be easily removed. More boards could then be placed at the top of the baskets and pressing could then resume to extract more liquid.

On the other hand, the built-up pressing bed (*Type 7*) consisted of two slab stones made of local limestone placed opposite each other, with their long faces parallel about 1.20 m apart. Each stone is a rectangular parallelepiped set horizontally on one of its two longest faces and is about 0.80 m to1.0 m high, 1.50 m to 2.0 m long and 0.20 m to 0.50 m thick. A groove about 0.10 m deep has been cut into each long broad inner face along its entire height. Opposite the space between the pair of stones, a niche was hewn in a standing monolithic stone to anchor a wooden beam. Two large blocks were sometimes placed side-by-side or one set behind another to serve as an upright.

5.3.4 Basket scale size versus capacity

The scale and size of the olive press elements have a direct impact on their capacity (Mattingly 1993: 485). This means that a sizable press allows large loads of olives to be pressed at once, though they can take a long time. Alternatively, the same press can process smaller loads of olives quickly due to its greater pressure. There is clearly an inverse relationship between capacity and time taken for processing. Increasing the level of oil production entails large loads being processed over long periods of time, and vice versa. The length of time and production between the two strategies are explicitly different.

Olive presses in Cyrenaica and elsewhere in the ancient Mediterranean are likely to have been far smaller in scale than those found in Spain and North Africa. Large-scale presses were clearly designed as a single load type, although they would have also been able to process smaller loads (Mattingly 1988a: 190). Their operating heights were higher, and the diameters of their press beds were much larger than Cyrenaican presses. In his comment on the load capacity of the massive North African presses, Mattingly (1988a: 182) suggests that there were two strategies for press operators to follow that could affect the carrying capacity of the press: the baskets of olive pulp could be placed below the press in fewer numbers, and their diameter, and thus their surface area, could be reduced, enabling higher pressures per square centimetre to be generated. The second choice seems more suitable for the small Cyrenaican presses, which obviously employed small baskets, and allowed users to apply a higher pressure to a relatively small quantity of olives. Thus, the implication to my mind is that the Cyrenaican press could process two loads in one working day. When larger presses in other parts of North Africa were used to press bigger stacks of larger baskets of pulped olives, the pressure applied would have been significantly decreased and the pressing time would have been extended. Such large presses may have been well-suited for use on substantial estates where a single large load could be pressed within 24 hours. While small presses require more workers per unit of the product produced, they were probably more suitable for processing two or more much smaller loads of olives per day from multiple small private farms.

Unfortunately, there are no ethnographic parallels to demonstrate that a small press with a short beam can process several loads. However, two pressings per day appears feasible. However, we need to bear in mind that, even in a small-scale press, the processing time was still quite lengthy. With a smaller capacity and a theoretically higher pressure exerted, we need to recognize that mechanically processing several loads in an ancient press would take longer than a modern press. The latter can generate a much greater pressure but with only a marginal difference in oil extraction (Mattingly 1988a: 182). In ancient presses, the labour and tasks involved in manipulating the stack of baskets must be taken into account when considering daily production capacity. We also need to consider the relationship between mill load and press capacity per pressing and per day. Taking all this into account I remain confident that Cyrenaican presses could process two loads per day.

5.3.5 Pressing-beds and eroded notches

The recent survey in the Gebel of Tarhuna recorded several examples with signs of notches inside the circular and square channels carved above the pressing surface (Ahmed 2019: 103). Brun (1986; 2004) argued that these eroded meanders resulted from the acidity of the olive oil over the long life of the pressing bed. Undoubtedly, olives were the leading cash crop of the Gebel, and so the vast majority of recorded presses were involved in olive oil production. Admittedly, it is probable that the eroded grooves are a result of the acids present in olive oil; however, it is puzzling to find that these acids only affected a minority of the many press floors found in the Gebel and elsewhere in North Africa (Brun 2004: 211–2). Strikingly, there is evidence of similar grooves at only one Cyrenaican site (Figure 5.6), though they are not as pronounced as those noted in Tripolitania. Not wishing to tackle the reason behind this type of erosion, Sehili (2009: 156) disagrees that this was a result of oil acidity. A. Wilson (personal communication) suggests that part of the explanation may be due to misidentification of wine presses as olive presses. Based on many examples of press beds that show signs of acid erosion found in different Mediterranean sites (Brun 2004: 211–2) I would suggest that these notches may depend on the precise geological composition of the stone and its reaction to acids.

Figure 5.6: Press bed ASD-P1. Note the clear difference between the central area and the margin.

5.3.6 Collecting vat

Unlike other pieces of standing pressing equipment, collecting receptacles and storage vats are generally missing or underrepresented from the survey record. This is mainly because most of these features were originally set into floors, and so were commonly covered or buried when the installation fell into disuse. The number of tanks recorded during the survey (Table 5.2 and Table AI.7) was therefore drastically lower than the number of other pressing elements.

After the resulting liquid was directed to a settling tank placed near the pressing bed, the final stage in which the oil was separated from the water could begin. Both ancient sources and the archaeological evidence attest to the decantation of olive oil. Since oil is less dense than water it floats to the top, so the following four methods fundamentally revolved around this principle (Frankel 1999: 174). The first method is to skim off the floating oil from the expressed liquid *amurca* using a shell or other shallow vessel (Cato, On Agriculture 66), which is then ladled into another vat reserved for cleaner oil. The process can then be repeated using a third vat to produce a higher quality product (Columella 12.52.11, 12). Unfortunately, the standing receptacle settling tanks rarely survive in the archaeological record, while those which were sunk below the press

No.	Site code	Shape	Shape & Dims.	Sg.	Tw.	O.	W.	Volume in cm²	Sediment-trap	Built-up	Rock-cut	Op. Sig.
1	BLG-CV1	C	65 wide × 75	✓	-	-	✓	3860	✓	-	✓	✓
2	BLG-CV2	R	60 × 100 × 30	✓	-	-	✓	3190	✓	-	✓	-
3	BLG-CV3	R	62 × 82 × 75	✓	-	-	✓	5245	✓	-	✓	✓
4	DJJ-CV1 DJJ-CV2 DJJ-CV3	R R R	50 × 70 × 20+ 70 × 100 × 30+ 230 × 110 × 35+	-	-	✓	-	1695+ 3530+ 9215+	? ? ?	- - -	✓ ✓ ✓	- - -
5	LAM-CV1	R	50 × 75 × 75+	✓		-	✓	4280+	-	✓	✓	✓
6	LAM-CV2	S	80 × 80 × 70 80 × 80 × 70	-	✓	-	✓	5825 5825	- -	✓ ✓	✓ ✓	✓ ✓
7	LAT-CV1	R R	50 × 55 × 50. 50 × 68 × 50	-	✓	✓	-	2630 3070	- -	✓ ✓		✓ ✓
8	LAT-CV2	R	45 × 65 × 46	✓	-	-	✓	2565	-	-	✓	✓
9	MAS-CV1	S R	42 × 49 × 43 47 × 65 × 42	-	✓	✓	-	1930 2500	✓ ✓	Made from a single stone		
10	MDS-CV1	R C	45 × 55 × 45 56 wide × 35	-	✓	✓	-	2295 1930	✓ -	- -	✓ ✓	- -
11	SDH-CV1	C	70 wide × 30+	✓	-	✓	-	2365+	-	-	✓	-
12	SDH-CV2 SDH-CV3	C C	45 wide × 60 40 wide × 45	-	✓	✓	-	2008 1445	✓ -	- -	✓ ✓	- -
13	SLT-CV1	S	100 × 100 × 60+	✓	-	-	?	7113+	-	-	✓	✓
14	SNB-CV1	R	70 × 85 × 130	✓	-	✓	-	8400	✓	-	✓	✓
15	SGG-CV1	R	80 × 120 × 30+	✓	-	-	✓	4361+	-	-	✓	-
16	SGG-CV2	R	*c.*70 × 50 × 80	✓	-	-	✓	4280	✓	✓	-	✓
18	STB-CV1	R	40 × 70 × 45	✓	-	✓	-	2500	✓	-	✓	✓
19	STB-CV2	R	30 × 60 × 35	✓	-	✓	-	1530	✓	-	✓	✓
20	TRK-CV1	R R	65 × 70 × 60 55 × 65 × 30+	-	✓	✓	-	4175 2253+	✓ ✓	- -	✓ ✓	✓ ✓
21	TRK-CV2	S R	70 × 70 × 40 60 × 65 × 42	-	✓	✓	-	3360 2945	✓ ✓	- -	✓ ✓	✓ ✓
22	ZHR-CV1	C R	55 × 20 60 × 70 × 30	-	✓	✓	-	1265 2500	-	Made from a single stone		

Table 5.2: Each of the recorded collecting tanks connected to an olive press. All measurements are in cm. The + symbol indicates the maximum observed dimension in cases where full measurement of a buried or destroyed feature was impossible. Abbreviations are as follows: Shape (C. = Circular, R. = Rectangular, S. = Square; Dims. = overall external dimensions (width × depth for circular, breadth × length × depth for rectangular); Sg. = Single tank; Tw. = Twin tanks; Op. Sig. = opus signinum lining.

room floor are often not discernible in survey fieldwork. Where they do survive, we can record a variety of types and shapes These collecting tanks were of different types and shapes (Table 5.3).

A second method is known as overflow decantation. In this the oil starts to rise above the collecting tank and flows out but water and solid refuse remain. This process may take place in either single or twin settling vats. The

Type	Rock-cut	Built-up	
	16	2	
Shape	Rectangular	Circular	Square
	11	5	2

Table 5.3: Type and shape of collecting vats.

latter approach was widely employed in olive oil presses in Syria and other parts of south-west Europe and North Africa (Frankel 1999: 175, T47121). In Cyrenaica, evidence of two or more adjoining collecting tanks has been found. Two twin collecting vats were recorded at al-Mhasi and Sidi Zehri. Both were divided into two almost equal compartments, and the floors of one or both were provided with a shallow depression. However, sometimes more than two settling tanks were used. The best example of this comes from Qasr Djaj, where a set of three rock-cut tanks were found connected to each other through outlets cut at the top of the dividing walls.

The other two methods of oil decantation are the underflow method, and a hybrid method which combines both overflow and underflow separation. In the former an outlet was positioned at the base of the collecting tank and the collected liquid was released. The dregs then flow out first as they are heavier than the oil. By controlling the flow, it is possible to separate the oil from the watery by-products. In the second method, the expressed liquid is first channelled to a tank with two separate chambers. As the liquid starts to rise up, the floating oil moves to the adjacent receptacle while the water can then be drained out to a separate vessel. The resulting oil then flows out to other connected tanks for further purification. To my knowledge, no evidence of either of these two techniques has been recovered in Cyrenaica. However, without giving any details, Frankel (1999: 175) points to the use of a possible overflow and underflow technique at Ras el-Hammam, 5 km southwest of Lepcis Magna.

Certain characteristics can be drawn for these features. Internally, the walls were vertical and in most cases a layer of waterproof mortar was applied throughout. In some cases, the collecting tank was placed against the pressing floor and was connected directly to another similar receptacle at the same level. One or both of these would have been provided with a sediment-trap. Twin tanks connected near the top of their walls were exclusively found in association with olive oil installations and indicate that the oil was normally separated by the overflow decantation method. When other evidence such as olive crushers is lacking, the presence of twin tanks in relation to the pressing bed may, to a large extent, indicate that the facility was related to olive oil production. Sometimes, a single collecting vessel with a bottom which usually had a small depression was also used, suggesting that it was probably connected to wine making. Only two examples have been found carved out of a single stone block followed by small numbers of built-up tanks, while the majority were hewn into the bedrock floor of the pressing area. The most numerous collecting tanks were rectangular, but circular and square shapes were also noted although in considerably lower numbers. In general, the depth of these collecting vessels varies from 0.20 m to 0.60 m. The volume of these recorded examples varies from 48 to 270 litres.

5.3.7 Counterweight block

The main characteristic of presses in Cyrenaica is the absolute rarity of the screw counterweights and therefore the lack of lever and screw presses. One example of a press with a screw mechanism has been found, at Qasr al-Hmeira, south of Balagrae. This counterweight block was discovered in a substantial building measuring 32 × 36 m made of large-dressed blocks and with a triangular arched doorway. On stylistic grounds the building can be dated to the early Roman period with the high-grade masonry suggesting elite ownership. Unfortunately, relatively recent clearances have largely obscured the internal arrangements of the building and the context to which the counterweight block belongs are not discernible.

The parallelepiped lever and windlass counterweight was the most regular type found throughout the region, and is apparently a variant unique to Cyrenaica. It was placed with its long axis parallel to and just under the press beam (Figure 5.7). The counterweight block was provided with two identical sockets, as well as another two narrow and shallow grooves in the lower edge of either the short or long sides of the block, usually extending across the two socket holes. A wooden peg or metal rod was inserted in this position to pass through a mortice cut in the lower part of the timber upright, to secure the windlass on the top of the counterweight. The windlass was connected to the beam by ropes. The counterweights are on average 1.70 m long, 0.60 m wide and 0.30 m high. The interval between the two vertical holes varied from 0.30 m to 1 m, with a normal distance of about 0.9 m. The underside grooves average 0.10 m in depth, 0.07 m in width and 0.70 m in length. Most of the time the grooves were cut longitudinally, and in a few examples the cuts are along the longer side and go right across the block.

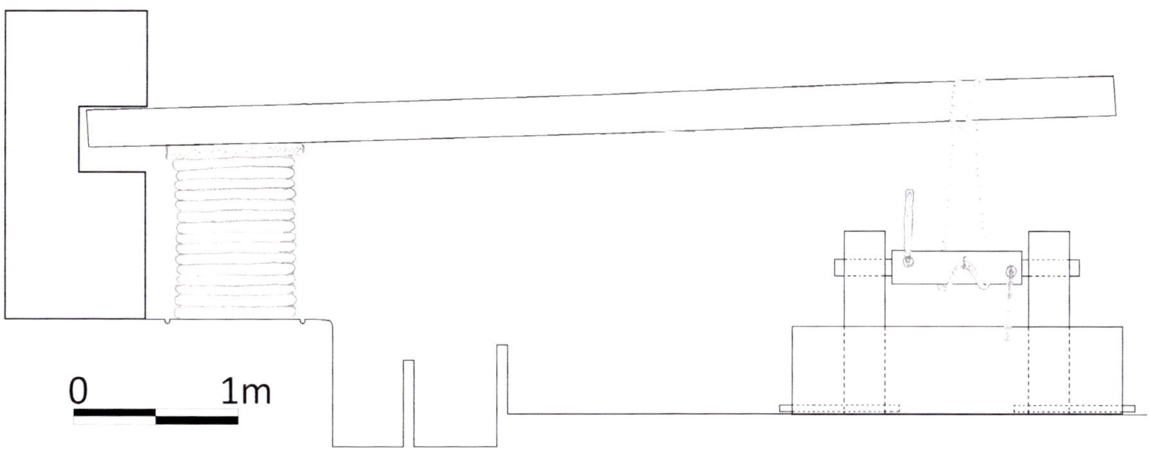

Figure 5.7: Section of the Cyrenaican press.

Another kind of counterweight block has two closed 'T' shaped sockets, with an average distance of about 0.7 m between each socket. These shallow holes were the bases used for fixing the windlass to the block. While a combination of closed and open 'T' shaped sockets was also used in the same block, the method by which the windlass mechanism was mounted remains enigmatic.

In general, the average weight of the Cyrenaican counterweights is 1.2 tonnes. This is broadly in line with those recorded in the Kasserine survey, in west-central Tunisia (1.1 tonnes, Mattingly and Hitchner 1993: Table 8) and in Provence, in south-eastern France (1.3 tonnes, Brun 1986: 248–50, Figs. 209–210), but slightly more than the examples found in Cherchell, in western Algeria (0.9 tonnes, Leveau 1984: 436-7). On the other hand, the evidence from the Gebel Tarhuna in Tripolitania shows extensive use of the larger Semana weight type, which ranges from 5 tonnes to 7.8 tonnes with an average 3.3 tonnes (Ahmed 2019: Table 4.9).

5.3.8 Lifting the counterweight block

The typical Cyrenaican counterweight demonstrates that the windlass was installed in a dissimilar way to those of the 'Senam type', which show a set of dove tail cuts applied in a standard array. In the Cyrenaican case, the counterweight block was placed with the long axis parallel to the press beam. The rectangular block was provided with two identical sockets and two narrow and shallow grooves in the lower edges of the block, usually extending across the two socket holes. A rod, presumably made of iron, was inserted in this position to pass through a mortice cut in the lower part of the timber uprights where they protruded through the base of the block, in order to secure them. Such a system will have prevented the counterweight from sitting exactly flush with the ground. It is possible that there was a slot cut in the floor directly below the counterweight to allow it to rest more evenly on the ground when not in operation and suspended below the beam. Careful excavation of press rooms is needed to check for this sort of feature below counterweight blocks. Even if not present, given that most of gearing up was done when the block was lifted off the ground, its uneven base may not have mattered much.

Close observation of the operation of a traditional lever press in south Tunisia, during which the counterweight was raised off the floor, led Mattingly (1993: 495. See also Vismara 2007: 73) to believe that the Roman weight was also lifted clear of the floor. Lifting the weight allows persistent pressure to be maintained over the baskets, especially if the press room is equipped with more than one lever press. In the meantime, it provides ample time for the milling and doing other tasks. The advantage here is that the process does not require a large labour force, in contrast to screw technology which demands continuous attention or repeated retightening of the device. Technically, applying a high pressure by means of a fixed windlass in the ground is possible, but the breaking point here is the ropes in case extra strain is applied. By contrast, when high force is applied to the mounted windlass on a counterweight block (a dead weight on the end) the weight block is lifted off the ground without difficulty. However, the failure points with respect to the processing power are once again the ropes and handspikes, both of which are employed in the pressing operation.

There are other potential problems in lifting the most commonly used Cyrenaican weight stone, Type 1, which weighs over 1 tonne. The operation of lifting the counterweight off the ground would have placed strains on the windlass and in particular the vertical supports that attached it to the counterweight block. Because the underside channel was shallow, there must have been a danger of the bracing support through the uprights breaking away. I would therefore say that although these grooves on the underside were intended to prevent upward movement of the wooden windlass posts (as previously suggested), it is possible that further supporting measures were needed. Perhaps the wooden uprights

Figure 5.8: A traditional press at Douiret in southern Tunisia in 1987. Mounting the windlass device.
Note wedging stones around the wooden post to secure the windlass device and an iron rod inserted into the underside *(Photo: D. Mattingly).*

Figure 5.9: A traditional press at Douiret in southern Tunisia in 1987. The way to connect the windlass to the beam press and the use of a handspike to apply pressure *(Photo: D. Mattingly).*

were slightly tapered or just thickened at their lower ends to make them more tightly fixed in the vertical holes through the counterweight blocks. end. Wedging other material such as stone or wooden wedges around the post would have been another means of adding further stability to the windlass device and in David Mattingly's photographs of the southern Tunisian traditional press, just such a reinforcement can be seen (Figure 5.8 and Figure 5.9).

5.3.9 Pressure estimation of the Cyrenaican press

Brun (1986: 246) estimated the operating pressure of presses in the Var region of Provence to be 5–7 kg/cm². Other calculations regarding ancient lever presses have also been obtained. At Volubilis, the maximum potential generation of pressure on the piled frails of crushed olives beneath the beam was 4.5 kg/cm², and in normal use would range from 2 to 4 kg/cm² (Alami Sounni 1982: 121–33). In Tripolitania presses generated only 1.1 kg/cm² (Oates 1953: 87), while presses in Portugal are estimated to have exerted less than 2 kg/cm² (Amouretti *et al.* 1984: 399-400). The pressures of a series of Lebanese presses were calculated to vary between 1.3 and 4.2 kg/cm² (Cresswell 1965: 45-52), while one Moroccan press generated a low pressure equivalent to only 0.3 kg/cm² (Mattingly 1988a: 183).

Conversely, archaeological data from Cyrenaican presses show that they were capable of generating a higher pressure than many other Mediterranean presses. In Cyrenaica, the distance from the back of the niche to the end of the counterweight block was normally 6 m. The counterweight block weighed approximately 1500 kg with the addition of the beam's weight itself (*c.*100 kg), and in accordance with the principle of the lever, theoretical calculations show that an operating pressure of about 5.3 kg/cm² could be exerted at the point of application on baskets of olive paste (Figure 5.10). This seems a considerable pressure in comparison to the relatively small size of the baskets used (which were less than 0.6 m in diameter), which means that a minimum of two loads could probably be processed in a working day (see above). The apparent differences in the pressure generated by the ancient presses underscores the possibility that pressing can easily be operated by following different processing strategies, and even by employing low-pressure installations (Mattingly 1988a: 183).

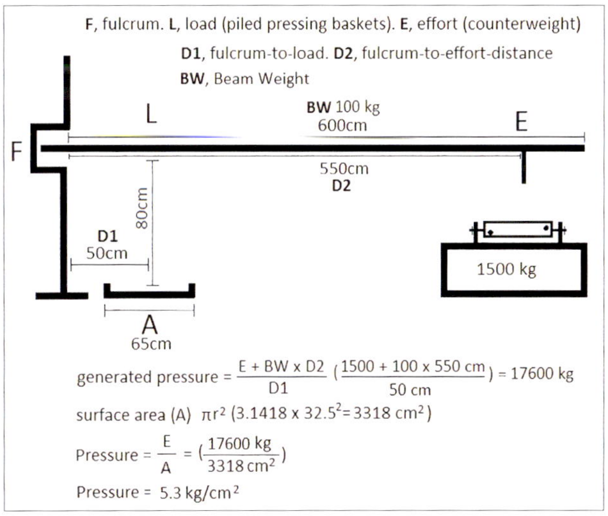

Figure 5.10: Calculation of pressure generated by a typical Cyrenaican lever and windlass press.

chapter six

SITE TYPOLOGY

6.1 Introduction

This chapter sets out an initial typology of settlements associated with olive oil production in Cyrenaica. Establishing a preliminary settlement type is a step towards attaining a relative basis for understanding the settlement pattern in rural Cyrenaica, which is not fully surveyed. Very little research has been conducted into the types and patterns of rural settlements, and thus their relationship with the urban centres is poorly understood. By contrast, many archaeological surveys have been conducted in Tripolitania (Ahmed 2019; Barker *et al.* 1996; Felici *et al.* 2006; 1954; Munzi *et al.* 2004; Musso 1998; Oates 1953; 1954; Rebuffat 1988; Sheldrick 2021) and other North African provinces (*Inter alia*, Baaziz 1986; De Vos 2000; Carlsen 1989; Leveau 1984; Hitchner 1988).

The limited research on Cyrenaican rural archaeology started with the fieldwork led by R. G. Goodchild, although his approach was not systematic. The resulting publications form a fundamental part of our knowledge on the Cyrenaican landscape and placed a special emphasis on an interesting type of defensive building known locally as a *qasr* (Goodchild 1951a; 1951b; 1953). This was followed by the collaborative work on Christian archaeology undertaken by R. G. Goodchild and J. B. Ward-Perkins in the region in the 1950s and 1960s. This was subsequently published in two separate volumes, *Justinianic Mosaics Pavements in Cyrenaican Churches* (Alföldi-Rosenbaum and Ward-Perkins 1980) and *Christian Monuments of Cyrenaica* (Ward-Perkins and Goodchild 2003). The latter work, although dependent on a selective approach which mainly focused on ecclesiastic evidence, provides useful descriptions of many different rural settlements.

Furthermore, the archaeological survey in the Wadi al-Kuf region under the direction of A. Abdussaid provided some interesting insights into farming sites in this hinterland region (Abdussaid *et al.* 1984). The survey zone covered around 100 km^2, where a total of 34 sites were recorded. Of these, 16 were associated with pressing elements used for olive oil and wine production. Despite the brevity of the published material (which is only in Arabic) and the basic discussion devoted to the chronology and function of the investigated sites, new economic information has been derived from a rugged terrain that has long been thought to have been used solely for defensive purposes.

In his pioneering research on the hinterlands of Tripolitania, Goodchild (1949: n. 31; Jimenez 2016: 171–2) used the term *qasr* (plural *qsur*) to describe a broad class of fortified sites. This term was commonly used by the locals of that region to refer to any ancient building of this type. The UNESCO survey of the Tripolitanian pre-desert area followed suit (Mattingly and Dore 1996: 127). The term was also used locally in Cyrenaica and was therefore adopted to refer to similar rural structures.

The study carried out by Emrage (2015) is the first systematic landscape survey in Cyrenaica. The Wadi al-Kuf Archaeological Survey (hereafter KAS) of *c.*1,350 km^2, recorded the remains of 55 sites and found a range of new evidence regarding the function of the recorded buildings in an undulating terrain cut by series of deep ravines which in antiquity formed a physical barrier between western and eastern Cyrenaica. The recorded buildings are generally divided into two main types. With respect to the physical appearance of the structures, the first type is classified into a civilian category which is divided into two types: fortified qasr and unfortified qasr-like buildings. These are associated with evidence relating to farming and manufacturing activity. The second type is of military character, judging by the absence of industrial and agricultural features and its topographical location. In addition, the size of this type of fortified structures is a key factor in its division into four sub-types: fort (more than 0.8 ha), fortlet with or without tower (0.1–0.5 ha), outpost (0.01–0.10 ha), and watchtower (0.01 ha and less) (Emrage 2015: 133–52).

Finally, the recent survey directed by O. Menozzi of Chieti University provided valuable information on rural settlement patterns within the territory of Cyrene. This project was launched as a response to an urgent need to map, remotely monitor and document rural sites that are increasingly under serious threat. Spatial analysis of the data collected from the targeted area, located between Messa (to the west) and al-Gubbah (to the east), provided intriguing information on the settlement types within Cyrene's territory and their distribution during the Late Antique period (Fossataro 2008; Menozzi 2012; Menozzi and Fossataro 2010; Menozzi *et al.* 2014; Saad *et al.* 2016). Although the sizes of the sites were not explicitly given, their extent and the presence/absence of certain types of public/Christian buildings were the main criteria in defining the settlement type of this designated area. These settlements were divided into three main types (Antonelli 2016: 54). They can be summarised as follows:

1. Pseudo-urban or minor settlements: with public and private buildings distributed in a regular manner as in large towns. They generally contained a large open space that was probably used for mundane and commercial purposes.
2. Secondary villages: smaller than the first category. Although they usually contained public buildings, their rural characteristics prevailed.
3. Scattered rural sites: the smallest category and widely represented by farms and *qsur*. Also associated with isolated churches.

My classification of the Cyrenaican settlement sites is a combination of the pattern proposed in the KAS survey (Emrage 2015: 143–52) and the Chieti University work (Antonelli 2016: 54). Nonetheless, it is by no means representative of the region, as both surveys were confined to relatively small areas. In addition, the KAS was mostly concerned with evidence of fortified sites. Concomitantly, while this study will generally use some types of settlement suggested by these last two studies, modifications have been made to certain terms. For example, 'small town' is used instead of 'pseudo-urban', and 'nucleated village' replaced 'secondary village'. In addition, some other terms such as agroville are proposed.

All the industrial and agricultural elements recorded during the survey were found in sites of civilian nature, usually in association with defensive structures (*qsur*) characterised by substantial outer walls and revetments and often surrounded by ditches. However, the isolated sites that appear to have been of military purpose, as indicated by architectural and topographic characteristics, geographical location and the apparent absence of industrial and agricultural activities, are not included here. My attempt in establishing a settlement typology also benefited from the classifications implemented in the pre-desert zone of Tripolitania (Mattingly and Dore 1996: 111–33) and in the Gebel Tarhuna survey (Ahmed 2019: 18–19).

It is worth mentioning that my survey mainly concentrated on gathering data related to olive oil and wine production and recorded other archaeological remains at a preliminary level. As a result of this limited data, the initial classification of settlement types in Cyrenaica (Table AI.10 and Figure AI.2) must be viewed as tentative. More extensive surveys are urgently needed in order to obtain a clearer understanding of settlement patterns and changes within a chronological framework. The provisional typology is based on 104 rural sites plus seven urban sites, many of which were first identified during my field survey. For full details of all sites visited during the survey, see Part II (Appendix II).

The degree of site preservation played an important role in identifying characteristics such as site extent and the number of pressing elements found on it. Accordingly, site typology is based on a combination of both the overall size of a settlement and the number of pressing elements. However, in most cases the two criteria were not strictly combined, with only one used in some circumstances.

It should be emphasised that the matters concerning the actual size of the sites, and to some extent their function, remain inconclusive. The state of surface preservation is solely dependent on the extent to which human and natural factors affected the sites, as these can sometimes totally obliterate the archaeological evidence (Mattingly 2011: 78). All the archaeological sites in the discussion contain evidence of olive-oil/wine presses. A high or low level of productivity at these sites was only applied to those in which crushing basins were found. Table 6.1 shows the number of mill mortars that were used to define productivity at each site type. However, other evidence of pressing elements, such as millstones

Type	Number of crushing basins	Productivity
Village (small town)	7 or more	High
	Less than 7	Low
Large fortified farms	4 or more	High
	Less than 4	Low
Small fortified farm	2–4	High
	Less than 2	Low
Large open farm	Over 3	High
	1–3	Low
Small open farm	4 or more	High
	Less than 4	Low

Table 6.1: Criteria for level of site productivity.

and counterweight blocks, were also recorded in the other sites (Appendix I, Table AI.10) suggesting that they were connected to olive oil production.

The following sections will describe the principal types of site recognised and present representative examples.

6.2 Towns

Generally, industrial evidence related to olive oil and wine production is relatively lacking in the Cyrenaican urban context. This apparent scarcity should not be seen as a definite characteristic of urban centres *per se*, as it can be explained in the main to the traditional focus of archaeological missions on monumental architecture and the glaring neglect of more mundane evidence, particularly evidence related to industrial activities.

Wilson's inventory study presented the most important industrial archaeological evidence found in the major towns of Cyrenaica (Wilson 2001a; 2004). Further information on industrial evidence was gleaned from the coastal site of Phycus, which seems to have become an important port in the late Roman period (Flemming 1971; Hesein 2015; Jones and Little 1971b). Aside from the ancient city of Tocra where evidence of crushing basins was found, though not in situ, the other large sites have yet to produce any elements that can be directly connected to olive oil production. The discovered evidence so far includes sunken vats whose internal walls were completely lined with a layer of hydraulic mortar, suggesting that they were most probably used for storing liquids. The recent discovery of the remains of a treading floor adjacent to the vats discovered at Tocra is strong evidence that they were used to store wine rather than oil.

While Hesein admitted that sunken vats were typically connected to wine production he hypothesised that many of them, particularly those located along the coast, could have been associated with fish-related production as well (Hesein 2014: 140). His interpretation of *garum* production and salted fish processing is based on parallel examples of different forms of vats found along the coast of many sites in North Africa (Arneur 2005), southern Spain and northern Morocco (Ponsich 1988; Trakadas 2004). While we generally accept that some of these vats were probably used for fish production, especially those located on the coastal sites, it remains probable that large numbers of them were used for other purposes. Deep round vats are a common feature in many inland sites, where several them have been found in close association with pressing facilities. This suggests that these vats were most likely used to store wine and/or olive oil.

It is worth mentioning that all the recorded pressing elements in the rural sites were surface finds and hence likely to date the last phase of the site. This is in striking contrast to the urban sites where similar elements were

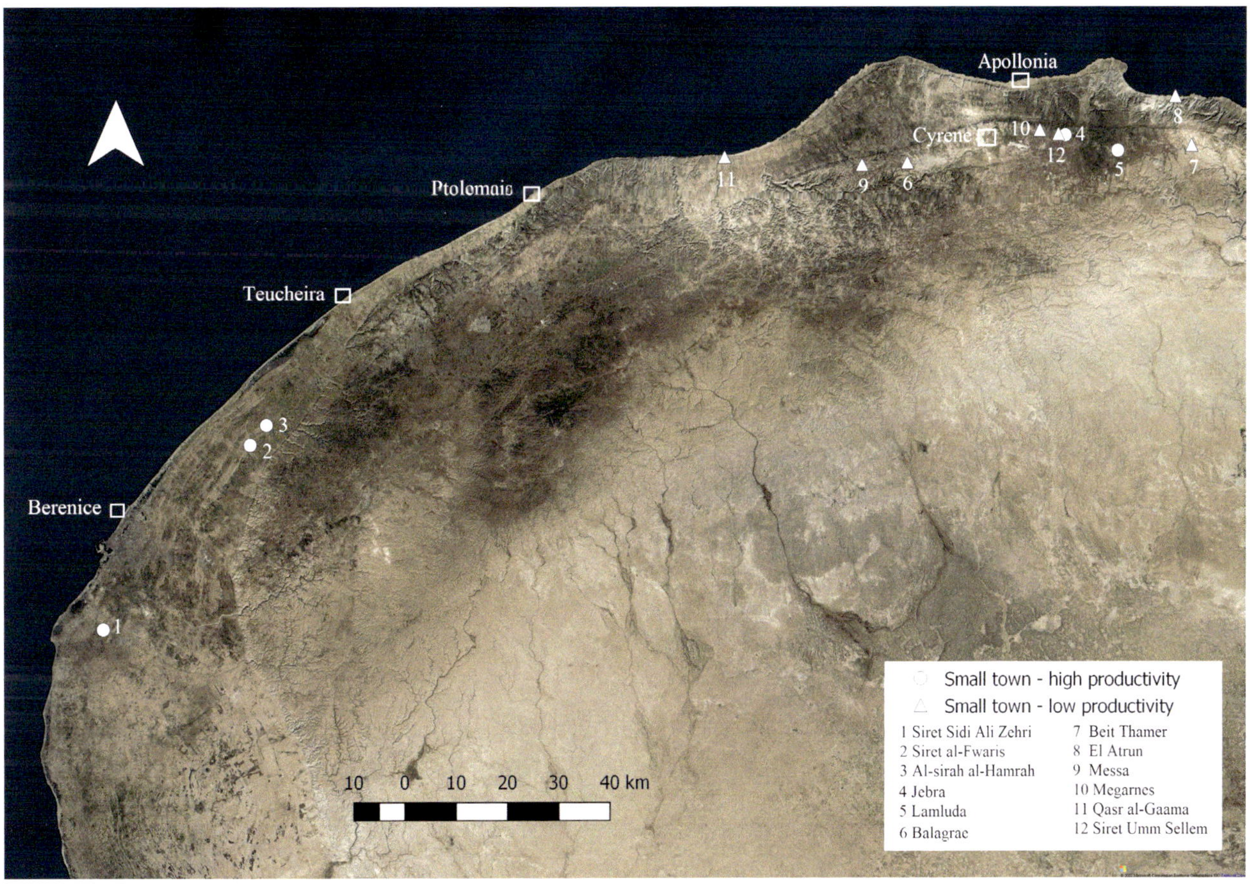

Figure 6.1: Towns, large and small, with evidence of pressing facilities.

almost absent. Although the visible remains in all the urban sites can be attributed to the late Roman and Byzantine periods, only a very few pressing elements were found.

In the light of current evidence, it seems that only limited oil and wine production was carried out in towns, with the majority therefore undertaken at rural sites. This supports Foxhall's argument that since olives and grapes were largely grown in the countryside, it would be more practical to process the substantial bulk of the crops within the rural sites rather than transport them over long distances to presses in towns (Foxhall 2007: 138–9).

6.3 Small Towns

The second category is related to small towns with urban characteristics, and from an olive production point of view, these can be divided into two main sub-types. The first is characterised by a very high level of productivity, while the second is associated with a limited amount of evidence of oil production, usually consisting of not more than three presses. Some of the former are about the same size as the latter or even larger, but here the scale of productivity rather than the overall site area is used to distinguish between the two (Figure 6.1).

These small towns often contained churches, baths and tombs. These secular and religious buildings were planned in a more or less regular manner, and most were built of ashlar masonry. Literary sources as well as the epigraphic and archaeological evidence indicate that some of these towns date back to the Classical period. Most of what is now visible is likely to relate to the late Roman period. Their geographical location seems to be closely related to the availability of fertile lands and water resources.

The archaeological evidence from Cyrenaica's rural settlements, particularly the upper plateau, reveals that churches were important components in the plans of small towns. A large number of churches have been recorded by previous work in the region (Duval 1989; Goodchild 1976; Reynolds 2003; Saad *et al.* 2016). Spatial analysis of the location and distribution of this type of building was recently conducted by Chieti University which found that most churches in the Gebel were located in small towns (Saad 2016: 44).

6.3.1 Agroville (high production small town)

An 'agroville' is a type of small town which possessed some of the characteristics of urban centres, but which processed a large volume of agricultural crops from the surrounding countryside (Mattingly and Hitchner 1995: 192). In my survey, sites which contained seven or more mill mortars (and hence evidence for 14+ presses) are classified as agrovilles as they indicate olive oil production on a massive scale (Figure 6.2). The survey has recorded five sites which could be identified as agrovilles (Figure 6.3). Two sites are located on the inland upper plateau, east of Cyrene, whilst the other three sites are concentrated in the Benghazi coastal plain to the west. All of these sites were near to the major cities.

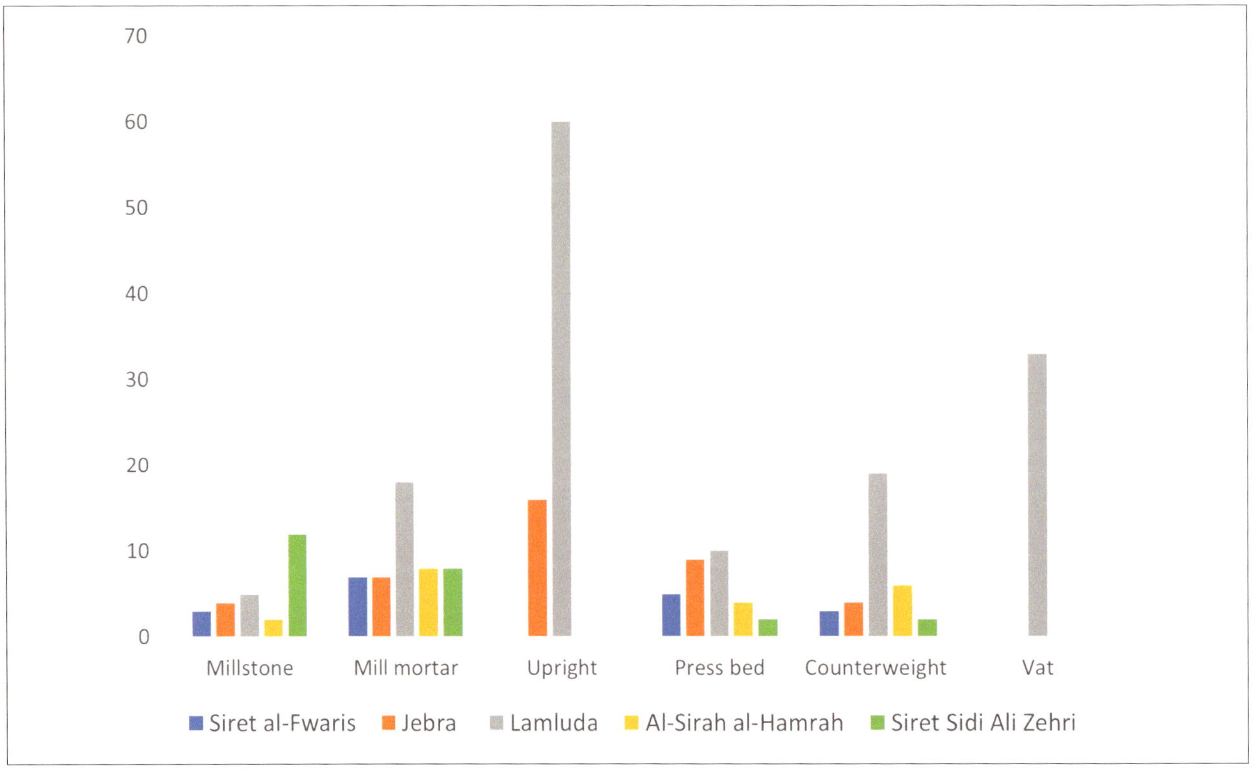

Figure 6.2: Pressing elements found in small towns linked to large-scale oil production.

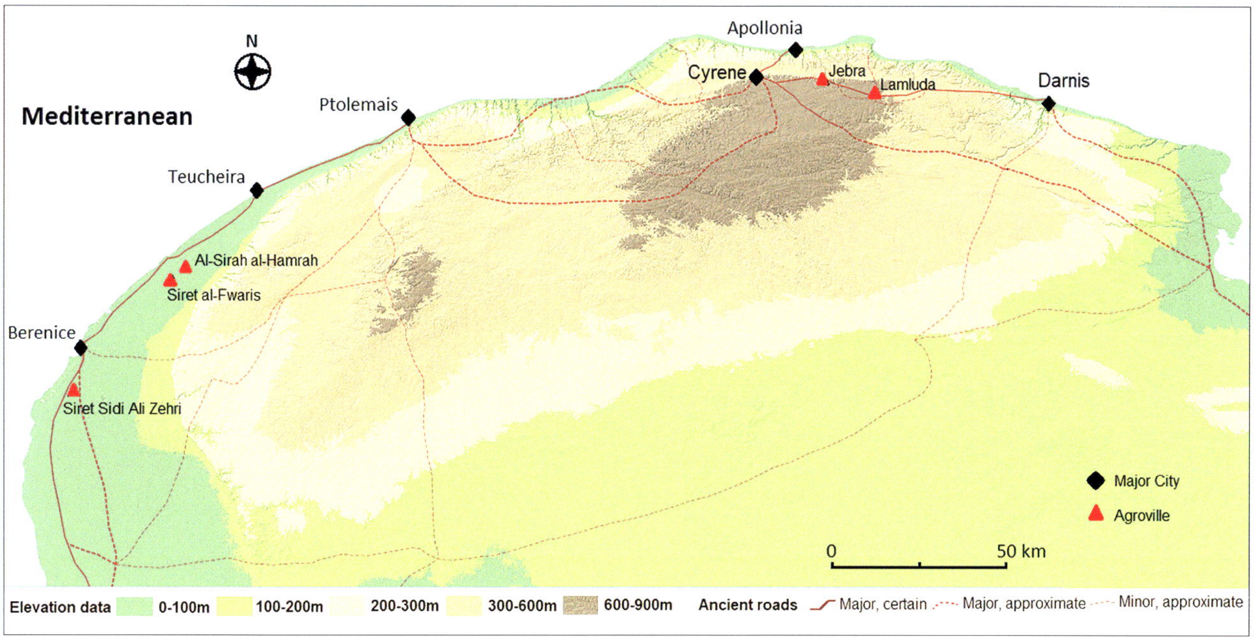

Figure 6.3: Location of agrovilles in relation to the major cities
(Source of the map: 2012 Ancient World Mapping Center).

The presence of such large agricultural centres is an indication that the surrounding lands were subject to intensive olive tree cultivation and reflects that the area specialised in oil production. This type of settlement is best represented by the site of Lamluda. The other sites dedicated to large-scale oil production are Siret al-Fwaris, Jebra, Al-Sirah al-Hamrah and Siret Sdidi Ali Zehri, though they possessed fewer pressing facilities than Lamluda.

To look at other examples close by, Kasr al-Guellal (Hitchner *et al.* 1990: 248), in the Tunisian high steppe, was more focused on grain, and contained ten small olive presses, along with a forum, church fort, cemetery and perhaps some public buildings (Hitchner 1988: 35). Further examples can be found in *Volubilis Colonia* (Akerraz and Lenoir 1981), Maduros (Christofle 1930) and Uchi Maius (Vismara 2007), though presses in these towns were established at a later date. Volubilis was a prosperous town between the second and third centuries AD and later its private houses were equipped with one or two oil presses (Wilson 2002: 299). Uchi Maius in northern Tunisia is a case of a major Roman town with monumental buildings, where the late phases have several presses inside, being to some extent repurposed for large-scale olive oil production (Vismara 2007: 510).

6.3.3.1 *Lamluda*

Lamluda lies on the upper plateau, 30 km east of Cyrene. It is generally agreed that 'Liminiade' of the early third century *Antonine Itinerary* (68, 2; 70, 8) must be the antecedent of the modern placename Lamluda (Pacho 1827: 125–6; Laronde 1987: 296, 321, no. 244, but see also Roques 1987: 11, no. 36 who argued that that name is valid for al-Gubbah). Lamluda is located in a fertile area on the main east-west road which linked the main towns and the city of Cyrene and was further directly connected by road with the port of Naustathmos (modern Ras al-Hilal). It contains a number of features normally found in urban centres: two churches, a probable bath and a discernible grid of dense street lines. Lamluda is the most impressive agroville (Figure 6.4), where 60 uprights (Buzaian 2009: no. 3) and 18 mill mortars were recorded that are predominantly connected to olive oil production (Appendix II: site no. 38). Nevertheless, some of them, like the one which was excavated by Goodchild in 1950s (Buzaian 2009), were more likely to have been for wine.

Of the early part of the town's life we know little except the bare fact of its existence, as attested by the *Antonine Itinerary* in the second and third centuries. There are three built-up tombs at Snibat el Awila, 6.5 km north of Lamluda, similar to those found in Messa and dated to the fourth century BC (Laronde 1987: 301; Stucchi 1975: 77). This strongly suggest that the territory in general was settled at least from the late Classical period. It seems likely that Lamluda as well as many other rural settlements were initially founded as simply organised agglomerations, and then transformed into proper towns between the end of the first century BC and the second century AD (Menozzi *et al.* 2014: 69). The great natural fertility of the lands around Cyrene and easy access to road networks were significant factors in determining the location of these early settlements and their development through the Roman period.

The site extends over *c.*20 ha and the plan has been partially recovered by the recent work of Chieti University (Menozzi *et al.* 2014: 71, Fig. 9). The grid, as far as it is known, consists of the basic *cardo* (A on Figure 6–4)

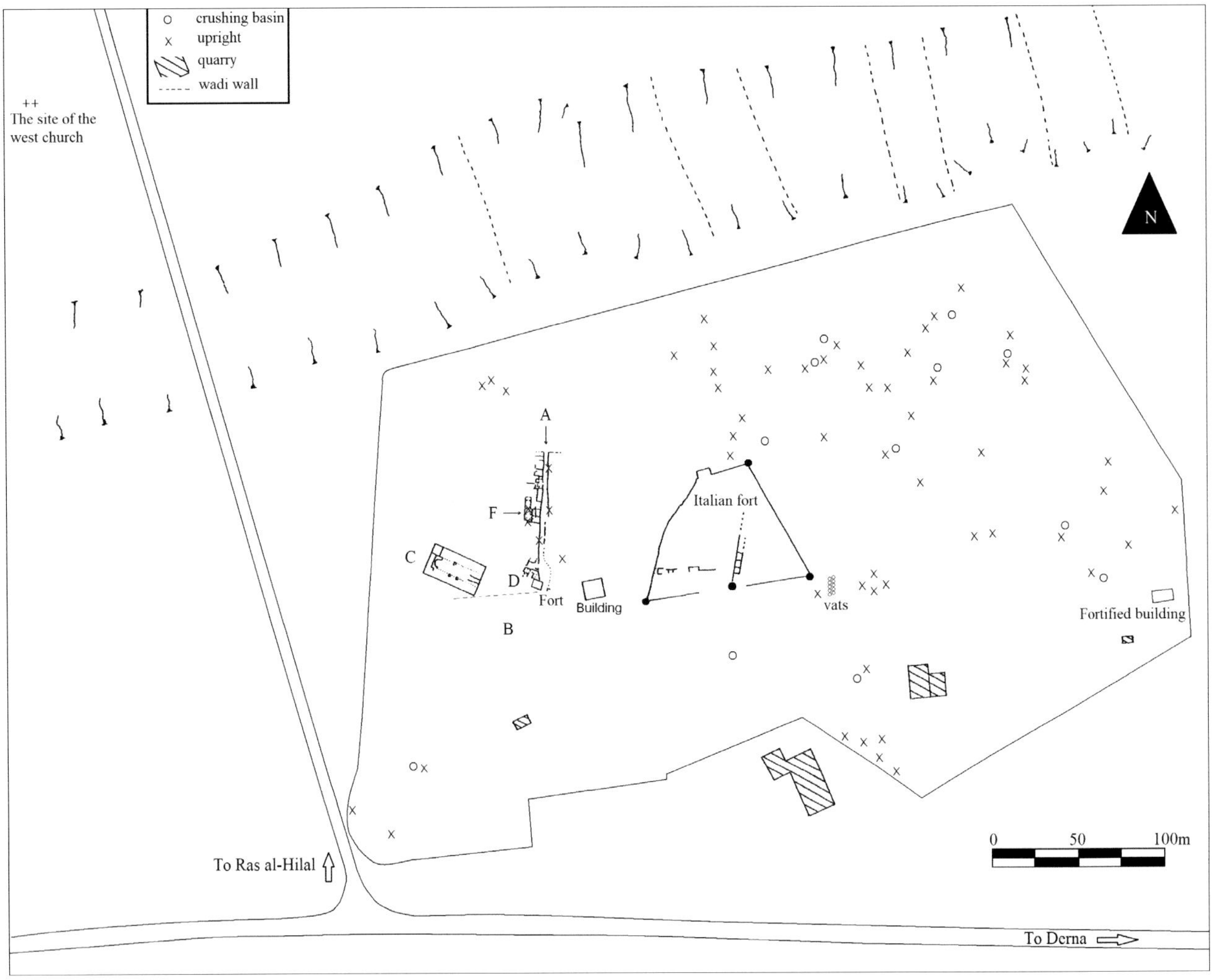

Figure 6.4: Lamluda. General plan of the site and the distribution of presses within the modern enclosure fence.

along the north-south axis and three *decumani* on the east-west axis. The former was located on the western side of the town and leads to an open area that possibly served as a market/caravanserai for the town.

Pottery evidence found at the site indicates that the initial settlement probably dated back to the second century BC (Menozzi 2014: 67). Some 43 small stelae made from local limestone were found in the cemetery area north-west of the site (Bacchielli 1987; Menozzi 2014; Bacchielli and Reynolds 1987). These stelae can be dated mainly to the early Roman period, and likely represent crude heads of Libyan characteristics. However, they feature names written in Greek or Latin letters, which may reflect the presence of a multicultural society with a distinct local influence.

The Byzantine use of the site is mainly represented by the east church and a fortified structure. The south-west corner seems to display the most obvious evidence that the town plan changed. This area was occupied by one of the *decumani* and the *forum* (B on figure 6–4). Before the southern end of the *cardo* stood a fortified building (D), which had evidently encroached upon the street and consequently reduced its width, thus restricting movement to and from the town (Menozzi 2014: 71). This encroachment can be seen as evidence of planning development between the fifth and sixth centuries.

In the 1950s Goodchild conducted limited clearance work in the western area of the town, which resulted in the discovery of a paved north-south street and a press room on its west side identified as having been used for olive oil extraction. However, the absence of a crushing facility, the extensive use of mortar lining in the pressing area and the existence of a large lined tank connected with a bell-shaped deep vat suggest that wine rather than oil was most probably produced here (Buzaian 2009). Moreover, the discovery of a group of 21 sunken *dolia* immediately north of the press room (Buzaian 2009: 47, 51; Oliva 2014: 72) may confirm the presence of wine production. Recent excavations in a building on the opposite side of the same street brought to light evidence of an additional group of sunken *dolia* (Menozzi *et al.* 2014: 72). Buried jars (*dolia defossa*) for fermentation, wine storage and other purposes were common in Early Roman Italian villas (e.g., Villa Regina, Boscoreali, Pollard 2016: 351, Fig. 17.6). However, they were rarely employed in North Africa, probably because of the warmer climate (Brun 2004, 6; Frankel 1999: 27).

Evidence from Volubilis clearly indicates that some presses were part of élite peristyle houses (Wilson 2002: 259). Limited excavation at Lamluda reduces our knowledge of the placement of the presses, but there is no evidence of architectural remains typical of élite houses in the associated rubble. Instead, the ample evidence for storage facilities and simple structures at Lamluda strongly suggests that the space was dedicated to industrial activities and the workers who ran these installations. These are known to exist in the town in the form of many single establishments rather than large oilery-type units.

6.3.3.2 Jebra and other agrovilles

Jebra is the other site located on the upper plateau that possessed a large number of pressing facilities (Appendix II: site no. 36). The site lies just 10 km west of Lamluda (Stucchi 1975: 77, 506), and housed at least 16 isolated units of olive oil presses in an area of *c.*6 hectares. There are no clear traces of élite residential buildings apart from a rectangular structure located in the north-west corner of the site. Its location on slightly raised ground and the use of large, squared blocks in the external walls suggest a building of defensive character (*qasr*). The early phase of the site was clearly represented by a group of monumental sarcophagus-tombs dated to the late Hellenistic period, with some evidence of later reuse in early Roman times (Menozzi *et al.* 2014: 67). There is a remarkable similarity between Lamluda and Jebra in their use of free-standing monolithic uprights (*Type 1*) associated with a box-like press-bed flanked on either side by two standing stone slabs (*Type 7*).

The location of the other three sites in the Benghazi coastal plan, which marked the far west end of Cyrenaica, demonstrates that it was of great agricultural potential, although annual rainfall here is significantly lower than on the upper plateau. Two sites were associated with a *qasr* (Al-Sirah al-Hamrah and Siret Sdidi Ali Zehri), and they seem to have been developed from pre-existing farms (third and fourth centuries AD).

The undefended site of Siret al-Fwaris seems to have been primarily established as an open settlement at some later time during the fifth or sixth century AD. This open settlement apparently benefitted from some of the surrounding fortified farms, which are located within a periphery of *c.*4 km. Three press rooms were detected in the eastern part of the settlement. Although they seem to have been incorporated into buildings, their layout cannot be discerned. The presses were located within rectangular rooms which varied in dimensions between 7–10 m long and 5-8 wide, and were all positioned along the northern side. The walls (0.75 m wide) of these press rooms were comprised of two faces of roughly-squared slabs set on their edges and a rubble of mud fill. A similar method of construction was also noted in the Al-Koefia oil press and in many other coastal sites west of Benghazi. In the western part was an elongated building measuring 20 × 6 m. This consisted of four rooms of unequal dimensions and a nearby cistern, just 3.5 m to the west. The two middle rooms were the largest (6 × 5.5 m). The southerly one (6 × 3.5 m) contained two circular vats (possibly more) with many fragments of *dolia* and tiles scattered around. This building can be identified as being used for the storage and distribution of oil and/ or wine.

6.3.2 Small towns with limited oil production

Seven small towns had only small numbers of pressing elements indicating only limited oil production. The biggest of these small towns covered *c.*20 ha, while they were more normally 5–10 ha while the largest number of crushing basins was at El Atrun, where three were recorded. Most of these sites were located on the upper plateau on or close to the major east-west ancient road.

6.3.2.1 Messa

One of the earliest of these settlements, founded by Cyrene, was Messa. As is the case of the similar small towns, it has never been excavated or systematically surveyed. Regrettably, at the end of 2014 the site was completely bulldozed and has gone forever (Figure 6.5). Little can be said about the layout of the site due to its ruinous condition (Appendix II: site no. 48). Moreover, documentation and publications on the site are very sparse. Nonetheless, these succinct accounts, in combination with my reconnaissance surveys in 2009 and 2010 and Google Earth imagery, allow us to sketch a plan of the town (Figure 6.6).

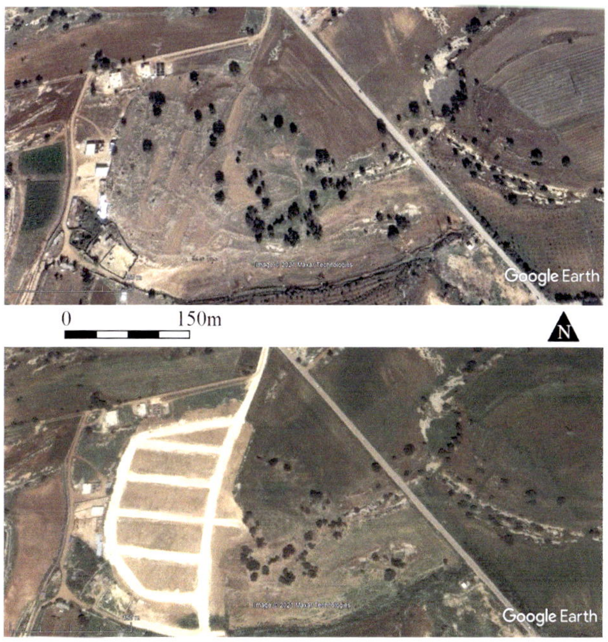

Figure 6.5: The site before and after destruction (*Google Earth © 2021 Maxar Technologies*).

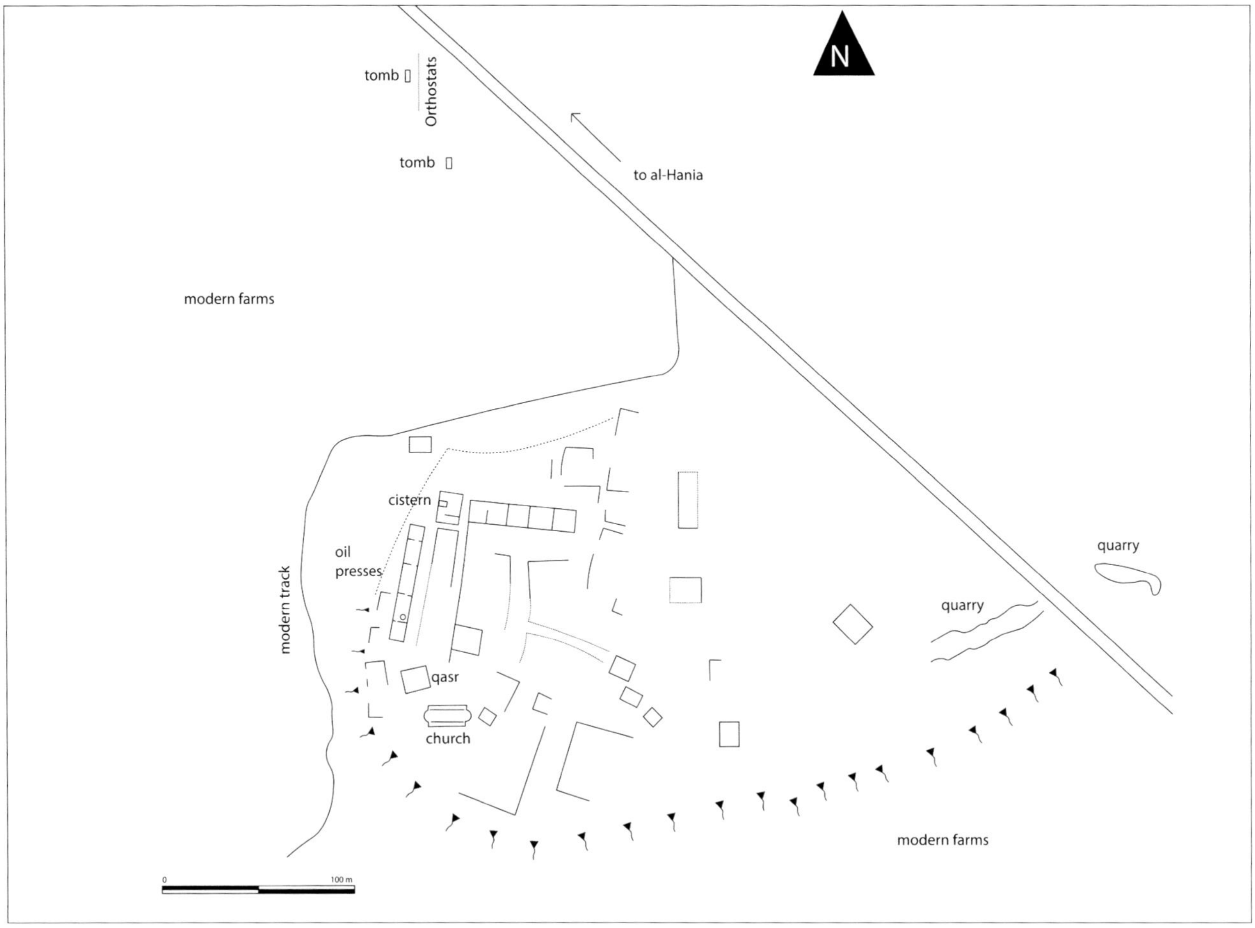

Figure 6.6: Messa. Sketch plan.

Even before its demolition, the site suffered from ploughing, land reclamation of land and pasturing. Ancient sources and archaeological discoveries plainly pointed out that the early history of the settlement is unquestionable, but the surface remains mostly related to the late Roman period.

The street layout is clearest along the western side of the town, where a series of wide, winding thoroughfares that intersected narrower, straight streets can be easily traced. These streets were bordered by the remains of a variety of buildings, including civilian, military and religious structures interspersed with industrial buildings related to olive oil production.

At the far north-west corner of the site were the remains of a rectangular building built of ashlar masonry. Farther south, a small underground cistern was roofed by means of a corbelled dome inserted into an open court building surrounded on three sides by a range of small rooms. This building was sited at the eastern end between two east-west streets running in parallel close to the western edge of the settlement. To the east of this building was an east-west range of five box-like structures, whose outer walls were made of two lines of rough square stones with no discernible internal arrangements. Near the southern limit of the settlement on top of a low hill was a substantial square building (*qasr*) with an outer wall built of large dressed stones which overlapped the same outline of an earlier building. Its strategic location in controlling the town and thick walls indicate that this was of defensive importance. A few metres to the south were the remains of a church heavily buried under its own rubble. To the north-west of the *qasr* a building of rectilinear plan was located. It consisted of at least five rectangular rooms, of which two contained crushing basins and other pressing elements connected to olive oil and wine production.

6.3.2.2 *Balagrae*

The second example of this category is represented by the site of Balagrae (Appendix II: site no. 7). The training excavations that Omar al-Mokhtar University conducted at the site between 2001 and 2006 have brought to light interesting information regarding industrial activities outside the major urban centres (Figure 6.7). These excavations unearthed the remains of mortar treading floors, lined collecting tanks and vats built in abandoned quarries which indicated the presence of industrial activity, most likely related to wine production (Buzaian and Bentaher 2006). The pottery and numismatic evidence found during the excavations suggest that industrial activity in this area began sometime in the early Roman period, and temporarily ceased following the

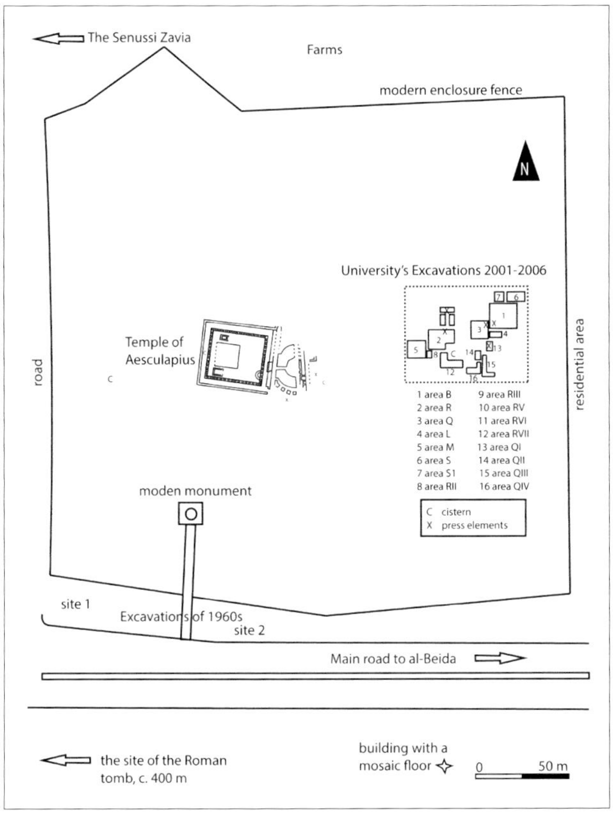

Figure 6.7: Balagrae. General plan shows the sanctuary and the locations of the previous excavations and recent discoveries.

earthquake of AD 365 (Bentaher and Buzaian 2010: 34). A number of late African red slip and Phocaean sherds buried under the rubble of one of the press rooms suggests that occupation resumed shortly after the catastrophe, and continued down to the seventh century AD.

It is still unfortunately true that excavation of wine and oil installations has rarely been undertaken in Cyrenaican archaeological excavations. Catani's research at Siret Qaserin el-Giamel is considered to be the first example of wine and oil installations scientifically excavated and securely dated to the second half of the fifth century AD (Catani 1976). The press at Balagrae is extremely important, as it represents only the second example of its kind from Roman Cyrenaica.

6.3.2.3 *The new Balagrae press*

The Balagrae press was unearthed in 2006 during the training excavations directed by A. Buzaian and F. Bentaher as part of Omar al-Mokhtar University's excavations at the ancient site of Balagrae (modern al-Beida). It is located some 100 m east of the temple of Asclepius within an area that had previously served as a quarry (Figure 6.7, areas 9–11). It represents part of a group of presses which appear to have been used for wine production (Bentaher and Buzaian 2010; Buzaian and Bentaher 2006). The excavation has revealed that the installation had at least three phases of construction (Figure 6.8). Each of these building phases presents changes in function, demonstrating that each phase was a distinct moment in the site's history.

Phase I

There is no evidence of the initial date of the press but this phase (Figure 6.8 A) can be dated to the first century AD when the whole surrounding area was developed for manufacturing activity (Bentaher and Buzaian 2010: 34). The press appears to be quite specialised with facilities for crushing and pressing olives – the rock-cut facilities for crushing were represented by a shallow circular trough (1), a crushing stone, pressing area (2), which was rectangular in shape, and a collecting tank (3). The entrance to the press was via a stepped opening at the northern end of the west wall. The crushing feature (1) was a circular depression 0.5-0.6 m wide and *c.*0.12 m deep, with a total diameter of *c.*2.3 m. A round lump of the bedrock was left uncut in the central area, *c.*1.2 m in diameter. It was flat on top at the same level as the surrounding floor. It is not possible to reconstruct the original design of this crushing feature, and the construction of a later wall on top of it (in phase II) seems to have largely destroyed it.

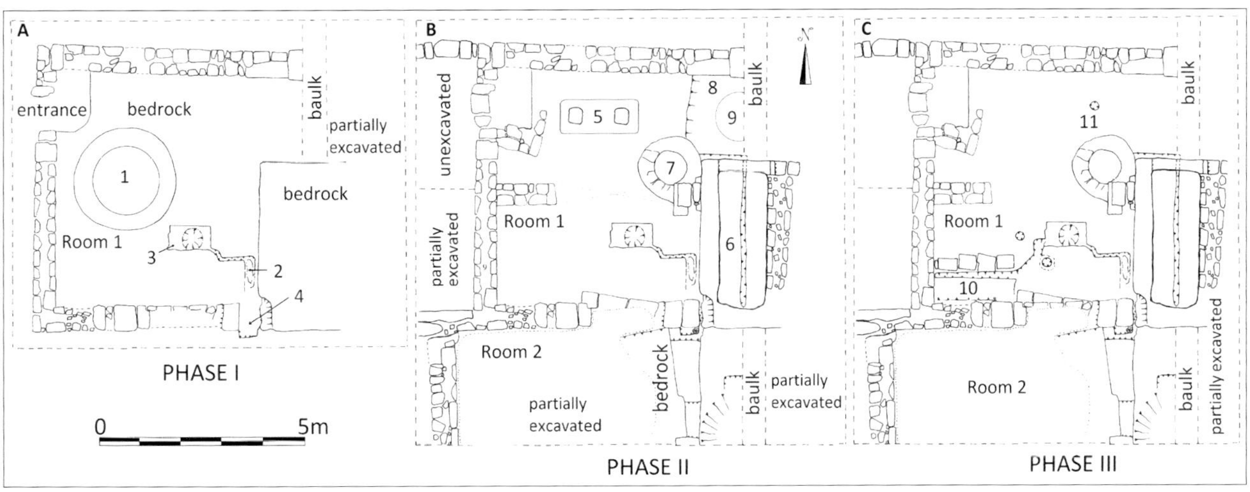

Figure 6.8: Balagare press. Three phases of construction.

The presence of the pressing bed shows that there had been a lever and weight press. The beam, which was probably weighted down by stones in boxes that were suspended on ropes, was anchored in the southern wall but was later blocked (4). Since no way of draining the collecting vat was found, the oil and watery lees were apparently removed directly from the vat using a cup or ladle.

Phase II

During phase II (Figure 6.8 B, Figure 6.9), the oil press was rebuilt and converted to a wine installation by hewing a substantial tank (6), a deep vat (7) and a press-bed (9). This interpretation is supported by the presence of a wall overlapping part of the crushing area. The press was also enlarged when another room on a higher level was added to the south. This room can be accessed through a doorway of two-stepped sill positioned in the middle of the southern wall of Room 1. Room 2 has only been partially uncovered, so nothing can be said about its internal arrangement. Dating evidence of this phase is virtually non-existent. However, the apparent density of third and fourth century AD African Red slip ware suggests that the surrounding area was largely developed during this period.

The large rock-cut tank (6) was located on the eastern side of Room 1. The tank was plastered with an impermeable layer of mortar, and an elongated shallow channel was cut in its floor. This was slightly inclined to the north and ended at a hole which opened into a narrow channel running against the tank from outside to end at the deep circular vat (7). This bell-shaped vat (Figure 6 10) was 2.1 m in depth by 1.3 metre in diameter at its widest point and contained a sediment-trap in its bottom (0.3 m wide and 0.15 m deep). The mouth of the vat was 0.8 m in diameter, with an approximate volume of 2 m^3. The walls of Room 1 were all covered with a white lime plaster similar to that noted in the large tank.

The grapes were first loaded in the large tank (6) to be trodden underfoot, and the resulting juice floated in the channel and was let out through a hole in the bottom where it discharged into the large vat (7). Secondary pressing of the grapes was carried out in phase II by use of a lever and windlass press placed along the northern wall. Here the remains of the trodden fruit were loaded into sacks and placed on the press-bed (9) to press out any additional liquid by using lever and windlass technology, which was evidenced by the typical Cyrenaican counterweight block (*Type 1*). The resulting liquid from the secondary pressing was also drained directly into the same large vat, with no evidence of an intermediate collecting vat. The must extracted from the secondary pressing generally yields inferior wines (Dar 2009: 68), so presumably the first must was drained

Figure 6.9: Balagrae. Some elements of the phase II press. Looking south. Scale 1 m.

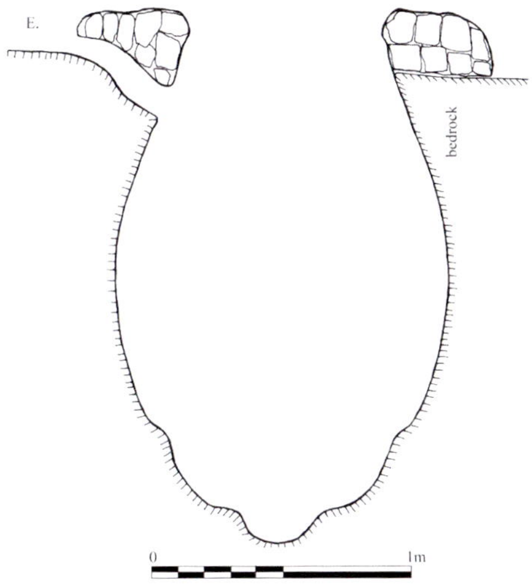

Figure 6.10: Balagrae. Vat (7).

between presses to create a higher quality product. The pressing beam was clearly anchored in the east wall just behind the press-bed, though its essential parts were missing. The location of the counterweight block shows that the beam was about 5.5 m long.

It is difficult to explain the use of a large deep tank for treading the grapes instead of the known shallow floor. While it is almost unknown in other installations, a similar arrangement has also been found at Wadi Senab (Gambini 1974–1975), Ghot Giaras (Bacchielli 1974–1975) and at Lamluda (Buzaian 2009). This suggests that this method of wine production was in some way different from that usually practised in a shallow treading floor.

Phase III

The phase II press ceased to function after the earthquake of AD 365. Ample evidence of this natural disaster has been found at Balagrae (Buzaian and Ben taher 2002: 130; Goodchild 1976: 229–32) and Cyrene (Stucchi 1965: 294), indicating that inhabited areas across the region were devastated. Room 2 fell out of use and the pressing beam no longer worked as the counterweight block was partly destroyed. The large tank (6) was filled with debris from the phase 2 buildings.

At some point in the early fifth century AD the press was brought back into use to produce wine, though on a much smaller scale (Figure 6.8 C). This date has been derived from a bronze coin (Figure 6.11) dated to the reign of Emperor Arcadius (AD 383-408) found under a voussoir from a nearby collapsed arch that was reused to build a U-shaped treading area (10) in the south-west corner of Room 1 (Figure 6.12). A shallow channel was cut along the axis of this treading floor that allowed the must to flow to the adjacent collecting tank (3) and to discharge it into the nearby large vat (7). Deposits filling the vat yielded some fragments of coarse pottery generally dated to the mid-seventh century AD, which suggests that the press went into disuse around the time of the Islamic conquest.

Figure 6.11: Balagrae. A coin depicts a bust of emperor Arcadius on the obverse found in the press.

Figure 6.12: Balagrae. The treading area (10) and the collecting vat (3). Looking east. Scale. 0.5 m.

6.3.2.4 Other small towns

Another five sites can be added to the group of small towns with marginal oil production (Appendix II: site no. 41). The first is the site of El Atrun (ancient Erythron), which is located 28 km east of Apollonia (Figure 6.13). It was not substantial in size, and indeed not much can be seen at the site due to the lack of wider excavations. However, according to Synesius (letter 67), the town was involved in a dispute with Darnis over the ownership of an old fort at a place called Hydrax. This indicates that the town enjoyed a considerable ecclesiastical power. Whether or not Erythron qualified for the title *polis*, the activities of at least three of its bishops and the existence of two churches, are confirmation that the town held a prominent ecclesiastical position and it may have become a pilgrimage site (Reynolds 2003: 231).

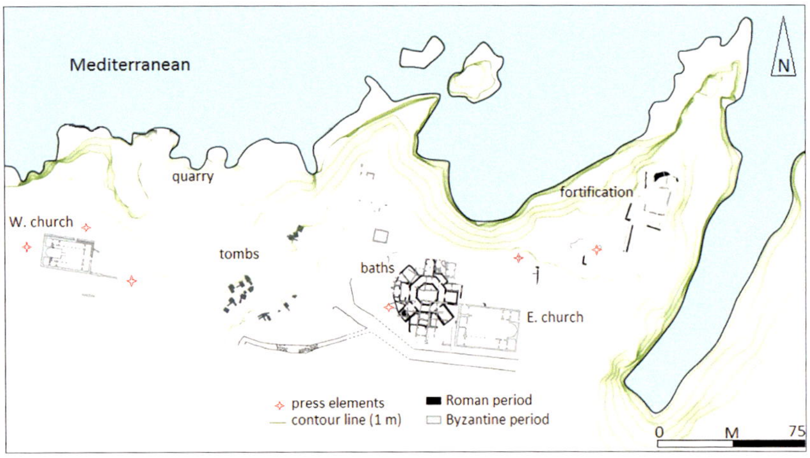

Figure 6.13: Erythron. General plan *(after Michel 2011: 207, fig. 2).*

In 2004, excavations immediately west of the East church uncovered part of an octagonal bath complex which probably dated to the third century AD, and which seems to have been abandoned in the early fourth century AD. Consequently, the complex served at a later date as a pottery rubbish tip which seems to have been associated with a pottery kiln found just off the *tepidarium* room. Studies of the assemblage found in the fill confirmed that lamps and transport amphorae, particularly Mid Roman Amphora 1, were manufactured there (Mazoul and Capelli 2011). Undoubtedly, this important discovery in combination with the previously known vessel types (Göransson 2007; Hesein 2015; Riley 1976; 1979; Mazou and Capelli 2011) will enrich our currently poor knowledge on local amphora production.

Three crushing basins, three milling stones, one counterweight and a number of deep vats were found dispersed across the site, with no clear relationship between any of them. Adjacent to the western side of the east church is clear evidence of a wine press installation with a cemented treading floor sloping towards two collecting vats. Furthermore, a bulldozing operation to the west of the West church found a rectangular plastered tank provided with a sediment-trap. The presence of these pressing facilities, which could have been used for olive oil and wine production, in the vicinity of the two churches may indicate that the industrial activities were under ecclesiastic control.

The second site is Mghernes on the upper plateau about 12 km east of Cyrene (Appendix II: site no. 49). Its wealth seems to have been based on the availability of both fertile land and an abundant water supply, which were key factors influencing the location of the site. The agricultural potential of this region is increased by the site's commanding position that allowed it to control a large area of the plateau east of Cyrene.

The site has never been excavated nor studied in detail, but the handful of upstanding remains are exceptionally preserved (Figure 6.14). Traces of outlying buildings and a widespread pottery scatter were evident beyond the modern enclosure fence, indicating that it was not less than 8 ha in size.

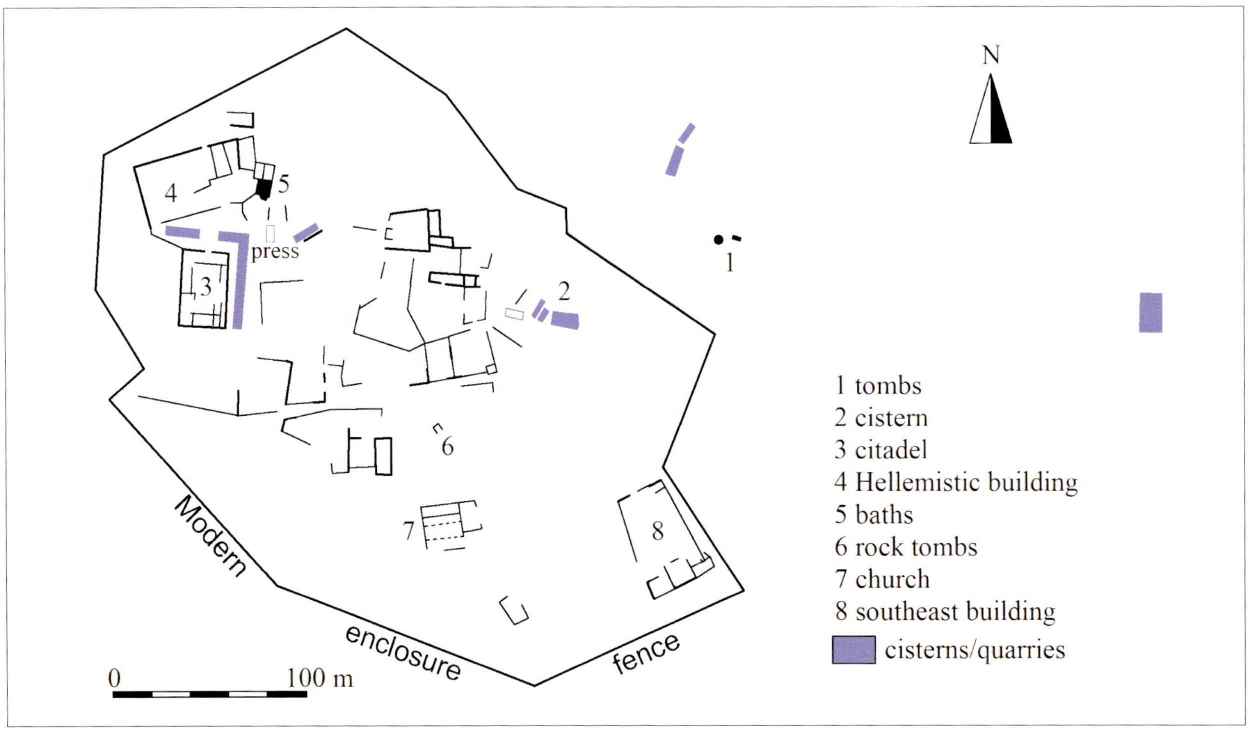

Figure 6.14: Mghernes. Sketch plan of the site *(Kenrick 2013: fig. 198).*

Figure 6.15: Umm Sellem. Google Earth imagery (2016) shows some of the archaeological remains at the ancient site *(Google Earth © 2021 Maxar Technologies).*

The third site is Umm Sellem which is located some 3.5 km east of Mghernes (Appendix II: site no. 104). A recent survey conducted by the expedition of the University of Chieti shows a long and continuous use of the site, with finds dating from at least the Hellenistic to the Late Roman periods (Menozzi *et al.* 2014: 67). The only features clearly attributable to the Hellenistic period were found around a group of quarries located at the far north-east end of the site. Parts of these quarries and the surrounding area were used as a cemetery where rock-cut tombs, two mausolea and numbers of sarcophagi can still be seen (Ward-Perkins and Goodchild 2003: 363).

The visible remains (Figure 6.15), were mainly located along the western edge of the settlement within an extensive but rather scattered area. These were all of Byzantine date and included a pair of churches (showing at least two phases of construction with apses placed on opposite orientations) sited near each other with a triconch building in the near vicinity. There were a number of oil presses in the north-east area of the settlement and further similar industrial installations were found between the east church and the fortified building to the south-east. The fortified building also incorporated presses and a tower and seems to have been the fortified residence of a wealthy owner (Ward-Perkins and Goodchild 2003: 363).

The location of this settlement in a fertile agricultural region is reflected through the ubiquitous remains of a field system and barrages across the landscape. The existence of two churches is a clear indication of the size of the settlement, which is difficult to determine with certainty due to the absence of an extensive survey of the site. However, the brief observation given by Ward-Perkins and Goodchild (2003), in addition to the notes recorded during my visit in 2009, clearly indicate that the settlement was substantial in size. In addition, the large number of the archaeological sites around the settlement of Umm Sellem is indicative of intensive agricultural exploitation in this region.

The remaining two sites, Beit Thamer and Qasr al-Gaama, are located at the eastern and western extremities of this group. Beit Thamer (Appendix II: site no. 15) has been almost entirely obscured by intrusive modern construction and agricultural expansion that has severely damaged the archaeological site and reduced it to a small knoll, which is also under severe threat. The remains of a late decorated tomb in an area known for its agricultural potential underscores its importance in late antiquity and indicates the existence of well-to-do individuals who could afford an expensive funeral monument. A boundary stone dated to the reign of Claudius (AD 41–54) found not far from the site, suggests that the domain had been under the control of the Ptolemaie in the surrounding area (SEG 26.1819; Reynolds 1971). These royal estates were seized by private individuals described as 'squatters' and were restored to the Romans to become *ager publicus Romani* after the death of Apion in 96 BC (Applebaum 1979: 110). It cannot be determined if the settlement was originally located within the limit of this *ager publicus* or near it.

Qasr al-Gaama (Appendix II: site no. 58) is a coastal site which was closely connected with the settlement site of Maaten el-Agla (ancient Kainopolis – Laronde (1983), but see also Jones and Little (1971b), who argued that the name is valid for al-Hania while Roques (1987: 117) identified it as Neapolis). The hilltop settlement is associated with a church embellished with a mosaic floor. At some time, its outer wall was consolidated by a sloping revetment (Ward-Perkins and Goodchild 2003: 399).

Farther north we located a cistern and several small structures which may have been connected with wine production. At the north-west corner were the remains of a rectangular tower-like structure, the walls of which had been strengthened by the addition of an outer sloping revetment. Towards the southern extremity of the site was a quarry that probably provided the settlement with most of its building stone. This settlement probably functioned as the administrative centre to a foreshore industrial and commercial area (Hesein 2015: 488). It bears evidence of at least 17 vats of various shapes and sizes, which were possibly involved in the manufacture of fish-related products (Hesein 2014: 135). Furthermore, its church must have served quite a large surrounding rural community.

6.4 Nucleated Settlement With or without Fortified Elements

Normally for this type of site, there is no evidence that a perimeter wall encircled these settlements (Mattingly *et al.* 2013: 183). Like fortified farms, many were commonly composed of clusters of buildings centred around a fortified structure (*qasr*), which was usually surrounded by a ditch. Nonetheless, the recent discovery of a curtain wall enclosing the settlement of Siret al-Bab, about 12 km north-west of Lamluda, demonstrates that perimeter walls were also constructed around some settlements, albeit probably not to any great extent. Based on the building techniques used, the wall was probably erected before the fifth century AD (Saad *et al.* 2016: 56).

Five out of six of these nucleated settlements, which occupied an area ≥ 5 ha, were concentrated in the Benghazi coastal plain between Berenice and Teucheira. Only one (Qasr Silu) was found farther east on the middle plateau, and all but one (Siret Leglad) were associated with a *qasr* (Figure 6.16).

Many examples of this type of settlement seem to have developed from earlier open farms. This view is entirely based on some diagnostic early to mid-Roman pottery dated between the first to third centuries AD, which included Italian Sigillata, Eastern Sigillata A and B and African Red Slip ware (Emrage 2015: 43, 166, 181; Bennett and Buzaian 2006: 39; Jones and Little 1971a: 67; Kenrick 2013b: 64. 66. 68). This early material clearly indicates that the sites relate to earlier structures, which were obscured or obliterated by later open farms and consequently became fortified farms by building or strengthening existing buildings – the *qsur* – around which settlements gradually filled out. Since the *qsur* replaced early open farms, they largely obscured or even totally obliterated their earlier vestiges.

Stucchi (1975, cited in Kenrick 2013b: 60) suggests that open farms were constructed of timber. In contrast to his view, there are two architectural features worth mentioning that might indicate the presence of pre-existing open-farm buildings executed in durable materials. Many of the fortified buildings showed two phases

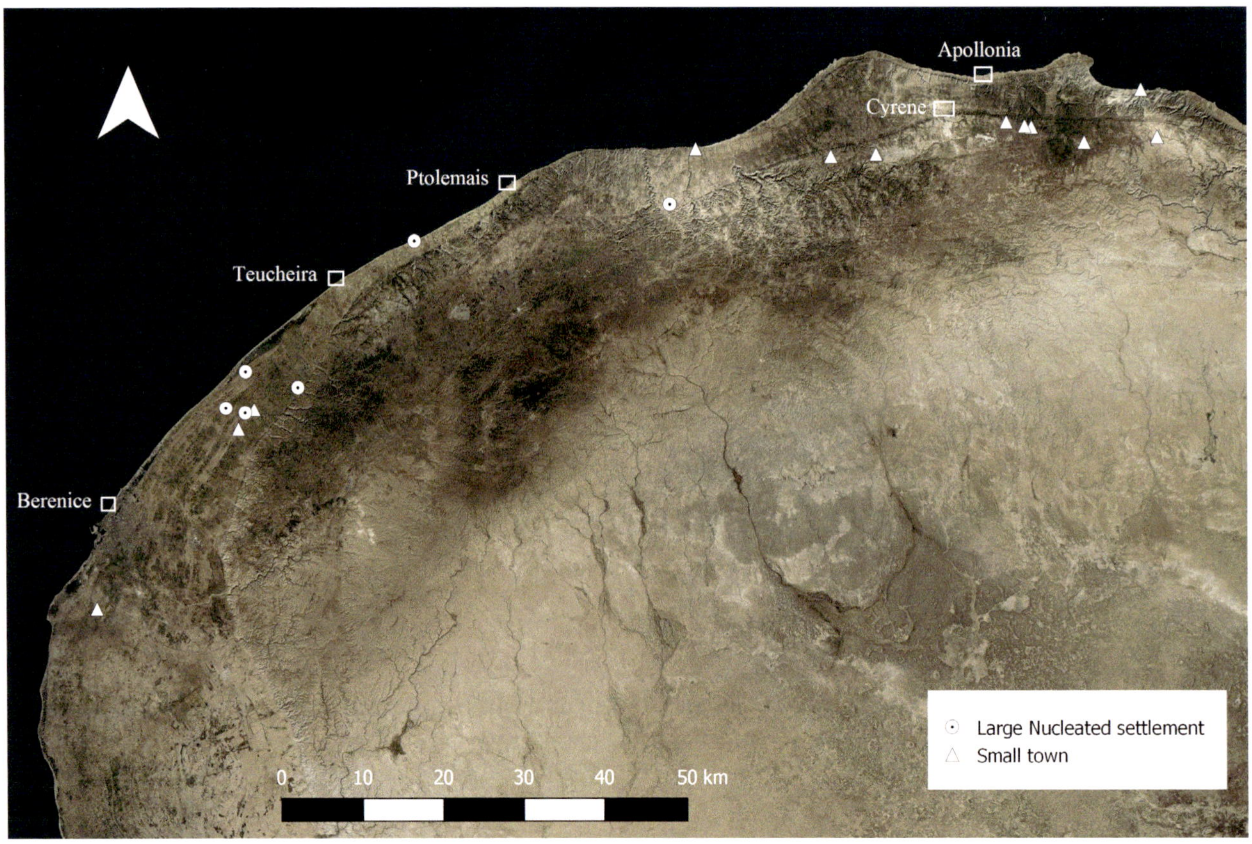

Figure 6.16: Distribution of nucleated settlements in relation to towns and small towns.

of construction, with early internal walls backed by a later revetment. In several cases, the inner walls were often prestigious constructions in ashlar masonry, with their external faces occasionally plastered (e.g. qasr Az-Zaarura and Qasr Sidi bu-Argoub, Emrage 2015: 266, 309 respectively). The later phase was represented by an outer sloping revetment which was made of rough blockwork less regular in character than that of the original walls and continuous round the whole building. The ashlar masonry of the inner walls with no remarkable thickness and only a single storey undoubtedly represented an early phase, likely an open farm building.

Recent observations provided by Kenrick during his survey for a new archaeological guide to Cyrenaica may support this hypothesis. Kenrick (2013b: 62) rightly spotted the presence of a crack in the west wall of the *qasr* of Az-Zaaroura, immediately south-west of the modern village of Messa, which was likely caused by seismic activity. Subsequently, a sloping revetment wall was added to strengthen the unstable wall. However, while this treatment indicates maintenance work had taken place, it does not necessarily mean that the function of the site had changed. This may lead us to assume that any similar feature noted elsewhere on any *qasr* structure equally represents a shoring work after a natural disaster event, and/or defensive measures on a private level without drastic changes to the function (*cf.* Kraeling (1960: 107) who advocated a state funding of this type of fortified buildings). Thus such revetments were later features added to earlier buildings as defensive measures in both marginal frontier zones as well as inland territories. Further example come from the fort of Hydrax at Ain Marah, mentioned by Syenesius in AD 411 (letter 67) as a ruined building which may have been destroyed by the earthquake of AD 365. Given the similar masonry style noted on the early phase wall in the *qsur* of Az-Zaaroura and al-Wushish (Kenrick 2013b: 60–2), I would instead place this constructional style very much earlier than the sixth century date suggested by Stucchi (1975: 529), and therefore propose that these buildings were primarily established as early open farms. However, this hypothesis remains open, and only excavations can help to date the earthquake(s) that affected these two *qsur* (and presumably many others).

Synesius wrote in his letters (13, 57, 62, 67, 69, 78, 94, 95, 104, 107, 108, 113, 122, 125, 130, 132, 134) during the late fourth and early fifth centuries AD about the frequent attacks of the local tribes. Security must therefore have been the dominant concern leading to the construction of these fortified buildings and the consequent nucleated settlements that were widely distributed across the region. While the agricultural and civilian nature of these site appear prevalent, their architectural appearance suggests that these *qsur* must have been intended for some sort of defensive function. Similar rural developments were noted in the pre-desert zone of Tripolitania (Mattingly and Dore 1996: 160–4) and in the Gebel Tarhuna (Ahmed 2019: 62), where by the third and fourth centuries AD respectively the *qsur* replaced unfortified farms and became increasingly the dominant form of settlement system.

A number of similar nucleated settlements lacking a *qasr* were probably built later in the settlement history of rural Cyrenaica. Scattered fine pottery sherds show no evidence of occupation earlier than the fifth century AD, which seems to reconcile with this view. The clear absence of defensive structures may be taken as indicative of a later expansion in areas that had not been previously settled. In the absence of a *qasr*, a fortified church building if available could have served as a refuge in times of crisis (Bonacasa Carra 1998: 68–72; Mattingly *et al.* 2013: 177; Saad *et al.* 2016: 40) Nevertheless, it is plausible to suggest that the advantages of adopting a nucleation system of settlement should not be overlooked as a tactical option to fulfil security measures in a potentially hostile landscape.

In general, the buildings in these settlements were humble and homogeneous. This suggests the absence of a large gap between different social strata, and indicates individual ownership by most villagers who mostly seem to have been engaged in land cultivation. On the other hand, small settlements may have been wholly owned by landlords. The houses were commonly small and two- to three-roomed. The outer walls were formed of two parallel lines of squared limestone and sandstone blocks with a core of stone chips and mud mortar. Floors were generally of beaten earth; mosaic or mortar floors were rare, and the internal walls were unplastered. Similar types of nucleated settlement whether associated with *qsur* or occurred in isolation were also noted in the Tripolitanian pre-desert area and appear to become a prevalent pattern in the middle and late phases of Romano-Libyan settlement (Mattingly and Dore 1996: 140–1).

6.4.1 The nucleated fortified settlement of Philino

Philino is a large settlement lying in open cultivated country close to the foot of the Gebel Akhdar (Figure 6.17), about 50 km north-east of Benghazi (Appendix II: site no. 56). The nearest known archaeological sites are Hadrianopolis, *c.*20 km to the north-west, and Tansoluk, *c.*15 km in the same direction. The settlement is located within an area of good agriculture potential called Rasm el-Hessan. It is worth noting that the modern local name for the site, Philino, is probably of Roman origin, though the precise ancient toponym is unknown.

Ancient sources are silent about the site of Philino. Although the site is of considerable size (*c.*21 ha.), it was not included in the accounts of modern travellers and investigators. This silence was perhaps due to the fact that the settlement was located off the main coastal route known at that time.

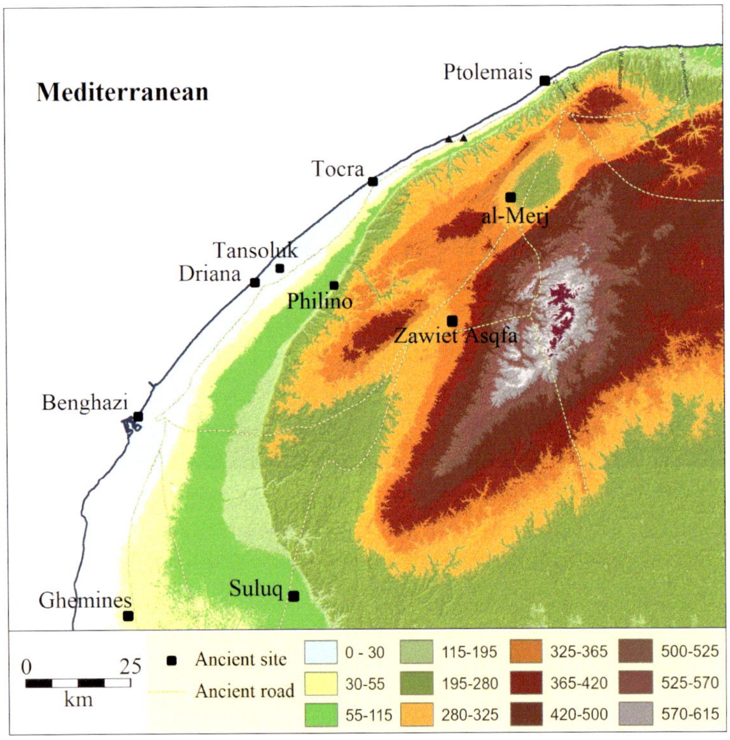

Figure 6.17: Coastal area around Benghazi and the location of Philino.

Figure 6.18: Philino. General plan.

The settlement's fairly poor state of preservation explains why it has not attracted attention before now. Although it is still free of overlying modern buildings, Philino has been extensively used as a ready source of building material over the past century. Part of the eastern section was swept away by erosion, and the site is currently used by locals as a cemetery which has led to the removal of the ruins.

For the time being, the locals use the site as a graveyard and the limits of the settlement have not been fully defined, as I was not allowed to investigate the surrounding modern farms in which traces of walls and pottery scatters can easily be detected.

The structural complexity of the phases of occupations and pottery scatters suggest activities continued until the Islamic conquest. However, without detailed excavations the chronology of the settlement must be treated as provisional. Figure 6.18 shows that the buildings were mainly concentrated around the core of the settlement and were haphazardly distributed without a regular network of streets.

Walls were chiefly built in a less monumental fashion. Two parallel lines of small rubble blocks were used, dressed only on the outer face. The centre of the wall was filled with a mixture of mud and stone chips. On average the walls were 0.60 m wide, and were not generally laid in straight lines (contrary to the appearance on the plan) and only survived to a maximum height of 0.4 m. No evidence has been found of any vestiges of the installation of the standing walls, and there are so far no remains of mosaic or mortar floors.

Approximately 1 km to the south-west of the settlement is a quarry located at the foothill of the Gebel. Vertical sides and cut marks can be seen in the base of the cutting, but no rock-cut tombs are visible or have been identified. It is worth mentioning here that a few buildings in the settlement employed ashlar blocks. This absence of finely dressed stones was probably because the use of large blocks was limited to the foundations, which are now mostly invisible. Another explanation for this is that the quarried stones were directed to destinations other than the settlement of Philino.

Water was supplied only by wells and cisterns, based on the presence of at least eight wells and a cistern which was associated with the houses. Shallow ground water, which was easy to reach by means of dug wells, has been known to be available in relative abundance in the Benghazi coastal plain and was also the main water supply in Teucheira (Goodchild 1967b: 264; Jones and Little 1971a: 53).

The settlement consisted of about 40 houses spread across an area of c.21 ha. Households, which all appear to have one storey and were of low-tatus, varied between 180 to 520 m^2, with a few occupying an area of up to 1,000 m^2. This considerable size may mean they were used for other functions than residential housing. Many of the houses were not isolated but semi-detached, and most were characterised by the existence of a large courtyard. This could be entered directly from their main door, and occupied the whole width of the front half of the building. The rear was occupied by a set of rooms opening into the courtyard. The number of rooms was not clear on the ground, but two to four were the most common arrangements noted. The complete absence of roof tiles suggests that roofs were flat and may have been made of wooden beams with poles or planking sealed with mud-mixed straw or seaweed.

The Qasr

The *qasr* was a prominent un-ditched building occupying a dominant position within the settlement. It was a sub-square structure measuring 21.40 × 22.50 m (Figure 6.19) and stood isolated on slightly raised ground in an area north-west of the settlement.

Two phases of construction were evident based on the double thickness of the outer walls. The original internal wall which varied in thickness from 0.8 to 1 m was fully constructed of small, faced blocks laid into two rows with rubble fill in the core. The outer wall was added from outside to give an overall thickness between 2 to 2.9 m, and was mainly built of large stone roughly trimmed and incorporated some blocks rich in marine shell fossils. The average size of the blocks was 0.9 × 0.5 × 0.4 m, roughly cut in the form of slabs and placed standing apart into two lines on edges. However, some sections of the external walls used medium-sized stones, reasonably well coursed (the average size is 0.35 × 0.35 × 0.25 m), roughly squared from the outside and set into two parallel lines with a fill of small stones and mud in between. The main entrance was probably located on the west wall, and there was no ditch surrounding the *qasr*.

Nothing is visible of the interior arrangements, except for traces of minor structures built up against the inner side of the first phase walls. These structures may have been storerooms, and open by arched doorways off a long passage. At least four isolated arches protrude from the fallen debris of stone. These arches are perhaps an indication of an upper storey, although no evidence of a staircase was detected to support this hypothesis.

It is evident that agricultural activity was the stimulus for the foundation of Philino, where natural fertile land and suitable levels of rainfall are available. The strategic position of the settlement also played an important role in linking the coastal plain with the plateau. This shows evidence of vigorous occupation in the large number of smaller settlements associated with a series of dams and irrigation systems. These extended far south to Zawiat Msus, which is marked as the southern limit of the defence of Roman Cyrenaica.

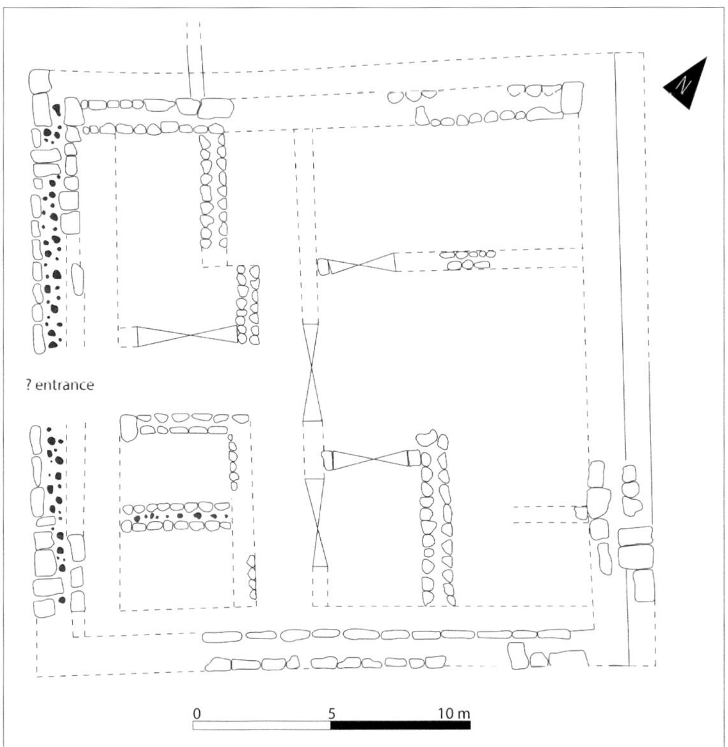

Figure 6.19: Philino. General plan of the *qasr*.

The press room

A square building located 100 m south of the qasr measuring (8 × 8 m). This was divided into two almost equal sections by a stub wall projecting from the north to a length of *c*.2.70 m. Three sides of the building, 0.55 m thick (southern, eastern and northern), were constructed from two lines of roughly squared stones with no attempt at coursing. The western wall, which was 0.9 m wide, was made of large and medium-sized ashlars made up of two parallel adjoining lines. A crushing stone was found embedded in a thick deposit of red clay which concealed the press room floor, indicating that it was used for olive oil production. No evidence of a standing upright stone was found in the room, which suggests that the beam was anchored in the wall. The considerable thickness of the western wall would make it a better candidate for securing the fixed end of the beam. It should be noted that there were additional pressing elements scattered across the settlement, particularly outside the fenced area in the north-west.

6.5 Fortified Farms

The term 'fortified' = *qasr* (plural. *qsur*) here refers to a building of defensive character which possessed a thick outer wall, ditch and revetment.

Since scientific excavations have not yet been conducted in these fortified *qsur* structures, our knowledge of their internal arrangements, functions and relations with the surrounding buildings and industrial installations are uncertain. Nevertheless, some clandestine excavations carried out in these *qsur* show evidence of a domestic nature and a clear absence of any elements that can be connected to industrial activity.

Regardless of their internal arrangements, a *qasr* that stands alone in a naturally defensive location with no signs of agricultural and industrial installations or other buildings is probably a site of military character (and thus not included in this book). Conversely, a *qasr* which is clearly associated with industrial features and other structural evidence implies a site of civilian character, though a defensive nature cannot be ruled out. The term 'fortified farm' is thus deemed expedient.

This work strictly uses 'fortified farm' to describe rural sites which possessed a defensive structure (*qasr*) associated with agricultural and industrial features and other functional buildings. The size of the farm played an important role in classifying it within the large or small category. In the meantime, the number of pressing elements found in each farm is used to distinguish a farm with an elevated level of oil production from that with a lower level of productivity. These fortified farms have been categorised as outlined below.

6.5.1 Large fortified farms

This is one of the main types of rural settlement, with 4 or more presses within an area ranging in size from 2 to 4 ha (Figure 6.20). In terms of size, this type occupies an area smaller than that of the nucleated fortified settlement and has a less nucleated layout. The type is distinguished by its agricultural character, as it was involved in olive oil and wine production. Some of these settlements have also produced early pottery sherds dating from the second century BC to the second century AD. They seem to have developed in much the same way as the nucleated settlements which replaced the open farms, but did not make the final transition into a nucleated settlement. However, these *qsur* could be viewed as prestige buildings constructed by local independent farmers who resisted the nucleation settlement system. The fortified building or the *qasr*, as the pottery sherds suggested, seem to have been built between the third and fourth centuries AD. This was probably a gradual shift from open to fortified farms and, more likely, prompted tribal raids from the desert. Nevertheless, security reasons naturally remain the most significant factor as the region became increasingly vulnerable to tribal forays (see above).

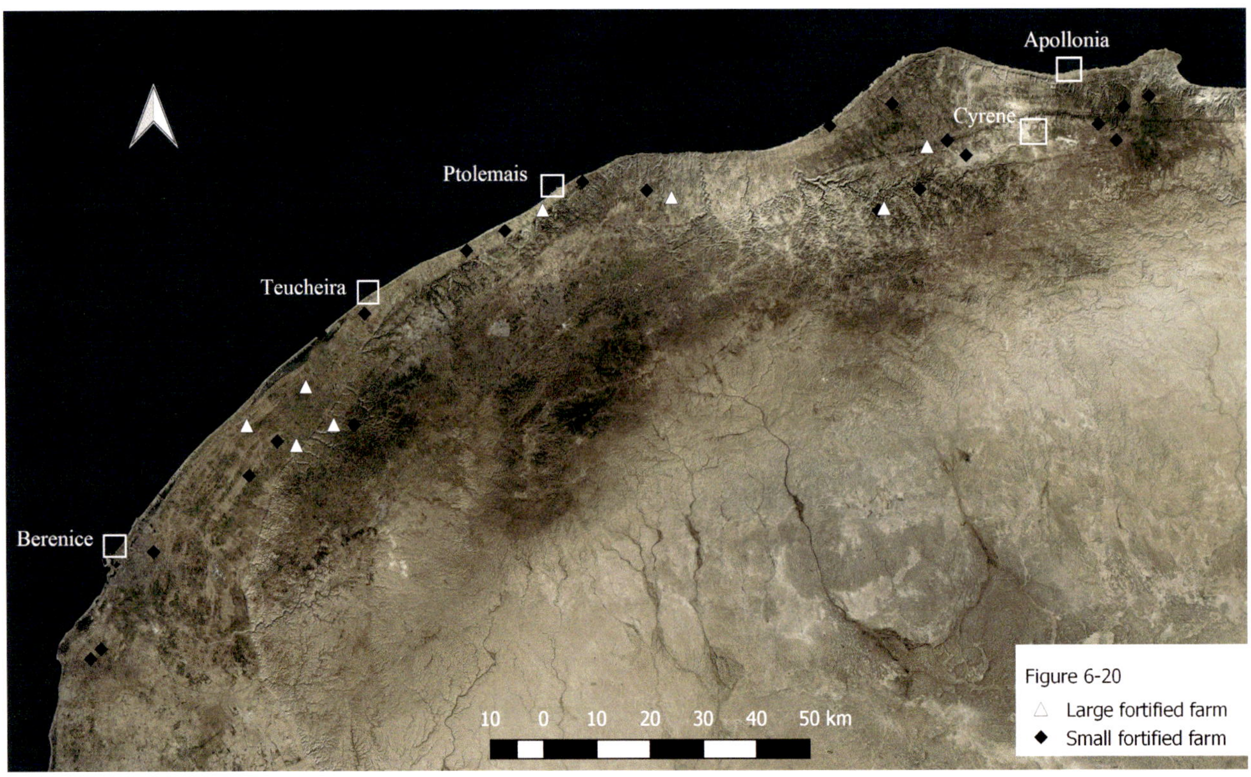

Figure 6.20: Distribution of large and small fortified farms with presses/mills.

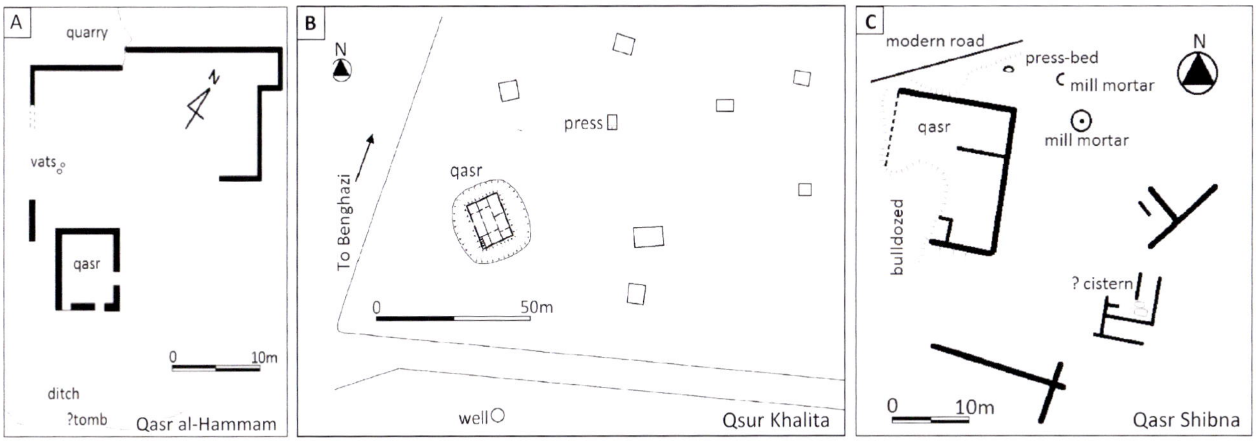

Figure 6.21: Comparative plans of three small fortified farms. Qasr al-Hammam (Emrage 2015: fig. 9.118) Qsur Khalita and Qasr Shibna plan *(Bennett and Buzaian 2006: fig. 4).*

Nevertheless, later datable pottery has been noted on the surface of many fortified farms, showing that evidence of occupation belonged conclusively to the period between the fifth and seventh centuries AD. The question is whether this represents continuity of defensive structures across the region or a later reuse. It is worth mentioning that fortified farms were fairly common in the sixth-century AD landscape of Apamea in central Syria (Decker 2006: 520).

Traces of various buildings were detected, though plans were difficult to discern without excavation. The poor state of all these fortified buildings and their associated outbuildings prevents us from gaining useful information regarding their layout. However, visible agricultural and domestic features included cisterns, wells, vats and presses, and possible barns. The walls were exclusively built of two faces of roughly tooled stone and a rubble of mud fill. Dressed blocks were used in the quoins of the buildings and as door jambs.

Some sites in this category possessed large numbers of pressing elements, and might have functioned as estate centres with a high capacity for oil production. Sites at Al-Mhasi (MAS) and Siret Sidi al-Agili (SAG) contained 11 and 8 crushing basins respectively within an area of about 2 ha. This represents the best example of a large fortified site characterised by a high number of oil production facilities. All these installations occurred in multiple small units, although their layout was not discernible.

Although the site Siret Milow (MLW) employed only four presses, it can also be placed into this category. The density of the rubble meant the site could not be examined in great detail, and future intensive and careful investigations may find additional crushing basins. Siret Milow covered roughly 2 ha and was located at the foot of the Gebel, *c.*4 km west of Ptolemais, on a low hill surrounded by fertile land. The crushing basins were scattered around the ditched *qasr* and largely obscured by the current use of the site as an animal shelter. At least six circular vats were found within a square room (8 × 8 m) at the north-east corner of the farm. These varied in diameter from 0.95 m to 1.2 m but their depth was not established as they were filled with stones. Three cone-shaped vats 0.7 m wide and 0.4 m deep were randomly inserted between these large vats. These large vats indicate the presence of a storage facility most likely related to wine, while the shallow vats could have served to hold amphora during the loading process.

6.5.2 Small fortified farm

This type is defined as a site with an area ranging in size from 0.5 to 1.5 ha, and includes sites with 1–4 crushing basins. Their architecture is similar to the large fortified farm sites, but on a reduced scale (Figure 6.21). However, there is a small group of small farms which employed ashlar masonry, as exemplified by Qasr al-Hammam (Figure 6.21A). The *qasr* was a rectangular building (9.65 × 7.55 m) surrounded by a ditch and built using recycled ashlar blocks (Emrage 2015: 87). An enclosure was added to the north of the main building, where a cistern and other industrial features represented by two vats and a possible beam socket stone were detected.

Where sites of this category had 2–4 crushing basins, they have been classified as small fortified farms with intensive oil productivity. Meanwhile, those with fewer than two have been grouped separately as small fortified farms with low levels of productivity (Figure 6.20).

Presses are located in separate rooms which were randomly distributed across the farm. A few of these farms, such as Jnan Ibrahim, contained a series of sunken *dolia*. This suggests the presence of industrial activity related to wine production.

6.5.2.1 *Qsur Khalita*

This is an example of a fortified farm controlling a large rangeland in open, relatively arid country located *c.*17 km west of Benghazi. A ditched *qasr* occupies a

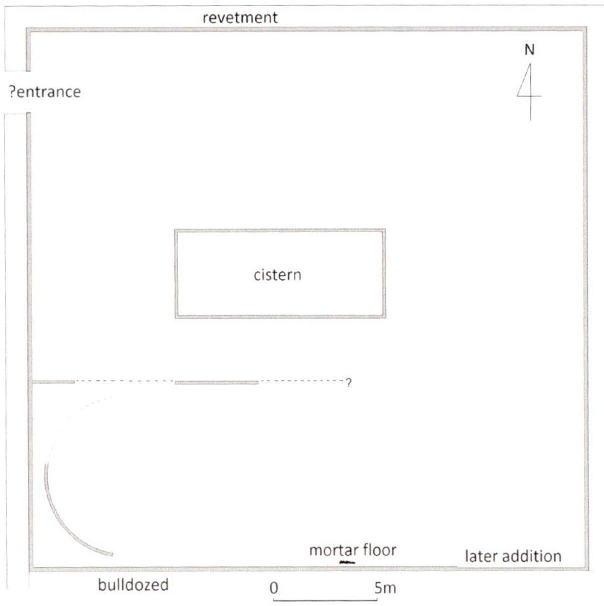

Figure 6.22: Gowt Bu-Esfia. A fortified building associated with an apsed hall.

low mound located on the south-west corner of the farm (Figure 6.21B). The interior arrangements were most clearly visible. In the middle of the west side an arched doorway gave access to a vestibule flanked on the left side by a small room on the right and the remains of a staircase to the upper floor on the other side. Another arched doorway on the opposite side of the main entrance gave access to a small courtyard with a series of small rooms grouped on three sides.

The clusters that surrounded the *qasr* included an oil press and a well, in addition to a group of buildings of different sizes. The press was located some 40 m north-east of the qasr. It measured 3.7 × 6.2 m, with a double press-bed placed near the southern wall and a counterweight block on the opposite side which was not found *in situ*. An upside-down crushing stone was found nearby, suggesting that crushing operations were conducted in a separate room. These buildings seem to have been distributed randomly, and were almost completely covered by all kinds of rubbish that effectively obscured their inner arrangements. However, some of their doorways, which were marked by two monolithic jambs, were still visible. The walls were made of double lines of medium squared stones and a rubble core.

In general, provision for a sufficient water supply in these fortified farms could be limited to shallow wells and cisterns. The former is considered to be the most common feature in the ancient sites of the coastal plain, while the latter were very frequent though found very commonly in the upper plateau settlements.

Some of these fortified farms were associated with chapels such as Siret Qasrin el-Giamel (Catani 1976). Church control over some oil and wine presses and possibly other productive installations has therefore been proposed (Wilson 2004: 145). Further evidence of an

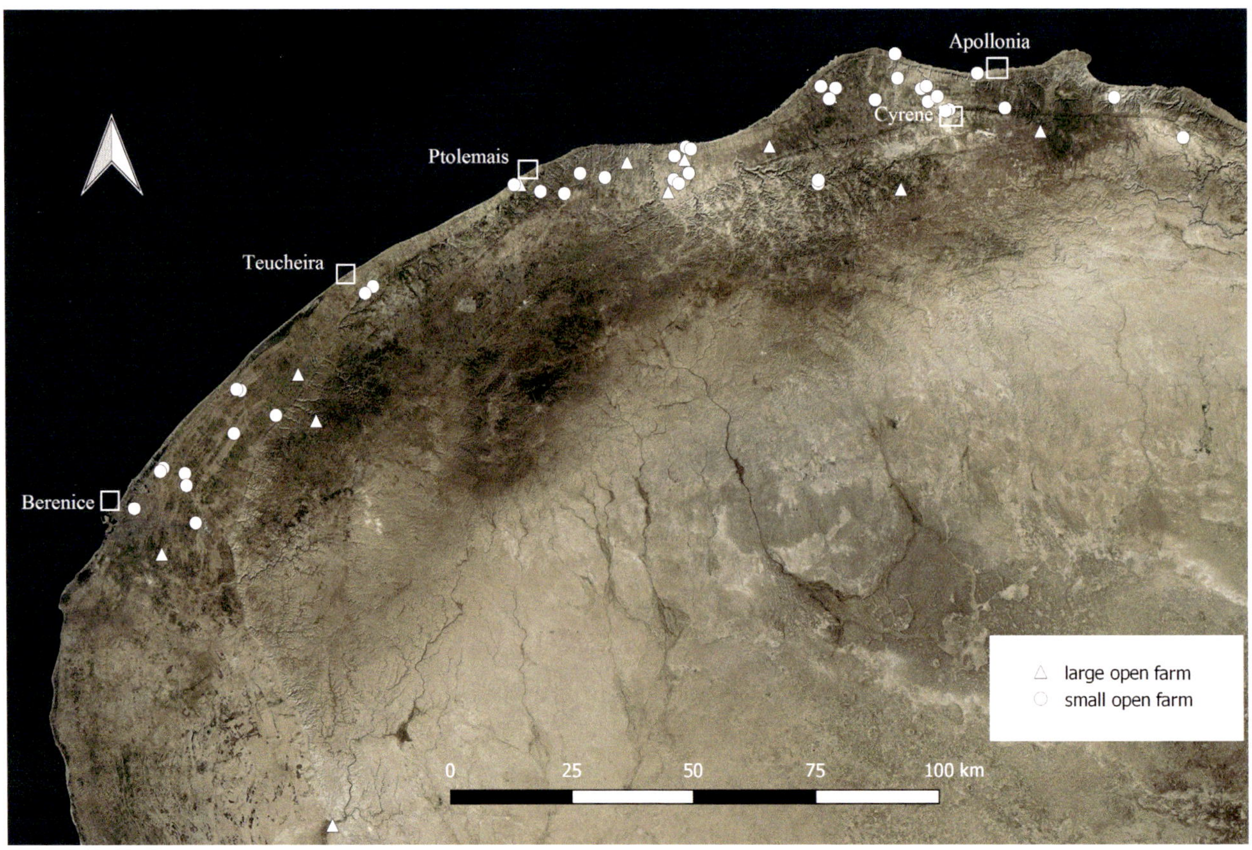

Figure 6.23: Distribution of Large and small open farms.

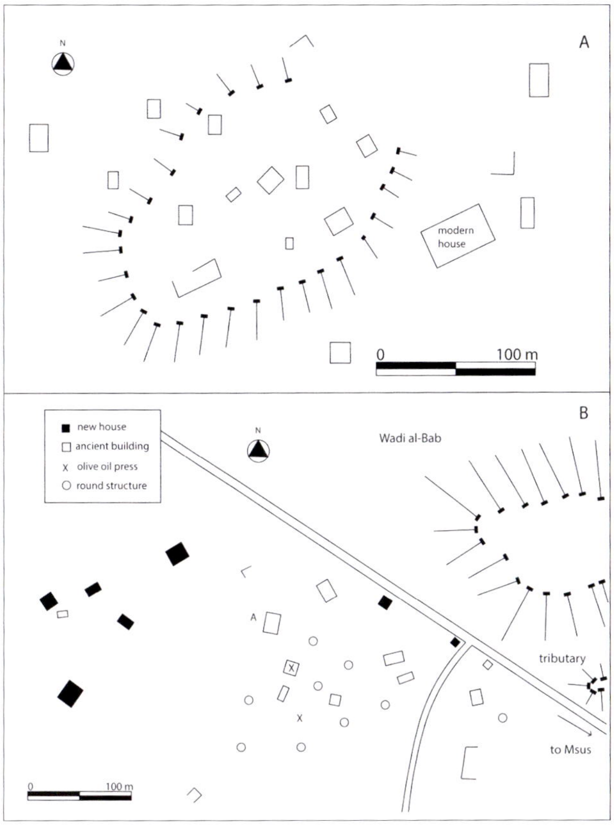

Figure 6.24: Sketch plan of the large open farm. A: Siret Sdoos and B Zawiat Wadi al-Bab.

ecclesiastical presence has been found in sites classified as small fortified farms, such as Siret Gowt Bu-Esfia (Figure 6.22) and Qsur Khalita. The latter only produced marble chancel posts, which suggests the existence of a religious building (Ward-Perkins and Goodchild 2003: 430). However, the ecclesiastical evidence in these small farms, as opposed to villages and nucleated settlements, is curious. The picture of these fortified buildings is far from complete, and only through scientific excavation and artefactual study will their function and ownership be fully understood.

6.6 Open Farm

This type of settlement consisted of groups of moderate structures distributed in a haphazard manner and lacking a fortified building. These open farms possibly benefited from the presence of other nearby fortified settlements and fortified farms. It is thus not too far-fetched to envisage that there was room in the fortified farms for the inhabitants of the neighbouring unfortified settlements. Those on the upper plateau were in close relation to the ridges of the wadis, and thus benefited from their natural protection.

In general, the open farm category predominated across the region (Figure 6.23). They were of remarkable density on the eastern part of the upper plateau. The Benghazi coastal plain was also marked by a considerable number of small farms, 10 of which have been found, while only two were recorded in the coastal strip west of Apollonia. Their frequency in rural Cyrenaica was perhaps a consequence of forming an alliance with a local tribe which had settled within the province's territory. The mention of the Maketae in the Decree of Anastasius (SEG IX. 356) and the Maurysioi in the Tarakenet inscription (SEG XX. 750a; Reynolds 2003: 416-7) suggests that the docile tribes played a vital role in this late development.

6.6.1 Large open farm

This sub-type consists of farms which varied in size from 2–6 ha and contained one to three crushing basins. In general, these were of a low level of productivity, except for two sites which were more likely farms with elevated levels of productivity, Siret Sdoos and Zawiat al-Bab (Figure 6.24, A and B).

6.6.2 Small open farm

This category of small farms was distributed all over the region, and occupied an area between 0.1 and 2 ha (Figure 6.25). These farms usually consisted of buildings with evidence of crushing basin presses, found singly or pairs. Their number normally varied from 1 to 2, with 4 at most.

Only 2 sites (Elwat Beia and Sidi al-Hrari) of this category were equipped with 4 crushing basins. These were therefore classified as farms with high levels of

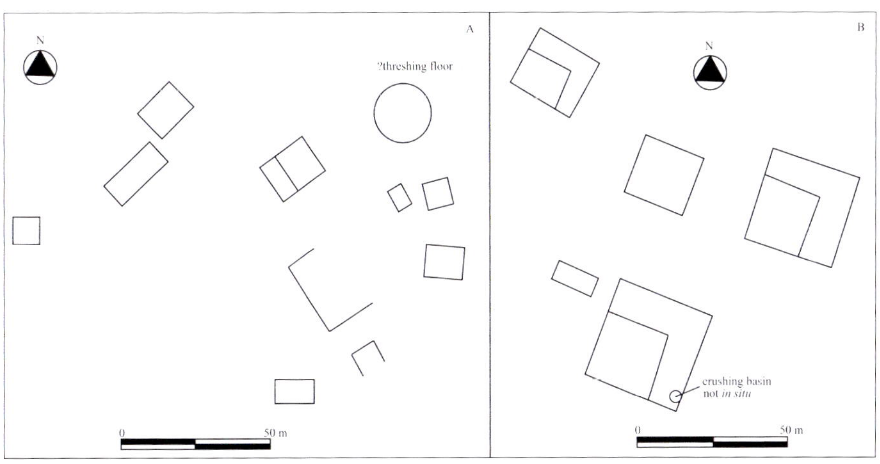

Figure 6.25: Sketch plan of small open farms. A: Siret al-Gabroon and B: Siret al-Hindawia.

productivity, while the other 31 farms furnished with 1–2 basins were deemed to have possessed low levels of productivity. It is noted that most of these open farms were sited in rocky areas and denuded mounds, to benefit from the surrounding fertile lands and field systems comprising cross wadi walls and other field irrigation features. Building materials and methods of construction were similar to those noted in the previous categories. Ashlar masonry was only found in Qasr al-Hmeira, where the only example of indirect screw technology was recorded.

6.7 Rock-cut Presses

There are several agricultural settlements which featured presses carved into troglodyte rock-cut chambers or either partially hewn into the living rock or into a rock slope.

All these installations were located on the upper plateau (Figure 6.26) and it seems likely that many were built from the first as underground olive-presses. This hypothesis is supported by the complete absence of any kind of underground olive or wine press in the coastal plain, despite the availability of numerous rock-cut tombs.

The site of Wadi Senab stands as a unique example in that it has evidence of human activity conducted in rock-cut shelters. These provide natural climate control in hot and cold weather and allow food to be stored for extended periods. A number of rock-cut chambers, including three separate olive press rooms and an open-air wine press, were found along the sides of the wadi (Figure 6.27). The scale of production in this troglodyte complex implies a surplus destined for the market.

This site covered an area of around 2 ha and housed two large caves with no clear evidence of habitation. Remains of a small bath complex were found immediately at the southern end of one of the large caves located on the west bank of the wadi. The later modification of part of the baths into an oil press room may indicate a change in the site's function during the late antique period, when such a luxurious facility gave way to industrial activities. Based on the pottery evidence, the site seems to have been continually occupied from the Hellenistic era down to the Byzantine period.

The region contains another troglodyte site in the ancient site of Slonta, 38 km to the south-west of Cyrene, although it seems that it was used for different purposes. It has been identified by Laronde (1987: 273) with Lasamices, mentioned in Antonine Itinerary (67, 6 and 70, 5). The site houses a rock-cut sanctuary with human and animal sculptures, and possibly served as a native cult centre surrounded by a large group of troglodyte shelters (Luni 1987). These workings of the rock perhaps belonged to the tribe of Lasaniki, whose land was centred around Lasamices between the Maketae to the west and the Psylles to the east. According to Ptolemy (IV, 4, 6), the Lasaniki used troglodyte shelters for either seasonal or sedentary occupation.

There is another range of isolated sites where the survey recorded a number of small installations involved in olive oil and wine production (Figure 6.28). Evidence of a settlement around these presses was not detected, since most of them are in areas where cultivation and modern development are rife. However, the scattered pottery indicates that some presses, such as the underground press in Tarakenet, were located adjacent to small settlements.

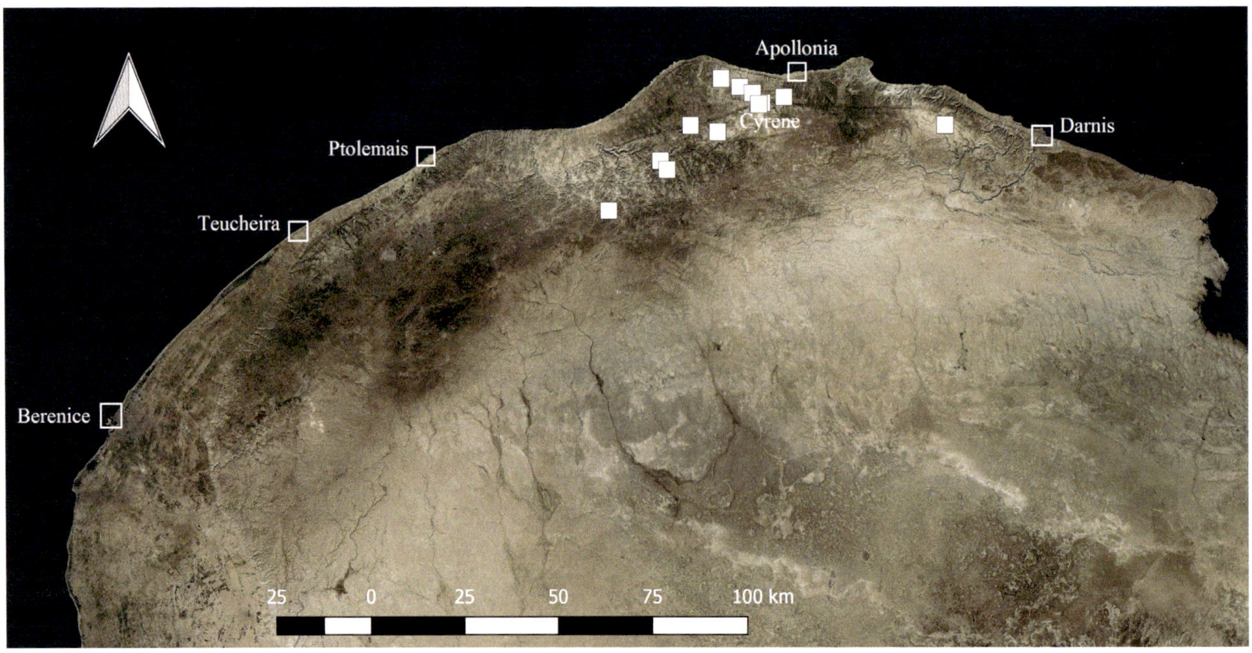

Figure 6.26: Distribution of rock-cut presses.

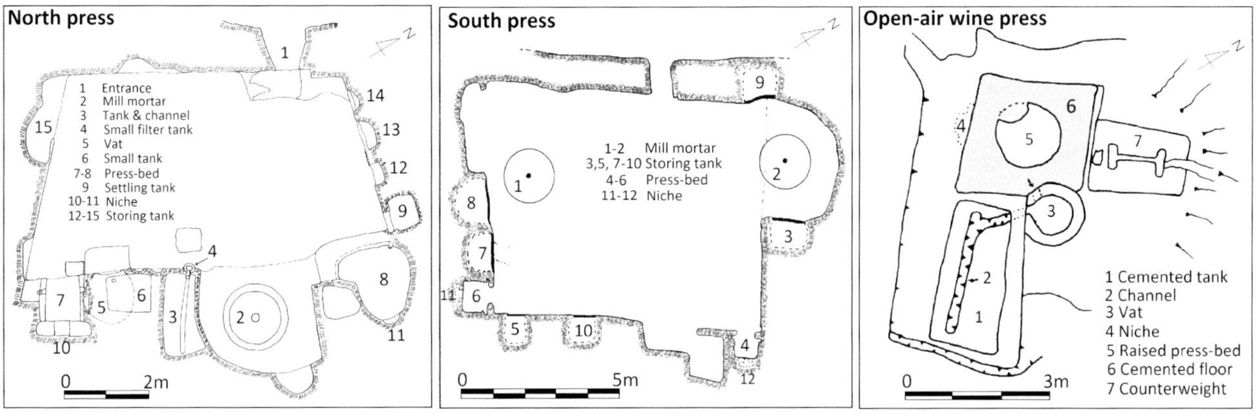

Figure 6.27: Wadi Senab. Plans for two rock-cut olive oil presses and one open-air wine press. *(The North press: Gambini 1975, fig. 1).*

Others, like those found in Qasr Stablous and Sidi Sharaf, were found near occupational areas and it seems that the availability of rocky mounds was a potent factor in their location. Another group of rock-cut presses was found in the suburbs of two major cities. The first was at Elwet Bia, 3 km west of Apollonia, where at least three rock-cut presses were found on top of a low rocky hill. Around these pressing installations were a few scattered buildings, although their layout was not discernible. The site possibly served as a production centre for the city of Apollonia. The second group was recorded in the periphery of Cyrene and consisted of three presses. A wine press was constructed in one of the tombs of the southern necropolis (see below). The other two presses located just east of the city (the Caf al-Nass and the newly-discovered press excavated by the Department of Antiquities) and seem to have originally been created for oil production.

Most of the recorded underground presses contained crushing basins cut in the living rock, which supports the view that these were originally intended to function as industrial installations. Establishing an underground wine and olive oil press or converting a rock-cut tomb into an industrial unit has the advantage of providing a suitable environment for processing wine in the summer and olives in the winter. Undoubtedly, creating a crushing basin in a rock-cut tomb requires steps which would leave unambiguous evidence that the tomb was converted into another function. The subsequent industrial use inevitably deformed the original layout of the tomb, where internal divisions must have been be cleared to create a suitable workspace. After this, certain industrial elements would have been made available for use as an oil/wine press.

Although the equipment and tools needed to make olive oil were in part different from those used for wine production, discrimination between the two is not archaeologically straightforward. Nonetheless, the existence of a crushing trough in the pressing area is one of the basic requirements for olive oil processing and is indeed considered the firmest archaeological evidence in favour of olive oil production. Building a mill mortar in such a situation is thus undoubtedly the most challenging task in converting rock-cut tomb. This awkward job can be achieved by either bringing in a prefabricated basin from

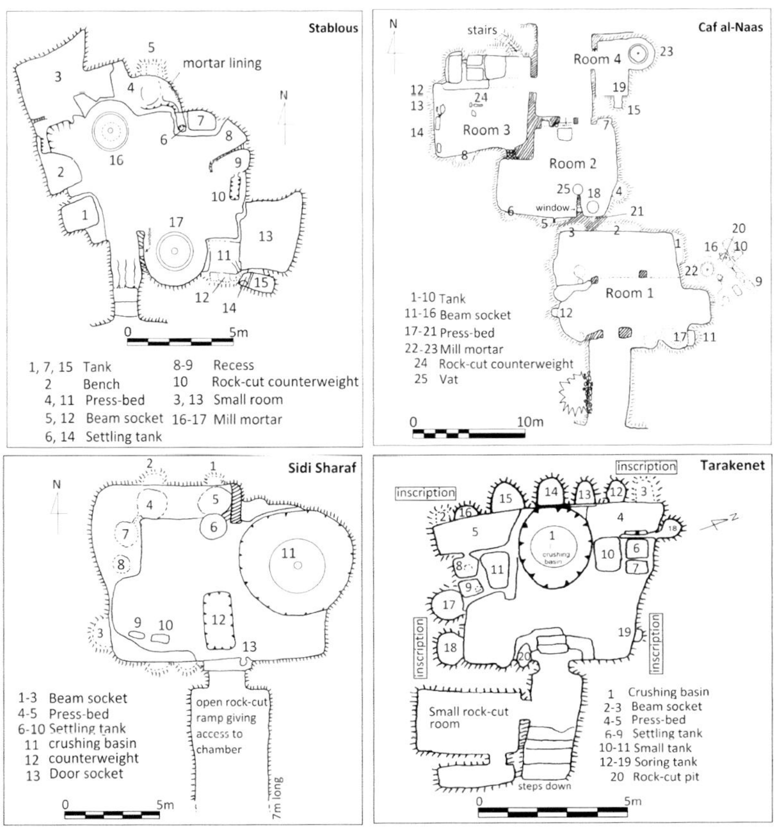

Figure 6.28: Comparative plans of isolated rock-cut presses.

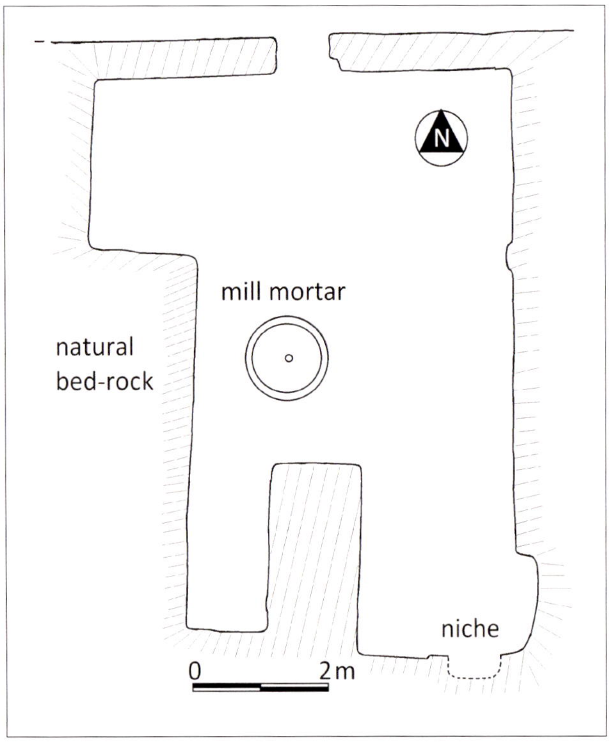

Figure 6.29: Plan of a tomb at Wadi Khargah converted into an oil press.

outside, or by cutting one into the living rock of the exposed surface or sides. A free-standing mill mortar was found in a tomb at Wadi Khargah north of al-Beida (Figure 6.29) where a high number of rock-cut tombs were cut into the rocky vertical sides of the wadi (see Appendix II: site no. 107). Here the original Roman-period tomb was later reconfigured to be used as an oil press. The original chamber was expanded by cutting down many of the *loculi* to create enough space for the crushing and pressing equipment. The entrance was widened to pass the basin inside the converted tomb. An example of a crushing basin carved into the living rock within a former tomb has not been recorded.

However, a wine press has been found inserted into an earlier tomb. The press was built in the rear of a late Hellenistic tomb of a 'Galleried Long Loculus Chambers' type located in the south necropolis of Cyrene which had been erroneously interpreted as a place to offer libations in memory of a loved one who had died (Cherstich 2005). This rock-cut press consisted of five functional components (Figure 6.30). A plastered treading-floor (1) measuring 1.9 × 0.95 m and 0.45 m deep. At its base, a T-shaped channel up to 1.2 m long, 0.15 wide and 0.1 m deep was cut to drain liquid into an adjacent collecting vat (2) 0.8 m in depth, and its bottom surface included a shallow sediment-trap. The mouth of the vat is round and ranged in diameter from 0.8 m at its top to 0.95 m at halfway down.

A secondary pressing of the grape was carried out here by means of a small lever and windlass press placed immediately next to the treading floor from the south. This was represented by an irregular cemented pressing floor (3) measuring *c.*1.95 × 1. 5 m and 0.15 m deep and equipped with a hole penetrating its north wall to empty liquid into vat (2). A T-shaped beam socket (4) was cut in the rock face just west of the pressing area and was positioned 0.6 m above the pressing floor. Farther east was a counterweight block measuring (1.15 m × 0.8 m and 0.35 m high) with two identical sockets (0.25 × 0.25 m) set 0.35 m apart with underside grooves. The distance between the counterweight and the niche suggests a beam length of about 4.3 m.

Christian crosses apparently of the late Roman period were found engraved in the north side of the entrance to the tomb (Figure 6.31). These offer relative dating evidence for the last phase of the tomb when it was converted into a wine press.

Figure 6.31: Crosses inscribed in the entrance of Tomb S1.

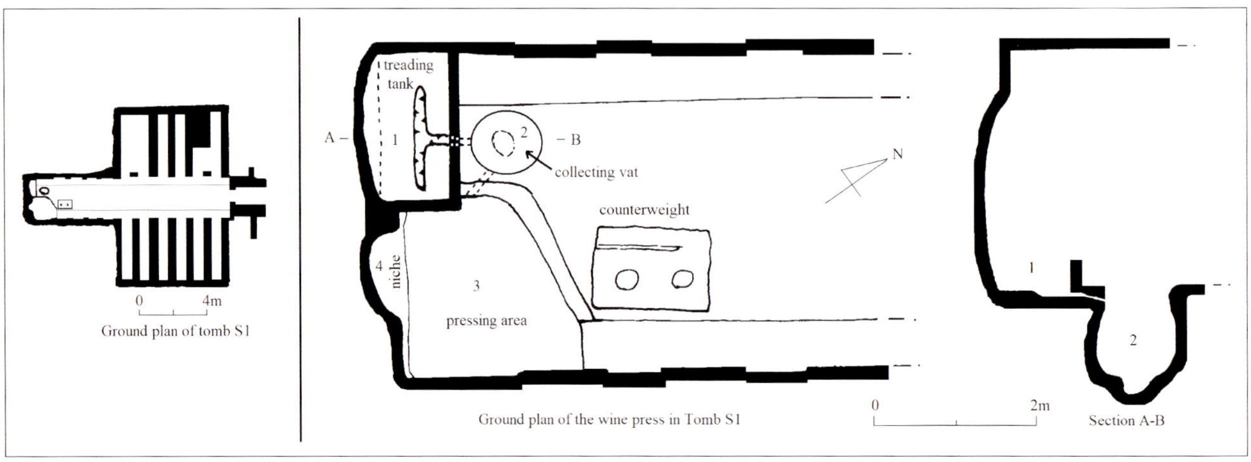

Figure 6.30: A wine press found in Tomb S1. *(After Cherstich 2005).*

6.8 Oilery

Olive oil presses in Tripolitania and some other North African regions were sometimes found in large buildings with multiple presses. These could range in number from 6 presses, as at Bir Sgaoun in Algeria, 20 km west from the border with Tunisia (Brun 2004: 220–1), to the 17 presses found at Senam Semana on the Tarhuna plateau of Tripolitania (Mattingly 1994: 142–43). Ahmed (2019: 52, Table 3.1) in his survey of the same area classified any complex containing at least five certain presses under the *oilery* category. *Oileries* in these regions clearly functioned as the focal installations of large agricultural estates.

Cyrenaica meanwhile exhibited a very different arrangement, whereby olive presses are mostly found in single units at sites, although some of these sites may contain a large number of individual presses (Table 6.2). The best example in Cyrenaica came from Lamluda, where the densest evidence for single pressing installations can be found scattered about on the surface of an area *c.*20 ha in extent. However, a large number of individual units were also noted in some comparatively small sites. For example, during the survey 11 crushing basins (probably equivalent to 12 presses) were recorded around Siret al-Mhassi, which occupied an area of only 2 ha. Using the term *oilery* to describe the rather scattered pattern of Cyrenaican presses is thus strictly speaking not conforming to the standard applied to the many oilery-type production units (with multiple presses in a single building) found in the Tripolitanian and Numidian regions. Nevertheless, there is one example that could perhaps be described with this term. This was the site of Sidi al-Hrari (HRR), where four crushing basins were all found within a single agricultural building 32.3 m long by 7.5 m wide which could imply the presence of 8 presses. This seems exceptional in Cyrenaica. In general, the *oilery* seems more likely a feature in a landscape dominated by large settlements of the estate type. Tripolitania is a case in point.

The *villa* type of settlement appeared to be a known feature in many rural sites across the Roman Empire and consisted of an independent farm associated with pressing facilities and occasionally paved with embellished mosaics. This type was not common in Roman Cyrenaica. In general, according to the literary evidence the term *villa* seems to have been confusing and had different meanings at different times. However, based on Varro (*De Re Rustica*, 3.2. 3–6; 6.12), the term can generally be applied to a complex of buildings in a rural or sub-urban context which was involved in agriculture as its primary economic activity (Mulvin 2004: 379). Nonetheless, the same building can combine two purposes as a residential part *pars urbana* and agricultural area *pars rustica* (Columella, *De Re Rustica* 6.1–23; Palladius, *De Re Rustica*). The layout and decorative aspects found in the residential parts and the low-quality architecture applied in the functional areas are considered the main criteria to differentiate between the two functions (Mulvin 2004: 381).

Based on information gathered during my survey, it thus seems that to date no evidence of the *villa* type of settlement can be assigned to this category with any

ID	Site code	Site name	Site type	No. crushing basins	No. presses	Size (hectares)
5	BIA	Elwat Beia	Small open farm	4	8	1.5
12	BSF	Siret Gowt Bu-Esfia	Small fortified farm	4	8	1.7
24	FWA	Siret al-Fwaris	Small town	7	9	11.5
34	HRR	Sidi al-Hrari	Small open farm	4	10	0.9
36	LAM	Lamluda	Small town	18	36	20
38	JEB	Jebra	Small town	7	8	6
41	LAT	El Atrun	Small town	3	6	2.4
44	MAS	Siret al-Mhassi	Large fortified farm	11	12	2
51	MLW	Siret Milow	Large fortified farm	4	6	2.1
64	SAG	Siret Sidi al-Agili	Large fortified farm	8	9	0.4
68	SDS	Siret Sdoos	Large open farm	3	6	2.2
86	SNB	Siret Wadi Senab	Troglodyte complex	4	8	1.9
88	SRH	Al-Sirah al-Hamrah	Small town	8	8	6.8
109	ZBD	Zawiat Wadi al-Bab	Large open farm	3	6	6.2
111	ZHR	Siret Sdidi Ali Zehri	Small town	8	8	27

Table 6.2: Sites of more than 6 presses and their sizes. Counting of presses is based on the minimum number of presses (MNP). Estimates are based on the presence of the crushing basin and other pressing elements.

certainty. The few examples which were exclusively derived from literature indicate that some estates must have existed in the region. These are represented by the so-called *villa rustica* at Samber, north-east of Cyrene, which was mentioned by White (1986: 106) without giving its exact location, the imperial villa-farm at Berteleis associated with the bases of several sunken *dolia* and at least two lined tanks (Ward-Perkins and Goodchild 2003: 230), and the estate of Synesius (letters 130 and 148) called (Anchemachus) in the southern extremity of Cyrenaica (Coster 1968: 120, 152, n. 9) which was only one of his many properties (Goodchild 1976: 240).

Furthermore, two more sites thought to have been maritime villas with their own anchorages were mentioned by Hesein (2015: 245-6). However, there were no monumental buildings with decorative elements such as painted walls or mosaic floors, and an additional revetment to the main building (SMSC1) was constructed with the presence of a circular vat (SMCS3) coated with a layer of hydraulic mortar. It is thus more likely that the site was a fortified farm (evidence of both defensive and industrial features was mentioned in the text but were dismissed by the author).

6.8.1 Round structures

A very few sites were associated with round structures ranging in diameter from 3.5 to 7 m (Table 6.3). The peripheral walls of these consisted of two parallel lines of roughly dressed small and medium stones and a rubble of mud fill. The thickness of the walls ranged from 0.6 to 0.7 m, with a preserved height up to 0.4 m and no sign of plastering on either the internal or external faces. The height of the walls was not fully established, and identification of these circular architectural features must remain uncertain.

However, their occurrence beside olive oil installations suggest that they were possibly used as a final collection point for olives awaiting crushing, or for the storage of solid refuse from olive oil production. Other circular areas of rock cleared surface which possibly served as a threshing floor were recorded in the proximity of two small open farms (Siret Batash and Siret al-Gabroon). They were located in the north-east corner of the site.

6.9 Distribution pattern of site types

A variation in the distribution of the sites in Cyrenaica was noted (Figure 6.32). The northern parts of Cyrenaica are characterised by sufficient rainfall to sustain agricultural activity, along with a few permanent water sources and abundant sedimentary plains. By contrast, settlements farther south in the steppe lands become progressively thinner due to the marked drought and scarcity of water resources. Rainfall, the nature of the region's geological formations and the associated availability of certain minerals consequently played an influential role in the geographical distribution of the population and settlement trends.

On the basis of the extent of the sites within the surveyed area, it is possible to define five main types of settlements apart from the major towns (Figure 6.33). Open farms seem to be the most attested type at almost 43% (45 out of 104 sites), followed by fortified farms which constitute around 30%. Out of 42 sites, about 40% present evident remains of fortifications within different types of settlements (six small towns, five nucleated villages and 31 fortified farms: eight large and 23 small). A total of ten rock-cut press sites have been recorded in the surveyed area; this type was confined to the Gebel region. A few of these were originally rock-cut tombs that were subsequently converted into presses, but it seems that many were founded from the start as underground olive-presses. This pattern from Gebel contrasts with the coastal zone where there is a complete absence of any kind of underground olive or wine press, despite the availability of numerous rock-cut tombs. Since processing of olives takes place for most part of the winter, a subterranean press seems more convenient in Gebel when temperatures would have been much lower those that in the coastal plain.

In the survey area, evidence of olive oil and wine production was identified in all the visited sites (111 sites). The archaeological evidence from Cyrenaica shows some differences in the distribution of presses across the coastal zone, upper plateau and pre-desert region (Table 6.4 and Figure 6.34). Rainfall seems to have played a significant role in this pattern while the variation in geographical relief in these zones was clearly a secondary factor (Figure 6.35). A large proportion of presses (60%) were found on the upper plateau which varies in elevation from 200 to about 800 m and

Id	Site name	Site code	Site type	Diameter	No.
24	Siret al-Fwaris	FWA	Small town 'agroville'	4.20 m	1
44	Siret al-Mhassi	MAS	small fortified farm	1–5.6 m 2–3.5 m	2
109	Zawiat Wadi al-Bab	ZBD	large open farm	7 m	2

Table 6.3: Locations and diameters of round structures.

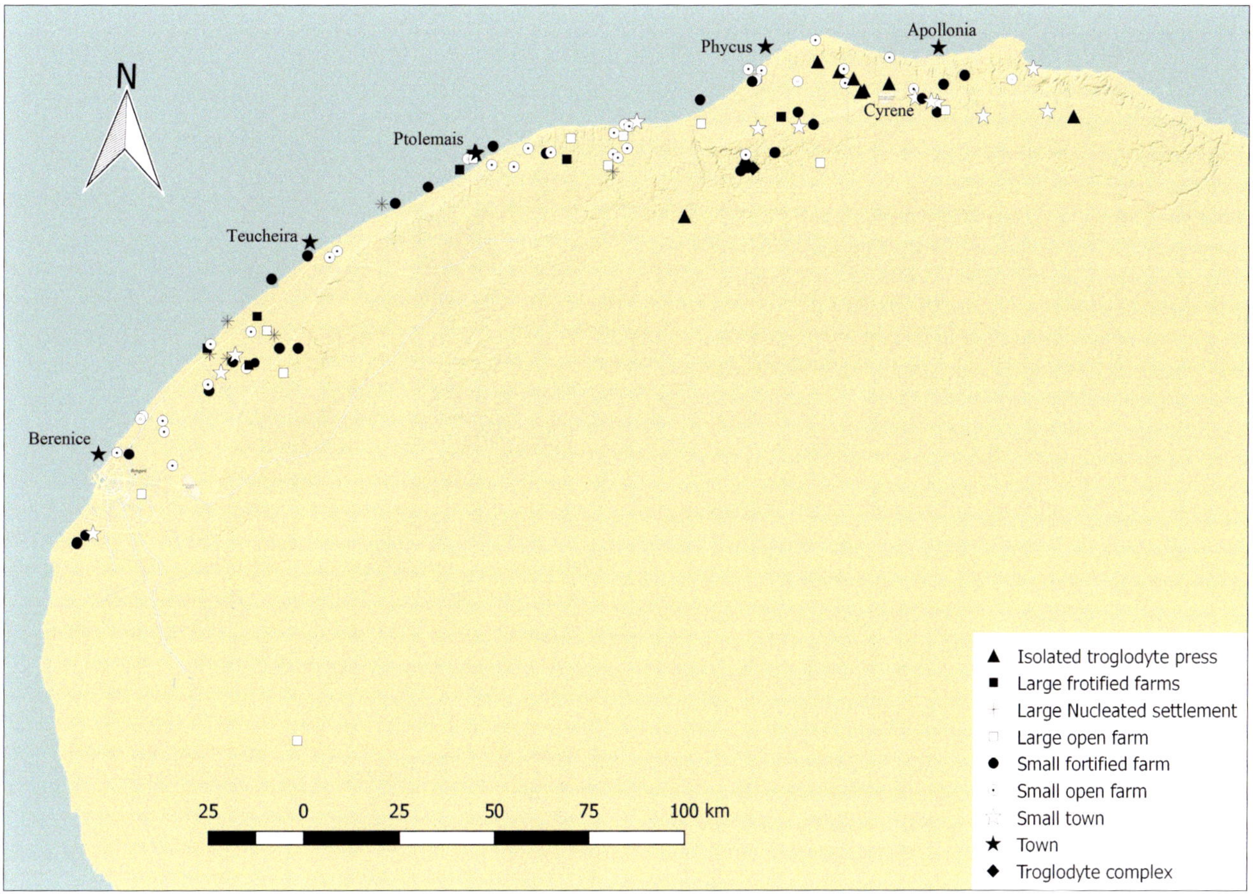

Figure 6.32: Distribution of site types in Cyrenaica.

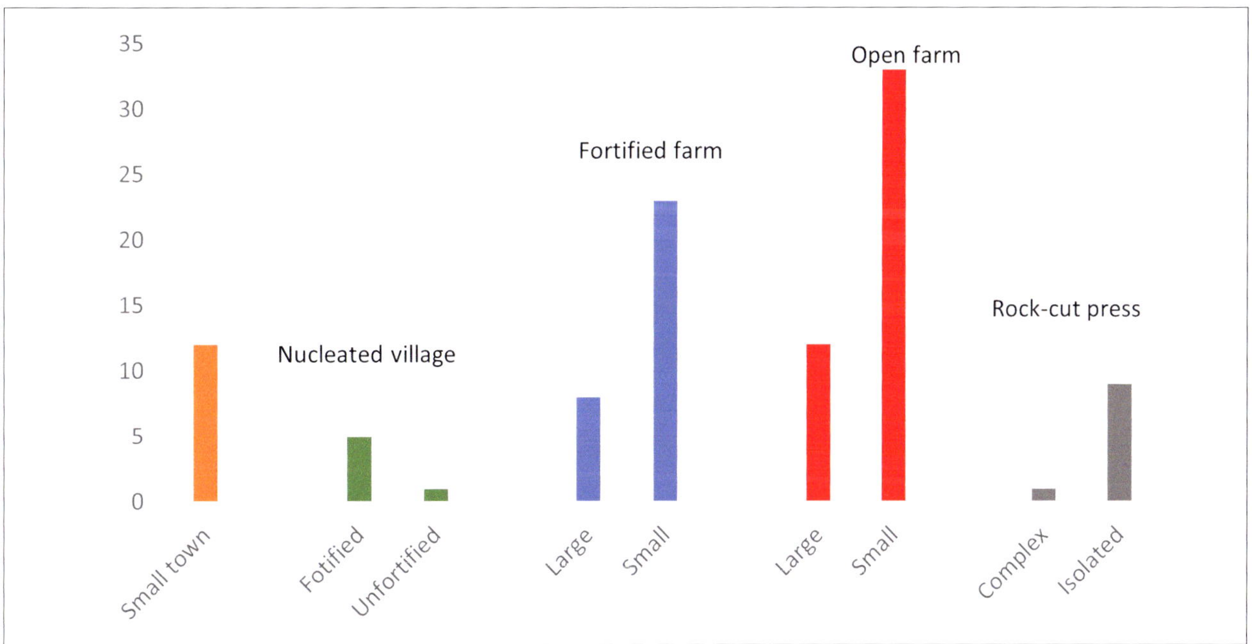

Figure 6.33: Types of settlement in Cyrenaica.

enjoys an annual rainfall ranging from 450 to 650 mm. The area of the upper plateau is roughly 10,000 km^2, or approximately 40% of the total surveyed area. However, the distribution of these presses in Gebel is more or less sporadic, and in a comparatively larger area if compared with the narrow coastal plain which only covers an area that extends across half of the upper plateau. Although the altitude in the latter region is less than 115 m and the annual rainfall varies from 250 to 400 mm, the proportion of presses found here (39%) indicates that the agricultural potential of the coastal plain and its involvement in olive oil production were particularly high. The

Region	Isohyet lines	No. of sites
Coastal plain	250 – 400 mm	41
Plateau	450 – 650 mm	62
Pre-desert	150 – 50 mm	01

Table 6.4: Rainfall isohyets in the main three regions of Cyrenaica (major centres and sites with urban contexts are not included).

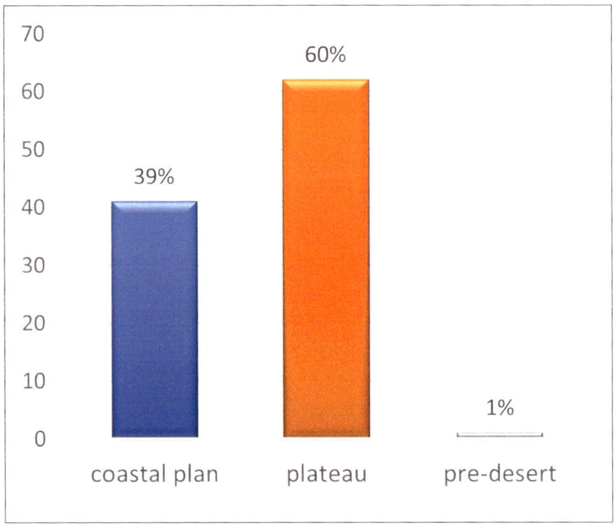

Figure 6.34: Percentage of presses recorded by surveys in the coastal plain, upper plateau of Gebel and pre-desert zone (major centres and sites within urban contexts are not included).

pre-desert zone, which represents 40% of the surveyed area, was apparently not engaged in oil or wine-making but at least its northern part of it was more likely used for cereal cultivation.

This is strikingly in contrast with the Tripolitanian pre-desert zone where the UNESCO Libyan Valleys Archaeological Survey (ULVS) suggested a large population and significant level of production (Barker *et al.* 1996: 14, 278–90; 1985: 129–32). Although the two areas are of comparatively similar environmental condition, they displayed different land-use behaviour.

Socio-political factors seem to have played a crucial role in this contrast between the two areas. By the late first century AD, the Roman authority had succeeded in sedentarising the local tribes of the interior of Tripolitania and followed some sort of policy to promote private landholding, most likely based on a tenancy system similar to those evidenced elsewhere in North Africa (Barker 1996: 348). One of the main results of this policy was the construction of a series of linear barriers, *clausurae*, in the narrow natural passages or defiles between the pre-desert and agricultural area in the Tripolitanian frontier zones. Many of these *clausurae* were found in different parts the pre-desert region of western Libya and southern Tunisia (Brogan 1971; 1980; Mattingly and Jones 1986). Their purpose was primarily to supervise transhumance and seasonal movements of local tribes, but they would later become of military significance as a result of increasing nomadic raids (Brogan 1980: 50). Most of these *clausurae*, which varied in length from 1–17 km, were associated with towers usually sited on several hilltops and breached by gates (Mattingly and Jones 1980: 89).

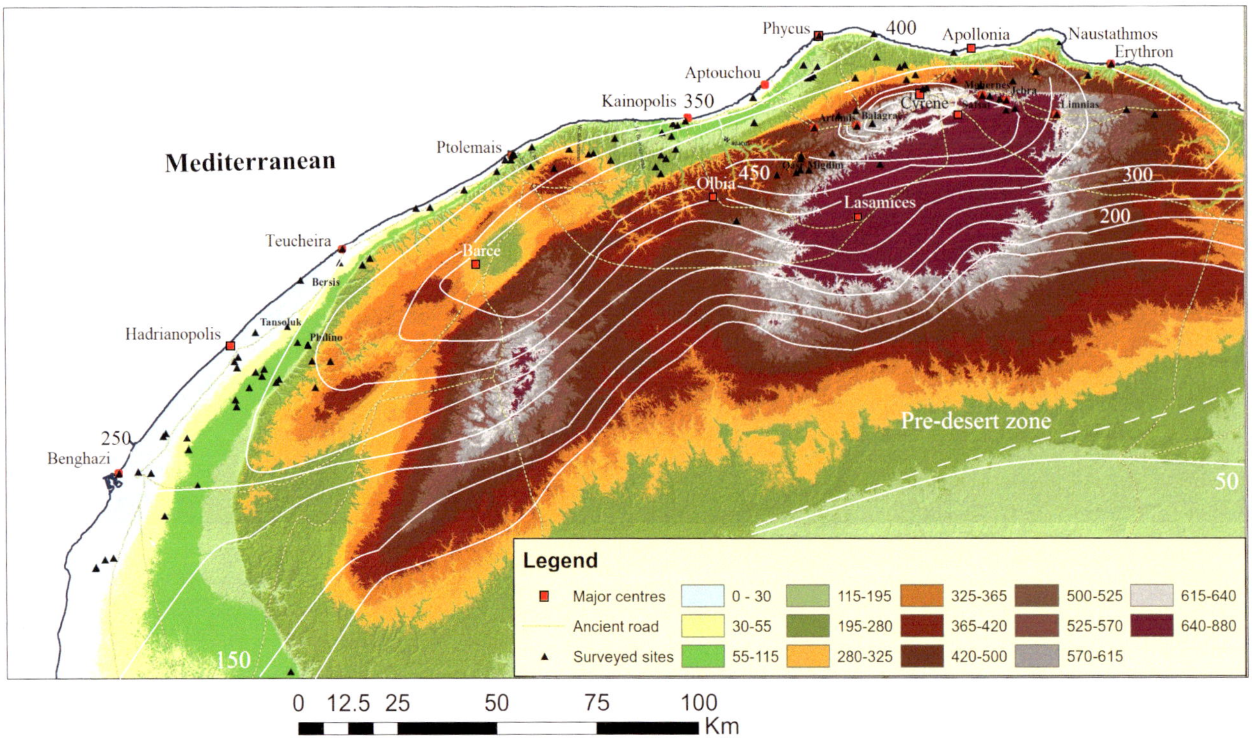

Figure 6.35: Recorded presses in relation to the modern average annum rainfall isohyets.

By contrast, in Cyrenaica, evidence of such linear barriers has not yet been found in the pre-desert region and settlement for the Libyan-Roman occupation beyond this line was virtually absent. Docile tribes were most likely settled within the interior between the coast in the north and the *limes* line in the south. A probable member of these tribes was Samphudion whose name was carved into a late Roman rock-cut oil press at Tarakenet (SEG XX. 705a and b). It appears that this person was a local inhabitant who held a military office over a possibly sedentarised Libyan group called the Marysii (Ward-Perkins and Goodchild 2003: 416).

The location of these presses was governed by ease of access from towns along the line of Roman roads, with others existing in the suburbs of towns. The majority of sites were equipped with one or two mill mortars (MNP=2-4 presses), while some possessed five or more (MNP= 10+) presses and a limited number contained more than nine presses (MNP=18+). While the last two categories may not strictly speaking be described as *oileries* since they were not found grouped in one building, their obvious density in some agrovillage settlements indicates large-scale oil production oriented to marketing.

While size was to an extent an important criterion for this classification, other factors such as the presence of utilitarian and religious structures were also taken into account. The analysis suggests that there were six main settlement types: towns, small towns, nucleated settlements, fortified settlements, open farms and rock-cut presses. All these sites produced evidence of pressing facilities, where some were characterised by large-scale capacity, indicating a high level of productivity which was fundamentally based on the number of crushing basins found in them. This suggests that a surplus of olive oil was being produced in these sites for marketing.

Relying principally on pottery scatters, some of the recorded settlements have been dated back to the Greek, Hellenistic and early Roman periods, while the majority were attributed to the late Roman period (Table 6.5).

The high density of rural settlements (fortified and open farms) in the late Roman period with evidence of industrial and agricultural activities presents a picture of general prosperity based on a polyculture economy of olive oil and wine production, animal husbandry and grain farming. Some of these rural settlements were perhaps more likely occupied by members of the indigenous population (Kenrick 2013b: 67).

Dates	Greek	Hellenistic	1st AD	2nd AD	3rd AD	4th AD	5th AD	6th AD	7th AD	No.	Productivity	
Town	✓	✓	✓	✓	✓	✓	✓	✓	✓	7	L	
Small town	✓	✓	✓	✓	✓	✓	✓	✓	✓	10	5 H	7 L
		✓	✓	✓	✓	✓	✓	✓	✓	2		
Nucleated village												
Fortified		✓	✓	✓	✓	✓	✓	✓	✓	5	L	
Unfortified												
				✓	✓	✓	✓	✓	✓	1		
Fortified farm												
Large		✓	✓	✓	✓	✓	✓	✓	✓	3	3 H	5 L
					✓	✓	✓	✓	✓	5		
Small		✓	✓	✓	✓	✓	✓	✓	✓	2	7 H	16 L
					✓	✓	✓	✓	✓	21		
Open farm												
Large		✓	✓	✓	✓	✓	✓	✓	✓	12	2 H	10 L
Small							✓	✓	✓	33	2 H	31 L
Rock-cut press												
Complex		✓	✓	✓	✓	✓	✓	✓	✓	1	H	-
Isolated						✓	✓	✓	✓	9	-	-

Table 6.5: Dating of urban and rural sites based on pottery evidence. All these sites show evidence related to the production of olive-oil/wine (H. High – L. Low).

chapter seven

OIL PRODUCTION AND ESTIMATING CYRENAICA'S POPULATION

A fundamental question in studies of the ancient Mediterranean is the size of the population. There are many uncertainties in trying to answer this question for ancient Cyrenaica, but I shall bring together estimates of rural production and the urban and rural populations. The purpose of these population calculations is to establish the scale of demand within Cyrenaica.

The first part of chapter provides an estimate of the maximum processing capacities of Roman-period olive presses in Cyrenaica and an estimate of the region's annual olive oil production, based on survey data. The second part estimates the urban and rural population of Roman Cyrenaica in the Mid-Roman period (from the early second to the end of the third centuries AD).

7.1 Oil Production Capacity

7.1.1 Introduction

Both oleoculture and viticulture are profoundly rooted in Mediterranean culture. Their primary products, oil and wine, were staples of ancient Mediterranean diets along with grain. At the same time, quantitative estimates of the volume of agricultural products in antiquity were recently introduced into the field of archaeology and provide a promising line of research for studies of the ancient economy. Frankel (1999: 38–40) succinctly summarised previous studies devoted to various aspects of this subject. By and large, the approach suggested by Mattingly (1988; 1993) in assessing the loading capacity of ancient olive presses remains of particular importance. He rightly remarks (1994: 92) that the figures he uses are exclusively based on measurements extracted from North African presses and are by no means suitable for comparison with other areas in the Mediterranean basin.

The estimate of annual olive oil production is based on measurements derived from the many presses which remain in a good state of preservation. Of particular significance are those measurements that can be used to reconstruct the basket size and operating height of the beam. In most cases this can be calculated, but it was impossible to estimate the surface area sizes of the type 7 pressing beds found exclusively in Lamluda, Jebra, Mghernes and Messa, or to identify whether the pressing process was conducted using basketry mats or wooden containers. To the best of my knowledge, no parallel example has yet been found outside the region. This suggests that it was of a type unique to Cyrenaica. Nevertheless, it seems very likely that this type of pressing bed was involved in olive oil production, although its method of operation remains enigmatic. Supporting evidence for its connection with olive oil production came from a number of press rooms recorded at the sites mentioned above. None of the recorded examples of type 7 press-beds have shown any sign of mortar plastering, which is usually associated with wine production. Furthermore, all the investigated uprights nominally associated with crushing basins were solely equipped with type 7 press-beds, while grooved circular channels and mortared floors were completely absent. Until future investigations produce evidence to the contrary, it can conservatively be assumed that at least half (76) of the press beds at the two nearly adjacent sites at Jebra and Lamluda were used to produce olive oil. Indeed, the majority of the other surveyed sites were located in areas which are even now considered especially suitable for both vine and olive cultivation.

A number of values are needed to calculate the size of a crushed olive load. These include:

- h the maximum height of the filled basketry mats stacked between the pressing bed and the press beam. The highest point closely corresponds with the base of the upper niche in the press upright.
- d the diameter of the press bed and therefore the maximum size of basket used to hold the pulped olives during the pressing process.

Defining the basket size of press bed type 7, which appears to lack the usual circular channel, was rather problematic (see the suggested solution below).

Thus, the oil yield per stack of the press can be calculated as:

Yield (kg) = *Volume* × 900 kg × 20 %

Yield (kg) = π × radius of basket stack × height of basket stack × 900 kg × 20 %

$$Yield\ (kg) = \pi \times ((d\text{-}0.04)/2)^2 \times (h\text{-}0.11 \times 90\ \%) \times 900\ kg \times 20\ \%$$

Below is an estimation of the load capacity for different types of Cyrenaican presses (estimation of the productive capacity of Cyrenaican presses in a bumper year).

7.1.2 Free-standing press-bed press

The average height of the base of the top niche was 0.80 m above the press-bed. A second bottom niche was rarely encountered in Cyrenaican presses, and formed only 7% of the recorded uprights at an average height of 0.40 m. This calculation is therefore only concerned with the height of the top niche (0.80 m). In this type of press with a free-standing press bed, the minimum and maximum internal diameters defined by the channel were 0.60 and 0.80 m, respectively. By allowing about 0.04 m of space around the internal edge of the channel, we can suggest that it is likely that the diameters of the frails used to contain the milled olives were between 0.56 m and 0.76 m. The stacked baskets were immediately flattened out during the pressing process so as not to conceal the channel. The maximum height of a pile of frails on the press-bed was 0.80 m – 0.11 m = 0.69 m (0.11 m is the thickness Mattingly (1988a: 185) proposed for the wooden lid *orbis* which was placed on top of the stacked baskets). The basket should take up some percentage of the stack of woven baskets. For the purpose of this calculation, it is assumed that an additional space of about 10% (= 0.07 m) of the stacked baskets was taken from the full operating height (0. 69 – 0.07 = 0.62 m).

The operating heights of Cyrenaican presses (max. 1.25 m) were notably lower than those of the Tripolitanian Gebel and Central Tunisia which reached maximum heights of 2.10 m and 1.85 m, respectively. It can be assumed that the stacked baskets in Cyrenaican presses were all loaded with pulped olives without any effect on the stability of the already low stack during the compression stage. Accordingly, if the possible height of the stack of full baskets of pulp was 0.62 m with a surface area of 0.25 – 0.45 m², then the total volume of this pile would be 0.15 – 0.28 m³. From the approximate 900 kg weight of 1 m³ of olive pulp (Mattingly 1988a: 185), it can be calculated that the press load would be equivalent to *c.*135 kg–250 kg of pulped olive. At a 20% return, this press load could have averaged an oil yield of 25–50 kg. Maximum production in this case would be between 1,500 and 4,500 kg of oil per year depending on a one to three-month processing season (Table 7.1).

Load size (kg olives)	Daily yield (kg oil)	30 days yield (kg oil)	60 days yield (kg oil)	90 days yield (kg oil)
250	50	1,500	3,000	4,500

Table 7.1: Maximum hypothetical oil yields for the free-standing press for a 30–90 day pressing season (one press per day).

7.1.3 Box-like press-bed built of two stone slabs from the site of Jebra (JEB-P1 and JEB-U1)

The niche for anchoring the fixed end of the beam was located 0.85 m above the press base. The pressing area of this press measured 0.80 × 1.1 m. Although the way that this kind of press-bed functioned remains uncertain, a stack of baskets was probably set within the limits of the defined pressing area. Assuming a maximum space of about 0.80 × 0.80 m, then the surface area would be 0.64 m². The total volume of this column, after subtracting the thickness of the *orbis* (0.85–0.11 = 0.74 m, in addition to 10% taken by the baskets = 0.66 m), would be 0.42 m³. The paste weighs *c.*375 kg, and at a 20% return this press load could yield around 75 kg of oil. Production could have totalled 6,750 kg of oil over 90 days or 2,250 kg over 30 days (Table 7.2).

Load size (kg olives)	Daily yield (kg oil)	30 days yield (kg oil)	60 days yield (kg oil)	90 days yield (kg oil)
375	75	2,250	4,500	6,750

Table 7.2: Maximum hypothetical oil yields of the box-like press-bed press for a 30–90 day pressing season (one press per day).

7.1.4 Double press-bed (type 4, MAS-P3)

A press bed with triple channels was found in Cyprus, and as a working hypothesis it is suggested that the middle channel was most likely used to hold frails after pressing in order to extract more oil by pouring on boiling water (Hadjisavvas 1990: 40, Figs. 62, 65). Further examples, though of two circles, were reported in Syria and the west-central part of the Balkan Peninsula. These were interpreted as being auxiliary press beds, as circular baskets were stacked on one of them before and after pressing (Frankel 1999: 91, T4266). In many cases, the diameter of the channel on the Cyrenaican examples of double press-beds apparently varied. Subsequently, it seems these presses employed two different basket sizes, as otherwise the wider frails would obstruct the channel of the smaller ones and vice versa.

This suggests another hypothesis that these press beds of two or sometimes three circular channels might have functioned simultaneously to hold frails, and pressure could have been applied by a single press beam (Figure 7.1). If we accept that this was the case, then we envisage a beam socket positioned mid-way between the two or three channels. A wooden slat could then easily be placed across the top of two adjacent stacked baskets in order to disperse the pressure of the press beam. A collecting tank, which was found alongside the press bed, most likely *in situ*, may serve to support this hypothesis (Figure 7.2).

None of the examples of double press-beds recorded in Cyrenaica were found in association with free-standing uprights or surviving walls into which niches were made. It was thus not possible to reconstruct the operating height at which the press was attached, although 0.80 m is a reasonable value for the maximum beam height across all the Cyrenaican presses. The flat woven mats would all be loaded with pulp, so the maximum height of the olive pulp on the press bed (with baskets and wooden lid) would be 0.62 m.

The internal diameters of the small and large circular channels are 0.58 m and 0.65 m, respectively. Allowing a 0.02 m space around the stacked baskets, the surface areas would be 0.23 m^2 and 0.29 m^2, respectively. The total volume of each column would be 0.14 m^3 and 0.18 m^3. A press load for each circular area would be (0.18 × 900) 160 kg for the large baskets and for the small baskets (0.14 × 900) 125 kg with a combined load of *c*.285 kg. At a 20% return, this press would yield *c*.55 kg oil.

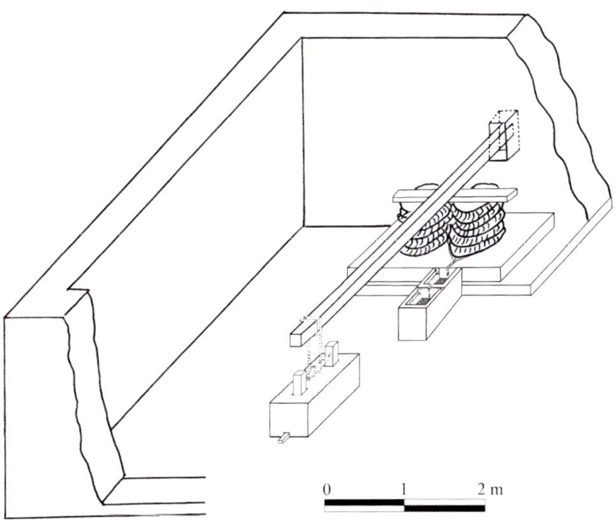

Figure 7.1: Reconstruction of a press with double press-bed.

Annual production of *c*.4,950 kg oil would be possible if the press was operated to capacity during the *c*.90 days of the pressing season and 1,650 kg oil if operated only for 30 days (Table 7.3).

Load size (kg olives)	Daily yield (kg oil)	30 days yield (kg oil)	60 days yield (kg oil)	90 days yield (kg oil)
285	55	1,650	3,300	4,950

Table 7.3: Maximum hypothetical oil yields of the double press-bed press for a 30–90 day pressing season (one press per day).

7.1.5 Discussion

There are clear differences in size and scale between the elements of Cyrenaican olive oil installations and those found in North Africa and other Mediterranean regions, meaning that their output must have differed (Figure 7.3). Presses in Tunisia and the Tripolitanian Gebel were much larger than the Cyrenaican examples and could have yielded between 5,000 and 10,000 kg (Hitchner and Mattingly 1991: 51) and 9,000 and 10,000 kg of oil, respectively (Mattingly 1988a: 193), per annum. However, smaller presses in the Tripolitanian pre-desert zone have been found that possessed a capacity in the range of 2,500 to 5,000 kg (Mattingly 1985: 41–2). Likewise, much smaller presses have been found in the Var region of Provence, south-eastern France, that produced barely 1,500–2,000 kg per annum (Brun 1986: 279–81).

Figure 7.2: Siret al-Mhassi. Press bed MAS-P3 delineated by a collecting tank. Looking south.

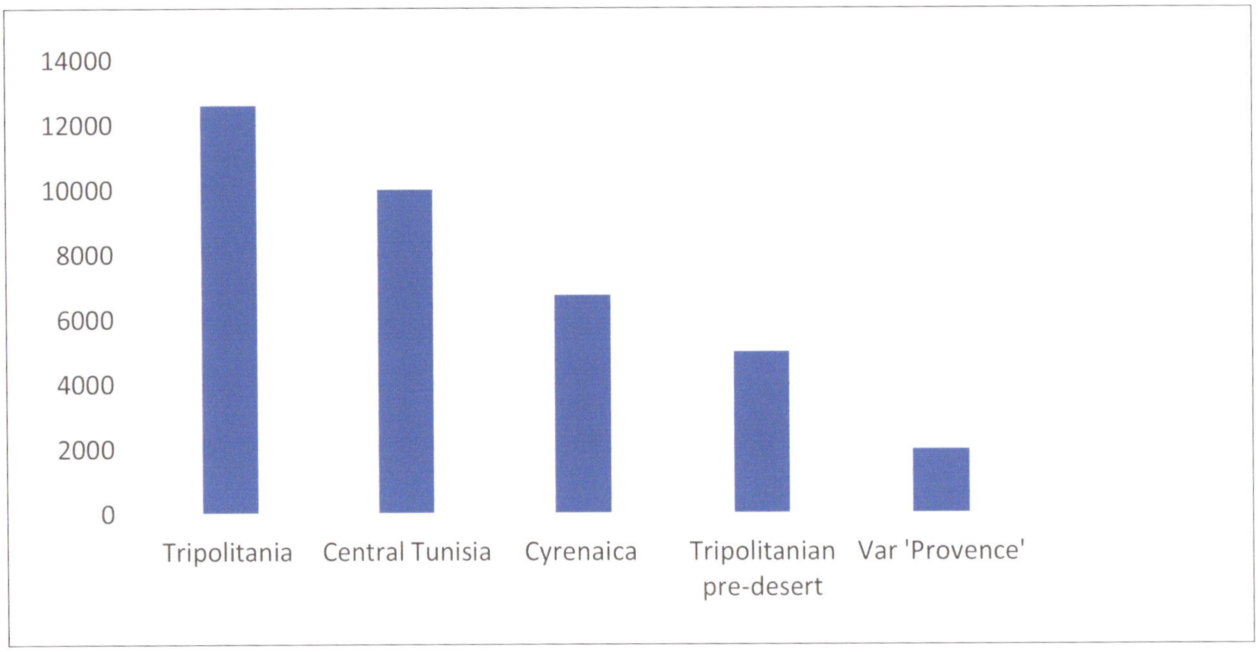

Figure 7.3: Estimated annual oil press yields from different regions.

Mattingly (1993: 496) believes that his maximum production figures may be underestimated and does not rule out the possibility that the largest North African presses might easily produce 18,000 kg of oil in bumper years. The same may be true here, and the figures on the Cyrenaican presses might be on the low side. Given their sizable counterweight blocks (which weighed in some cases in excess of 2–3 tonnes), their relatively short beam lengths (5–6 m) and the position of the pressing beds immediately under the fixed end of the *prelum* of many Cyrenaican presses, then the maximum output of these presses could have been higher than the estimates above. This is because presses of these characteristics could have generated quite high pressures (about 5.3 kg/cm^2) over a relatively small basket. This would have significantly reduced the processing time compared to the North African presses, which are assumed to have processed one load per day. On this basis, it is possible that Cyrenaican presses could have processed two loads of olives in 24 hours; if this was the case, a maximum of 10,000 litres of oil per year could have been feasible for these presses.

Nonetheless, the capacity of the Cyrenaican presses seems less impressive than their more westerly North African counterparts. However, the ample archaeological evidence for this kind of industrial installation suggests that olives and the grapes were suitable crops for the Cyrenaican landscape, and that they were of great importance to the ancient population.

My survey has recorded a minimum of 265 presses, which suggests an estimated density of around 0.01 per km^2. The density of olive presses in Cyrenaica is considerably lower than in Tripolitania and northern Syria; in the former province, the density was 0.5 per km^2 (Mattingly 1988d: 35), while the latter was far higher with 1.5 presses per km^2 (Decker 2001: 81). However, the most important factors affecting these numbers are the more intensive methods of the latter surveys and the visibility of press elements between different regions.

Mattingly (1993: 492) does not give this matter much weight in estimating annual production due to the variability of bi-annual olive tree output. Rather than investing in building new presses, a smaller number of olive presses with an extended processing period may perhaps be a better way to cope with a variable harvest. Large-scale production may have been possible on the basis that it was highly likely Cyrenaican presses were capable of processing two loads per day.

If we combine the production of the oil presses from the site of Lamluda alone, where 60 uprights were recorded (Figure 6.2) and assume that at least half of them operated contemporaneously producing oil, it is possible that they could process *c.*300,000–360,000 litres of olive oil in peak production years (at two loads per day with a maximum capacity in the range of 10,000–12,000 litres). This implies the processing of at least 1.5–1.8 million kg of olives during the good years of production. Unfortunately, there is no ancient literary evidence relating to the yields of productive trees in Cyrenaica.

However, modern information on oleoculture may provide valuable hints regarding the productivity of olive trees in antiquity. Lewis (as cited in Hill 1960: 291–2) states that in the 1950s, dry-farmed olive trees in the Jefara Plain, northern Tripolitania, had a density ranging from 33 to 50 trees/ha and an average yield of 17.5 kg of olives/tree. Figures from Cyrenaica from between 1956-1958 indicated a total of 1.5 million wild olive trees found on 15,000 ha and 0.5 million cultivated

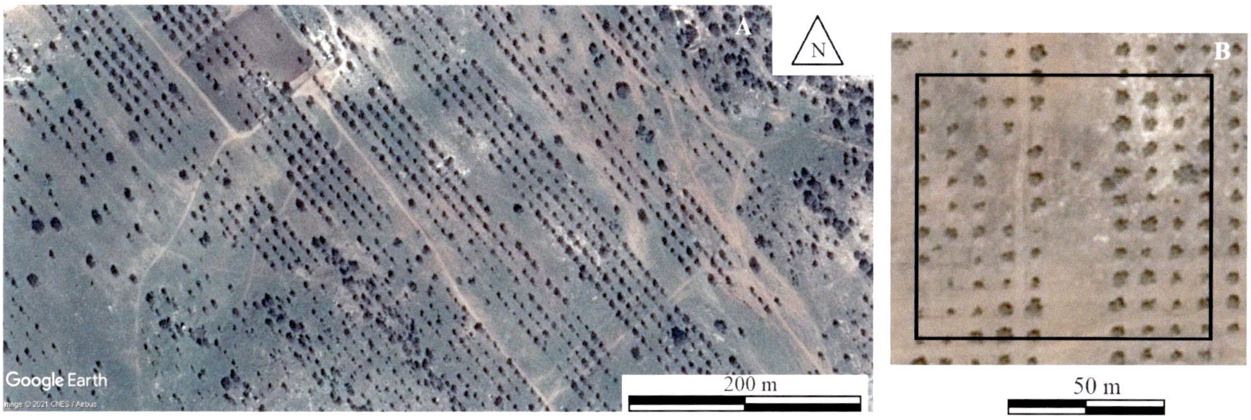

Figure 7.4: (A) Rows of olive trees in a modern farm at Taknis (Google Earth 2016). (B) Taknis. Planting density per hectare with a wider spacing left in the middle between the two main vertical rows where intercultivation is usually practised.

trees on 2,500 ha with an average density of 100 and 200 trees/ha, respectively (Kroeller 1958, Table 9). The picture is similar today for the wild olive trees; however, modern (cultivated) orchards in the region are now found to have a nominal density of just 100 per ha. Satellite images of modern olive orchards in the Taknis area (Figure 7.4 A and B), 30 km east of al-Marj, indicate that the spacing between the trees is around 10 m, with a density of some 100 trees/ha. Further evidence of what possibly represents ghost impressions of ancient tree pits from Lamluda (Figure 7.5 and Figure 7.6) reveal a probable dryland olive plantation at *c.*7 m to 13 m spacing (over 125 trees/ha). Environmental factors, such as annual rainfall and temperature, may have had a significant effect on the difference in planting density between the two areas. Bearing in mind the olive tree's biennial bearing cycle, the average yield for productive trees in Cyrenaica is 20 kg of olives per tree (4 kg oil/tree). Lamluda would then need some 75,000–90,000 mature trees (around 750–900 hectares) in full production to feed its presses to capacity. This is a considerable amount of olives, and was most probably obtained from small groves and dispersed medium-sized farms across larger areas rather than a few vast estates.

7.2 Estimating the Ancient Population of Cyrenaica

Ancient populations can be divided into two main categories: agricultural and non-agricultural. The bulk of the agricultural population normally live in rural areas, while urban centres are usually lesser and are dominated by the non-agricultural population. However, a mixture of both categories can be found living side by side, meaning that any attempt to differentiate between them is futile. Nonetheless, in order to estimate the whole population of a given region and validate the results, any calculation of the population of the urban centres should

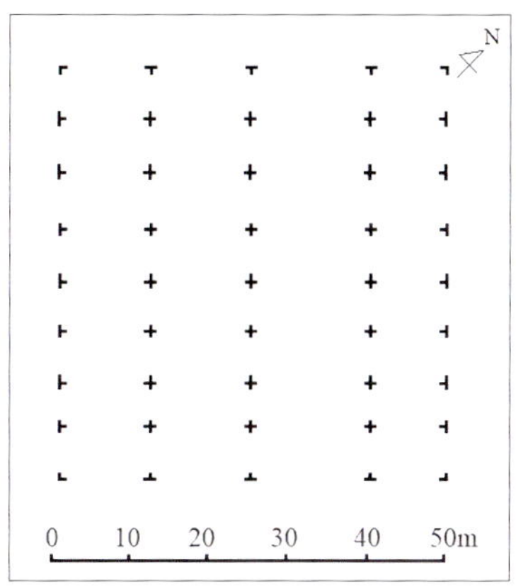

Figure 7.5 (left): Possible ghost impressions of ancient olive tree pits just 0.4 km south of Lamluda (*Google Earth © 2021 CNES/Airbus*).

Figure 7.6 (right): The probable olive grove shows planting density in ¼ hectare (overall density is around 125 trees/ha). Note the difference of the spacing of the tree pits between the vertical and the horizontal rows, *c.* 7 m and 13 m, respectively.

be assessed independently from the rural sites. Presumably, the average city has a population much greater than that of individual rural settlements, although cumulatively these can sometimes be larger.

Two models will be used in this estimation of Roman Cyrenaica's population. The first approach will calculate the urban population from household counts and area size, while the second will estimate the carrying capacity of local farmland per km². The first model was proposed by Wilson in 2011, while the second was suggested by Mattingly in 2011. Both originated from data collected during archaeological survey projects conducted in different Roman Mediterranean regions.

Wilsons's approach estimates a population from the areas allotted for residential purposes located within defined city walls. The difficulty in applying this method is when we are dealing with undefended cities and the existence of immediate extramural populations. A lack of perimeter walls could be compensated for by reliable population density multipliers, while the surrounding population can be overlooked since this approach aims to establish a minimum rather than a maximum population (Wilson 2011: 170).

Meanwhile, Mattingly's model is based on rural population densities per km², where rough figures of the capacity of different site categories are suggested; however, he stresses that his figures do not form reliable pointers to population levels across larger regions (Mattingly 2011: 15). In any given area, the quality and quantity of data largely depend upon the number of recovered sites and their overall size. Expecting a high level of site recovery is wishful thinking. Extensive and intensive survey are the two main methods used in this approach, but factors such as funding, human resources and security are important points which should be discussed in considerable detail before a final decision is taken in any archaeological survey project. This leads to a compromise in choice for both extensive and intensive surveying methods in order to enhance the data reliability and the balance between data quantity and quality.

7.2.1 Counting the urban population

For the urban demographics, Wilson's population estimates for the Roman period, as based on the known size of the major Cyrenaican cities, will be used (Table 7.4). It is worth noting that Applebaum (1979: 100) estimated the population of Cyrene in the Classical period as about 50,000 people (Applebaum 1979: 100). In his attempt to estimate the population of the same city in the Hellenistic period, Laronde disputes a population of 30,000 to 35,000 people based on an average density of 120–145 people per ha across 250 ha (not far from the figure proposed by Wilson for Roman Cyrene though in an area of only 123 ha at 200/ha) and states that this figure for the population is substantially underestimated. He instead

City	Area in hectares	Population
Cyrene	123	25,000
Ptolemais	217	30,000
Teucheira	41	6,000
Berenice	-	10,000
*Apollonia	-	4,000
*Barce	-	3,000
*Hadrianopolis	-	3,000
Total		**81,000**

Table 7.4: The population of the major Cyrenaican cities. *Source: Wilson 2011: table 7.9. The asterix (*) denotes my estimation.*

suggests a slightly higher population density of 133.3/ha over an intramural area of 750 ha, which gives a population for the Hellenistic city of not less than 100,000 inhabitants (Laronde 1987: 342). However, the estimation of the intramural area proposed by Laronde (750 ha) seems to be over-generous (White 1998: 605), unless the population of the extramural habitation and suburbs were also included in his calculation. Furthermore, one could argue that even if we accept that the city expanded over a considerable area, it should consider the rolling nature of its terrain and that a large amount of its space was divided between religious (the sanctuary of Apollo) and secular (the agora and other entertainment buildings) activities. This leads to one envisaging that there was far less space for residential housing; furthermore, the city was largely depopulated as a consequence of the Jewish revolt. Thus, Wilson's figure of 25,000 inhabitants seems reasonable, and will be maintained in my calculations. For Ptolemais, Malkowski (2012: 93–100) calculates 30,000 people on the basis of the daily volume of water that could be delivered by the aqueducts. This estimation is identical to Wilson's figure, which is based on the population density of the area within the city wall. The city of Apollonia was not included in Wilson's estimation. While the walled area of Apollonia is measured at *c.*12.5 ha, an area of *c.*2.5 ha was given over to a monumentally-sized public space and uninhabitable terrain. Subsequently, at a density figure of 400 people per hectare for ancient cities, the remaining walled area (10 ha) probably accommodated a total population of *c.*4,000. There are no suitable data on the size of Barce and Hadrianopolis, but I consider them to be more minor cities and propose a population of 3,000 each.

7.2.2 Counting the rural population

Two case studies have been used here to identify the type and the number of sites they contain that consequently allow the calculation of the ancient rural populations that lived within them. The first area is located in the

Benghazi coastal strip between Berenice and Teucheira. Here, the topography is generally flat and covered by the rich *terra rossa* soil with an annual average rainfall of around 300 mm. Rich fertile soil is deposited here after torrential rainwater flows through numerous wadis, bisecting the escarpments from the north. This soil is suitable for both agricultural and pastoral purposes. The second case study covered an area of 100 km^2 and was aimed to draw a comparison with the figures previously extracted from the first area. It lies in the Wadi al-Kuf region in the middle plateau, and receives relatively large amounts of annual rainfall of up to 500 mm. Unlike the Benghazi coastal plain, the Wadi al-Kuf landscape is characterised by rugged terrain interspersed by fertile lands and dissected by a series of wadi systems. By estimating the approximate number of inhabitants in each area through these two case studies, an average population can be estimated that should eventually help to calculate the entire population of the region.

The survey in the first case study covered a sample area of 125 km^2 (2,500 ha) located south of Driana, 30 km east of Benghazi. The survey was selective and primarily focused on standing structures and recorded no fewer than 14 sites of varying size and function (Figure 7.7). These 14 sites included one small town, three nucleated villages, three large fortified farms, three small fortified farms, a large open farm and three small open farms. Other features found in the sample area included two quarries, an isolated cistern, an aqueduct, and numerous traces of field systems. The low level of site recovery is because this part of the coastal plain was largely cleared during land reclamation works in the mid-1970s, work that has largely obscured a number of other sites. Nevertheless, the widely scattered pottery (mainly late Roman) is highly suggestive that occupation was widespread, and that the area was highly populated.

The reasonable state of preservation of the nucleated village of Philino (Figures 6.17 and 6.18) allows one to count 40 one-storied houses in an undefended area of *c*.20 ha. Household sizes varied between 180 to 520 m^2, with two to four rooms usually occupied on one side of an open courtyard. These are clearly different from Wilson's (2011: 172) urban two-storied houses, each of which accommodated 4 to 10 persons with a 100 m^2 ground floor area and 5 to 7 rooms on each floor. The considerable size of the houses at Philino, with their much larger courtyards and smaller rooms, indicate that agricultural, as well as residential, activities were

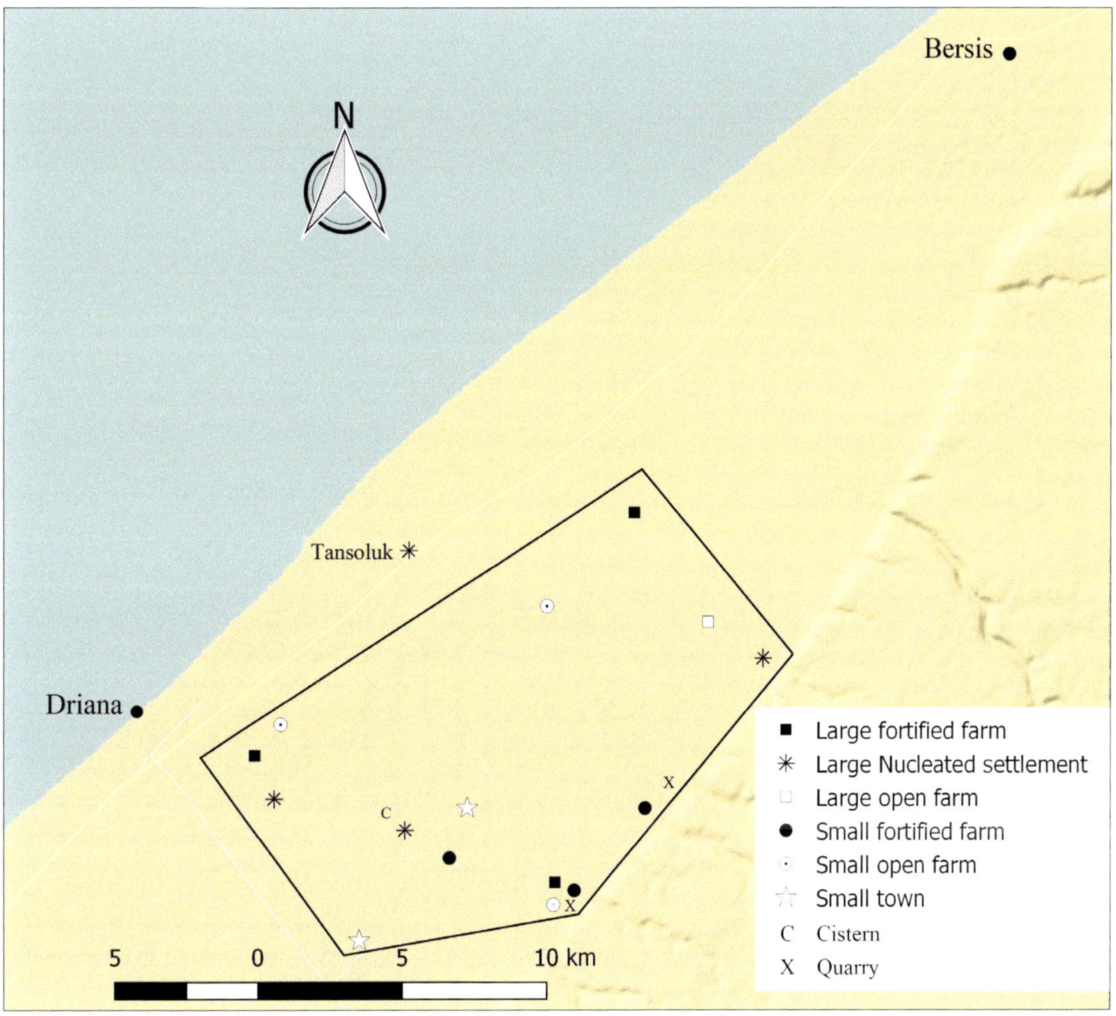

Figure 7.7: The area of detailed survey, Benghazi coastal plain.

practised within the same spaces. Each house in Philino could thus have accommodated the nucleus of a family consisting of around five to seven members per household, with five being almost certainly on the low side. Assuming that half of the site was used for residential area, animal pens, threshing floors and other agricultural and industrial activities (*c.*10 ha), these household numbers give population density figures of between 20 and 28 inhabitants per hectare (Table 7.5).

People/household	5–7
Population of site	200–280
Density per hectare	20–28

Table 7.5: Population ranges for the site of Philino.

These density numbers are unique to Philino, but can be applied to other similar nucleated sites. Therefore, a minimum number of 200 will be used in my calculation as an estimation for the villages identified in each of the two case studies.

Assuming broad contemporaneity of the sites recorded in the sampling area (which produced diagnostic pottery broadly dating from the first to the seventh centuries AD), we can use the figures calculated for the nucleated site of Philino plus those proposed by Mattingly (2011: 82, table 4.2) from the Kasserine survey. This gives a total for the first case study area of 1,670 inhabitants across 125 km^2 or 13.36 people per km^2 (Table 7.6).

Evaluating the population in the second area relied entirely on the basic information given in the study by Abdussaid and others in 1984. The survey recorded 34 sites in an area measuring around 100 km^2 (fairly similar to the area in the first case study). While the report does not mention the size and the type of the recorded sites, the text and the integrated plans give some clues as to their functions and the area which they covered. By quoting the same population figures used above for each category of recorded sites, while suggesting a figure of 10 men for the military outpost, we get the estimate presented in Table 7.7 with a population density of 18.15 people per km^2.

Although the two selected areas were of about the same size, the number of recorded sites in the second area was much higher. Conversely, the total population within each area does not seem to be significantly different (13.36 versus 18.15 people per km^2), with an average population density of approximately 17 people per km^2. The total surveyed area covers an area of around 30,000 km^2, but includes thousands of square kilometres of almost empty land. If we take the

Type of site	Population nos. per site	No. of sites	Total people	Total people per km^2
Small town	1000	1	1000	8
Village	200	3	600	4.8
Large fortified farm	10	3	30	0.24
Small fortified farm	5	3	15	0.12
Large open farm	10	1	10	0.08
Small open farm	5	3	15	0.12
Total		**14**	**1670**	**13.36**

Table 7.6: Site numbers and population estimates in a sample survey of 125 km^2 in the Benghazi coastal plain.

Type of site	Population nos. per site	No. of sites	Total people	Total people per km^2
Small town	1000	1	1000	10
Village	200	3	600	6
Large fortified farm	10	7	70	0.7
Small fortified farm	5	7	35	0.35
Large open farm	10	4	40	0.4
Small open farm	5	10	50	0.5
Military outpost	10	2	20	0.2
Total		**34**	**1815**	**18.15**

Table 7.7: Numbers of sites and population estimates of sites recorded in a sample survey carried out in the Wadi al-Kuf area by the Department of Libyan Antiquities at Shahat *(Abdussaid et al. 1984).*

habitable area of land as half of this and use the figures from the two sample areas as low and high population models we can calculate an estimated range for the rural population of 200,400 to 272,250 inhabitants (15,000 × 13.36 and 15,000 × 18.15 respectively) with a median figure of 236,325.

7.2.3 Counting military deployments, pastoral people and Marmarica

Presumably, there were some military deployment residents in and around the major cities of Cyrenaica, but estimating their size is an issue that encompasses numerous difficulties directly related to the apparent paucity of our sources. Therefore, the dearth of evidence makes any estimate of the total military deployment in Cyrenaica highly speculative. Cyrenaica was always dependent on foreign troops to suppress any attempt to disrupt its stability. Due to the geographical proximity to Egypt, Cyrenaican security becomes inevitably dependent on Egypt, which consequently led to political domination over the region for the vast majority of ancient history (Goodchild and Reynolds 1962: 41).

Nevertheless, some inscriptions have been discovered in different sites of Cyrenaica that may help to shed some light on the presence of a number of military troops. One came from Corinclanum (modern Ajedibya), which exhibited the names of soldiers thought to belong to the *Cohors I Apamenorum* which defeated the Marmaridae and the Garamantes in the mid-first century AD. After the war, the Cohort probably remained in Cyrene with a number of its units deployed in different parts of the region, including Corinclanum (SEG. IX, 775, 776, 778, 782 and 794; Ferri 1926). Two inscriptions were found in Cyrene and dated to around the early third century AD. The inscribed names were most probably linked to the *Cohors I Macedonica* of the reign of Severus that was initially dispatched to put down the Jewish revolt of 115-7 AD and remained thereafter (Goodchild and Reynolds 1962: 37-9). The rebellion spread over a wide area of Cyrenaica and was thought to have caused a great loss of the population (Orosius VII. 12, 6) to the extent that it became necessary to bring new settlers to repopulate the region (Applebaum 1979: 270, 287; Goodchild 1976: 219). According to Cassius Dio (LXVIII, 32, 1–2), who lived between AD 155–235, this turmoil resulted in the deaths of around 222,000 people. The last two inscriptions were found at Ptolemais and are believed to bear names of soldiers of the *Legio III Augusta* and are broadly dated between the early third to fourth centuries AD (Goodchild and Reynolds 1962: 39–41).

The Roman army consisted of legionaries and auxiliaries, but the exact numbers of men in a legion is still debated. MacMullen (1980: 451) suggested, that by the early Roman empire, that a number of 6,000 soldiers was likely, a figure which is generally accepted. By Diocletian's time, this number had been reduced to 1,000 soldiers (Overtoom 2014: 3). What might be noted from the above-mentioned early-mid Roman inscriptions is that these military troops were neither contemporaries nor permanent, but rather dispatched on a temporary basis to restore order in case of any of the troubles that were frequently caused by political conflicts or local tribal forays. Therefore, in order to keep the estimate more conservative, the total manpower stationed in Cyrenaica at one time (from the second to third centuries AD) could have been, in my view, around 6,000, plus at least another 2,000 of local troops as the region probably had its own garrison from the first century AD, though it was probably a small one (Goodchild 1953: 65). This brings the total up to 8,000 men.

Next to these 8,000 soldiers, we should also take into account a further number of pastoral people and allies or docile local tribes that must have existed. The numbers of such people are much harder to estimate since evidence of their occupation is almost entirely absent. Nonetheless, in order to arrive at some reasonable figure, there is no alternative but to assume as a guess that they would not have exceeded 5,000 people.

An attempt to estimate the demography of Marmarica has been made and added to the total population. It is worth noting that in the mid second century AD, according to the Geography of Claudius Ptolemy (IV, 4, 4), the region east of Derna was administratively under Egypt. Nevertheless, adding the inhabitants of Marmarica to the total population of Cyrenaica was based on the fact that the region has not yet shown any evidence of olive oil production. A lack of evidence of large-scale oil production in Egypt suggests that Cyrenaica was the main source of this commodity. Archaeological evidence from Berenice suggests only a little commercial contact with Egypt (Riley 1979: 412-6). Unless otherwise altered by future archaeological investigation, this situation also seems likely to be applicable to Marmarica. It is worth noting, though at a later date, that according to the Arab traveller Al-Idrisi (310–11), who lived between AD 1100-1165, olive oil was exported to Egypt via the port of Tolmeita (ancient Ptolemais). A French trade statistic dated to 1850 mentioned a consignment of about 1375 tons of olive oil with other agricultural products shipped from Cyrenaica to Egypt (Wright 1982: 22).

Owing to the meagre evidence with regards the population of the ancient inhabitants of Marmarica, the number cannot be determined with confidence. Over sixty sites, ranging from fortified settlements, to farmsteads, farms and villages have been identified during the recent survey conducted by L. Hulin in the area east of Tobruk (Hulin 2008; Hulin *et al.* 2009; Hulin *et al.* 2010). The project was abruptly curtailed by the

Type of population	Approximate total population
Urban	81,000
Rural	250,000
Marmarica	8,000
Militants, pastorals and local tribes	8,000
Total	**347,000**

Table 7.8: Estimated number of population in whole Cyrenaica.

revolution in 2011, but the available data, in addition to the apparent aridity of the region, suggest that it is unlikely that the population was high. O. Bates (1914: 32) estimated the population of Marmarica in the early twentieth century at 8,000, and it does not seem too far-fetched to assume that this figure is the same as it was in ancient times.

Finally, by combining the estimates for urban and rural Cyrenaica, Marmarica and the military (Table 7.8), a total population of somewhere in the region of 333,325 inhabitants is proposed. This number is, however, much lower than the 628,000 people that Laronde suggested for Hellenistic Cyrenaica (Laronde 1987: 342). Although Laronde agrees there was widespread havoc caused by the Jewish revolution, which took place at a later date, he is somewhat doubtful about its supposed death toll. In the meantime, he upholds the impression that the Hellenistic period apparently marked the peak of the region's population (Laronde 1987: 342).

7.3 Conclusion

Since the survey was selective, further systematic fieldwork is still required. At present, it is impossible to know exactly how many olive presses were present in Cyrenaica. However, one might expect that the number of estimated presses (265) is a low figure, given the lack of excavation, poor survival and frequent invisibility of remains in surveys. Many presses are buried under the debris of collapsed buildings, while several archaeological sites are reported to contain presses but have never been visited, while others cannot be accessed as they are located within fenced private properties. Furthermore, more pressing elements were brought to light, during the recent unauthorised land reclamation and uncontrolled construction activity, that were not included in the context of this study (statistics are not available).

By using the press dimensions taken in the field, my estimated figures indicate that the number of 265 presses distributed in the whole region could have produced a total output of between *c.*2,650,000–3,180,000 million litres of olive oil during the peak years, when processing work might last for three months. In addition, the available surveyed data suggests that the hypothetical region's population stood at about 333,000. By taking the calculation, proposed by Mattingly (1988d: 34), that the average Roman consumed 20 litres of olive oil per year, then Cyrenaica's population may have demanded around 6,666,000 litres of oil annually during the Roman period. Subsequently, the scale of the total production of olive oil in the region would have been enough to supply *c.*130,000–160,000 people each year.

chapter eight

EVIDENCE OF OLIVE OIL/WINE LOCAL AMPHORA PRODUCTION AND LONG-DISTANCE TRADE

This overview of regional amphora production in Cyrenaica focusses on the locations of the known amphora production centres. The fabrics and typologies of Cyrenaican amphorae, as well as their regional and inter-regional geographical distribution pattern, are examined, to help gain an understanding of the economic activity of the area in the wider context of the Roman economy.

8.1 Introduction

An amphora is a large, two-handled, ceramic container for transporting and storing commodities, such as olive oil, wine, citrus fruits and fish sauce, that were traded around the Mediterranean regions and beyond. They preserve well in the archaeological record and have distinctive morphological and technical characteristics that allow their provenances to be identified. They can thus play a key role in furthering our understanding of the ancient economy specifically on regional and inter-regional patterns of trade.

Excavations at Monte Testaccio in Rome (Dressel 1878; Manacorda 1977, Panella 1973; Rodriguez-Almeida 1975) brought to light huge numbers of amphorae. These were almost exclusively olive oil containers and other types were probably recycled to hold olive oil. Commodities, particularly olive oil (Carandini 1970), inundated the city of Rome and were mainly imported from southern Spain, Africa Proconsularis and Tripolitania. The use of a methodological approach in both excavations and field survey work, accompanied by a quantitative analysis of amphora from the western Mediterranean, provides an interesting picture of significant ancient maritime trade with kaleidoscopic patterns of exchange. Rome's economic ties with southern Spain, northern Africa and the rest of the Early Roman western Mediterranean provinces are clear due to the widespread and dense diffusion of established types from these regions.

By contrast, the situation in the Eastern Mediterranean is still far from clear with very few assemblages published. In Cyrenaica, despite the long-established missions at sites such as Cyrene and Apollonia, there are only two studies on ceramics: Berenice (Riley 1979) and Euesperides (Göransson 2007). Much more work on amphorae from large pottery assemblages from many more sites is badly needed, along with the use of a more quantitative approach.

The sizable olive presses found in North Africa illustrate how the region's agricultural potential motivated investors, who successfully directed their efforts towards this lucrative business. The maritime olive oil trade flourished from the end of the second century AD and imports of North African olive oil into Rome became more frequent. This is evidenced by the frequent occurrence of Tripolitanian amphorae I-III and the Tunisian African I and II. The third century AD saw peak production of Tripolitanian amphora III, which represented 30% of all the Roman North African amphorae found in the Monte Testaccio (Ahmed 2019: 152). Meanwhile imports were predominantly of Africana IB amphorae (mainly produced in Tunisia), which accounts for 60% of the total amphorae found (Remesal Rodriguez 2004).

8.2 Pottery Kilns in Cyrenaica

To date a total of 27 kilns have been discovered in the region distributed between 9 coastal sites (Figure 8.1). Only seven of them (or eight if the Hellenistic kiln at Tocra is included) have been confirmed with confidence as possessing amphora kilns (Table 8 1). Strikingly, while the inland landscape is characterised by the widespread distribution of Roman-period farming settlements of various sizes, pottery production sites have not yet been found in the region beyond the coastal strip area. This apparent concentration of evidence for the kiln sites in the littoral area indicates that these very likely served both local and hinterland production sites. Indeed, the

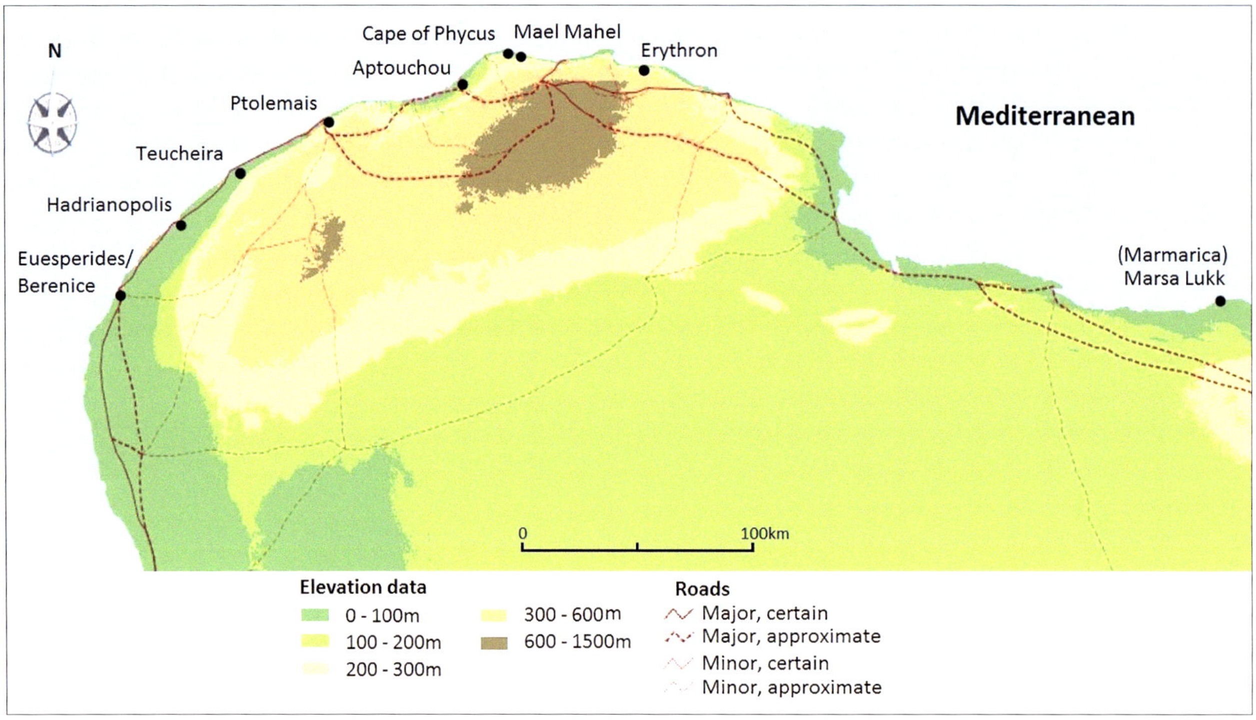

Figure 8.1: Pottery kilns in Cyrenaica and Marmarica. There are additional kilns from Marmarica but their locations are not available *(Source of the map: 2012 Ancient World Mapping Center).*

Site name	No. of kilns	Feature name	Shape			Possible products	Date
			R	C	O		
Euesperides	1	-		✓		Cyrenaica amphorae 3 & B	4th BC
Berenice	6	(a) kiln			✓	tiles, bricks & large vessels	2nd to 1st BC
		(b) kiln	✓			tiles, bricks & large vessels	2nd to 1st BC
		(c) kiln			✓	?	Early – mid 3rd AD
		(d) kiln	✓			lamp	3rd to 4th AD
		(e) kiln	✓			lamp	3rd to 4th AD
		(f) kiln		✓		?	3rd AD
Hadrianopolis	1	-		✓		?	Mid 1st AD
Teucheira	2	-	✓			Early Roman amphora?	Hellenistic/Early Roman
		-		✓		pottery	Roman
		kiln site				MR8, 9 & 10	Mid-Roman
Ptolemais	5	K1	✓			lamp	Late Roman
		K3	✓			bricks	Late Roman
		K4	✓			bricks	Late Roman
		K5	✓			bricks	Late Roman
		-	✓			? lime	Late Roman
Apollonia	1	kiln site				MR8	Mid-Roman
						cooking ware	Mid-Roman
Mahel Mael	3		2		✓	MR1 amphora	Mid-Roman
Cape of Phycus	4		2	✓	✓	MR1 & MR8 amphorae	Mid-Roman
Aptouchou	3		3			MR1 amphora	Mid-Roman
Erythron	1		✓			MR1 & MR8 amphorae	Mid-Roman
Total	**27**		**17**	**5**	**4**		

Table 8.1: The identified kilns and kiln sites in Cyrenaica with products specified. R = Rectangular; C = Circular; O = Oval.

abundant evidence of inland oil presses strongly suggests that most of these facilities were located much farther away from the sea, and their products would have arrived at the coast in skins to be transferred into amphorae for export.

8.2.1 Greek and Hellenistic kilns

Evidence for pottery production sites in Cyrenaica is meagre, and the current state of knowledge in this field is fairly poor. Excavation in 1996 at the northern limit of Euesperides brought to light one early kiln complex set into the bedrock, which consisted of three circular firing chambers, a well and a rock-cut tank (Buzaian and Lloyd 1996: 134). Waste material, including deformed and misfired amphorae recovered from the kiln and the surrounding area, indicates that Cyrenaican amphora 3 and B amphora forms at least were produced here (Göransson 2007: 60, 76, fig. 20). Finds retrieved from the kiln suggest that the complex was active between the early fourth century to the mid-third century BC (Buzaian and Lloyd 1996: 136). It is probable that the kiln was later used for lime production. The rescue excavations at the site of Berenice, which took place between 1971 and 1975 under the auspices of the Libyan Department of Antiquities and the Society for Libyan Studies in London, have brought to light the remains of six kilns of different shape and size. The two earliest kilns (Kilns A & B) were found within building K1, which may have been a production centre for large vessels, tiles and bricks (Lloyd 1977: 62, 211). It seems that both kilns functioned at the same time between the second to first centuries BC. Kiln A was oval in shape with a maximum diameter of 1.4 m, and was built of mixed materials, including pot sherds and overfired clay fragments. Kiln B meanwhile was probably rectangular in plan, with walls executed by two rows of baked mud brick backed by a surrounding wall of rubble and mud. The remaining four kilns were dated back between third to fourth centuries AD. Two of them were severely damaged with no evidence of their products, while the others seem to have been dedicated to lamp production.

8.2.2 Roman kilns

During the early 1970s an archaeological survey conducted by G. Jones and J. Little in the Driana (Hadrianopolis) area, 30 km west of Tocra, identified one circular kiln. Scattered pottery around the kiln was dated from the second to third centuries AD (Jones and Little 1971a). The kiln's 6.8 m diameter makes it amongst the largest circular Roman pottery kilns known. From a comparative perspective, it is larger than the Ain Scersciara kiln in the Tripolitanian Gebel, which is 6.0 m in diameter (Goodchild 1976: 88), and far exceeds the largest kilns in Tunisia (4.9 m, Bonifay 2004: 29). Given the substantial diameter of the Hadrianopolis kiln, it is highly probable that it was used for amphora production. The kiln's proposed date is concurrent with the occurrence of the local MR8 amphora. Further systematic surveys and excavations are required to ascertain which ceramic types were produced here.

There have also been further three discoveries of kilns farther east, at Teucheira. The first kiln site lies outside the city wall, some 200m north-west of the west gate, and was discovered by Wright in 1960. Initial analysis of the pottery sherds collected from the waste dump led him to suggest the kiln had been operated in the first century AD (Wright 1963). When J. Riley excavated the kiln site, the structure *per se* was not found, but a large assemblage of coarse pottery sherds was recovered that dated the site to the late second and third centuries AD (Riley 1976; 1979b). Three local amphora types were found here: MR8, 9 and 10.

Two other kilns were excavated by Benghazi University within the walls of the ancient city. The first was a quadrangular kiln (2.6 × 2.2 m) with a stokehole (0.80 m wide) on the north side. A pedestal placed off-centre towards the middle of the firing chamber suggests that clay bars formed the floor on which the pottery was stacked. The internal walls were built of three parallel lines of fired clay blocks, which were backed by two squared limestone and sandstone blocks filled with mud and rubble (Buzaian 2000: 62–3, fig. 2). A large quantity of pottery wasters, including a deformed *lagynos* spout and a double-rolled amphora handle, as well as fragments of discoidal loom weights, were found in the kiln. These suggest that it was active during the late Hellenistic and early Roman periods (Bentaher 1994: 237–8). The kiln waster of a double-barrelled handle (*cf.* Buzaian 2000: fig. 32) is very intriguing, and despite the lack of a complete profile its similarity to the Early Roman Amphora 1 and 4 from Berenice (Riley 1979a: 145–6, D104 and 149–51, D118) is marked and I would suggest that it was probably influenced by the Koan amphora. It is worth noting, however, that this type of double handle is not an exclusive characteristic feature of the Koan amphora. It also appeared on its successor type, the Dressel 2–4, which was produced in many different regions including Kos itself (Göransson 2007: 153, 155).

The second kiln was circular, *c.*1.1 m in diameter, and dated approximately to the late second to early third centuries AD, and survived to a maximum height of 0.55 m. The structure was clearly prefabricated and then sunk into the ground. Its walls were constructed from three coils varying from 3 to 5 cm thick (Buzaian 2000: 69, figs. 11–12). Two small red-slip bowls were recovered from the kiln (Bentaher 1994: 243), one of which was uncharacteristically oxidised and discoloured near the rim, indicating that the kiln was most likely used for firing pottery. Although this is consistent with the general belief that round kilns were usually used for pottery making (Peacock 1982: 31), the size here is crucial and it is likely that amphorae kilns are wider in diameter than those used for table ware.

Fifteen spreads of ashy soil and wasters, mainly second- and third-century amphorae and coarse pottery, have been reported from the northern and eastern districts of the city of Ptolemais some 35 km east of Tocra (Wilson 2002: 253). Furthermore, the remains of six kilns have been identified at the so-called 'Villa with a View' recently discovered by the Polish Archaeological Expedition. These kilns clearly represented a short-lived second phase of artisanal activity within earlier residential buildings, and probably date to the fifth century AD (Żelazowski 2012: 144). All these kilns are rectangular in plan, though they vary in size. Evidence of production waste and portable finds was lacking, as it was obvious that this production centre had been thoroughly cleaned. However, remains of bricks found near Kilns K3 and K5 suggest that they could have been used for firing this kind of building material (Żelazowski 2011: 20). There is evidence that quadrangular kilns were commonly used for firing bricks alongside large vessels such as amphorae and *dolia* (Peacock 1982: 69, 130). It is thus reasonable to argue that amphorae may have been produced in them too. This evidence of pottery manufacturing, though not yet adequately scrutinised, indicates that Ptolemais was probably an important centre for processing agricultural products.

Ten amphora kilns have been discovered in a recent survey of the area between Apollonia and Phycus (Hesein 2015: 172, 8–9). Analysis of pottery sherds collected from these areas, including wasters, indicates that MR1 and MR8 were produced here (two types of amphorae were produced in the Cape of Phycus kilns, while only MR1 amphorae seem to have been produced at Aptouchou and Mahel Mael). Future archaeological surveys will undoubtedly bring to light additional kiln-sites along the whole length of the coastal strip. These new kiln sites enrich our knowledge of previously known amphora production sites in the region. Furthermore, an excavation in 2010 conducted by the French mission and carried out within the ancient city of Apollonia, shed more light on amphora production in Cyrenaica (Mazou 2016). This area of excavation was located on the north-east of the city, by the shoreline, and not far from a row of rock-cut chambers that resemble warehouses. Although the kiln was not found in this area, the excavation revealed compact dumps of ash, fired bricks and tiles mixed with large amounts of pottery sherds. This pottery assemblage includes 84 sherds of MR8 amphora, of which 15 sherds were overfired, strongly suggesting that this type of amphora was produced here. Strikingly, due to the sherds being found within the city walls and not outside them, it would suggest that this location could well have been the centre of production in the region, since the city was also a major port.

Recent excavations by the French archaeological mission at Erythron (25 km to the east of Apollonia), just west of the east church, have identified a ceramic production site. A kiln has been found within a Roman bath complex which had been abandoned at the end of the third/beginning of the fourth century AD (Mazou and Capelli 2011). The quantity of misfired amphorae (mainly Mid Roman 1 amphorae type) and lamp fragments found near the kiln confirms that these were its main products.

Kiln amphora sites are also well attested in Marmarica to the east. A recent survey carried out by L. Hulin along the coastal area east of Tobruk recorded eleven sites and provided evidence of vast spreads of pottery and amphorae wasters including eight kilns (Hulin 2008; 2009). These ranged in date from the third to seventh centuries AD, and were circular in plan (in contrast to the majority of quadrangular kilns found in Cyrenaica). They were also all located by the sea, apart from one site which laid 7 km inland. This abundance of amphora kiln sites can serve as proxy evidence for agricultural production. While these were possibly coincident with the agricultural and/or fish processing industries, presses or tanks were not detected in the surveyed area. Empty amphora production directed at the Egyptian and Cyrenaican markets is worth considering, although the possibility that Marmarica produced commodities for export in the amphora should not be discounted. Papyri evidence (*Papyrus Vaticanus Graecus II*) attests to wine production along the coast between Marmarica and Cyrenaica, suggesting that the production of these kiln was possibly also connected with wine production in this region. This papyrus, which reported an extract of cadastral records from the area of Cherrhonesos (modern Ras al-Teen), *c.*45 km east of Darnis (modern Derna), was written between AD 189-190 and reports cadastral and juridical records in around 190 scrolls. It is possible to assume that viticulture was continued along the western Mamarican coast and farther west in the area of the Pentapolis, between Darnis and Apollonia, down to the Byzantine period. It must be noted, however, that characterising the Marmarican amphora fabrics and types is an essential step before we can start searching for them to the east and west.

In general, Cyrenaican kilns were mostly of the up-draught type. These were able to attain temperatures of *c.*1000°C, and although dated to Hellenistic and Roman periods, they concurrently occurred in different shapes (quadrangular, circular and oval-shaped), the choice of shape seems to have no chronological significance. Most Cyrenaican kilns were rectangular in plan, although a few examples are either round or oval-shaped. Though by no means conclusive, the rectangular kiln was thought to be designed for amphorae-, *dolia*- and brick-making, while the other shapes seem to be better suited for pottery-making (Peacock 1982: 69). Some of the quadrangular kilns were equipped with pedestals that would have supported a raised clay perforated floor on which pottery could be stacked. No direct evidence of the superstructure has been preserved.

The discovered kilns are exclusively located on the coast, in or near to the urban centres, and are not at oil/wine producing sites which are nearly all situated farther inland. Their dates spanned the Hellenistic to the late Roman periods. There is a complete absence of Greek amphora kilns in Cyrenaica, which may in part be attributed to the lack of excavations. It may suggest also that olive oil and wine in Greek time were produced on a domestic level using rudimentary equipment. Meanwhile, Roman amphora production was a consequence of surplus olive oil and wine production, and involved the use of presses.

8.3 The Distribution of Kiln Kites in Cyrenaica

All the kilns discovered in Cyrenaica so far have been located along the coast in the immediate vicinity of port sites, and no single example has yet been detected inland beyond the line of the coastal harbours. The abundance of archaeological remains relating to oil and winemaking leads me to believe that many of the discovered kilns produced amphorae for transporting these perishable commodities. If the surplus found its way to the overseas markets, it is reasonable to assume that it would have been helpful to have kilns close to ports. Locating amphora kiln sites near the coast would reduce the risk of the containers breaking on the journey from the production site, often inland, and provide accessibility to regional and inter-regional markets.

Indeed, oil and other goods were likely transported to the coast in goat skins, then unloaded in warehouses (*horrea*) or storage facilities before being transferred to locally produced amphorae for onward travel by sea. The transfer of oil and wine in goat skins is much easier and safer than transport in amphorae, especially across difficult terrain and uneven roads, minimising collateral damage.

The pottery production sites appear to have been primarily affected by the availability of suitable clays deposited at the mouths of the wadis. On the other hand, apart from the kilns at Hadrianopolis and Latrun, the kiln sites lacked permanent water sources. They compensated for this by digging wells. Indeed, wells are a common feature in the coastal plains due to the shallow depth of ground water level (5-7 m deep). For instance, at the Cape of Phycus (el-Mamluh), 25 km west of Apollonia, four kilns were supplied from a well located some 60 m to the south which is still in use today (Hesein 2015: 391).

The distribution of these kilns is much denser in the eastern sector of the region than in the west. This likely reflects a greater specialisation in oil and wine production on the upper plateau, though the density of olive presses in the two areas is notably different. In fact, a total number of 112 out of 164 crushing basins was recorded in western Cyrenaica (west of Wadi al Kuf). This suggests that oleoculture was also intensively cultivated in western Cyrenaica and the apparent low number of kilns found is due to the lack of archaeological field works.

This situation corresponds closely with the situation in the Guadalquivir Valley, southern Spain, and in central Tunisia, where kilns are also concentrated on the navigable rivers and coast, respectively. In Baetica, at least 100 amphorae kiln sites presently identified (Ponsich 1991) were intentionally located along the banks of the Guadalquivir river. Meanwhile, olive trees and oil presses were widely distributed across the land beyond the valley, and the oil produced was transported down to collection points near the main course of the River Guadalquivir or at its major southern tributary, Genil (Mattingly 1988d: 43, no. 46). The distribution of many amphora kiln sites along the central Tunisian coast, including the cities of Leptiminus in the Sahel region and Meninx in the Gulf of Gabes, indicates that these cities played an important role in organizing exports of oil and wine from inland farms (Wilson 2002: 262).

A different situation can be observed in the territory of Lepcis Magna in Tripolitania, which was one of the ancient Mediterranean world's major olive oil producers. There was a close relationship between olive oil manufacture and amphorae production here, with some 35 amphora kilns identified in the hinterland of Lepcis within or around large estates which specialised in olive oil production (Ahmed 2019: 48, 146).

8.4 Local Amphora Fabrics, Typologies and Distribution Patterns

The distribution patterns of amphorae produced at kiln sites in Cyrenaica can be used to establish the area's regional and inter-regional economic ties over time. Before addressing this matter, it is important to identify the fabrics and typologies of Cyrenaican transport containers, as well as their distribution patterns across the region. The distribution patterns of local amphorae are based on published material originating from systematic excavations and recent surveys.

Our knowledge on the Hellenistic and early Roman Cyrenaican fabrics is chiefly based on the two established descriptions of fabrics and vessel morphology from Berenice and Euesperides. The first study by J. Riley is on coarse pottery from Berenice (Riley 1979a), while the second is on amphorae from Euesperides, carried out by K. Göransson (2007). Both Euesperides and Berenice are located within the modern city of Benghazi. More invaluable information has been recently published by Mazou (2016) on fabric analyses of samples of local MR1 and MR8 amphora from different production centres and overseas sites.

Since this study exclusively deals with olive oil production, only a succinct account of these various types is given below with specific focus only on those which were probably used for oil transportation.

8.5 Types of Cyrenaican Amphorae

So far, thirteen Cyrenaican amphora types, plus an intermediate class, have been identified in the excavated assemblages from Euesperides, Berenice, Teucheira, Cape of Phycus, Aptouchou and Mahel Mael, Apollonia and Erythron. These Cyrenaican amphorae can be divided into three main groups generally dated from the fifth century BC to the end of the third century AD, while the only locally produced transport vessel from the late Roman period, is treated here separately. Group One was found at Euesperides (Table 8.2 and Figure 8.2) and consisted of five main coeval amphora types (Cyrenaican amphora types 1, 2, 3, 4 and B) with some variety in their forms, especially in the rim zone (Cyrenaican amphora 3-4). Out of these five classes, Cyrenaican Amphorae 1 and 2 morphologically correspond to the Hellenistic amphorae 1 and 2 from Berenice (cf. Riley 1979a, 119, D1–12 and 122, D13–15). Group Two (ER 12–14), dated to the early Roman period, was mainly identified in Berenice (Table 8.3 and Figure 8.3). The first two are ER12 and 13 amphorae assigned to the second half of the first century AD and seem to have imitated the Koan amphora. Meanwhile, ER14 amphora possessed a rather shorter neck and occurred at Berenice in the first and second centuries AD. It was also frequented at the third century AD Tocra kiln site. Group Three (Table 8.4 and Figure 8.4) is composed of four types dated to the mid-Roman period (MR1, 8, 9 and 10 amphorae). MR1 was a common product from the kilns found in the Cape of Phycus, Aptouchou, Mahel Mael and Erythron. This type of amphora has been recorded in many different sites across Cyrenaica, including

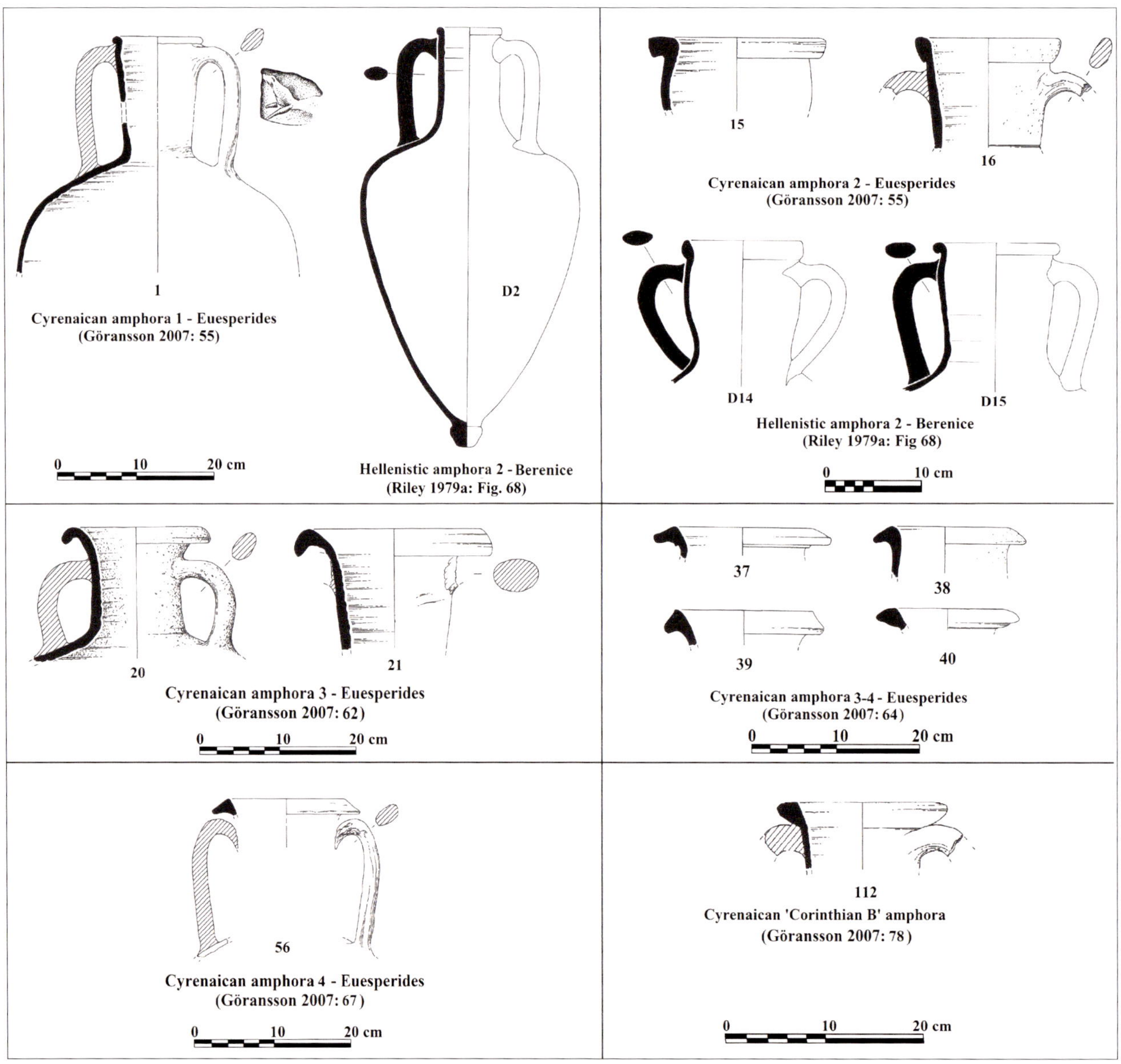

Figure 8.2: Selected local Hellenistic Cyrenaican amphorae from Euesperides and Berenice.

No.	Amphora Type	Notes
1	Cyrenaica Amphora 1 **Euesperides**	Fabric: CYR A, B & C (Göransson 2007: 51–54).
	Hellenistic Amphora 1 **Berenice**	Fabric: Benghazi 2 (Riley 1979a: 119–120).
2	Cyrenaica Amphora 2 **Euesperides**	Fabric: CYR A, B & C (Göransson 2007: 57–58).
	Hellenistic Amphora 2 **Berenice**	Fabric: Benghazi 1, 4 & 5 (Riley 1979a: 122).
3	Cyrenaica Amphora 3 **Euesperides**	Fabric: CYR A & B s (Göransson 2007: 60–62).
4	Cyrenaica Amphora 4 **Euesperides**	Fabric: CYR A–C (Göransson 2007: 65–71).
5	Cyrenaican B Amphora **Euesperides**	Fabric: CYR A, B & C (Göransson 2007: 75–78).

Table 8.2: Group One. Types and fabrics of local amphorae from Euesperides during the Hellenistic period with some types continued in Berenice to the early Roman period.

Berenice and Teucheira. Sherds of MR1 were also recorded at other sites during recent archaeological survey projects, including Ptolemais, Apollonia (Hesein 2015, fig. 5.17) and Qasr Aqeela, 8 km east of Qasr Beni Gdem (Emrage 2015: 157–8, fig. 6.1). It thus seems safe to assume that this type was just as important as MR8 amphora (see below) and was possibly exported outside the region. However, a lack of final publications on well-stratified and quantified pottery finds at sites impedes a full appreciation of the importance of this type, at both the regional and inter-regional levels. Meanwhile, the two remaining types, MR9 and 10, share roughly similar morphological characteristics with a vertical thickened and elongated rim, which in the latter can be thickened, rounded and much shorter, and have a concave outer face. They also possess a cylindrical neck which has a carination below the rim where the upper part of the handles is attached. The rough ovoid handles are attached from the carination and onto the shoulders.

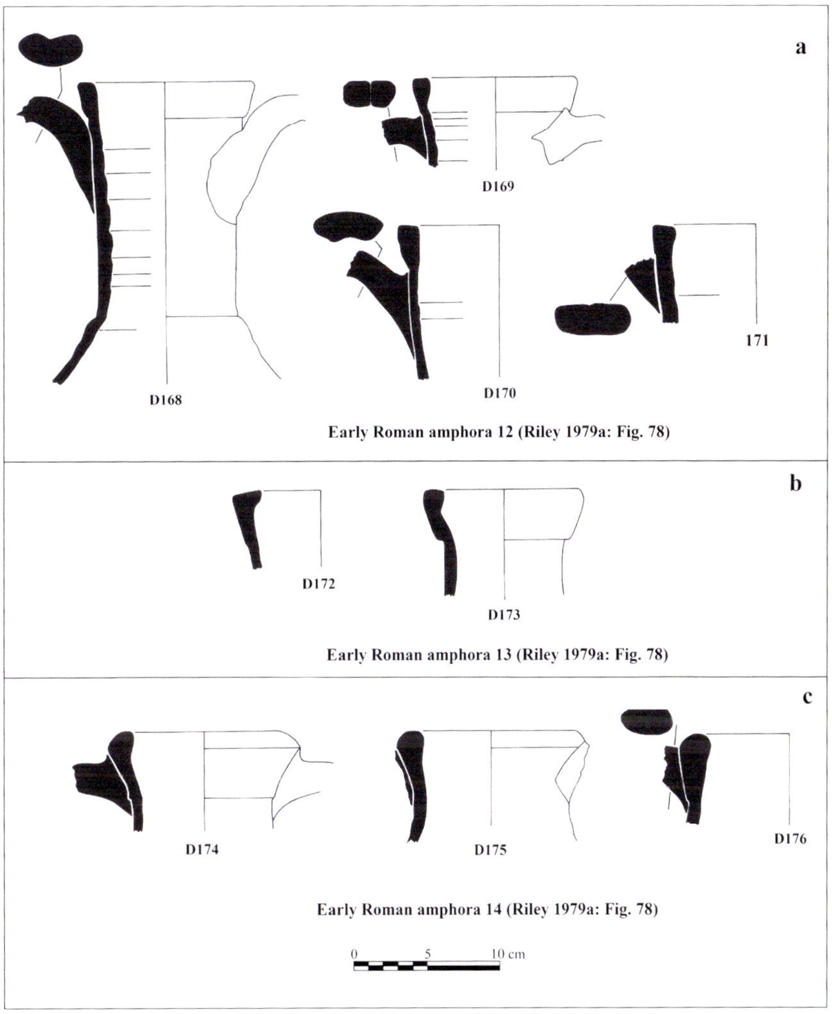

Figure 8.3: Early Roman Cyrenaican amphorae from Berenice.

No.	Amphora Type	Notes
1	Early Roman 12 amphora **Berenice**	Fabric: Orange to brown containing white and pale grey grits. Imitation of Koan amphora Riley 1979a: 168).
2	Early Roman 13 amphora **Berenice**	Fabric: ?
3	Early Roman 14 amphora **Berenice** A4 amphora **Teucheira**	Fabric: Benghazi 5. (Riley 1979a: 170–1; Riley 1979b: 56–57).

Table 8.3: Group Two. Types and fabrics of local amphorae from Berenice and Teucheira dated from first to third centuries AD.

Figure 8.4: Cyrenaican Mid-Roman amphorae 1, 8–10.

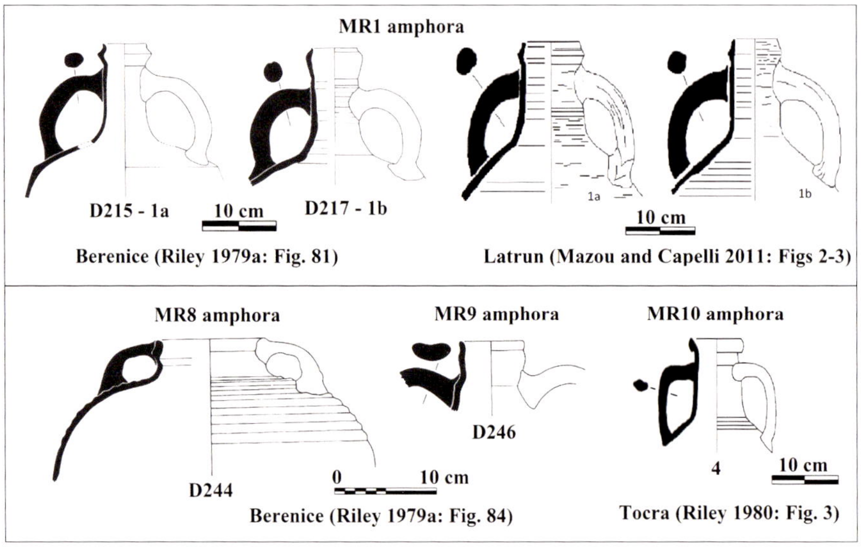

With the exception of MR8 amphora, the general shape of types in these three groups, which featured narrow mouths and long necks, seems to favour wine. Indeed, the Cyrenaican Amphorae 1 and 4 types are clearly modelled on Chian and Greco-Italic amphorae respectively, which were very widespread across the Mediterranean and used for wine transportation.

No.	Amphora Type	Notes
1	Mid Roman Amphora 1	(Hesein 2015: 172–178)
	Cape of Phycus, Aptouchou and Mahel Mael	
	Erythron	(Mazou and Capelli 2011; Mazou 2016)
2	Mid Roman Amphora 8	
	Berenice	Fabric: Benghazi 5 (Riley 1979a: 193)
	A1 amphora **Teucheira**	Fabric: Tocra 2 (Riley 1979b: 54; Mazou 2016)
	Cape of Phycus	Fabric: Apollonia fabric? (Hesein 2015: 180)
	Apollonia	Fabric: Apollonia fabric (Mazou 2016)
	Erythron	Fabric: Latrun fabric (Mazou and Capelli 2011; Mazou 2016)
3	Mid Roman Amphora 9	Fabric: Benghazi 5
	Berenice	(Riley 1979a: 194)
	Teucheira	(Riley 1979b: 54, 56)
4	Mid Roman Amphora 10	Fabric: Tocra 2
	Teucheira	(Riley 1979b: 54)

Table 8.4: Group Three. Types and fabrics of local Mid-Roman amphorae from different Cyrenaican sites.

8.5.1 Cyrenaica Mid Roman amphora 8

The main features of this amphora include its short vertical neck, thickened flanged rim and broad corrugated shoulder. The rim diameters of amphora from Tocra range from 0.11 to 0.12 m. Amphorae of this type were mostly produced in workshops in Berenice (local fabric 5), Teucheira (local fabric 2), the Cape of Phycus, Apollonia and Erthrun. They were mainly produced in the first half of the third century AD. They were the most common amphora at the Tocra kiln site, comprising 45% of the total amphora RBH (rim, bas and handle). Fewer were found at Berenice, where they made up only 3.6% of the total amphorae in the mid-third century AD (Riley 1979a: 193; 1980: 54). The discovery of new MR8 amphora production centres in other Cyrenaican sites suggests that this type was widely produced and may have been in use earlier than Riley proposed.

This is perhaps the only amphora type that can be attributed with some confidence to the production of olive oil. Wilson (2004: no. 15) suggested that the morphology of the neck might indicate that it had contained oil, while *garum* also remained a possibility. He supported his argument by pointing out that the production date of this amphora was broadly contemporary with a consignment of oil exported from Cyrenaica to Aquileia in north-east Italy recorded in the *Digest* (19.2.61.1) and find of the amphora in this region. This connection was previously refuted by Riley (1979a: 415) due to the obvious absence of the MR8 amphora before the second century AD when the consignment was exported. Given the short gap between the date of the consignment and the first occurrence of MR8 amphora, I would agree with Wilson's hypothesis.

The MR8 amphora type is increasingly being recognised in many sites around the Mediterranean (Figure 8.5), and the overall distribution seems to have been concentrated in the centre of the western part of the Mediterranean. The amphora is found in limited quantities in Rome, Ostia (Rizzo 2014: 292–93), and in various locations of northern Italy: Milan (Paniale1990: 380), Turin (Mazou 2016: 192), Brescia (Bruno 2002: 277–307, figs. 38 and 39), Angera near Lake Maggiore (Bruno 2002: 277–307), Trieste (Auriemma *et al.* 2012: 225–298), Aquileia, Oderzo, Concordia dia Sagittaria (Degrassi and Maggi 1991: 26–29) and Padua (Cipriano *et al.* 1997: 99–109, fig. 2–3). Farther west, this amphora type is reported from Saintes-Maries-de-la-Mer, in southern France (Long 2011: 116, fig. 27, 2). It is also known at Zaton near Zadar on Dalmatia's coast (Wilson *et al.* 2013), which is located on the sea route to Aquileia. This suggests that part of the cargo may have been unloaded here, or that Zadar might have imported oil for its own use. Only one example is found in North Africa at Lepcis Magna (Bonifay and Capelli 2013: 67–150, fig. 9, no. 25). Further evidence of the same amphora type is found in the Eastern Mediterranean: in Alexandria, at Kom el-Dikka site (Mazou 2016: 192) and Bouto, in the Nile Delta (Mazou 2016: 192) and in Crete at Knossos (Hayes 1983: 97–169). Nevertheless, these locations represent a tiny fraction of the whole Roman Empire and much more work needs to be done on materials from other sites across the Mediterranean.

8.5.2 Fabrics of MR8 amphora

Recently, L. Mazou (2016) carried out archaeometric (thin section) analyses under a microscope focussing on 13 samples of MR8 amphora. These samples came from Tocra, Apollonia, Latrun and Ptolemais. Examination also included samples of consumption sites outside Cyrenaica, from Ostia and Turin in Italy, and Saintes-Maries de la Mer in France. Descriptions of fabrics from these sites is given in some detail below and is solely based on Mazou's study.

The three samples from Tocra are similar to each other and can be distinguished from those of Apollonia by a more calcareous matrix and by clear abundant of quartz. The Glauconite and iron oxides are rare, while mica and flint are very occasional. Both tourmaline and amphibole are present. It is also noted that limonitic nodules and unmixed red clay are relatively common.

The Ptolemais sample is quite different from the others. The matrix is limestone. It has a hard and compact texture with angular limestone inclusions, which are partially disconnected. Some fragments of flint are noted. Fine inclusions are moderately abundant. Glauconite and mica are relatively common. Igneous and metamorphic rocks, such as, amphibole, epidote and rutile are rare.

The two samples of Apollonia are characterised by a rather fine and fairly compact matrix of orange-brown to orange-red and sometimes orange-yellow in colour. There are numerous fine white inclusions composed of crystals of calcite and microfossils. It is also noted that there is a presence of dark gray inclusions and rare red ferric nodules (Mazou 2016: 190). Microscopic examination shows a matrix rich in iron, while calcareous elements include rare radioles of echinoids and fragments of molluscs. There are also relatively abundant inclusions of silicates (<0.1 mm). Meanwhile, quartz is quite abundant, in addition to rare mica and occasional epidote and zircon. Iron oxides are also noted, though rather scarce and small (Mazou 2016: 194). MR8 samples from the kilns at the Cape of Phycus were not available when Mazou conducted his study. However, the proximity of this production centre to Apollonia and their location in the same local geology, suggesting that both fabrics are closely related to each other.

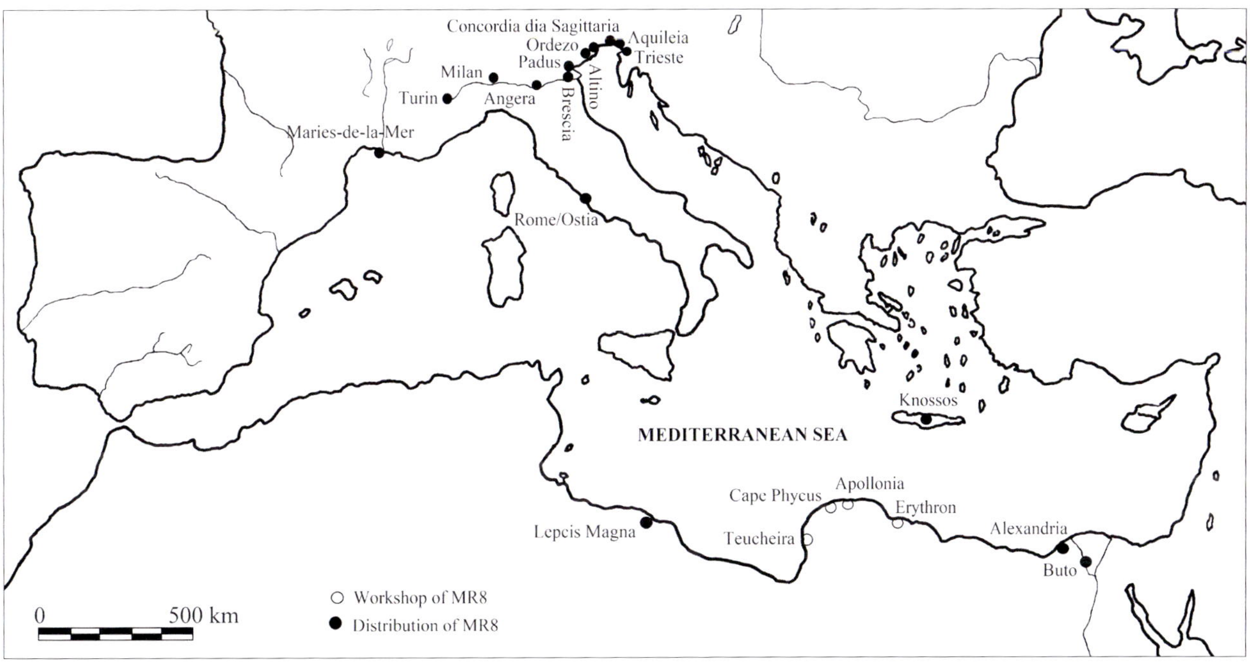

Figure 8.5: Workshop and distribution map of MR8 Amphora and its kiln sites.

The three MR8 samples from Latrun matched MR1 amphora samples and other categories found in the other workshop sites[1] (Mazou and Capelli 2011). Therefore, for an assemblage comprising only body sherds, it is difficult to determine the exact type of an amphora. These fabrics are characterised by relatively low inclusions. Quartz is frequent and mica is generally absent or rare, while glauconite and clay nodules, rich in iron, occur regularly (Mazou 2016: 195).

The two samples from Ostia are not too similar as one shows a partially calcareous matrix and relatively scarce inclusions, among which rare fragments of flint. It is only partly comparable to the fabrics of Apollonia or Latrun. The other sample is quite isolated. It has a matrix rich in iron, semi-vitrified and partially oxidized towards the margins. Fine inclusions of silicates are abundant, while limestone fragments (and flint) are rare. The Turin sample is similar to the Apollonia fabric, but it is distinguished by slightly better sized inclusions (bimodal distribution) and by the presence of some fragments of flint. The sample of Saintes Maries de la Mer, is very different, characterized by many fine inclusions of quartz. It is possibly related to the production of Tocra. Mazou (2016: 195) observed that the samples from sites in Italy and France were variable fabrics that cannot be matched to the Cyrenaican productions just described.

In general, the analyses demonstrated that all the studied samples of MR8 amphora, found in the different sites of Cyrenaica, form a relatively homogeneous group, characterised by inclusions mainly composed of calcareous elements of dimensions up to 0.5mm (rounded or rarely angular fragments of biomicrites and biosparites, planktonic and benthonic foraminifera, bioclasts, calcite individuals), and quartz individuals <0.1mm in size (Mazou 2016: 194). The calcareous elements (visible to the naked eye in the form of small white dots) are often not very dissociated, which indicates firing temperatures lower than 900°C. The matrix is quite rich in iron, with a limestone component more or less abundant. It is in most cases well oxidised throughout the cross section (the macroscopic color varies from red, to a more rarely seen yellow-orange).

Finally, the late Roman local LR9 amphora type from Berenice is the only transport vessel which could be dated to this period. No complete profile of this type has been found. The rim is vertical or slightly flared (Riley 1979a: 228). The ubiquitous evidence of oil and wine presses, which probably date to the late Roman period, is in striking contrast with the obvious dearth of local late Roman amphora production.

8.6 Stamped Handles

Finds of stamped Cyrenaican amphorae are uncommon. Six stamped handles were recorded during excavations at Euesperides. They were all faint, but three of them bore Greek letters (ΣΙ, Φ, ΣΛ), and one was stamped with a figural stamp that may have represented a donkey's head (Göransson 2007: 54, 66). It is not known to which type of amphora these handles belong, but it is generally believed they were attached to vessels used to transport wine. The same rarity of locally stamped amphorae was noted at Berenice, where only seven stamps were found on the Hellenistic amphora 1 which was thought to be the descendent of the Cyrenaican amphora 1 from Euesperides. This type probably contained silphium juice (at least before the second century BC), but it has also been suggested that it could equally have contained oil, wine or dates (Riley 1979a: 120). The stamps from Berenice (Table 8.5) seem to represent Greek names, although it is unclear whether they represent the owners of the production site or the manufacturers. Five stamps on handles of possibly local Hellenistic amphora 1 were found in Alexandria, suggesting that there was some sort of contact between the two regions. The scale of this trade, and the kind of goods imported, is still unknown due to the lack of quantifiable studies of stratified Hellenistic amphorae from Alexandria (Riley 1979a: 408-9).

A scarcity of stamps has also been noted on Tripolitanian amphorae where they were present on only about 1% of the total produced amphorae (Ahmed 2019: 150). Tripolitanian stamps often depicted what may have been initials (*tria nomina*), although some of them seem to refer to imperial estates. Other stamps, ending with the letters 'CV' (*clarissimus vir* = a man of senatorial rank), are thought to be related to amphorae

No.	Stamp	Amp. no.
1	φΙΛΩΝΟΣ	D5
2	ΦΙΛΩΝΟΣ	D6
3	ΦΙΛΙΣΚΟ	D7
4	ΦΙΛΙΣ (ΚΟΥ)	D8
5	ΡΑΔΑΝΟΥ	D9
6	Π enclosing O	D10
7	ΚΑΡИΗ[ΑΣ	D12

Table 8.5: List of local amphora stamps from Berenice *(Riley 1979a: 120–1, pls. XXII).*

[1] It is worth mentioning that Cyrenaica MR1 amphora is an imitation of a type found in different Mediterranean regions. Tripolitania and Byzacena have been put forward as possible source areas for the MR1 amphora on account of its frequency there (Panella 1974: 471). The discovery of a number of workshops in Sicily led some to believe that south Italy was a major producer of the MR1 amphora (Freed and Wilson 1999: 268; Wilson 2000: 361-3). The fabric is typical of the sedimentary geology of Cyrenaica and can be distinguished from the volcanic-rich inclusions of Sicilian clay texture and the metamorphic elements in the Tunisia fabric (Capelli and Bonifay 2007).

stamped on behalf of the leading Lepcitanian families. This suggests that the elites organised the production of olive oil and the supply (and the production) of amphora for their own, and possibly other, estates (Ahmed 2019: 150-151).

8.7 Types of Imported Amphorae

8.7.1 Imported amphorae in Euesperides and Berenice

This section examines the imported amphorae to Cyrenaica, which is characterised by a widespread distribution of different types of imported amphorae. Information is very limited and only represented from two sites: Euesperides, from the Greek period (Göransson 2007), and its successor, Berenice, from the Hellenistic period down to the Byzantine time (Riley 1979a). Although imported amphorae types identified in these two sites are varied and contained different substances, the discussion here is confined only to those thought to have been used for transporting olive oil. The interpretation, expressed below, should be viewed as a working hypothesis that is, inevitably, dependent on a slender body of evidence awaiting further data.

The pottery finds from excavations at Euesperides (1996–2006) mainly cover the period from the fifth century BC until its abandonment during the middle of the third century BC. In general, local or regional amphorae make up approximately a third of the quantified assemblage (34%, 161 out of 480), while imported amphorae comprise 66% (319 out of 480) of the total RBH amphorae in the fully quantified contexts (Figure 8.6). About 72% of them were of Greek origin, while the remaining 5% came from the Punic world.

Corinthian A was the first amphora type generally believed to have transported olive oil (Göransson 2007: 82–9). This type was very rare at Euesperides and mainly belonged to the fourth century BC. The four class of Aegean amphorae (Chian 'West Aegean', Samian 'East Aegean, Koan and Rhodian 'South Aegean) represent the second imported amphora type present at Euesperides, where they make up 10% of the total amphora RBH (49 out of 481). Samian amphora is occasionally stamped, and olive oil is generally supposed to have been the main contents, but it has been suggested that this form also carried wine from Samos (Göransson 2007: 150). It was produced from the sixth century through to the first century BC, and possibly continued well into the third century AD. This type was infrequently stamped, occurring in Euesperides between the mid-fourth to mid-third centuries BC (Göransson 2007: 149–50). While the amphora was absent from the Berenice excavations, the Salmani tombs in the vicinity yielded only one complete example, and another which was found farther east, off the coast of Apollonia. A few imported amphora sherds in this class characterised by mushroom-shaped rims were generally believed to come from different South Aegean sites, including Kos (Göransson 2007: 163). Solokha 1 is the name given to an amphora which belongs to this group that was found near Nikopol in eastern Ukraine, but its fabric is typical of those classified as 'Southern Aegean amphorae' with their distinctive mushroom-shaped rims. Finally, there is a small group of amphorae primarily categorised as being of South Aegean origin, on the basis of their fabrics, but which, in the meantime, cannot be assigned to a specific type typical of that region (Göransson 2007: 165).

The third amphora type found in Euesperides was the magnificent Cypriot basket-handled amphora (65 to 80 litres), which was rare (2 out of 481) and occurred

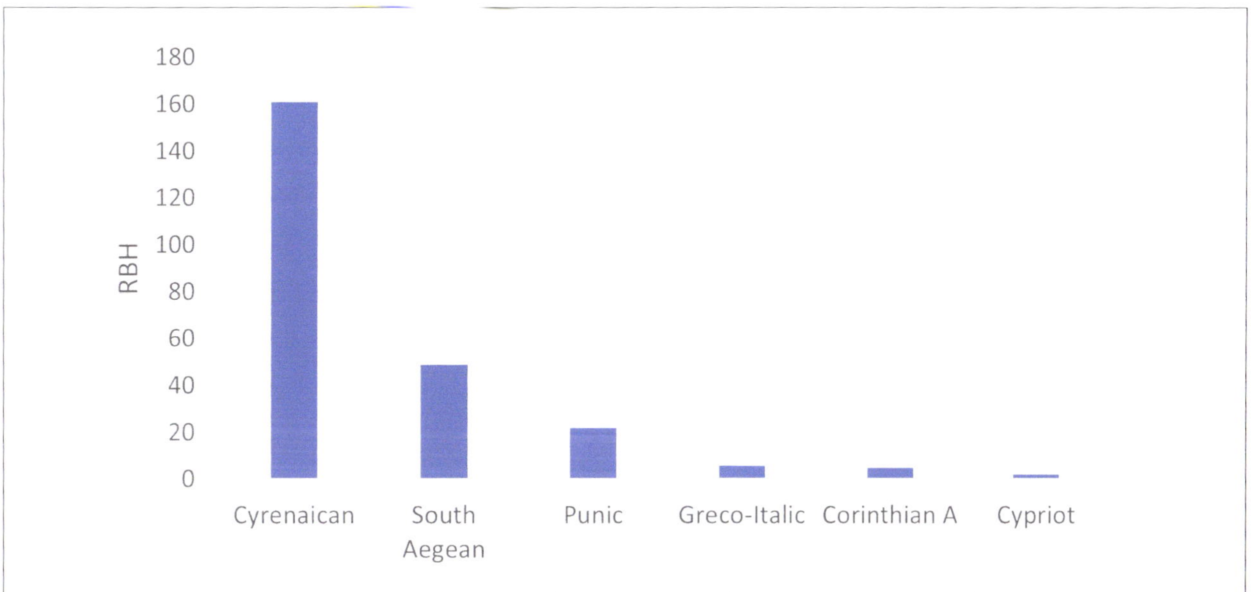

Figure 8.6: Relative proportions of RBH of Cyrenaican and imported amphorae in the fully quantified contexts at Euesperides *(author's graph, data from Göransson 2007).*

in the first half of the third century BC. Gjerstad (1960 cited in Göransson 2007: 170) tentatively suggested that this type was of Cypriot origin, mainly based on the frequency of its occurrence. In addition, he pointed out that the same amphora was also found in Rhodes, Egypt and the Levant. This type is usually thought to have contained olive oil, but it could also have contained wine or other commodities, as well (Leidwanger 2007: 29).

Finally, there is also a small quantity of Punic amphorae represented by nine types found at both Euesperides and Berenice. These were imported from North Africa, western Sicily and even the Straits of Gibraltar (Göransson 2007: 220). Several types indeed share comparable characteristics, such as the open mouth and the short or sometimes absent neck and handles attached onto an almost perfectly cylindrical body (Bonifay 2007: 144; Göransson 2007: 175). It is generally believed that the wide mouth is suitable for filling and emptying viscous liquids like *garum* and salted fish, although olive oil (Bonifay 2007: 143) and wine (Wilson 2003: 147) must also have been transported in different types.

Some of the imported Hellenistic amphorae which flowed into Euesperides seem to have continued flowing into Berenice, its successor city. In the Hellenistic period (Figure 8.7), imported amphorae only account for a very small part of the overall demand (12% – 19 out of 164). North African amphorae, which were probably used for oil, were very rare and made up only 5% (only one sherd out of 19) of the total imports. This trend seems to have continued in the wake of early Roman control of Cyrenaica (in the late first century BC), except that a few North African amphora-born products started to appear among the other amphorae imported into Berenice.

During the Hellenistic period, up to the early-to-mid first century AD, Berenice seems to follow the traditions of its predecessor city, Euesperides, by producing Berenice Hellenistic amphorae 1 and 2. These were the forerunner types of Cyrenaican Amphorae 1 and 2. The former was most common in the Hellenistic and Augustan periods (comprising 58% of all identifiable RBH amphorae – 67 out of 115), but became rare in the mid-to-late part of the first century AD. Fulford (1989: 175) proposed that the morphology of Berenice Hellenistic local amphora, and indeed their prototypes from Euesperides (which were not available when Fulford prepared his study), suggested that they were used as containers for liquids, probably wine. However, he doubted they would have been exported in large quantities.

It is likely that wine was carried in most of the imported amphorae in this period. This is not to contradict what has already been suggested regarding the morphology of Cyrenaican amphorae, which also seems to favour wine. It is not clear whether this was due to shortages in the local supply or for reasons of quality. These local amphorae could, however, have also been used to transport olive oil.

The second half of the first and early second centuries AD saw a marked increase in imports, which comprised about 76% (338 out of 446 sherds) of the total amphorae imported into Berenice (Figure 8.8a). East Mediterranean amphorae comprised 62% of the total identifiable RBH imported amphora (210 out of 338), and Cretan amphora (MR2 Amphora), which was associated commonly with wine, dominated with 51% (107 out 210). Meanwhile, west Mediterranean amphorae comprised a relatively high proportion of the imports (Figure 8.8b) and made up 38% of the imported amphorae (128 out of 338). Although Dressel 20 generally originated with major oil producers, *garum* was probably the prime contents, while wine has also been suggested as a secondary commodity (Riley 1979a: 413). However, there is a high possibility that these Spanish amphorae, found at Berenice, carried *garum* (Riley 1979a: 159). Dressel 5 (ER Amphora 5) from Istria, at the head of the Adriatic Sea, was also present at Berenice. It was not particularly common, comprising just 5% of the total RBH amphora in this period. Oil was probably the main content, but the amphora may also have contained wine, *mulsum* (spiced honey wine) and *garum* (Riley 1979a: 153).

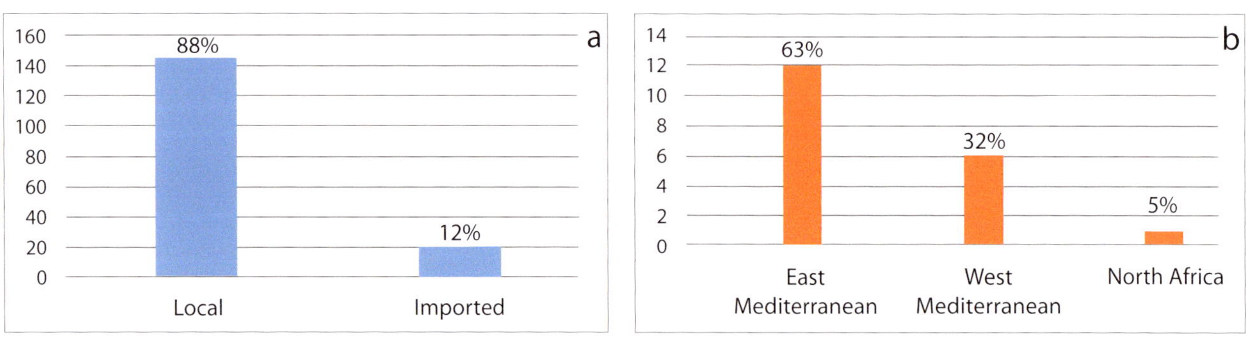

Figure 8.7: The relative proportion of the collected amphora sherds found in Berenice. Graph (a) presents the total amphora sherds in the Hellenistic period, (b) the total imported amphora sherds from the same period *(author's graph, data from Riley 1979).*

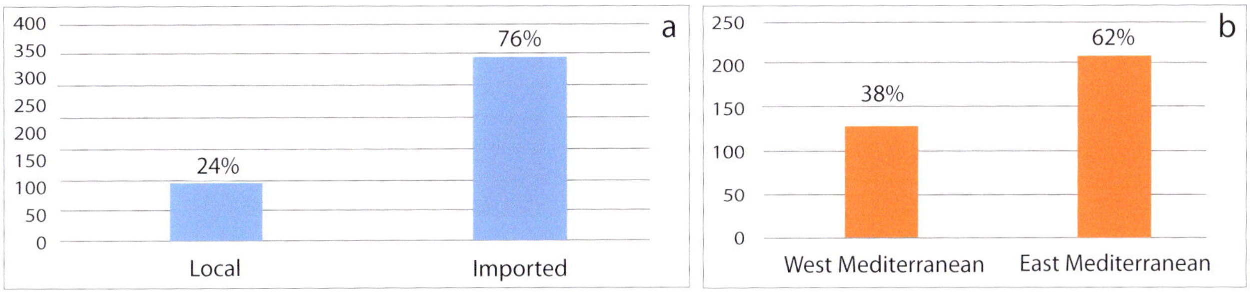

Figure 8.8: The relative proportion of the collected amphorae from Berenice in the second half of the first and early second century AD. Graph (a) presents imported and local amphorae of the total collected sherds, (b) sources of the identifiable RBH imported amphorae to Berenice in the same period *(author's graph, data from Riley 1979).*

The three amphora types, which were manufactured locally in the first century AD (ER Amphora 12, 13 and 14), were uncommon (Riley 1979a: 114), comprising only 4% of total RBH amphora found in the first century AD deposits (24 out of 629).

During the second century AD the pendulum seems to have swung a considerable distance towards eastern Mediterranean markets (Figure 8.9), as their amphorae comprised about 82% of the total identifiable amphorae imported into Berenice (196 out of 238). Imports from North Africa comprised 8% (18 out of 238), showing the same trend as the preceding period.

The amphora assemblage from the third century AD Berenice (Figure 8.10) clearly shows a distinct preference for eastern Mediterranean products over all other imports (86% – 462 out of 536). Western Mediterranean material, mainly North African, was minimal in this period and represented only 74 containers

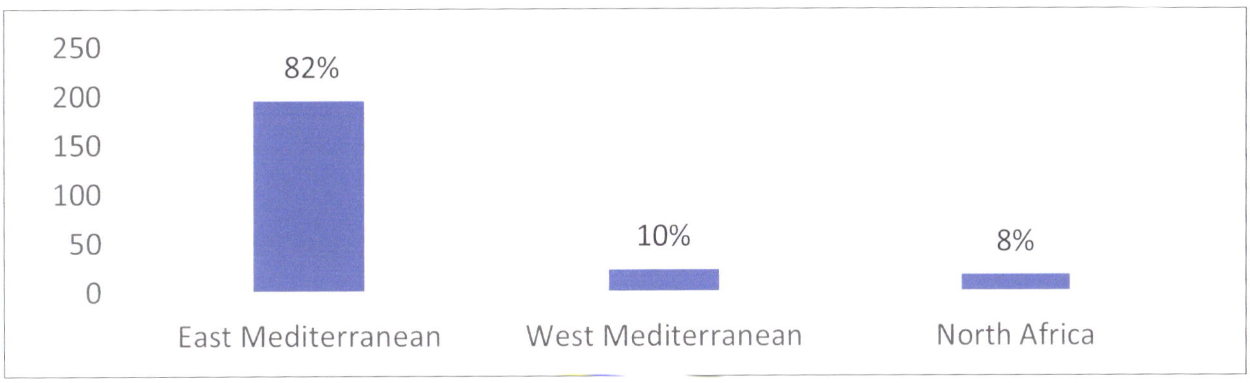

Figure 8.9: The relative proportion of the collected imported amphorae from Berenice in the second century AD *(author's graph, data from Riley 1979).*

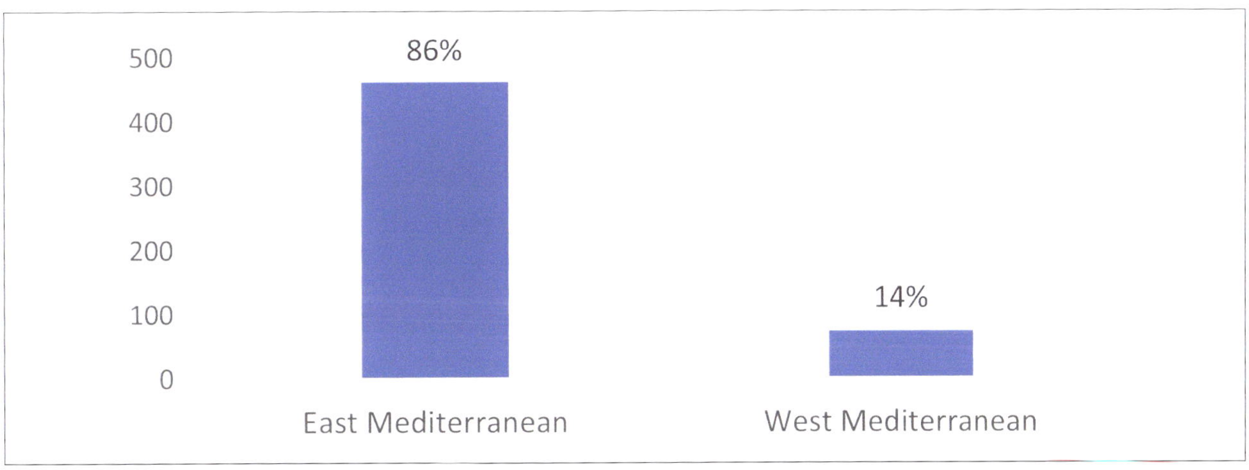

Figure 8.10: The relative proportion of the collected imported amphorae from Berenice in the third century AD *(author's graph, data from Riley 1979).*

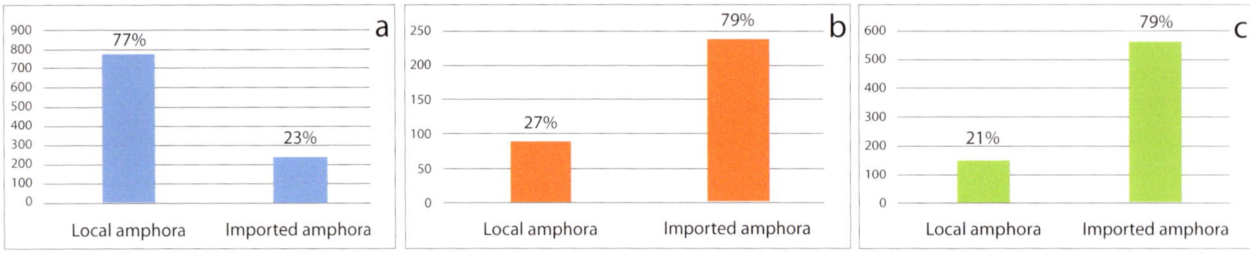

Figure 8.11: The relative proportion of the collected amphora sherds found in Berenice. Graph (a) presents the total amphora sherds in the early second to the end of the third centuries AD, (b) the identifiable amphora RBH in the second century AD, (c) the total amphora sherds in the third century AD *(author's graph, data from Riley 1979).*

(14% – 74 out of 536). 13 were of Africano Grandi Amphora (MR Amphora 16) from the Sahel region of Tunisia, 10 were of Tripolitanian origin and 4 came from Ostia LX. It is at this time (i.e. in the mid-third century AD) that North Africa became the dominant supplier of olive oil to Rome, and to many other important markets in the western Mediterranean region (Williams and Carreras 1995: 234).

Evidence of amphora production centres in Cyrenaica during the mid-Roman period (from the early second to the end of the third centuries AD) remains significant (Figure 8.11). As evidenced by artefactual finds and archaeological remains, Cyrenaica had the resources needed to make its own amphora (MR1 and 8). However, the trickle of imported containers into Berenice continued during this period, making up around 23% of all identifiable amphorae sherds (234 out of 1008). In the meantime, local amphorae from Berenice comprised a relatively low 27% (89 out of 327) of identifiable RBH amphorae fragments, found in the second century AD, and made up 21% of the following century's assemblage (145 out of 681 '536 + 145') of the total amphora sherds belonging to this period.

The last chronological grouping of imported amphorae found in Berenice spans the period of the fourth to the mid-seventh centuries AD (Figure 8.12). The Aegean/north-east Mediterranean area accounts for 94% of the total identifiable imported amphorae (405 out of 429). Tabulated results of Late Roman amphora finds from Berenice indicated that LR1 and LR2 were the most popular amphorae on the site. Both olive oil and wine have been suggested as the prime products in both vessels (Karagiorgou 2001: 146), while Opaiţ (2004) suggests that LR2 most probably carried olive-oil. LR1 amphora was produced in the Roman provinces of Cilicia and Cyprus and it accounts for over 71% (289 out of 405) of the total Late Roman amphorae from Berenice. It also occurs in most coastal sites from Boreum (modern Marsa-el-Brega) in the west to the Gulf of Bomba in the east, as well as inland with spot-finds that include Ajdabiya Qasr el Atallat (Riley 1979a: 213, fig. 42) and Lamluda (Menozzi *et al.* 2014 75). Aegean LR2 was the second most common amphora in Berenice (8% – 32 out of 405). This type was quite possibly manufactured in a number of production centres throughout Chios and Cnidos (Opaiţ 2004) and at Kounoupi in the Argolid (Munn 1985). North African amphorae (LR8a and b) was represented in very low quantities (1% – 6 out of 429), and oil would seem to have been the likely contents of this amphora (Riley 1979a: 228).

The recent recovery of LR1 amphora at the site of Lamluda led Menozzi to suggest that the presence of

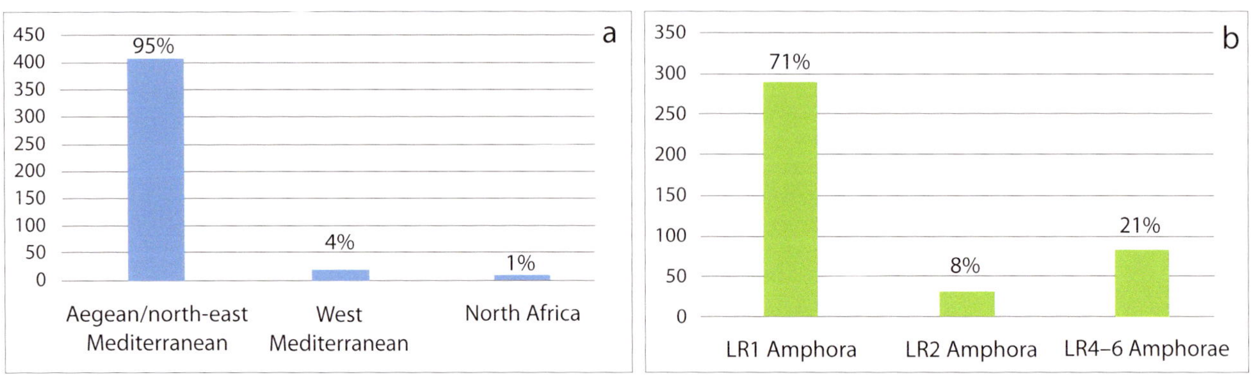

Figure 8.12: (a) The relative proportion of the total collected amphora sherds found in Berenice from fourth to mid-seventh centuries AD, (b) The total Aegean and East Mediterranean amphora sherds from the same periods *(author's graph, data from Riley 1979).*

this type of amphora may be connected with the *milita annona* supply to the military garrisons based in Cyrenaica (Menozzi *et al.* 2014 75–6). This is based on the strategic position of the site at a crossroads and along the Roman *limes*. This hypothesis is in line with Wilson (2001: 39) who is sceptical about the role of Late Roman Cyrenaica in Mediterranean trade. He assumes that exchange patterns involved mainly one-way traffic trade, heavily reliant on imports, and that some of the imported items may have arrived as provisions for military garrisons. I would first argue here that the layout of Lamluda, as in the Roman period, was predominantly occupied by pressing facilities, apart from a small, fortified *qasr*. Any kind of military activity within the site would thus have been impossible unless this took place in the surrounding area. Secondly, the contents of LR1 amphorae could have been either imported directly to the local markets or exchanged between the locals and mobilised soldiers (Karagiorgou 2001: 153; Poulter 1999: 43). Since the LR1 amphora occurred concurrently with the Cypriot and Late Roman C/Phocaean Red Slip Ware in all Cyrenaican sites, it is reasonable to assume that these finewares were conveyed as an additional complement to the main cargoes carried onboard ships. If that is so, this more likely alludes to systematic private trade with no military implications.

8.8 Maritime Routes

Analysing the sources of the traded amphorae found at Euesperides and Berenice provided useful information about the maritime routes that connected Cyrenaica to the eastern and western Mediterranean. It has been suggested that Campanian wine may not have been exported directly to Cyrenaica from Campania (Fulford 1987). The same pattern is also suggested by Fulford regarding the Rhodian wine imported into Cyrenaica (1989: 173). A shipwreck dating back to the mid-first century BC was discovered just off the coast of Alexandria. It was loaded with hundreds of amphorae from southern Italy, as well as some Cretan and Rhodian amphorae (Clement 1999). The ship seems to have first sailed from Italy to Crete, after which it continued to Rhodes and was finally destined for Alexandria (Göransson 2007: 214). On the contrary, epigraphic evidence (Fraser 1951; Reynolds 1968; Wilson 2013) complemented by results obtained from archaeological excavations at Euesperides (Göransson 2007) suggest that this was not so. Since Greco-Italic amphorae were also produced in different regions, wine from Campania may have first been brought to Sicily and southern Italy, and then redistributed to Cyrenaica (Göransson 2007: 117; see also Hesein 2015: 334). Despite the absence of any Greco-Italic amphorae with an Italian or Sicilian origin in Apollonia, South Aegean Knidian and Koan wine amphorae are reported to be common there. They may have reached the region via Crete and the nearby port of Phycus (Göoransson 2007: 227-8, 232). This seems to support Fulford (1987), who suggested that Italian products reached Cyrenaica via the Aegean route but not directly from Sicily.

Based on the very large number of B amphorae at Euesperides, Göransson (2007: 223–4) suggests sailing directly from Corcyra in the north-west coast in the Ionian Sea. In the meantime, he also does not rule out the possibility that during the Hellenistic period there were entrepôts in the trade with Cyrenaica via the port of Alexandria and Syracuse and Gela in Sicily. A general assessment of the sources of the imported fineware pottery and amphora from Euesperides and Berenice led Lloyd (1968: 64) to suggest that products of the Black Sea region and many other remote areas were brought via Naucratis/Alexandria. However, the complete absence of Egyptian amphorae at Euesperides during the Ptolemaic period (Göransson 2007: 229) seems to refute this view due to the difficulty of sailing between the two destinations (Fulford 1989: 171).

Moreover, the amphora assemblage found by the French excavations at Apollonia suggests that Crete may have been an important centre of transhipping for eastern Cyrenaica given the proximity between the two regions. Unfortunately, the amphorae recovered from Apollonia are not yet published. This means no safe conclusions can be drawn about the types and frequency of amphorae from this site. Cretan amphorae were absent in Euesperides (Göransson 2007: 227). Meanwhile Attic Black-glazed wares were abundant, and were likely traded goods shipped along with the Aegean amphorae that entered primarily via the port of Attica, Piraeus, but not Crete. Although Crete formed a united region with Cyrenaica in 74 BC, it seems that no significant commercial contact took place until the late first century AD (Riley 1979a: 411).

In addition to multiple wind directions, there was the factor of the movement of currents in the sea that had, to a lesser degree, influenced cross-Mediterranean ancient trade (Smith and le Roux 2013: 230). The anti-clockwise current is the most prevalent current in the Mediterranean basin. This current flows eastwards from the Atlantic into the Mediterranean. Once there, it passes through the Straits of Gibraltar, heading south along the coast-line of North Africa, and then turns northwards along the coast of the Levant and Turkey, to meet with the Black Sea current. From there it flows towards the Greek and Italian coasts, heading South to Spain and finally ending up at Gibraltar (Aubet 156–7).

8.9 Discussion

Archaeological evidence from Euesperides and Berenice, in the form of amphora finds from the Classical, Hellenistic, Roman and late Roman periods, indicates that Cyrenaica relied on the West and the Aegean at least partially to supply some of its olive oil and wine consumption needs. Amphora and other ceramic finds show a wide range of long-distance trading contacts with both the Greek Aegean and the Punic world.

The archaeological material from Euesperides represents a short period of time spanning from the fifth to the mid-third centuries BC and provides only a brief idea about patterns of trade. However, these analyses indicate that the bulk of imports came from the eastern Mediterranean, particularly the Aegean world. The amphorae from this part of the Mediterranean would have been imported from areas famous for olive oil such as Corinth, although in comparatively low quantities (Wilson 2006: 147). Wine was apparently the most in-demand product and it is not easy to tell whether this was due to a shortage in the local supply, reasons of quality or taste. It should be noted, however, that there was a clear increase in the importation of oil between the second and third centuries AD (Hesein 2015: 304–6). This is in striking contrast with the Cyrenaican olive oil consignment exported to Aquileia sometime in the second century AD (*Digest* 19.2.61.1). However, while this implies that olive oil was locally manufactured and found its way to the overseas market, it can only be taken as a casual case and it makes little sense for large scale export. At the same time, there were other products of western Mediterranean origins, including Punic amphorae. These were mainly from Tunisia, western Sicily and possibly the Iberian Peninsula.

Unfortunately, the amphora-based study of economic trends in Cyrenaica is limited to Euesperides and Berenice. There is an obvious void created by the absence of comparable quantitative studies from Teucheira, Ptolemais Cyrene and its port, Apollonia. The latter was the most important regional port city until the end of the third century AD, when Ptolemais superseded it to become the metropolis of Libya Superior until the end of the fifth century. Apollonia then took the lead again as the capital of the region until the arrival of the Arab armies in the mid-seventh century AD.

Evidence of western Mediterranean amphorae in Late Roman Cyrenaica is minimal. This is in contrast to the fineware vessels which were particularly abundant. African Red Slip wares from Berenice made up the majority of the total imported finewares at around 73% (1182 out of 1629 sherds), while quantities of Tripolitanian Red Slip wares were generally low with 8% of the total imports (125 out of 1629 sherds) (Kenrick 1985: 255). The limited number of western Mediterranean amphorae in Cyrenaica indicates that imports from these areas were insignificant. By contrast, east-west trade was strong. Evidence of eastern amphorae is common in Carthage, where LR1 amphora comprises 8% of the total amphorae RBH, while LR2 has also been noted (Riley 1979a 213, 217).

The low frequency of imported oil amphora in the late Roman period and, indeed, in most preceding periods, in contrast to the high frequency of wine transporting vessels, suggests that this commodity was not required in Cyrenaica due to the local production of a similar product. The number of recorded olive oil presses which likely belonged to this period strongly suggests that oil was produced on a fairly large scale. Nonetheless, since olive harvests normally varied substantially biennially it is expected that oil may have been imported to compensate the local shortage in lean years.

As evidenced from the preceding periods, local clay was suitable for manufacturing amphorae and many local types were produced, albeit not on a wide scale. Unfortunately, no local transportation of amphorae for either oil or wine has yet been categorically identified in late Roman Cyrenaica. It should be emphasised, however, that a lack of local amphora in this period can be explained by the complete absence of systematic field surveys. Unlike fine pottery and certain forms of coarse ware, amphorae tended to evolve at a slow pace. Therefore, their forms generally have a long life and slow evolutions (Callender 1965). For instance some forms of the local Mid-Roman amphorae, such as MR8 amphora, persisted during the late Roman period without observable change. It is therefore possible that many of these vessels, as found in later contexts and regarded as residual or fortuitous, could ultimately prove to be contemporaneous.

On the other hand, there has been a glaring bias towards urban archaeology and a neglect of rural sites. Furthermore, the situation is made worse by the deliberate obliteration of the uppermost layers in most urban excavations in order to reach down to the more attractive and splendid classical architectural monuments (Wilson 2001a: 28). Without firm ceramic evidence we must look for other reasons to explain the lack of late Roman local amphorae. It could be that animal skins were used as an alternative. The transportation of liquids, such as olive oil and wine, in animal skins, from production sites which were often located in the hinterland, and then on to the ports, was probably common practice (Marlière and Costa 2007). *Ostraca* dated to the fourth century AD, found in the Circular Harbour of Carthage (Peña 1998) record the arrival of a consignment of olive oil in skins at the port. The skins are unsuitable for long-distance maritime transport or long-term storage (Peña 1998: 216) so were probably transferred to amphorae. Animal skins filled with oil and wine can be unloaded quickly and easily. Moreover, they are flexible and cart capacity would be greater than if loaded with amphorae (see Brun 2003b, 100-1). The use of skins is affected by the availability of livestock in the region, and Cyrenaica is renowned in this respect (Herod. IV, 155; Hom. *Od.*, IV, 85-9; Pind., IX *Pyth.*, 6). Unfortunately, such perishable materials are rarely preserved in archaeological contexts, and leave scarce evidence of their use. It is worth mentioning that hides were among the products exported by Cyrenaica (Applebaum 1979: 129). Interestingly, the large number of terracotta figurines found on the slope of the acropolis at Cyrene represent standing female figures wearing typically 'Libyan' stiff cloaks, perhaps made of animal skins (Fabbricotti 1993: 30, fig. 11; Bacchielli and Uhlenbrock 2000). If olive-oil and/or wine were exclusively transported in skins, we would then be sceptical about export of Cyrenaican olive oil at the Late Roman period. It was more likely being mainly consumed within Cyrenaica, where local and regional transportation in skins was sufficient. If it was not destined for overseas markets, there was no need for amphorae for maritime transport.

In the meantime, imported amphora could have been reused for transportation and storage. A second-century shipwreck discovered off the coast of Grado in Italy was loaded with some 600 amphorae, African types for olive oil, which had been reused to transport salted fish (Auriemma 2000). Another example comes from Tomis, on the west coast of the Black Sea, where more than a hundred LR2 amphorae have been found in a storeroom. Chemical analysis has proven that they contained viscous commodities and painted marks were interpreted as evidence that they had been reused a number of times in short and long-distance commerce (Karagiorgou 2009). In Cyrenaica, LR1 amphorae were found in association with the vats discovered at Berenice. This type was probably reused again for transportation (Lloyd 1977: 148), at least on the intra-regional level.

Wooden barrels, which were mainly used for wine, could be another possibility, although these were more suited to northern Europe where timber is available in abundance.

8.10 Conclusion

The new evidence of amphora kiln sites, especially those recently found in the area between Apollonia and Phycus, has greatly increased our knowledge of the previously known local amphora production. It is significant that the discovered kiln sites in Cyrenaica that produced amphorae for oil and wine, were all located on the coast near the main port towns. Meanwhile, olive oil producing sites were found much farther inland. The kilns were mostly attached to sites which were not characterised by high levels of olive-oil production capacities.

There still is a general lack of much-needed research on the classification of local Cyrenaican amphorae types and fabric analysis. We need to distinguish imported from local types. Until ceramic analysis and quantification, of large amphora assemblages recovered from the excavations, have been carried out in urban centres and rural sites alike, such issues will remain obscure.

Surplus oil was available in the markets of Roman Cyrenaica, forming an important and lucrative source of income for many farmers. With reference to Synesius' account (letter 148) that Cyrenaican olive oil was not outstanding in quality, it may have been exported primarily as lamp oil. The number of sites with multiple presses, particularly in Lamluda, is indicative of the large-scale production in olive-oil destined for local market consumption. However, the scale of surplus production, in most cases, was most likely small, and trade in oil was mainly intra-regional.

chapter nine

CONCLUSION

Rural sites in Cyrenaica have often been overlooked in favour of urban ones. However, these rural sites, large and small, were pivotal in the economic and sociocultural life of Cyrenaica. This survey focused on the discovery and investigation of rural sites with particular attention to the evidence from those connected to olive oil production. It is now possible to place these field survey results on olive oil production in Cyrenaica within the broader context of the Roman economy.

9.1 Types and Characteristics of Cyrenaican Pressing Elements

The evidence gathered in this study has allowed for the establishment of a new, detailed typology for mill mortars and millstones, uprights, press beds and counterweights (Chapters 3 and 4). All of those pressing elements have been classified and illustrated by examining, measuring, and by estimation of weight.

Cyrenaican pressing equipment had distinctive characteristics (Chapter 5) when compared to those found elsewhere in North Africa. Although both regions exhibited the lever and windlass type of press, Cyrenaican examples appear to have been smaller and with lower scale production. The press structures found in Tripolitania and the central Tunisian steppe were larger, with a different way of supporting the lever/beam. The pair of orthostats (*arbores*) known in Tripolitania and Tunisia (Mattingly and Hitchner 1993: 446–51), and in Northern Palestine (Frankel *et al.* 1994: 42–3), where the fixed end of the beam was held, are not found in Cyrenaica. Instead, there are three main methods by which the head of the beam was pinned: in a niche cut into the face of a large block (sometimes two joined block stones); carved into a section of a rock face; or located in a socket built into a wall. Most the uprights were equipped with one beam socket, so the height of the beam could not be adjusted during the pressing process. However, a few uprights with two niches were found, indicating that operating height could also be adjusted.

Cyrenaican presses mostly generated pressure by the use of a windlass mounted on a parallelepiped counterweight block (*Type 1*) which broadly belongs to the Semana weight type. The diverse fitting arrangements to mount a windlass device were completely different from those found in North Africa and other Mediterranean regions. In addition, this counterweight block was distinct in its position, as it was placed in line with the pressing beam. Moreover, beam length in Cyrenaican presses was shorter than those in North Africa. However, the usual position of the uprights in most Cyrenaican presses is beside the pressing beds; a similar arrangement was also reported from Istria (Matijasić 1993: 254). This, combined with the small size of baskets used in Cyrenaican presses, meant the generated pressure would be higher than in installations in North Africa and the other Mediterranean regions, and thus two loads of crushed olives per day could possibly have been processed. The *Type 1* counterweight block seems to be unique to Cyrenaica, although a similar type was found in Methana, from where it possibly originated. A counterweight with a T-shaped socket hole was also found in Cyrenaica, either hewed into the bedrock or cut into a monolithic stone. So far, no similar examples have been detected in other Mediterranean regions and they appear to be specific to Cyrenaica.

Pressing beds in Cyrenaica also varied in form, from built up or rock cut box-like pressing areas to circular grooves carved into a monolithic slab or made of a pavement of *opus siginnum* (which was more likely connected to wine production). The *Type 4* pressing bed is an intriguing form. It was made of a large monolithic slab with two (sometimes three) circular channels. Parallel examples from Cyprus suggest that this type of pressing bed was possibly operated by one pressing beam. Other types of press beds, which were box-like in shape and either entirely cut into the bedrock (*Type 6*) or built into walls (*Type 7*), were also recorded and seem to be confined to Cyrenaica. This suggests that Cyrenaica had its own unique structural characteristics, which were different from those found in other Mediterranean regions.

In other parts of North Africa the construction of presses and mills was standardised as has been noted by Mattingly and Hitchner in the Kasserine region (Hitchner *et al.* 1990: 251–2) and in the Tarhuna plateau, in Tripolitania (Ahmed 2019: 105). However, similar evidence was not detected in Cyrenaica. This region presents a significant variety of press/mill elements, which suggests that press-construction along with pressing elements were created by very localised craftsmen, indicating a degree of conservatism.

9.2 Windlass versus Screw Technology

The study shows that Cyrenaica was almost entirely dependent on the traditional lever and windlass technique, as for the rest of North Africa (apart from Morocco), Crete, Methana and Istria/Dalmatia for the development of lever and screw presses (Figure 9.1). There were three different kinds of presses which generally belonged to Brun's class A2. All pressing beams were secured in a niche either cut into a standing single block, into bedrock or even simply housed in a socket built into a wall.

The use of lever and screw pressing technology in wine and olive oil presses was known from the late first century BC and several enhanced models were already applied by the middle of the following century (Mattingly 1996: 585). Nevertheless, the diffusion of the screw mechanism remained limited across the early Roman world and it was not until the Late Antique period that the technology was widely employed. By the third century AD, the screw mechanism became common in Spain, Italy and southern France. Soon after the screw technology had become widespread over almost all of the Late Antique eastern Mediterranean. Remains of lever presses attached to screw mechanisms were found in the regions of North Syria, Palestine, Cyprus, Egypt and Turkey. The use of direct screw presses appears to have been fairly widespread in Palestine (Frankel 1997), Jordan (Frankel 1999: 28; Khalil and Al-Nammari 2000) and Egypt (Bigi 2016; Rodziewicz 1998), while lever and screw presses seem to have been more common in Cyprus (Hadjisavvas 1992), North Syria (Callot 1984) and the Anatolian region (Lewit 2012: 140).

Mattingly (1996) and Lewit (2007) provided a seminal discussion on the factors that probably led to the diffusion of screw technology in the eastern Mediterranean, in stark contrast with the situation in North Africa which was characterised by a rigid adherence to the windlass mechanism. The two areas, though they were not contemporary, showed an impressive commercial scale of olive oil/wine production. Throughout the first to third centuries AD, North Africa was one of the principal suppliers of olive oil across the Mediterranean world. By the fourth century AD, the trade had moved to the eastern Mediterranean where producers in Palestine and north Syria took the lead in this lucrative industry alongside substantial population growth. It is interesting to note that the Tripolitanian pre-desert region also witnessed population growth during the late Roman period (Barker and Gilbertson 1996: 349), but olive oil/wine continued to be produced by employing the windlass mechanism without the need to change to screw press technology.

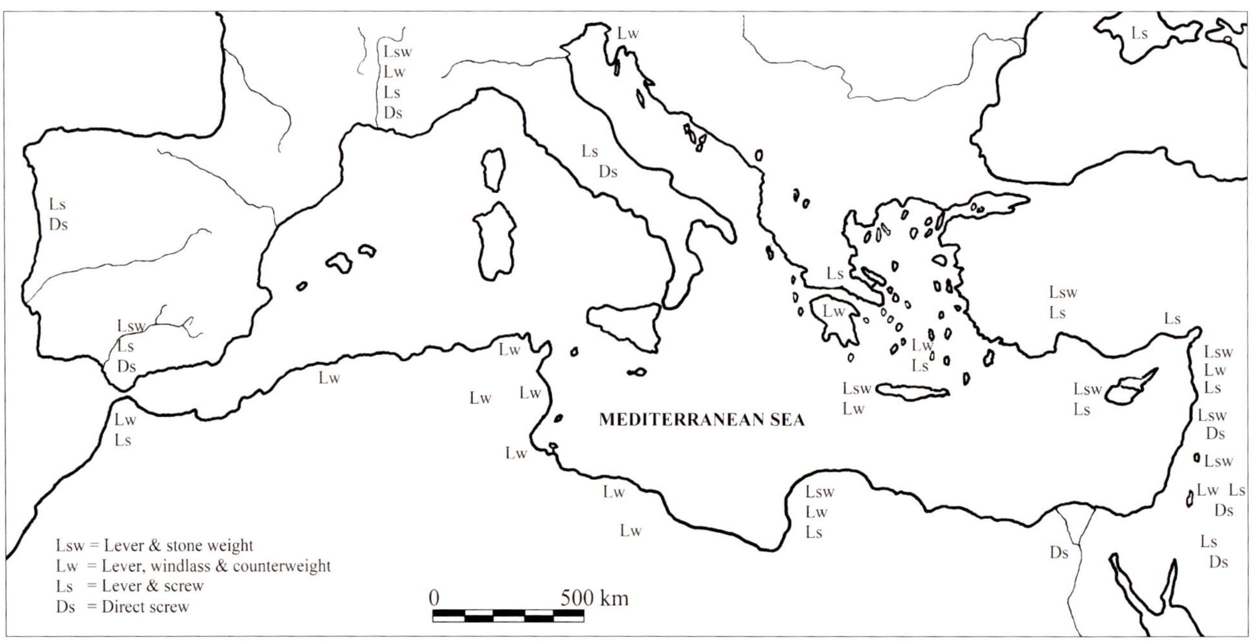

Figure 9.1: Distribution of press types in the Roman Mediterranean.

There is little doubt that agricultural expansion in marginal lands encouraged investors to build new installations capable of exceeding purely domestic consumption and meeting the demands of a market-oriented economy (Mattingly 1988c: 157). This led some scholars (Amouretti *et al.* 1984: 418–20; Forbes 1992: 99; Frankel *et al.* 1994: 50; White 1984: 32) to argue that this could only be achieved with the adoption of the screw mechanism, as they regarded it as more efficient than the lever and windlass press, either when applied to the lever or used as a direct press. They believe that the choice of the long-established lever and windlass pressing technique is inefficient for a large demand, and therefore screw technology was a more practical option in terms of available space increasing output. It is true that direct screw machinery, unlike lever and/or screw technology, occupies less space (Lewit 2007: 127), but it has been viewed as being rather awkward to operate (Mattingly 1996: 584). Furthermore, it needs greater manpower for operation, and thus increases operating costs. According to Mattingly (1993: 495), the lever press can be run by one person while a screw press requires more people to turn the screw (Amouretti *et al.* 1984: 418–20; Lewit 2007: 128). It is reasonable to argue that a direct screw press allows the process to continue without any interruption for rotating baskets and adjustments in operating height (Frankel 2009: 7). Nevertheless, an empirical study of a traditional press still in operation in 1987 in southern Tunisia demonstrated that pausing the pressing process and rebuilding the stack of baskets would not result in any significant delay in operation (Mattingly 1993: 495).

In the Late Roman period, both Methana (Foxhall 2007: 195; van Andel and Runnels 1987: 113) and Istria (Matijasić 1993: 258) seem to have enjoyed a high degree of specialisation in olive oil production and a share in the overseas market. Like North Africa, the two regions exclusively maintained lever and windlass technology, and did not follow the other east Mediterranean regions in adapting the screw technique. If we accept that political instability led North Africa to lose its long-distance trade with the urban markets, particularly Rome, the major consumer, (Reddé 1988: 80), perhaps there was no impetus to employ screw technology. However, this explanation cannot be applied to Methana and Istria where conditions were favourable for the adoption of a change in technology. Accordingly, it is logical to conclude that the choice of efficiency of an existing technology outweighed the need for technical change (Mattingly 1996: 594). Furthermore, it is hard to believe that Synesius a bishop of Ptolemais who lived in Alexandria in AD 403–405, had never seen or heard of the screw technology that was widely used there. This is perhaps a strong refutation of Brun's hypothesis that educated and wealthy landowners were more likely to be a vital factor in adopting the screw technology (Brun 2004: 161–7). Wilson (2004: 150) believes that there is no necessary link between educated individuals and their influence on the level of private or civic wealth or state investment in the region. Equally, Brun (2004: 210) is also in disagreement with the notion posited by Lewit (2007: 135–6) that the small holder but not tenants or absentee landlords would be a greater stimulus to improving and investment in agricultural equipment. Archaeological evidence from Cyrenaica suggests that the agglomerated pattern of settlement in the region is fairly similar to that detected in the Levantine regions. The ample evidence of imported finewares (Emrage 2015: 166–7; Hesein 2015: 311–2; Kenrick 2013a: 63–4), the presence of houses (Abdussaid *et al.* 1984; Hesein 2015: 158–60) bathhouses (Luni 1974/75: 266–76; Ward-Perkins and Goodchild 2003: 295, 311, 373, 391, 393) and churches embellished with mosaic pavements (Rosenbaum and Ward-Perkins 1980; Ward-Perkins and Goodchild 2003) found in many rural sites of Cyrenaica suggest communities that were closely connected to their land. These communities evidently were directly involved in the process of production, but enjoyed a similar quality of life to their urban brethren.

According to Shereshevski (1991:2), ecclesiastical control over aspects of economic life in Palestine led to the accumulation of capital in the hands of priests, who would not have been eager to invest in mundane projects. Based on archaeological evidence, Leone (2001) concluded that the church in the late Roman and Byzantine Tripolitania and Tunisia was deeply involved in urban and rural economic life and its control may also have extended to ownership of oil production facilities. In ancient Cyrenaica, unlike Tripolitania and Tunisia, there is neither literary nor archaeological evidence to extrapolate the pattern of exploitation of the land or the socio economic system, which leaves this matter open to question. Nonetheless, Wilson (2004: 145) referred to the remains of industrial installations found within the premises of the monastery of Qasrin el-Giamel to suggest that there was possibly some sort of ecclesiastic role within the Cyrenaican economy.

Even if this hypothesis is accepted, the situation in Palestine was clearly different from that evidenced on the ground and displays a rather stark contrast to that noticed in Cyrenaica if we broadly accept that the two regions were 'state-like institutions', as Alston (2004: 128) prefers to call the economies that were under the church's domain. Thus, the prosperity underlying population growth in Palestine cannot be attributed to any specific factor.

Undoubtedly, geographical factors represented by the proximity of olive-producing regions to the largest centres of consumption in the ancient world (Rome and later Constantinople) were an important catalyst in intensifying the cultivation of olives and investment in the olive oil industry. For example, we see Spanish oil flowing into Rome in impressive quantities from the beginning of the first century AD, which was subsequently replaced by the Tripolitanian and African products. These production centres, unlike Cyrenaica, were not far from Rome. The same trend occurred when the pendulum swung the other way to the eastern Mediterranean and Constantinople became the capital of the empire. Again, Cyrenaica would not have been able to compete in any way with Cyprus, Palestine and Syria, since these were geographically located closer to the capital of the empire with its enormous population and large potential for consumption.

The late widespread distribution of the screw technology in the Levant, Cyprus and Egypt is notable and supports Mattingly's hypothesis. Conceivably, the strong momentum given by the geographical proximity of these regions to Constantinople, the new political and economic capital of the Roman empire, may be considered an additional factor. Nonetheless, retaining the traditional technology in Methana, despite its close proximity to Constantinople, suggests that a geographical location near attractive markets does not necessarily lead to technological change. Again, as in North Africa, archaeological evidence from Methana and Istria indicates these regions were primary olive oil producers from the Classical down to the late Roman periods. The density of pressing equipment found approaches that found in the key oil regions of the Roman Empire (Foxhall 2007: 186, 202), and employing the windlass mechanism was an active choice with no attempt to change to the screw technique. This is in contrast with Cyprus which was also not far from the metropolitan centre of the Byzantine Empire. Viticulture in Cyprus was known from the early second millennium BC (Karageorghis 1993: 32) and the island was renowned for its wine making (Pliny, NH. xiv, 9,7; Strabo 14.6.5), which formed a major part of its culture throughout history. While by no means conclusive, it is perhaps logical to assume that the geographical proximity of the province to Constantinople, the new powerful unitary state, and the establishment of well-used long-distance trade links that paved the way for applying the screw technique was a response to meet the increasing demands of the new powers emerging in the region. However, the geographical proximity of Istria and Methana to Constantinople confounds this hypothesis.

Alternatively, this may in part be the result of the availability of ample timber resources in these regions, as making a screw device requires timber in order to develop the carpentry skills required (Mattingly (1996: 589). Olive oil production in Egypt never produced a surplus (Kingsley and Decker 2001: 5) and all the press remains found were connected to wine production. In the meantime, Egyptian wine was produced and traded, though quite limited quantities, throughout the Mediterranean in the fourth to fifth centuries (Kingsley and Decker 2001: 4; Haas 2001: 52; 2006: 38) and farther afield (Banaji 2001: 111, 132; Wilson 2004: 151). Wineries that employed direct screw presses were found in the Mareotis region (Lewit 2007: 123). Direct screw presses, of course, have obviated the need for a long press beam, which would have had to be imported, as almost no long timber would have been found in Egypt at the time. However, the use of screw technology in Egypt, which lacked good timber supplies, seems more likely to have relied on the existence of woodworkers familiar with water-lifting devices from the third century BC (Wilson 2001b: 234). Strikingly, the screw technology in Egypt seems not to extend farther east to Cyrenaica despite the physical proximity and the strong political influence.

The case in Italy was essentially different in that oleoculture, unlike viticulture, was always local in its orientation (Mattingly 1988d: 49). France, in this respect, also seems not to have deviated from the Italian trajectory (Frankel 1999: 93). In both countries, there was simply a progressive evolution when screw technology was initially employed in wine manufacturing and then used for oil production. With the exception of the Methana region of Greece (Foxhall 1997) and Istria/Dalamatia (Matijasic 1993: 254–7), which exhibit a picture comparable to that found in North Africa, a similar account emerges for the eastern Mediterranean. Syria (Decker 2001: 78), Palestine (Kingsley 2001) and Cyprus (Karageorghis 1993) were already well-established wine centres; therefore, their transfer to the lever and screw technique should be placed within the wider context of the evolutionary process. This contradicts the proponents of the belief that technological change need not necessarily be continuous and linearly progressive (Foxhall 2007: 132; Greene 1990). However, it should be borne in mind that more advanced technology does not necessarily mean better efficiency or enhanced performance (Mattingly 1996: 584).

African wealth was derived mainly from the massive production of, and trade, in olive oils, which was probably of greater significance as an export than wine (Carandini 1970; Mattingly 1985). Recent ceramic studies have shown that other African amphora types were also used to transport fish and wine products (Ben Lazreg *et al.* 1995; Bonifay 2004) but their export seems to have been smaller than that of oil. It has been also suggested that the distribution mechanism of ARS wares was probably associated with the grain and textile trade rather than amphora exports (Bonifay 2004: 477–9). In addition, there are many installations that have been interpreted as oil presses, but they could be better seen as having been used for wine-making (Brun 2004). Nevertheless, the available ceramic studies seem not to have altered the olive boom model (Martin 2008). The African explosion in production, accompanied by brisk oil trade, leaves no room to envisage the possibility that the region was effectively isolated from the rest of the

Mediterranean. The region was undoubtedly a major oil producer, and the traditional lever windlass presses were clearly geared for large surpluses. It was not deemed obsolete, but rather endured due to the lack of any need for change.

Both northern Morocco and, at a later date, northern Syria, remained exceptional cases of regions that used screw technology. The straightforward explanation for the penetration of such technology into these two regions was due to their geographical proximity to Spain and Palestine, respectively, where screw technology was already well established. The question which remains unanswered is why the application of screw technology in Morocco and Syria was confined to the traditional lever and weight presses rather than completely switching to direct screw technology, as was almost entirely prevalent in Palestine and the north-west Mediterranean regions. Perhaps it is coincidence that the development of the screw mechanism in Spain probably took place around the third century (Mattingly 1996: 589), a time in which the African provinces became the largest producers of olive oil (Ahmed 2019: 152). Spain no longer held a solid foothold in the greater Mediterranean olive oil markets, thus considerable investment was directed towards viticultural activity, to which its soils were well suited.

One of the reasons for the continued use of the lever and windlass press technology over the screw mechanism is that it is less labour-intensive and once going, it can be left to run unattended, unlike the screw press (Wilson 2008). Another plausible explanation for the absence of screw technology among the major known olive oil producers (with the exception of Spain) and the maintenance of the traditional lever and windlass technique in the North African regions lies mainly in the fact that their economy was primarily that of a large-scale, specialised manufacturer of olive oil. This is in line with Mattingly (1996: 595) in arguing that the introduction of screw technology into regions known principally for wine making accounts for its subsequent use in the olive oil industry.

9.3 Oil or Wine Presses?

It has sometimes been claimed that presses for oil production could also be used for making wine (Peacock and Williams 1991: 34). While this seems to be reasonable, oil production needs special kinds of apparatus not necessarily required for wine manufacturing, such as crushing basins. This pressing element was encountered in almost all the recorded sites. Therefore, it is truly convincing that these presses were, certainly, connected to olive oil production. Ancient literary accounts suggest that the production of wine and olive oil was almost equal and that many presses were probably multi-purpose (Brun 2004a: 53–6). Nevertheless, most of the archaeological excavations to date have interpreted the press remains as being used for olive oil production rather than wine-making. It is still difficult to distinguish between wine and oil presses and Hobson (2015: 70, 99) stated that this challenge puzzled the survey archaeologist as well as the excavator. However, during excavations there will always be opportunities to collect environmental samples. These are often of great potential value and can offer useful information towards definite interpretations. In relation to Cyrenaica (Chapter 2), as most of the sites visited during the survey produced an unprecedented number of millstones and mill mortars recorded, it is unquestionable that those recorded presses were used for olive oil production.

The initial investigation of wine production evidence suggests that this activity was also found in Cyrenaica. Presses used to process wines were mainly hewn from rock surfaces and consisted of two essential functional components: a treading-floor (usually plastered) and a collecting tank. A mechanical lever and windlass press was often utilised to extract more juice from the grape skins.

Archaeological evidence of wine production was mainly concentrated in the upper escarpments of the Gebel. However, unlike olive oil, a few installations were also found within some coastal cities (Wilson 2001a). Use of presses suggests a production that exceeds subsistence needs and thus has a clear commercial potential. Evidence of more wine amphora types being produced in Cyrenaica might suggest that the output of wine would have been higher than that of olive oil.

9.4 Types of Rural Settlements in Cyrenaica

In relation to defining types and characteristics of pressing elements my work has established a typology of rural settlements of Cyrenaica (Chapter 6). The region appears to have witnessed changing settlement patterns with an increased number of buildings that were defensive in character. This seems to have taken place between the third to fourth centuries AD, and in almost a similar way to that found in the Tripolitanian hinterland (Ahmed 2019; Felici et al. 2006) and pre-desert regions (Barker *et al.* 1996; Mattingly 1995). The study revealed regional variation of settlement types in terms of form, size and level of oil production. Lamluda stands as a unique example of a site of high-level productivity. The village was a centre for the intensive production of olive oil and wine throughout the fourth to seventh centuries AD, probably without interruption (Buzaian, 2009; Goodchild and Ward-Perkins, 2003; Menozzi and Antonelli, 2014: 71–2; Wilson, 2004: 149). Similarly, other small towns such as Jebra, Umm Sellem (Menozzi *et al.* 2014: 71), Siret al-Fwaris and Al-Sirah al-Hamrah are good examples of larger villages managing the agricultural exploitation of the region in the Late Roman period.

The number of rural sites had clearly grown in late antiquity to exceed that of the Hellenistic and early Roman periods. In the Benghazi coastal strip, the survey shows that this area, during the Roman period, was a focus of important agricultural activity, particularly for olive oil production, with a pattern of increased settlement and reoccupation of earlier sites in the third-fourth to sixth centuries AD. An increase in the number of rural sites occupied, their size, and the intensity of land use has also been noted by surveys conducted on the Wadi al-Kuf area (Abdussaid *et al.* 1983; Emrage 2015) and east of Cyrene (Saad *et al.* 2016).

Most of the rural settlements are of utilitarian character and the architecture and decoration of some buildings (public or private) built during the third and sixth centuries suggest a prosperous, although not exceedingly wealthy, community. A few of them provided, from the surface, evidence of luxurious materials (e.g., mosaic floors and bath-buildings). Examples of this are the lavish bath-house in Wadi Senab (Luni in Attiya 1975), although this might have been from an earlier date before it was converted into a press, the monastic complex and its associated winery building at Gaserin al-Gemel (Catani 1976; 1998), the figurative mosaic found at Qasr Bandis (Ward-Perkins and Goodchild 2003: 393-5) and the recent discovery of a building at Wadi Khargah furnished with a polychrome mosaic floor with round medallions in which Greek inscriptions were apparent (F. Khalifa, pers. com.).

9.5 Landownership

In Cyrenaica, the rural population lived mainly in villages of moderate size (5–20 ha), but these were less densely populated than the towns. This may imply a lack of centralised control over production. During the Byzantine period, spoliation of building materials was a common practice in both the eastern and western Mediterranean (De Vos 2013; Wilson 2004: 146). Cyrenaica was not exceptional and the grandiose building enterprises that marked the Imperial period were limited to churches which exclusively absorbed imports of marble in the Byzantine period (Harrison 1985).

We cannot actually demonstrate that there was no large land ownership and imperial estates in Cyrenaica, as noted in Tripolitania. It seems that both large and imperial estates did exist (as attested by epigraphic evidence for instance), but their form and organisation were clearly different from those found in Tripolitania. Some distinguished philanthropists are recorded in epigraphic evidence dating from the late Hellenistic to the early Roman periods, and these people are likely to have belonged to a high-ranking class in Cyrenaican society (SEG 20. 729; SEG 26. 1817; SEG 9. 417; SEG 28. 1539, 1540; SEG 9.354). For the time being, unequivocal textual and epigraphic evidence from the mid-Roman period onward is absent, suggesting that affluent powerful elites were less evident than those of Tripolitania and Alexandria (Wilson 2004: 152). There was possibly an elite in the cities holding the position of power and who made money from the land. They must have owned land and possessed rural estates, but individual estates may not have been quite as big in suburban areas. We know that Synesius was a member of the urban elite and owned several rural estates (letters 130 and 148; Goodchild 1976: 240). The amount of land he owned as an absentee landlord was quite significant, though he appears not to have spent much time visiting his estates. That may be the key difference between the Cyrenaican elites who were more urban based.

Certainly, the little evidence from field survey does not allow us at present to reconstruct the tenure pattern on the land. In Cyrenaica, there seems to be considerable regional variation in rural settlement patterns, so that there are a number of site types that are quite big and could be estate centres of large productive units. There are also many small sites that seem to have been small farms. It is not yet clear whether these large sites were communal centres in which groups of people lived together, shared labour and security, or were controlled by rich individuals permanently living in urban centres but operated by dependent tenants. They may have used bailiffs or tenants on the land for the cultivation and production of food and cash crops. The same arguments apply to the small sites, which could either be privately owned small farms, or were under the control of a neighbouring urban community. With respect to the latter, arbitration was sought from Synesius over the ownership of Hydrax between Erythron and Darnis (Synesius, letter 67) a well recorded dispute between communities rather than individual land owners.

However, there was seemingly a middle-class group which was involved in trading and manufacturing activities. This may explain the relatively small size of the olive oil presses and be indicative of a low level of capital investment in olive production. This is in line with Mattingly's remark that most of the ancient olive oil presses are expected to be smaller in scale than those owned by Italian and African aristocratic elites (Mattingly 1993: 435). Nonetheless, the widespread distribution of imported fine red slip-ware throughout rural settlements is a striking trend. These finewares, from Phocaea, in western Turkey, Cyprus and, to a far lesser extent, Tunisia, certainly reflect commercial penetration into rural Cyrenaica. The import of such luxurious goods is an indication of a prosperous middle-class society that existed well above the basic subsistence threshold.

9.6 Capacity of Cyrenaican Presses

The careful measurement of Cyrenaican press elements has allowed for tentative estimates of the production capacity of Cyrenaican olive oil presses (see Chapter 7). The capacity has been estimated by extrapolation from the height above the press floor of wall niches of holes in uprights and the diameter of press beds, and ranges from about 4,500 to 6,750 kg of oil over a 90-day pressing season in good years. If the idea that Cyrenaican presses could process two loads per day is accepted, then the maximum annual capacity could reach 12,000 kg of oil. By contrast, Mattingly (1993) suggested that the maximum capacity of presses in the Tripolitanian Gebel was up to 18,000 kg of oil per season and they were more densely distributed (Mattingly 1988d) than in Cyrenaica. However, the output of presses in Provence in south-eastern France (Brun 1986) and the Tripolitanian pre-desert (Mattingly 1985) were much lower than that in Cyrenaica with a total annual olive oil output (in peak years) that may have only reached between 2,000 to 5,000 kg of oil.

Mattingly (1988d: 34) calculated that the average Roman consumed 20 litres of oil per year, which means that Cyrenaica's estimated population of *c.*333,000 may have demanded around 6,660,000 litres of oil annually during the Roman period. The production capacity of the 265 recorded olive oil presses, assuming they functioned simultaneously, was an estimated *c.*2.6–3.2 million litres of olive oil during the annual pressing season (at two loads per day with a maximum capacity in the range of 10,000–12,000 litres of oil in a good year). This would have been enough to supply *c.*130,000–160,000 people with oil each year. Therefore, the output of the Cyrenaican oil presses calculated here is tentative, and it is perhaps too early to judge how important these industries were to the economic life of the province. Surely the recorded preses are only a fraction of the total presses that existed.

9.7 Local Amphorae

The evidence from local amphorae manufacturing explored in Chapter 8 indicates that Cyrenaican amphorae were mostly oriented towards the intraregional market. There is no quantitative study to suggest any significant degree of trade, but the regional distribution of MR8 amphorae suggests that the region enjoyed a good level of growth. The economy of the rural sites in Cyrenaica was presumably dependent on short-distance trade. For example, Lamluda had a ready market for its agricultural produce in the nearby city of Cyrene (Wilson 2004: 149). According to the archaeological evidence, kilns were only identified along the coast. This situation is similar to that in Tunisia, but again different from Tripolitania, where a larger number of kilns were concentrated farther inland.

The data collected suggest that Cyrenaica did not produce enough olive oil to satisfy its own needs. There is no conclusive literary and archaeological evidence that it exported regular surpluses, though there are some suggestive hints. A reference to a shipment of olive oil to Aquilea (*digesta*), probably dating to the first half of the second century AD, is indicative of an established oil industry and alludes to the potential for creating a surplus. This, with the limited distribution of MR8 amphora in Ostia and Rome, the Veneto region in northern Italy and the Adriatic (Wilson *et al.* 2012: 368), suggest that a surplus in bumper years would probably have been shipped to destinations throughout the Mediterranean. However, this should be taken on its own as a possible rare occurrence of small-scale export. A shortage in the supply of oil during a bad year was likely to see oil being secured from overseas markets, as suggested by the presence of North African MR16 amphora (Riley 1979a: 200–3). If we consider the strong tendency of the olive tree for biennial fruiting, it cannot be ruled out that from time to time, as a result of the great demand for this essential commodity, Cyrenaican oil found its way to the overseas markets.

In contrast, we have little evidence that this situation persisted into the Late Roman period. This is because our information on local amphora from this period is almost nil. Meanwhile, imported late Roman amphorae, such as LR2 and LR8 amphorae which are thought to have contained oil (Karagiorgou 2001: 147), have been found at many Cyrenaican sites (Riley 1979a: 218, fig. 44, 228). Nonetheless, one can put forward the idea that the production of the MR8 amphora type continued well into the later periods but archaeologically has not yet received the attention that it deserves and is still seen as residual.

Overall, ceramic evidence indicates that local amphorae were manufactured from the Hellenistic period and with the recent discoveries of amphora kilns dating back to the Roman period, it can be said that Cyrenaica produced, to some extent, its own transport vessels. The presence and distribution of the MR8 amphora type may have been related to the olive trade. This type of transporting vessel, along with MR1, MR9 and MR10 amphorae, were manufactured in different centres along the littoral of Cyrenaica, slightly away from the hinterland where olive cultivation thrived, and which thus implies export. It is possible to reuse the imported amphorae and re-export them at least on the local level. Additionally, the possibility that oil and wine were distributed locally and even exported in perishable containers cannot be ruled out, thus escaping detection.

9.8 Wider Implications for Studies of Ancient Olive Oil Production and Trade

Several scholars have argued that Cyrenaica suffered extensively from the Jewish Revolt in AD 115-7, and much more substantial damage from the major earthquake of AD 365. Consequently, the region experienced significant economic decline and seems not to have enjoyed any subsequent revival of its fortunes. Wilson has argued this point quite strongly:

> *Cyrenaica did not see the emergence of a super-rich aristocracy to the same degree, perhaps because it had no large urban port of the scale of Alexandria, and because the rural instability of the region required defence and inhibited investment in the productive infrastructure of estates.*
>
> *Cyrenaica, therefore, perhaps provides a model for what happens to provinces when their strategic and economic importance drops below the threshold that warrants the close attention of an empire only able to deal with a limited number of crises. Once the state is no longer able to protect the region against incursion, there is a severe knock-on effect on private investment in agricultural production, commerce and trade.*
>
> (Wilson 2004: 152)

This traditional picture of a declining economy is strongly echoed in earlier studies (Goodchild 1968; Jones 1985; Lloyd 1990; Reynolds 1977; Stucchi 1975). However, it principally stems from the virtual absence of any archaeological evidence. Consequently, this hypothesis was suggested as a compromise solution until the recovery of more conclusive archaeological data (Hesein 2015: 343). Cyrenaica was heavily affected by the tremor of the mid-fourth century AD, frequent tribal forays, migratory locusts and the outbreak of plague. The frequency of the tribal raids increased in the late fourth and early fifth centuries with no sign of opposition by standing troops. In AD 405, these raids penetrated the hinterland, besieged Cyrene and set fire to crops (Synesius, letter 130). Despite the sombre description given in the *Catastasis* of Synesius in the early fifth century AD, it is possible that the repeated raids against urban centres of Cyrenaica had little initial impact on the region as a whole. Goodchild sometimes wrote of Synesius' letters as telling one side of the story, which was largely corrupted by his 'personal animosities' (Goodchild 1976: 195).

By the late fourth century AD, the southern perimeter wall of Cyrene was reduced when the portico's wall of the forum was heightened to form part of a fortress (Goodchild 1964: 44). Nevertheless, archaeological evidence seems to suggest that the city enjoyed relative prosperity (Goodchild 1976: 226). The Hellenistic walls of Ptolemais were abandoned and compensated for by a system of blockhouse forts and houses (Kraeling 1962: 100–4, 147–8; Ward-Perkins *et al.* 1986). This implies that the city lacked the population and garrison to defend the long ramparts. However, its aqueduct was restored (Procopius, *De Aedificiis*, VI. 2,11) and thus the city, to some extent, flourished, even when it was no longer the metropolitan representative of the region. Procopius also mentioned the reinforcement of the perimeter defences of Teucheira (*De Aedificiis*, VI. 2,4) and Berenice (*De Aedificiis*, VI. 2,5). Additionally, Borium, the last city towards the west, also received an extensive new circuit (*De Aedificiis*, VI. 2,12). These ambitious defensive rebuilding programs are in drastic contrast to the idea that tribal incursions were not as constant as narrated in the previous two centuries (Goodchild and Ward-Perkins 2003: 3). It is now widely believed that the farming communities in the Tripolitanian pre-desert region predominantly comprised indigenous Libyans, Romanised and/or Punicised to a certain degree, and not settlers from outside the region (Mattingly and Hitchner 1995: 194). Mattingly (1996: 334) argues that if the local tribes did not actually eliminate '*qasr* communities' then the two sides must have reached an agreement and that as Roman authority collapsed, they developed into an independent or semi-independent tribal confederation. It is likely that a similar pattern of events applied in Cyrenaica. It is worth noting that this notion was refuted by Goodchild (1976: 184–5, 206), although he suggested elsewhere (1976: 196) that a number of fortified farms were perhaps constructed and occupied by allied tribes, such as the Maci. Samphodion, who is known on an inscription from Tarakenet (Goodchild and Ward-Perkins 2003: 415–7) to have had military as well as civic responsibilities, was likely a chief of a Libyan tribe that had recently moved into the region. Samphodion perhaps belonged to the Marysoi, who possibly formed one of the forces that joined Heraclius in his war against Phocas in AD 610 (John of Nikiou CVII, 2). This may justify the conclusion that the region survived and fell only to the Arab armies of the mid-seventh century. Fentress and Wilson (2016) argued that it was Saharan invaders who actually posed a serious threat to Roman authority in North Africa. Therefore, a perspective worthy of consideration is that the conflict in Cyrenaica could be more appropriately framed as between the Romano-Libyans of the Gebel Akhdar and the Saharan tribes to the south.

The growing evidence from both urban and rural archaeological excavations and recent surveys (although the associated finds have not yet been fully analysed) supports the impression that there appears to have been a period of reasonable prosperity following the economic crisis of the third century AD (this has also been suggested by Goodchild and Ward-Perkins 2003: 4; Roques 1985). Occupation of the countryside covers a large part of classical antiquity, but with some intensification in the fourth through to the seventh centuries AD (Abdussaid *et al.* 1983; Akab 2010; 1984; Emrage, 2015; Hesein, 2015; Saad *et al.* 2016). This is evident from the abundance of imported pottery that continued to arrive both at urban and rural sites. However, the economic structure seems likely to have been embedded in a regional economy rather than having developed primarily in relation to overseas markets.

It is hoped that this volume will help stimulate greater informed debate about the mechanisms that underpin olive oil/wine production and economic performance and trade in Cyrenaica but due to the sheer geographical size of the area under discussion, these observations are not necessarily conclusive and further information and lengthier exegeses are required.

Whether olive oil production was regularly traded to a wider market seems unlikely, but a consignment mentioned in the *Digest* hints that future research may find some evidence of exported Cyrenaican olive oil at more Mediterranean sites. Further fieldwork on equally urban and rural sites and local amphora is necessary to develop this concept.

The production of amphorae in Cyrenaica was obviously related to that of olive oil (and wine). Urgent research priorities include the excavation of key sites such as Lamluda and Jebra and recently recorded amphora kiln sites (Hesein 2015: 172, 8–9) which will improve our knowledge of the Cyrenaican amphora typological series.

Marine archaeology and the excavation of shipwrecks off the coast of Cyrenaica are an invaluable mine of information as to the associated economic performance. In Cyrenaica, this field of archaeology has not yet attracted the attention it deserves. Very little work has been conducted in this regard with only four wrecks reported to the east of Benghazi (Parker 1992) and at least two others at the foot of the Gulf of Sirte, *c.*600 km east of Tripoli (Preece 2000).

Synthetic micro-regional and localised studies by different authors are desperately needed. These will subsequently form the ground upon which to view, in a broader context, patterns of Cyrenaica with other different regions.

It need hardly be emphasised that this work has been sufficient only to give a broad overall view of olive oil production in Roman Cyrenaica. It would require years of archaeological research and excavation across the entire region if we are to be able to date the abundant olive oil/wine presses scattered throughout the region with any accuracy. Meanwhile, this work may serve as a stimulus to further research.

Finally, Libya does not yet have a Sites and Monuments Record of its heritage assets. Threats to archaeological sites, in the light of increasing social and economic change, are at their peak. Therefore, a national SMR is urgently needed for the Department of Antiquities to be able to manage, monitor and hence protect these priceless heritage assets.

BIBLIOGRAPHY

Ancient sources

Al-Idrisi. *Kitab Nuzhat Al Mushtaq fi Ikhtiraq Al Afaq.* Volume 1, Religious Culture Library, Cairo – Egypt (in Arabic). Available at: https://ia600204.us.archive.org/13/items/nuzht-almushtaq/nuzht-almushtaq.pdf, (accessed: 6 May 2022).

Aristotle, *The History of Animals.* Book V. Translated by D'Arcy Wentworth Thompson. Available at: http://penelope.uchicago.edu/aristotle/histanimals5.html (accessed: 6 May 2022)

Cato and Varro (1934). *On Agriculture.* Translated by W. D. Hooper and Harrison Boyd Ash, The Loeb Classical Library No. 283, William Heinmann Ltd, Cambridge.

Columella (1955). *On Agriculture, Volume III, Books 10–12. On Trees.* Translated by E. S. Forster and Edward H. Heffner, Loeb Classical Library No. 408, William Heinemann Ltd, Cambridge.

Dio Casius. *Roman History, Epitome* LXVIII. Available at: http://penelope.uchicago.edu/Thayer/e/roman/texts/cassius_dio/68*.html (accessed: 6 May 2022).

Diodorus of Sicily (1967), *Books III.* Translated by C. H. Oldfather, the Loeb Classical Library, William Heinemann Ltd, Cambridge.

Diodorus of Siculus. *The Library History* (1935). Published in Vol. II of the Loeb Classical Library. Available at: http://penelope.uchicago.edu/Thayer/E/Roman/Texts/Diodorus_Siculus/4B*.html (accessed: 6 May 2022).

Expotitio Totius Mundi et Gentium (1966). Introduction, texte critique, traduction, notes et commentaire, par Jean Rougé, Paris : Éditions du Cerf.

Geoponica sive cassiani bassi scholastici eclogae (1895). Ed. H. Beckh: Teubner.

Herodotus (1950). *The History*, Books 3–4. Translated by A. D. Godley, The Loeb Classical Library, William Heinemann Ltd, Cambridge.

Palladius: *Opus Agriculturae. The Work of Farming.* (2013). Translated by John G. Fitch. Prospect Books.

Pauli Orosii: *Historiae Adversum Paganos* Libri VII. Based on the edition by C. Zangemeister (1899). Available at: http://www.attalus.org/latin/orosius.html (accessed: 6 May 2022).

Pliny (1949–54). *Natural History* (vols. 1–5, 9). Translated by: H. Rackham, Harvard University Press.

Pliny. *Natural History*. Book XIV.

Procopius, *Buildings*. Text and Translation on LacusCurtius. Available at: http://penelope.uchicago.edu/Thayer/E/Roman/Texts/Procopius/Buildings/home.html (accessed: 6 May 2022).

Scylax, *Pseudo – Skylax's Periplous.* (2011). Translated by G. Shipley, Bristol Phoenix press.

SEG. *Supplementum Epigraphicum Graecum*: IX (1938). Volumen nonum, Pasc. I. Lugduni Batavorum, Apud A. W. Sijthoff.

Strabo, *Geography*. Book XIV. Available at: http://penelope.uchicago.edu/Thayer/E/Roman/Texts/Strabo/14F*.html (accessed: 6 May 2022).

Strabo (1949). *The Geography of Strabo*, Book XVII. Translated by H. L. Jones, the Loeb Classical Library, William Heinemann Ltd, Cambridge.

Synesius. *The Letters of Synesius of Cyrene* (1926). Translated by: A. FitzGerald. Oxford University Press.

The Chronicle of John, Bishop of Nikiu. Translated from Zotenberg's Ethiopic text by R. H. Charles. Text and Translation Society, Williams and Norgate (1913). English Translation. Available at: https://archive.org/stream/JohnOfNikiuChronicle1916/John_of_Nikiu_Chronicle_1916#page/n5/mode/1up/search/Herac (accessed: 6 May 2022).

Modern references

Abdrbba, M. O. (2019). *Outside the Walls: Cyrene's Suburban Zone between the Greek and Roman Eras*. Unpublished PhD Thesis submitted to the University of Leicester. Available at: https://hdl.handle.net/2381/43788 (accessed: 6 May 2022)

Abdussaid, A., Abdalnaby, S., Gweidr, R., Farag, S., Hsoona, A. Al-Mzeini, A. (1984). *Research Project in the National Park of al-Kuf.* Damascus: Arab Centre for the Studies of Arid zones and Dry lands (in Arabic).

Addyman, P. (1962). 'The archaeology of the Sbeitla area: interim report'. *Brathay Exploration Group, Annual and Account of Expedition*: 60–77.

Addyman, P. and Simpson, G. (1966). 'The archaeology of the Sbeitla area: second interim report'. *Brathay Exploration Group, Annual and Account of Expedition*: 153–170.

Ahmed, A. M. Mftah (2019). *Rural Settlements and Economis Activity: Olive oil, wine and amphorae production on the Tarhuna Plateau during the Roman Period.* Society for Libyan Studies Open Access Monograph 1. London: Society for Libyan Studies.

Akab, S. (2010). 'Olive presses on the territory near Cyrene'. In M. Luni (ed.), *Cirene e la Cirenaica in età greca e romana.* Monografie di Archeologia Libica 30: 25–30.

Akerraz, A. and Lenoir, M. (1981–2). 'Les huileries de Volubilis'. *Bulletin d'Archeologie Marocaine* 14: 69–120.

Alston, R. (2004). 'Writing the economic history for the late antique east: a review'. In S. Kingsley and M. Decker (eds), 'Economy and Exchange in the East Mediterranean during the Late Antiquity'. *Ancient East and West* 3.1: 124–136.

Amouretti, M.-C. (1986). 'Le pain el l'huile dans la Grèce antique'. *Annales Litteraires de l'Uuniversité de Besancon* 328.

Anderson-Stojanović, V. R. (2007). 'Olive oil production at the Isthmus of Corinth'. *Historia Antiqua* 15: 89–98.

Applebaum, S. (1979). *Studies in Judaism in Late Antiquity. Jews and Greeks in Ancient Cyrene.* Leiden: Brill.

Attiya, B., Stucchi, S., Bacchielli, L. Luni, M., Gambini, W. and Purcaro, V. (1974–1975). 'Prima escursione nello Uadi Senab e nel Got Giaras', *Libya Antiqua* 11–12: 251–296.

Aubet, M. E. (1993). *The Phoenicians and the West: Politics, Colonies and Trade.* Cambridge: Cambridge University Press.

Auriemma, R. (2000). 'Le anfore del relitto di Grado e il loro contento'. *Mélanges de l'École Française de Rome Antiquité* 112: 27–51.

Auriemma, R., Degrassi, V. and Quirie, E. (2012). 'Produzione e circolazione di anfore in Adriatico tra III e IV secolo: dati da contesti emblematici'. In C.S. Fiorello (ed), *Ceramica Romana Nella Publia Adriatica.* Bari: Egnazia: 255–298.

Autret, C. (2012). 'Cyprus and Cilicia: amphora production, trade and relations in the early Roman era'. In A. Georgiou (ed.), *Cyprus an Island of Culture, Society and Social Relations from the Bronze Age to the Venetian Period.* Oxford: Oxbow Books: 251–267.

Ayalon, E. (2009). 'The open-air oil press at Zur Natan'. In E. Ayalon, R. Frankel and A. Kloner (eds), *Oil and Wine Presses in Israel from the Hellenistic, Roman and Byzaintine Periods.* BAR International Series 1972, Oxford: BAR: 163–165.

Ayalon, E., Frankel, R. and Kloner, A. (2009). 'A Byzantine (?) oil press in Samaria-Sepaste'. In E. Ayalon, R. Frankel and A. Kloner (eds), *Oil and Wine Presses in Israel from the Hellenistic, Roman and Byzantine Periods*, BAR International Series 1972, Oxford: BAR:159-165.

Bacchielli, L. (1974-1975). 'La sistemazione agrarian e gli insediamenti umani'. *Libya Antiqua* 11–12: 254–265.

Bacchielli, L., Reynolds, J. and Rees, B. (1992). 'La tomba deli Demetria a Cirene'. *Quaderni di archeologia della Libia* 15: 5–22.

Bacchielli, L. and Uhlenbrock, J. (2000). 'Dal "Giardino delle terrecotte" Al Santuario delle Nymphai'. In M. E. Micheli and A. Santucci (eds) *Il Santuario della Nymphai Chthoniai a Cirene. Il Sito e le Terrecotte.* Monografie di Archeologia Libica *25.* Rome: Bretschneider: 17–22.

Baird, D. (2004). 'Settlement expansion on the Konya Plain, Anatolia: 5th–7th Centuries A.D.'. In W. Bowden, L. Lavan and C. Machado (eds), *The Late Antique Countryside. Late Antique Archaeology 2.* Leiden: Brill: 219-246.

Banaji, J. (2001). *Agrarian Change in Late Antiquity: Gold, Labour and Aristocratic Dominance.* Oxford: Oxford University Press.

Bar, D. (2002). 'Was there a 3rd-c. economic crisis in Palestine?'. In J. Humphrey (ed.), *The Roman and Byzantine Near East*, Vol. 3, Supplement 49. Portsmouth, RI: *Journal of Roman Archaeology*: 43–54.

Barker, G. W. W. (1979). 'Economic life at Berenice'. In J. A. Lloyd (ed.), *Excavations at Sidi Khrebish Benghazi (Berenice)*, volume 2. Supplements to *Libya Antiqua* 5. Tripoli: Department of Antiquities: 1–49.

Barker, G. W. W. (1985). 'Agricultural organisation in classical Cyrenaica: the potential of subsistence and survey data'. In G. Barker, J. Lloyd and J, Reynolds (eds), *Cyrenaica in Antiquity.* Society for Libyan Studies, Occasional Papers I. BAR International Series 236, Oxford: BAR: 121–134.

Barker, G., Basell, L., Brooks, I. a Burn, L., Cartwright, C., Cole, F., Davison, J., Farr, L. Grün, R., Hamilton, R., Hunt, C., Inglis, R., Jacobs, Z., Leitch, V., Morales, J., Morley, I., Morley, M., Pawley, S., Pryor,

A., Rabett, R., Reynolds, T., El-Rishi, H., Roberts, R., Simpson, D., Stimpson, C. Touati, M. and van der Veen, M. (2008). 'The Cyrenaican Prehistory Project 2008: the second season of investigations of the Haua Fteah cave and its landscape, and further results from the initial (2007) fieldwork'. *Libyan Studies* 39: 175–221.

Barthel, C. (2017). 'Apollonia-Sozousa in late antiquity: some remarks on the *caput provinciae* of Libya Superior'. *Libyan Studies* 48: 159–168.

Ben Baaziz, S. (1985). 'Les huileries de la haute vallée de l'oued el Htab'. *Africa* 9: 69–85.

Ben Baaziz, S. (1991). 'Les huileries de la Tunisie antique'. *Cah Tun* 43: 39–64.

Benkhaial, A. S. (1995). 'Agriculture and animal husbandry'. In A. M. Bolegma and S. K. Al-Gzeiri (eds) *Al-Jamaheria: Study in Geography* (in Arabic). Tripoli: Dar Al-Jamaheria: 545–627.

Bennett, J. and Coockson, B. (2009). 'Hendek Kale: a Late Roman multiple lever press site in western Asia Minor'. *Antiquity* 83: 319–320.

Bennett, P. and Buzaian, A. (2006). 'A preliminary survey of Gasr Shibna, Benghazi'. *Libyan Studies* 37: 31–44.

Bentaher, F. and Buzaian, A. (2006). 'Excavations of Garyounis University at Tocra 1997-2002'. In E. Fabbricotti and O. Menozzi (eds), *Cirenaica: Sudi, Scavi e Scoperte* (Parte I: *Nuovi Dati da Citta e Territorio*). BAR International Series 1488, Oxford: BAR: 163–172.

Bentaher, F. and Buzaian, A. (2010). 'Roman wine production in Cyrenaica; new evidence from Balagrae (al-Beida)'. In M. Luni (ed.), *Cirene e la Cirenaica nell'antichità*. Monografie di Archeologia Libica - XXX. Rome: L'Erma di Bretschneider: 31–35.

Bernhardsen, T. (2002). *Geography Information System: An Introduction* (3rd edition). New York: John Wiley and Sons.

Bigi, L. (2016). 'Oil production at Dionysias and in Fayum tradition and technological innovation across the Ptolemaic and Roman periods'. In N. Mugnai, J. Nikolaus, N. Ray (eds), *De Africa Romaque: Merging Cultures across North Africa*. Society for Libyan Studies Conference Volume 1. London: Society for Libyan Studies: 145–156.

Bintliff, J. L. (1997). 'Regional survey, demography and the rise of complex societies in the Aegean: Core-periphery, neo-Malthusian, and other interpretive models'. *Journal of Field Archaeology* 24: 8–38.

Blackman, D. (1998). 'Archaeology in Greeece 1997–98'. *Archaeological Reports* 44: 1–28.

Bonifay, M. (2003). 'La ceramique africaine, un indice du développement économique?. *Antiquité Tardive* 11: 113-128.

Bonifay, M. (2007). 'Ceramic Production in Africa During Late Antiquity: Continuity and Change'. In L. Lavan, E. Zanini, and A. C. Sarantis (eds), *Technology in Transition: AD 300-650*. Leiden: Brill: 141–158.

Bonifay, M., Capelli, C. (2013). 'Les Thermes du Levant a Leptis Magna: quatre contexts ceramiques des IIIe et IVe s.'. *Antiquites Africaines* 49: 67–150.

Brehony, J. A. N. (1960). 'Semi-nomadism In the Jebel Tarhuna'. In S. G. Willimot and J. I. Clark (eds) *Field Studies in Libya*. Research Paper Series No. 4, Department of Geography, Durham Colleges in the University of Durham: 60–69.

Brogan, O. and Smith, D. J. (1984). *Ghirza. A Libyan Settlement in the Roman Period* (Libyan Antiquities Series I). Tripoli: Department of Antiquities.

Brøndsted, J. (1928). 'La basilique de Cinq Martyrs à Kapljuç'. In E. Dyggve and J. Brøndsted (eds), *Recherche à Salone*, I. Copenhagen: J. H. Schultz imprimerie de l'Université: 34–195.

Brun, J.-P. (1986). *L'oléiculture antique en Provence, les huileries du départment du Var*. Paris: Revue Archéologique de Narbonnaise, Supplément 15, Centre National de la Recherche Scientifique.

Brun, J.-P. (1993). 'Les innovations techniques et leur diffusion dans les pressoirs'. In M.-C. Amouretti and J.-P. Brun (eds), *La Production du Vin et de l'Huile en Méditerranée*. Athens-Paris: Boccard: 539–550.

Brun, J.-P. (2003a). *Archéologie du Vin et de l'Huile: De la Préhistoire à l'Époque Hellénistique*. Paris: Éditions Errance.

Brun, J.-P. (2003b). *Le Vin et l'Huile dans la Meditérranée Antique. Viticulture, Oléiculture et Procédés de Fabrication*. Paris: Éditions Errance.

Brun, J.-P. (2004). *Archéologie du Vin et de l'Huile dans l'Empire Romain*. Paris: Editions Érrance.

Brun, J.-P. (forthcoming). 'Wine and oil production in the VAR region, 50 years on'. In D. Van Limbergen, E. Dodd, M. Stella Busana (eds), *Vine-growing and winemaking in the Roman world*. Rome: Peeters Publishers/Academia Belgica.

Bruno, B. (2002). 'Importazione e consumo di derrate nel tempio: l'evidenza delle anfore'. ROSSI: 277-307.

Bukechiem, A. A. (1993). 'Utilisation of groundwater in Jebel el-Akhdar, north-east Libya, as a basis of agriculture improvement with special emphasis on the El-Merj plain'. *Libyan Studies* 24: 121–142.

Burns, T. S. and Eadie, J. W. (eds) (2001). *Urban Centers and Rural Contexts in Late Antiquity*. East Lansing: Michigan State University Press.

Buzaian, A. (2000). 'Excavations at Tocra (1985–1992)'. *Libyan Studies* 31: 59-102.

Buzaian, A. (2009). 'A forgotten press building at Lamluda'. *Libyan Studies* 40: 47–54.

Buzaian, A. and Bentaher, F. (2002). 'Preliminary report on two seasons of excavations at Balagrae (al-Beida)'. *Libyan Studies* 33: 125–131.

Buzaian, A. and Bentaher, F. (2006). 'Excavations at Balagrae (al-Beida) 2001-2003'. In E. Fabbricotti and O. Menozzi (eds), *Cirenaica: Studi, Scavi da Città e*

Scoperte. Parte I: Nuovi dati da cità territorio. BAR International Series 1488, Oxford: BAR: 153–162.

Callender, M. H. (1965). *Roman Amphorae.* London: Oxford University Press for University of Durham.

Callot, O. (1984). *Huileries Antiques de Syrie du Nord.* Paris: P. Geuthner.

Camperio, M. (1881). 'Una gita in Cirenaica'. *L'Esploratore* 5: 14–58.

Camps-Farber, H. (1953). L*'Oliver et l'Huile dans l'Afrique Romaine.* Algeria: Direction de l'Interieur et de Beaux-Arts.

Camps-Farber, H. (1985). 'L'oliver et son importance économique dans l'Afrique du Nord Antique, in: l'Huile d'Olive en Méditerranée'. *Histoire, Antropolgie, Économie de l'Antiquité à nos jours. Actes de la Table Ronde de CGroupement d'Intérêt Scientifique (G.I.S.) «Sciences Humaines sur l'Aire Mediterraneene» et de la Chambre de Commerce et d'Industrie de Marseille.* Aix Marseille: Institut de recherches et d'études sur les mondes arabes et musulmans, Institut de recherches méditerranéennes, Université de Provence: 53–78.

Capelli, C. and Bonifay, M. (2007). 'Archéométrie et archéologie des céramiques africaines: une approche pluridisciplinaire'. In M. Bonifay, and J.-C. Tréglia, (eds), *Late Roman Coarse Wares, Cooking Wares and Amphorae in the Mediterranean: Archaeology and Archaeometry.* Vol. 1. BAR International Series 1662, Oxford: BAR: 551–568.

Carter, T. H. (1963). 'Reconnaissance in Cyrenaica'. *Expedition* 5: 18–27.

Catani, E. (1976), 'I frantoi della fattoria bizantina di El-Beida'. *Quaderni di Archeologia della Libia* 8: 435–448.

Catani, E. (1978). 'Pavimento con iscrizione musiva cristiana da El-Beida (Cyrenaica)'. In L. Gasperini (ed.), *Scretti Storico-Epigrafici in Memoria di Marcello Zamblli*, Rome: Centro Editorial Internazionale, Universita di Maccerata: 69–85.

Catani, E. (1998). 'Fasi edilizie e techniche murarie della fattoria paleo-bizantina di Siret el Giamel nella chora Cirenea'. In E. Catani and S. Marengo (eds), *La Cirenaica in Età Antica*, Pisa - Rome: Isttituti Editoriali e Poligrafici Internazionali: 113–135.

Cherstich, L. (2005). 'The tomb S1 of Cyrene: from the Hellenistic phase to the Christian re-use'. In C. Briault, J. Green, A. Kaldelis and A. Stellatou (eds), *Symposium on Mediterranean Archaeology* 2003. BAR. Oxford: BAR: 33–38.

Chevrollier, F. (2016). 'From Cyrene to Gortyn. Notes on the relationship between Crete and Cyrenaica under Roman domination (1st century BC–4th century AD)'. In J. E. Francis and A. Kouremenos (eds), *Roman Crete: New Perspectives.* Oxford & Philadelphia: Oxbow Books: 11–26.

Christofle, M. (1930). *Essai de Restitution d'un Moulin à Huile de l'Époque Romaine à Madaure (Constantine).* Alger: J. Carbonel (A).

Cipriano, S., Mazzocchin, S. and Paspore, P. (1997). 'Nuove considerazioni sui commerci del territorio patavino in eta` imperiale. Analisi di alcune tipologie d'anfore da scavi recenti'. *Quaderni di Archeologia del Veneto* 13: 99–109.

Coster, C. H. (1968). *Late Roman Studies.* MA: Harvard University Press.

Dahari, U. (1998). 'Horbat Tinshemet, Church of St. Bacchus'. *Excavations and Surveys in Israel* 18: 67–68.

Dar, S. 1986. *Landscape and Pattern: An Archaeological Survey of Samaria 800 BCE–636 CE.* BAR International Series 308, 2 vols. Oxford: BAR.

Dar, S. (1999). *Sumaqa: A Roman and Byzantine Jewish village on Mount Carmel, Israel.* BAR International Series 815. Oxford: BAR.

Decker, M. (2008). 'Water into wine: Trade and technology in Late Antiquity'. In L. Lavan, E. Zanini and A, Sarantis (eds), *Technology in Transition A.D. 300-650. Late Antique Archaeology.* Volume 4. Leiden: Brill: 65–92.

Degrassi, V. and Maggi, P. (1991). 'La struttura: il pozzo e I suoi reperti'. *Aquileia romana.Vita pubblica e privata, Catalogo della mostra,* Venezia: 26–29.

De Martino, G. (1912). *Tripoli, Cirene e Cartagine.* 2nd edition. Bologne: Zanichelli.

Dent, J. S., Lloyd, J. A. and Riley, J. A. (1983). 'Some Hellenistic and Roman tombs from Benghazi'. *Libya Antiqua* 11–13: 131–212.

Dennis, G. (1870). 'On recent excavations in the Greek cemeteries of the Cyrenaica'. *Transactions of the Royal Society of Literature.* Second Series, Volume 9: 135–182.

Desio, A. (1968). 'History of geologic exploration of Cyrenaica'. In F. T. Barr (ed.), *Geology and Archaeology of Northern Cyrenaica, Libya.* Tenth Annual Field Conference. Tripoli: Petroleum Exploration Society of Libya: 79–114.

De Vos, M. (2000). *Rus Africum: Tterra, Acqua, Olio nell'Africa Settentrionale: Scavo e Ricognizionenei Dintorni di Dougga (Alto Tell Tunisino).* Trento: Università degli Studi di Trento/Institut National du Patrimoine de Tunis.

Drachmann, A. G. (1932). *Ancient Oil Mills and Presses.* Danske Videnskalernes Selskab Arcaeologisk Kunsthistoriske Meddeleser, Bind 1, Kopenhaven.

Dressel, H. (1878). 'Ricerche sul Monte Testaccio'. *Annali dell'Instituto di Corrispondenza. Archeologica,* 1878: 118–192.

Edwik, A. A. (2007). *Oil Dependency, Economic Diversification and Development: A Case Study of Libya.* Research Institute for the Built and Human Environment School of the Built Environment. University of Salford. PhD Thesis. Available at: http://usir.salford.ac.uk/2189/ (accessed: 14 May 2022)

Eitam, D. (1980). The Production of Oil and Wine in Mount Ephraim in the Iron Age. Unpublished MA thesis, Tel Aviv University (in Hebrew).

Empereur, J.-Y. and Garlan, Y. (1986). 'Recherches sur les amphores grecques'. *Bulletin de Correspondence Hellénique*, Supplément 13: 515–531.

Empereur, J.-Y. and Picon, M. (1989). 'Les régions de production d'amphores imperiales en Mediterrranée orientale'. In *Amphores Romaines et Histoire Économique : Dix Ans de Recherche*, Actes du colloque de Sienne, 22-24 mai 1986. Rome: École Française de Rome 114: 223–248.

Emrage, A. (2015). *Roman Fortified Farms (Qsur) and Military Sites in the Region of the Wadi al-Kuf, Cyrenaica (Eastern Libya)*. Unpublished PhD Thesis submitted to the University of Leicester. Available at: http://hdl.handle.net/2381/32210 (accessed: 10 May 2022)

Fantoli, A. (1952). *Le Pioggie della Libia*. Rome: Ministero dell' Africa Italiana, Ispettorato Meteorologico.

Felici, F., Munzi, M., and Tantillo, I. (2006). 'Austuriani e Laguatan in Tripolitania'. *L'Africa romana* 16 (1): 591–688.

Fentress, E. and Wilson, A. (2016). 'The Saharan Berber Diaspora and the Southern Frontiers of Byzantine North Africa'. In Susan T. Stevens and Jonathan P. Conant (eds), *North Africa under Byzantium and early Islam ca. 500–800*. Trustees for Harvard University, Washington, D.C.: 41–64.

Ferrarini, F. (1993). 'Osservazioni su due tipologie di anfore della media eta` imperiale da Altino'. *Quaderni di Archeologia del Veneto* 9: 157–164.

Ferri, S. (1926). 'Firme di legionary della Siria nella Gran Sirte'. *Rivista della Tripolitania* 2 :192–363.

Flemming, N. (1971). *Cities in the Sea: an Exploration of Ancient Cities Beneath the Mediterranean*. New York: The New English Library.

Food and Agriculture Organization of the United Nations (1969a). *Development of Tribal Lands* and *Settlements Project*, General Report. Report to Libyan Government. Volume 1. Libyan Funds-in-Trust, Rome (in Arabic). Available at: http://www.fao.org/docrep/field/009/89724e/89724e01.pdf (accessed: 30 May 2022)

Food and Agriculture Organization of the United Nations (1969b). *Development of Tribal Lands* and *Settlements Project*, Final Report of Experts, Soil and Water Surveys. Report to Libyan Government. Volume 3. Libyan Funds-in-Trust, Rome (in Arabic). Available at: http://www.fao.org/docrep/field/009/89724e/89724e03.pdf (accessed: 30 May 2022)

Foot, H. (1964). *A Start in Freedom*. London: Hodder and Stoughton.

Forbes, H. A. and Foxhall, L. (1978). 'The queen of all trees: preliminary notes on archaeology of the olive'. *Expedition* 21, I: 37–47.

Foss, C. (1994). 'The Lycian coast in the Byzantine age'. *Dumbarton Oaks Papers*, Volume 48: 1–52.

Foxhall, L. (1993). 'Oil extraction and processing equipment in classical Greece'. In M.-C. Amouretti and J.-P. Brun (eds), *La Production du Vin et de l'Huile en Méditerrnanée*. Paris: Boccard: 183–200.

Foxhall, L. (1997). 'Ancient farmsteads, other agricultural sites and equipment'. In C. Mee, H. Forbes (eds), *A Rough and Rocky Place. TheLandscape and Settlement History of the Methana Peninsula, Greece. Results of the Methana Survey Project*: 257–268.

Foxhall, L. (2007). *Olive Cultivation in Ancient Greece: Seeking the Ancient Economy*. Oxford – New York: Oxford University Press.

Franchetti, L. (1914). *La Missione Franchetti in Trpolitania (Il Gebèl); Indagini Econmico-Agrarie della Commissione Inviata in Tripolitania dalla Società Italiana per lo Studio della Libia*. Firenze - Milan: Frattelli Treves.

Frankel, R. (1994). 'Ancient oil mills and presses in the Land of Israel'. In E. Ayalon (ed.), *History and Technology of Olive Oil in the Holy Land*. Tel Aviv: Eretz Idrael Museum: 19–89.

Frankel, R. (1997). 'Presses for oil and wine in the southern Levant in the Byzantine period'. *Dumbarton Oaks Papers*, Volume 51: 73–84.

Frankel, R. (1999). *Wine and Oil Production in Antiquity in Israel and Other Mediterranean Countries*. Sheffield: Sheffield Academic Press.

Frankel, R. (2016). 'Oil and wine production'. In G. L. Irby (ed.), *A Companion to Science, Technology, and Medicine in Ancient Greece and Rome*, Volume 1, Chichester: Wiley Blackwell: 550–569.

Fraser, P. M. (1950). 'Hadrian and Cyrene'. *Journal of Roman Studies* 40: 77–87.

Freed, J. and Wilson, R. (1999). 'Sicilian Naxian wine amphoras: a new look at wine in North Africa'. *American Journal of Archaeology* 103: 268–85.

Fuks, A. (1961). 'Aspects of the Jewish Revolt in A.D. 115- 117'. *Journal of Roman Studies* 51: 98–104.

Fulford, M. G. (1989). 'To east and west: the Mediterranean trade of Cyrenaica and Tripolitania in antiquity'. *Libyan Studies* 20: 169–191.

Fulford, M. G. and Peacock, D. P. S. (eds). (1984). *The Avenue du Président Habib Bourguiba, Salammbô: The Pottery and Other Ceramic Objects from the Site, Excavations at Carthage: the British Mission, Volume. 1, 2*. Sheffield: The British Academy from the Department of Prehistory and Archaeology, University of Sheffield.

Gambini, V. (1974-1975). 'Due impianti per frantoi'. *Libya Antiqua* 11–12: 277–286.

Gardiner, A. (1972). *Egypt of the Pharaohs*. Oxford: Oxford University Press.

Goodchild, R. G. (1949). 'The *limes Tripolitanus* in the light of recent discoveries'. *Journal of Roman Studies* 39: 81–95.

Goodchild, R. G. (1953). 'The Roman and Byzantine *limes* in Cyrenaica'. *Journal of Roman Studies* 43: 65–76.

Goodchild, R. G. (1967a). 'The forum of Ptolemais (Cyrenaica)'. *Quaderni di Archeologia della Libia* 5: 47–51.

Goodchild, R. G. (1967b). 'Byzantines, Berbers and Arabs in seventh century Libya' *Antiquity* 41: 115–124.

Goodchild, R. G. (1968). 'Graeco-Roman Cyrenaica'. In F.T Barr (ed.): *The geology and archaeology of northern Cyrenaica, Libya.* Petrol. Explor. Soc. of Libya. 10th annual field conference: 23–40.

Goodchild, R. G. (1976). *Libyan Studies, Select Papers by R. G. Goodchild.* J. M. Reynolds (ed.). London: Paul Elek.

Goodchild, R. G. (1981). *Cyrene and Apollonia.* Tripoli: Department of Antiquities.

Goodchild, R. G. and Reynolds, J. M. (1962). 'Some military inscriptions from Cyrenaica'. *Papers of the British School at Rome* 30: 37–46.

Göransson, K. (2007). *The Transport Amphorae from Euesperides: The Maritime Trade of a Cyrenaican City 400–250 BC.* Lund: Lund University.

Greene, K. (1990). 'Perspective of Roman technology'. *Oxford Journal of Archaeology* 9.2: 209–19.

Greene, K. (1992). 'How was technology transferred in the Roman world?'. In M. Wood and F. Queiroga (eds). *Current Research on the Romanization of the Western Provinces*, BAR S575, Oxford: BAR: 101–105.

Gregory, J. W. (1911). 'The geology of Cyrenaica'. *Quarterly of the Journal of the Geographical Society of London* 67: 572–615.

Habsburg, K., Kila, J. and Walda, H. (2011). Mission Report. 2. Civil-Military Assessment for Libyan Heritage. By Blue Shield and International Military Cultural Resources Work Group 'IMCuRWG'. 12 to 16 November 2011.

Hadjisavvas, S. (1985). 'Excavations at the 'Tombs of the Kings', Kato Paphos' In V. Karageorghis (ed.), *Archaeology in Cyprus 1960–1985.* Nicosia: AG Leventis Foundation: 262–268.

Hadjisavvas, S. (1992). *Olive Oil Production in Cyprus from the Bronze Age to the Byzantine Period.* Nicosia: Paul Åström.

Hadjisavvas, S. (1993). 'Perforated monoliths: myths and reality'. In M.-C. Amouretti and J.-P. Brun (eds), *La Production du Vin et de l'Huile en Méditerrnanée.* Paris: Boccard: 137–149.

Haimann, G. (1882). 'La Cirenaica'. *Bolletino della Societa Geographica Italiana*, Série 2, Volume 7. Rome: Stabilimento Giuseppe Civelli: 87–90.

Hallett, D. (2002). *Petroleum Geology of Libya.* Amsterdam: Elsevier.

Hamilton, J. (1856). *Wanderings in North Africa.* London: John Murray.

Hayes, J. (1983). 'The Villa Dionisos Excavations, Knossos: the pottery'. *Annual of the British School at Athens* 78: 97–169.

Hesein, M. A. H. (2014). 'Ancient marine resource exploitation in the coastal strip of Cyrenaica: Some evidence of fish-related industry in Cyrenaica?'. In E. Botte and V. Leitch (eds), *Fish & Ships, Production and Commerce of Salsamenta During Antiquity.* Publications du Centre Camille Jullian: Aix-en-Provence: 129–141.

Hesein, M. A. H. (2015). *Bridging the Eastern and Western Mediterranean: The Roman Harbour Sites on the Coast of Cyrenaica, North-Eastern Libya.* Unpublished PhD Thesis submitted to the University of Leicester. Available at: http://hdl.handle.net/2381/33017 (accessed: 10 June 2015)

Hill, R. W. (1960), *Some Problems of Economic Geography in Northern Tripolitania: a Study of Agriculture and Irrigation on the Jefara Plain,* Durham theses, Durham University. Available at: Durham E-Theses. Available at: http://etheses.dur.ac.uk/8358/ (accessed: 15 May 2022)

Hitchner, R. B. (1988). 'The Kasserine Arcaheological Survey, 1982-1986'. *Antiquités africaines* 24: 7–41.

Hitchner, R. B., Ellis, S., Graham A., Mattingly, D. and Neuru, L. (1990). 'The Kasserine Arrchaeological Survey. 1987'. *Antiquités africaines* 26: 231–259.

Hitchner, R. B. and Mattingly, D. J. (1991). 'Fruits of empire. The production of olive oil in Roman Africa'. *National Geographic Research and Exploration* 7: 36–55.

Hobson, M. (2015). The North African Boom: Evaluating Economic Growth in the Roman Province of Africa Proconsularis (146 B.C. – A.D. 439). *Journal of Roman Archaeology*, Supplementary series; no. 100. Portsmouth: Rhode Island.

Hulin, H. (2008). 'Western Marmarica Coastal Survey 2008: a preliminary report'. *Libyan Studies* 39: 299–314.

Hulin, L., Timby, J. and Mutri, G. (2009). 'The western Marmarica coastal survey 2009: preliminary report'. *Libyan Studies* 40: 178–187.

Hulin, L., Timby, J. Muftah, A. M. and Mutri, G. (2010). 'Western Marmarica coastal survey 2010: preliminary report'. *Libyan Studies* 41: 155–162.

Humphery, J., Oleson, J. and Sherwood, A. (1998). *Greek and Roman Technology : A Sourcebook. Annotated Translations of Greek and Latin Texts and Documents.* London: Routledge.

Hunt, C., Elrishi, H. and Hassan, A. (2002). 'Reconnaissance investigation of the palynology of Holocene wadi in Cyrenaica, Libya'. *Libyan Studies* 33: 1–7.

Johnson, D. L. (1973). *Jabal al-Akhdar, Cyrenaica: an Historical Geography of Settlement and Livelihood.* Department of Geography Research. Paper no. 148, Chicago: University of Chicago Press.

Jones, B. and Little, J. (1971a). 'Hadrianopolis'. *Libya Antiqua*, 8: 53–75.

Jones, B. and Little, J. (1971b). 'Coastal settlement in Cyrenaica'. *Journal of Roman Studies* 61: 64–79.

Karageorghis, V. (1993). 'The history of in Cyprus. A brief survey'. In *Vines and Wines in Cyprus - 4000 years of Tradition*, Limassol: Vine Products Commision: 31–45.

Karagiorgou, O. (2001). 'LR2 container for the military *annona* on the Danubian border?'. In S. Kingsley D. and Michael (eds), *Economy and Exchange in the East Mediterranean during Late Antiquity.* Proceedings of a Conference at Somerville College, Oxford, 29 May, 1999. Oxford: The Information Press Eynsham: 129–166.

Karagiorgou, O. (2009). 'Mapping trade by the amphora'. In M. M. Mango (ed.), *Byzantine Trade, 4th-12th Centuries: The Archaeology of Local, Regional and International Exchange: Papers of the Thirty-eight Spring Symposium of Byzantine Studies*, St. John's College, University of Oxford, March 2004. Society for the Promotion of Byzantine Studies – Publication 14. Bodmin, Cornwall: MPG Books Ltd: 37–58.

Keay, N. (1989). 'The amphorae'. In M. Fulford and M. Hall (eds), *Excavations at Sabratha 1948–1951, Volume 2 The Finds, Part 1. The Amphorae, Coarse Pottery and Building Materials.* London: Society for Libyan Studies: 5–85.

Kenrick, P. M. (1985). 'Patterns of trade in fine pottery at Berenice'. In G. Barker, J. Lloyd and J. Reynolds (eds), *Cyrenaica in Antiquity.* BAR International Series 236, Oxford: BAR: 249–257.

Kenrick, P. M. (2013a). *Libya Archaeological Guides: Cyrenaica.* London: Society for Libyan Studies, Silphium Press.

Kenrick, P. M. (2013b). 'Ancient sites in rural Cyrenaica: a partial update'. *Libyan Studies* 44: 57–72.

Khalifa, F. (2010). Tombs at the Settlement of Wadi Ein Khargah, Cyrenaica (West of al-Beida): Architectural study. Unpublished MA dissertation submitted to the Benghazi University (in Arabic).

Khalil, L. A. and Al-Nammari, F. M. (2000). 'Two large wine presses at Khirbet Yajux, Jordan'. Bulletin of the American Schools of Oriental Research 318: 41–49.

Kingsley, S. A. (2001). 'The Economic Impact of the Palestinian Wine Trade in Late Antiquity'. In S. Kingsley D. and Michael (eds), *Economy and Exchange in the East Mediterranean during Late Antiquity.* Proceedings of a Conference at Somerville College, Oxford, 29 May, 1999. Oxford: The Information Press Eynsham: 44–68.

Kingsley, S. and Decker, M. (2001). 'New Rome, new theories on inter-regional exchange. An introduction to the East Mediterranean economy in Late Antiquity'. In S. Kingsley D. and Michael (eds), *Economy and Exchange in the East Mediterranean during Late Antiquity.* Proceedings of a Conference at Somerville College, Oxford, 29 May, 1999. Oxford: The Information Press Eynsham: 1–27.

Kloner, A. and Sagiv, N. (1993). 'The olive presses of Hellenistic Maresha, Israel'. In M.-C. Amouretti and J.-P. Brun (eds), *La Production du Vin et de l'Huile en Méditerranée.* Paris: Boccard: 119–136.

Kraeling, C. H. (1960). P*tolemais, City of the Libyan Pentapolis.* Chicago, Illinois: The University of Chicago Press.

Kroeller, E. H. (1958). *Agricultura Statistics in Cyrenaica 1954-1958.* Benghazi : Provincial Government of Cyrenaica, Nazarat of Agriculture and Forests, Statistics Section.

Łajtar, A. (2012). 'Greek inscriptions discovered during archaeological works of the Polish mission'. In J. Żelazowski (ed.), *Ptolemais in Cyrenaica. Studies in Memory of Tomasz Mikocki.* Warsaw: University of Warsaw, Institute of Archaeology: 253–271.

Lanfranchi, R. E. (2009). *I Torchi per la Pressatura delle Olive. I Ritrovamenti nel Territorio di Dougga.* Unpublished PhD thesis submitted to the Universtà degli Studi di Trento.

Laporte, J.-P. (1983). 'Fermes, huileries et pressoirs de Grand Kabylie'. *BCTH* ns 19, fasc B: 127-146.

Laronde, A. (1983). 'Kainopolis de Cyrénaïque et la géographie historique'. *Comptes Rendues de l'Académie des Inscriptions et Belles-Lettres* 127: 67-85.

Laronde, A. (1984). 'Environmental change or stability, with special emphasis on the Roman agricultural development of Libyan Roman economy, prior the Arab conquest'. (Working document prepared at the request of UNESCO). Available at: http://unesdoc.unesco.org/images/0005/000585/058591EB.pdf (accessed: 12 May 2022).

Laronde, A. (1987). *Cyrène et la Libye Hellénistique. 'Libykai Historiai' de l'Époque Republicaine au Principat d'Auguste.* Paris: Centre National de la Recherche Scientifique.

Leake, B. E. (2011). *The Life and Work of Professor J. W. Gregory FRS (1864–1932): Geologist, Writer and Explorer.* London: Geological Society Memoirs 34.

Leveau P. (1984). *Caesarea de Maurétanie: une Ville Romaine et ses Campagnes.* (Collection de l'École française de Rome 70), Rome: École française de Rome.

Leveau P. (1985). 'Pressoirs ă huile autour de Caesarea de Maurétanie (Cherchel, Algérie). Problèmes d'interpretation historique'. In *Histoires des Techniques et Sources Documentaries. Méthodes d'Approche et Experimentation en Region Méditerranée.* Aix-en-Provence: 193–197.

Lewit, T. (2007). 'Absent-minded landlords and innovating peasants? The press in Africa and the Eastern Mediterranean'. In L. Lavan, E. Zarini and A. Sarantis (eds), *Technology in Transition A.D. 300-650* (Late Antique Archaeology, 4, cil. (n. 7). Leiden: Brill Academic Publishers: 119–139.

Little, O. M. (1945). *Handbook on Cyrenaica: Geology of Cyrenaica.* Part 1, British Military Adminstration (Cyrenaica).

Lloyd, J. A. (1990). 'The cities of Cyrenaica in the third century AD'. In G. Lincea (ed.), *Atti del Convegni Lincei. Giornata Lincea sull Archaeologia Cirenaica* (Rome, 3 Novembre 1987). Rome: Accademia Nazionale dei Lincei: 40–53.

Lloyd, J. A. (1977), (ed.). *'Excavations at Sidi Khrebish, Benghazi (Berenice)', Buildings, Coins, Inscriptions, Architectural Decoration.* Volume 1, Supplements to *Libya Antiqua* 5. Tripoli: Department of Antiquities.

Lloyd, J. A. (1985). 'Some aspects of urban development at Euesperides/Berenice'. In G. Barker, J. Lloyd and J. Reynolds (eds) *Cyrenaica in Antiquity.* BAR, International Series 236, Oxford: BAR: 49–66.

Lloyd, J. A. (2002). 'The development of trade between Cyrenaica and Italy in the Hellenistic and Roman periods'. *Quaderni di Archeologia della Libya* 16: 151–163.

Long, L. (2011). 'Recherches sous-marines au large des Saintes-Maries-dela- Mer (Bouches-du-Rhône). Sur les traces de l'avant-port maritime d'Arles'. *SFECAG,* Actes du congrès d'Arles: 97–118.

Cherstich, L., Menozzi, O., Antonelli, S., Cherstich, I., (2018). 'A 'living' necropolis: change and reuse in the cemeteries of Cyrene'. *Libyan Studies* 49: 121–152.

Luni, M. (1987). 'Il santuario rupestre *libya* delle "Immagini" a Slonta (Cirenaica). testimonianze della cultura *libya* in ambiente greco-romano: originalità e dipendenza'. *Quaderni di Archeologia della Libia* 12: 415–458.

MacMullen, (1980). 'How big was the Roman imperial army?'. *Klio* 62: 451–460.

Małkowski, W (2012). 'Investigation of the aqueduct of Ptolemias using GPS RTK survey equipment'. In J. Żelazowski (ed.), *Ptolemais in Cyrenaica.* Studies in Memory of Tomasz Mikocki. Warsaw: University of Warsaw, Institute of Archaeology: 93–99.

Matijasić, R. 1993. 'Oil and wine production in Istria and Dalmatia in Classical Antiquity and the early Middle Ages'. In M.-C. Amouretti and J.-P. Brun (eds), *La Production du Vin et de l'Huile en Méditerrnanée.* Paris: Boccard: 247–261.

Mattingly, D. J. (1985). 'Olive oil production in Roman Tripolitania'. In D. J. Buck and D. J. Mattingly (eds), *Town and Country in Roman Tripolitania: Papers in Honour of Olwen Hackett.* BAR International Series 274, Oxford: BAR: 27–46.

Mattingly, D. J. (1988a). 'Megalithic madness and measurement or how many olives could an olive press press?'. *Oxford Journal of Archaeology* 7.2: 177–195.

Mattingly, D. J. (1988b). 'The olive boom. Oil surpluses, wealth and power in Roman Tripolitania'. *Libyan Studies* 19: 21–41.

Mattingly, D. J. (1988c). 'Olea mediterranea?'. *Journal of Roman Archaeology* 1: 153-161.

Mattingly, D. J. (1988d). 'Oil for export: a comparative study of Roman olive oil production in Libya, Spain and Tunisia'. *Journal of Roman Archaeology* 1: 33–56.

Mattingly, D. J. (1990). 'Paintings, presses and perfume production at Pompeii'. *Oxford Journal of Archaeology* 9.1: 71-90.

Mattingly, D. J. (1993). 'Maximum figures and maximizing strategies of oil production? Further thoughts on the processing capacity of Roman olive presses'. In M.-C. Amouretti and J.-P. Brun (eds), *La Production du Vin et de l'Huile en Méditerranée.* Paris: Boccard: 483–498.

Mattingly, D. J. (1994). 'Regional variation in Roman oleoculture: some problems of comparability'. In J. Carlsen, P. Ørsted, and J. E. Skydsgaard (eds), *Landuse in the Roman Empire.* Analecta Romana Instituti Danici Supplement 22: 91–106.

Mattingly, D. J. (1996). 'Olive presses in Roman Africa: technical evolution or stagnation? '. In M. Khanoussi, P. Ruggeri and C. Vismara (eds), *L'Africa Romana. Atti del XI convegno di studio* (Cartagine, 15–18 dicembre 1994), Ozeieri: 2 Torchietto: 577–595.

Mattingly, D. J. (2009). 'A new study of olive oil (and wine?) production in northern Tunisia'. *Journal of Roman Archaeology* 22: 715–720.

Mattingly, D. J. (2011). 'Calculating plough-zone demographics. Some insights from arid-zone surveys'. In A. Bowman and A. Wilson (eds), *Settlement, Urbanization, and Population.* Oxford: Oxford University Press: 76–96.

Mattingly, D. J. and Hitchner, R. B. (1993). 'Technical specifications of some North African olive presses of Roman date'. In Amouretti and Brun (eds), *La Production du Vin et de l'Huile en Méditerranée.* Paris: Boccard: 439–462.

Mattingly, D. J. and Hitchner, R. B (1995). 'Roman Africa: An archaeological review'. *Journal of Roman Studies* 85: 165–213.

Mattingly, D. J. and Dore, J. (1996). 'Romano-Libyan settlement: typology and chronology', In G. Barker (ed.). *Farming the Desert, the UNESCO Libyan Valleys Archaeological Survey. Volume 1: Synthesis.* London: Society for Libyan Studies – Department of Antiquities: 111–158.

Mattingly, D. J. and Zenatti, M. (1984). 'The excavation of building Lm 4E: the olive press'. *Libyan Studies* 15: 13–18.

Mazou, F. (2016). 'Une production d'Amphores Benghazi Mid Roman 8 à Apollonia de Cyrénaïque'. *Études Libyennes* 3. Paris, Editions Riveneuve: 187–205.

Mazou, L. and Capelli, C. (2011). 'A local production of Mid Roman 1 amphorae at Latrun, Cyrenaica'. *Libyan Studies* 42: 73–76.

McBurney, C. M. and Hey, R. W. (1955). *Prehistory and Pleistocene Geology in Cyrenaican Libya: A Record of Two Seasons' Geological and Archeological Fieldwork in the Gebel Akhdar Hills, with a Summary of Prehistoric Finds from Neighboring Territories.* Cambridge: Cambridge University Press.

McLachlan, K. (1982). 'Strategies for agricultural development in Libya'. In J. A. Allan (ed.), Libya

Since Independence: Economic and Political Development. London: Routledge: 9–24.

Menozzi, O. and Antonelli, S. with contributions by Cinalli, A., Mancini and Agostini, S. (2014). 'Lamluda: from the excavation to the archaeometric analysis'. *Libyan Studies* 45: 65–84.

Meunier, J. (1941). 'L'huilerie romaine de Kherbet-Agoub (Perigotville)'. *Bulletin de la Societé Historique et Géographique de la Region de Setif* 2: 35–41.

Michel, V. (2011). 'Nouvelles recherches en Cyrénaïque: les thermes romains d'Érythron, Latrun'. In Comptes rendus des séances de *l'Académie des Inscriptions et Belles-Lettres*, (janvier-mars), Paris: 205–220.

Morizot, P. (1993). 'L'Aures et l'olivier'. *Antiquités Africaines* 29 : 177–240.

Mrabet, A. (2000). *Carte National des Sites Archeologiques et des Monuments historiques*, Kettana 157. Tunis: Ministere de la Culture, Institut National du Patrimoine. Available at: http://www.inp.rnrt.tn/Carte_archeo/pdf/Fr/157KatanaFr.pdf (accessed: 28 June 2022)

Munzi, M. (2012). 'Italian archaeologists in colonial Tripolitania'. *Libyan Studies* 43: 81-110.

Munzi, M., Felici, F., Matoug, J., Sjostrom, I. and Zocchi, A. (2016). 'The Lepcitanian landscape across the ages: the survey between Ras el-Mergheb and Ras el-Hammam (2007, 2009, 2013). *Libyan Studies* 47: 67–116.

Narducci, G. (1934). *La Colonizzazione della Cirenaica nell'Anticha e nell Presenta*. Benghazi: Fratelli Pavone.

Opait, A. (2010). 'On the origin of Carthage LR amphora 1'. In S. Menchelli, S. Santoro, M. Pasquinucci and G. Guiducci (eds), *LRCW3 Late Roman Coarse Wares, Cooking Wares and Amphorae in the Mediterranean: Archaeology and Archaeometry. Comparison between Western and Eastern Mediterranean*. BAR International Series 2185, Volume II, Oxford: BAR: 1015–1022.

Overtoom, N. L. (2014). 'Was the Roman imperial army small? A comparative study of ancient imperial military forces'. *Classical Association of the Middle West and South Annual Conference*, Waco, Texas, April 2014: 1:14. Available at: https://unm.academia.edu/NikolausOvertoom (accessed: 12 May 2022)

Pacho, J.-R. (1827). *Relation d'un Voyage dans la Marmarique, la Cyrénäique et les Oasis d'Audjelah et de Maradeh*. Paris: Librairie de Firmin Didot, Père et Files.

Paniale, P. (1990). Contenitori da transport, in *Milano capitale dell'Imperto Romano*, 286-702 d.C., Catalogo della mostra, Milano: 380–382.

Pansiot, F. P. and Rebour, H. (1961). *Improvements in Olive Cultivation*. Rome: FAO.

Parker, A. (1992). *Ancient Shipwrecks of the Mediterranean and the Roman Provinces*. BAR, International Series 580, Oxford: BAR.

Peacock, D. (1982). *Pottery in the Roman World: an Ethnoarchaeological Approach*. London and New York: Longman.

Peacock, D. P. S. (1984). 'Petrology and origins'. In M. G. Fulford and D. P. S. Peacock (eds), *Excavations at Carthage: The British Mission Volume I, 2. The Avenue du President Habib Bourguiba, Salammbo: The Pottery and Other Ceramic Objects from the Site*. Sheffield: University of Sheffield: 6–28.

Peacock, D. P. S. (1994). 'The amphorae: typology, fabric and chronology'. In M. G. Fulford and D. P. S. Peacock (eds), *Excavations at Carthage: The British Mission Volume II, 2. The Circular Harbour, North Side, the Pottery*. Oxford: University Press: 42–52.

Peacock, D. and Williams, D. (1986). *Amphorae and Roman Economy: An Introductory Guide*. London and New York: Longman Archaeology Series.

Pedley, J. G. (1979). 'The Byzantine baths'. In J. H. Humphrey (ed.) *Apollonia, the Port of Cyrene: Excavations by the University of Michigan 1965–1967*. Supplements to *Libya Antiqua* 4. Tripoli: Department of Antiquities: 225–243.

Pelling, R. and Al Hassy, S. (1997). 'The macroscopic plant remains from Euesperides (Benghazi): an interim report'. *Libyan Studies* 28: 1–4.

Peña, J.T. (1998). 'The mobilization of state olive oil in Roman Africa: the evidence of late 4th-c. ostraca from Carthage'. In *Carthage Papers: the Early Colony's Economy, Water Supply, a Private Bath, and the Mobilization of State Olive Oil* (*Journal of Roman Archaeology Supplement* 28): 117-238.

Pesce, G. (1950). *Il 'Palazzo delle Colonne' in Tolmaida di Cirenaica*. Monografia di Archeologia Libica II. Rome: L'Erma.

Pollard, N. (2016). 'Villas'. In A. E. Cooley (ed.), *A Companion to Roman Italy*. Oxford: Wiley-Blackwell: 330-354.

Ponsich, M. (1974). *Implantation Rurale Antique sur le Bas-Guadalquivir (Seville Séville-Alcalá del Rio-Lora-Carmona)*. Paris: Boccard.

Ponsich, M. (1991). *Implantation Rurale Antique sur le Bas-Guadalquivir. Écija, Dos Hermanas, Los Palacios y Villafranca, Lebrija, Sanlúcar de Barramedea*. Madrid: Editorial Casa de Velázquez.

Porath, Y. (2009). 'Olive oil press at Kh. Kafritha (Qiryat 'Ata)'. In E. Ayalon, R. Frankel. A. Kloner, *Oil and Wine Presses in Israel from the Hellenistic, Roman and Byzantine Periods*. BAR International Series 1972, Oxford: BAR: 99–100.

Poulter, A. (1999). 'The excavations and the social and economic context'. In A. Poulter, R. Flanker and J. Shepherd, *Nicopolis ad Istrum: A Roman to Early Byzantine City: The Pottery and Glass*. London: Leicester University Press for the Society of Antiquaries of London: 3–53.

Preece, C (2000). 'Marsa-el-Brega: a fatal port of call. Evidence for shipwreck, anchorage and trade in antiquity in the Gulf of Sirte'. *Libyan Studies* 31: 29–57.

Raju, T. S. (1980). 'Hydrology and water balance of the Benghazi plain'. In M. J. Salem and M. Busrweil (eds), *The Geology of Libya* 2, London: Academic Press: 671–683.

Rautman, M. (2000). 'The busy countryside of Late Roman Cyprus'. *Report of the Department of Antiquities Cyprus,* Ministry of Communications and Works. Department of Antiquities, Cyprus: 317–331.

Rebuffat, R., Joulia, J. C., Mouthel, G. and Lenoir, E. (1987). 'Note préliminaire sur les grands thermes d'Apollonia'. *Libya Antiqua* 15–16: 263-277.

Reddé, M. 1(988). *Prospections de Vallees du Nord de la Libye (1979-1980): la Région de Syrte à l'Époque Romaine.* Paris: École Normale Supérieure.

Remesal Rodriguez, J. 2004. 'L'Afrique au Testaccio'. *L'Africa Romana* 15: 1077–1090.

Renfrew, C. and Bahn, P. (1991). *Archaeology: Theories, Methods and Practice.* London: Thames and Hudson Ltd.

Riley, J. A. (1979a). 'The coarse pottery from Berenice'. In J. A. Lloyd (ed.) *Excavations at Sidi Khrebish Benghazi (Berenice)* vol. 2. Supplements to *Libya Antiqua* 5, Tripoli; Department of Antiquities: 91–467.

Riley, J. A.(1979b). 'The petrological investigation of Roman and Islamic ceramics from Cyrenaica'. *Libyan Studies* 10: 35–46.

Riley, J. A. (1980). 'Amphoras in the Apollonia Museum store'. *Libyan Studies* 12: 75–78.

Riley, J. A. (1983). 'Excavation of a kiln site at Tocra, Libya in August 1974'. *Libya Antiqua* 13–14: 235-263.

Rizzo, G. (2014). 'Le anfore, Ostia e i commerci mediterranei'. In C. Panella and G. Rizzo (eds), *Ostia* VI. *Le terme del nuotatore. I saggi nell'area NE. Le Anfore, Ostia e i commerci mediterranei.* Studi Miscellanei 38: 65–481.

Robert, J. and L. Robert (1964). 'Bulletin Épigraphique'. *Revue des Études Grecques,* tome 77, fascicule 364–365, Janvier-juin 1964: 127–259.

Rodriguez-Almeida, E. (1975). 'Bolli anforari di Monte Testaccio'. *Bullettino della Commissione Archeologica Comunale di Roma* 84 (1974–1975): 199–248.

Rodriguez-Almeida, E. (1984). *Il Monte Testaccio: Ambiente, Sioria, Materiali.* Rome: Qasar.

Rodrígue-Almeida, E. (1989). *Los Tituli Picti de las Ánforas Olearias de la Bética I.* Madrid: Editorial de la Universidad Complutense.

Rodziewicz, M. (1998). 'Classification of wineries from Mareotis'. In J.-Y. Empereur (ed.), *Commerce et Artisan dans l'Alexandrie Hellénistique et Romaine. Paris: Bulletin de Correspondance Hellénique,* Supplement 33: 27-36.

Romanelli, P. (1943) *La Cirenaica Romana 96 a.C.–642 d.C.* Verbania: L'Erma,.

Roques, D. (1975). *Le Système Portuaire de Cyrène: Phykous et Apollonia.* Unpublished Ph.D. Thesis submitted to the Université de Paris-VI Sorbonne.

Roques, D. (1985). 'L'economie de la Cyrenaique au Bas-Empire'. In G. Barker, J. Lloyd and J, Reynolds (eds), *Cyrenaica in Antiquity.* Society for Libyan Studies, Occasional Papers I. BAR International Series 236. Oxford: BAR: 387–394.

Roques, D. (1987). *Synésios de Cyrène et la Cyrènaïque du Bas-Empire.* Paris: Études d'Antiquités Africaines.

Roques, D. (1999). 'Ports et campagnes de Cyrène: d'Apollonia a Phycous'. In A. Laronde and J.-J. Maffre (eds). *Cités, Ports et Campagnes de la Cyrénaïque Gréco-Romaine.* Actes de la journée d'étude sur la Cyrénaïque; à Paris le 21 novembre 1992. *Karthago Revue d'Archeologie Mediterraneenne* 24: 187–195.

Rosenbaum, E. and Ward-Perkins J. B. (1980). *Justinianic Mosaic Pavements in Cyrenaican Churches.* Volume 14 of Monografie di Archeologia Libica. Rome: L'Erma di Bretschneider.

Rostovtzeff, M. (1941). *The Social and Economic History of the Hellenistic World.* Volume I. Oxford: Clarendon Press.

Sehili, S. (2009). *Huileries Antiques de Jebel Semmama: Région de Kasserine: Secteur Couvert par la Feuille Topographique au 1/50000e de J. Semmama,* no. 076. Tunis: Centre de Publication Universitaire.

Sheldrick, N. (2021). *Building the Countryside: Rural Architecture and Settlement in Tripolitania during the Roman and Late Antique Periods.* London: Society for Libyan Studies.

Smith, A. M. and le Roux, M. (2013). 'The Phoenicians and the dangers inherent to sailing on the Mediterranean Sea in antiquity'. *Ekklesiastikos Pharos* 95, N.S. 24: 319–331.

Smith, D. and Crow, J. (1998). 'The Hellenistic and Byzantine Defences of Tocra (Taucheira)'. *Libyan Studies* 29: 35–82.

Smith, R. and Porcher, A. (1864). *History of the Recent Discoveries at Cyrene, Made During an Expedition to the Cyrenaica in 1860-61, Under the Auspices of Her Majesty's Government.* London: Day.

Stucchi, S. (1965) *L'agorà di Cirene,* vol. 1. *Monografie di Archeologia Libica* 7. I. Rome: L'Erma di Bretschneider.

Stucchi, S. (1975). *Architettura Cirenaica. Monografie di Archeologia Libica* 9. Rome: L'Erma di Bretschneider.

Tate, G., (1992). *Les Campagnes de la Syrie du Nord du IIe au VIIe siècle.* Beyrouth: Presses de l'IFPO.

Tchalenko, G., (1958). *Villages Antique de la Syrie du Nord. Le Massif du Bélus à l'Époque Romaine.* Paris: P. Geuthner.

Tusa, S. (2010). 'Rapporto preliminare della missione italiana per lo studio dell'archeologia costiera e subacquea in Cirenaica (2003-2008)'. *Libya Antiqua* 5: 211–236.

Tusa, S. (2011). 'Archeologia costiera e subacquea in Cirenaica (2003-2008)'. In Ensoli, S. (ed.). *For the Preservation of the Cultural Heritage in Libya: A Dialogue among Institutions.* Proceedings of Conference 1–2 July 2011. Rome: Fabrizio Serra Editore: 63–76.

Tyree, E. and Stefanoudaki, E. (1996). 'The olive pit and Roman oil making'. *The Biblical Archaeologist* 3, American Schools of Oriental Research: 171–178.

Van der Veen. M., Grant, A. and Barker, G. (1996). 'Romano-Libyan agriculture: crops and animals', In G. Barker (ed.). *Farming the Desert, the UNESCO Libyan Valleys Archaeological Survey. Volume 1: Synthesis.* London: Society for Libyan Studies – Department of Antiquities: 227–263.

Vanhaverbeke, H., Martens, F., Waelkens, M. and Poblome, J. (2004). 'Late Antiquity in the territory of Sagalassos (Pisidia)'. In W. Bowden, L. Lavan and C. Machado (eds), *The Late Antique Countryside. Late Antique Archaeology 2,* Leiden: Brill: 247–279.

Vetter, T., Rieger, A-K. and Nicolay, A. (2009). 'Ancient rainwater harvesting systems in the north-eastern Marmarica (north-western Egypt)'. Libyan Studies 40: 9–23.

Vismara, C. (2007). 'L'olio di Uchi Maius'. In C. Vismara (ed.), *Uchi Maius 3: I Frantoi: Miscellanea.* Sassari: Editrice Democratica Sarda: 429–482.

Vossen, P. (2007). 'Olive oil: history, production, and characteristics of the world's classic oils'. *HortScience* Vol. 42 (5): 1093–1100.

Walker, S. (2002). 'Hadrian and the renewal of Cyrene'. *Libyan Studies* 33: 45–56.

Ward-Perkins, J. B. and Goodchild (2003). *Christian Monuments of Cyrenaica.* London: Society for Libyan Studies.

Ward-Perkins, J. B., Little, J. H. and Mattingly, D. J. (1986). 'Town houses at Ptolemais, Cyrenaica: a summary report of survey and excavation work in 1971, 1978–1979'. *Libyan Studies* 17: 109–153.

Weber, T. M. and Berger, F. (2016). 'The western chôra and necropolis of Ptolemais'. *Libya Antiqua*, new series 9: 23–40.

White, D. (1998). 'Static versus reactive defense: an in-progress case study of the Apollonia and Cyrene fortifications'. In E. Catani and S. Marengo (eds), *La Cirenaica in Età Antica.* Pisa – Rome: Isttituti Editoriali e Poligrafici Internazionali: 579–622.

White, K. (1975). *Farm Equipment of the Roman World.* Cambridge: Cambridge University Press.

White, K. (1984). *Greek and Roman Technology.* New York: Cornell University Press.

Wilson, A. (2001a). 'Urban economies of Late Antique Cyrenaica'. In S. Kingsley D. and Michael (eds), *Economy and Exchange in the East Mediterranean during Late Antiquity.* Proceedings of a Conference at Somerville College, Oxford, 29 May 1999. Oxford: The Information Press Eynsham: 28–43.

Wilson, A. (2001b) 'Water-mills at Amida: Ammianus Marcellinus 18.8.11'. *Classical Quarterly* 51.1, Cambridge University Press: 231–236.

Wilson, A. (2002). 'Urban production in the Roman world: the view from North Africa'. *Papers of the British School at Rome* 70: 231–273.

Wilson, A., (2004). 'Cyrenaica and the late antique economy'. *Ancient West and East*, volume 3.1: 143–154.

Wilson, A. (2006). 'New light on a Greek city: archaeology and history at Euesperides'. In E. Fabbricotti and O. Menozzi (eds), *Cirenaica: Sudi, Scavi e Scoperte, Parte I: Nuovi Dati da Citta e Territorio.* BAR International Series 1488, Oxford: BAR: 141–152.

Wilson, A. (2008). 'Machines'. In J. P. Oleson (ed.), *Handbook of Engineering and Technology in the Classical World.* Oxford: Oxford University Press: 337–366.

Wilson, A. (2016). 'Euesperides (Benghazi): Summary of excavations 1999–2006'. *Libya Antiqua*, new series 6: 577–579.

Wilson, A., Bennett, P., Buzaian, A., Buttrey, T., Göransson, K., Hall, C., Kattenberg, A., Scott, R., Swift, K. and Zimi, E. (2002). 'Euesperides (Benghazi: preliminary report on the spring 2002 season'. *Libyan Studies* 33: 85–123.

Wilson, A. Bennett, P., Buzaian, A., Found, B., Göransen, K., Guinness, A. Hardly, J., Holman, J., Kattenberg, A., Morley, G., al-Mugasbi, M., Swift, K., Vaughan-Williams, A., Wootton, W. and Zimi, E. (2005). 'Euesperides 2005: preliminary report on the spring 2005 season'. *Libyan Studies* 36: 135–182.

Wilson, A., Schörle, K. and Rice, C. (2012). 'Roman ports and Mediteranean connectivity'. In S. Keay (ed.), *Rome, Portus and the Mediterranean.* Rome: Archaeological Monograph of the British School at Rome, Volume 21: 367–391.

Wright, J. (1969). *Libya.* London: Ernest Benn Limited.

Wright, J. (1982). *Libya, a Modem History.* Baltimore: Johns Hopkins University Press.

Wright, J. (2005). *Travellers in Libya.* London: Society for Libyan Studies, Silphium Press.

Żelazowski, J. (2012). 'General remarks on Polish excavations in Ptolemais'. In J. Żelazowski (ed.), *Ptolemais in Cyrenaica. Studies in Memory of Tomasz Mikocki.* Warsaw: University of Warsaw, Institute of Archaeology: 121–156.

Żelazowski, J., Rekowska-Ruszkowska, M., Kowarska, Z., Szymon, L., Krzysztof C., Rosłoniec, L., Jaworski, P., Misiewicz, K., Lewartowski, K., Yacoub, G., Bogacki, M., Małkowski, W. and Polak, Z. (2011). 'Polish archaeological research in Ptolemais (Libya) in 2007–2009. Preliminary report'. *Światowit*, 8 (49), fasc. A. (2009/2010): 9–55.

Zohary, D. and Spiegal-Roy, P. (1975). 'Beginning of fruit growing in the old world'. *Science* 187: 319–327.

معاصر الزيتون القديمة وإنتاج الزيت في إقليم كيرينايكي (شمال شرق ليبيا)

أحمد مصطفى أحمد بوزيان

جمعية االدراسات الليبية

يتناول هذا الكتاب إنتاج زيت الزيتون في كيرينايكي (شمال شرق ليبيا) في الفترة ما بين منتصف إلى أواخر العصر الروماني. يرى العديد من المختصين بأن المنطقة قد شهدت تدهورًا اقتصاديًا منذ القرن الثالث الميلادي فصاعدًا، ويقدم الكتاب بخصوص ذلك معلومات جديدة مهمة حول هذا النقاش لكون كيرينايكي تتمتع بموقع مهم يربط بين شرق البحر المتوسط وغربه وشمال إفريقيا بالعالم الإغريقي. يتعرض الكتاب أيضًا إلى مناقشة مدى إسهام الأدلة الأثرية من كيرينايكي في فهمنا لشبكات الاتجار عبر البحر المتوسط وأنماطها والدور الذي قام به الإقليم على نطاق تجاري أوسع.

على الرغم من وجود قدر كبير من المعلومات حول إنتاج زيت الزيتون قديمًا في شمال إفريقيا، إلا أن الدراسات المتعلقة بتقنية عصره في كيرينايكي تبدو نادرة للغاية، ولم يتم ربطها بتقنيات التصنيع المستخدمة في باقي إفريقيا الرومانية، ولهذا تعد هذه الدراسة محاولة لإثبات أهمية هذه الصناعة في اقتصاد الإقليم وذلك من خلال التقصي ولأول مرة عن الأدلة الأثرية المتعلقة بإنتاج زيت الزيتون في كيرينايكي. تركز الدراسة على تصنيف أنواع المعاصر والتعرف على خصائصها وتقنيتها وقدرتها الإنتاجية خلال الفترة من منتصف العصر الروماني إلى أواخره. يهدف هذا البحث إلى فحص الأدلة الأثرية التي جُمعت خلال العمل الميداني والمشتملة على بيانات من حوالي 107 مواقع ريفية ضمن منطقة جغرافية واسعة تغطي مساحة ما يقرب من 30.000 كيلومتر مربع. بالإضافة إلى تحديد أنواع عناصر معاصر الزيتون في الإقليم، تتناول الدراسة كذلك تصنيف أنواع الموقع التي وجدت فيها. تُجري الدراسة علاوة على ذلك تقييم لحجم الإنتاج وعلاقة ذلك بالإنتاج المحلي من الأمفورات، لمعرفة مدى إسهام إنتاج الإقليم لزيت الزيتون في اقتصاد شمال إفريقيا والبحر المتوسط. ينقسم الكتاب إلى جزأين: يحتوي الجزء الرئيس منه على تسعة فصول. يتناول الفصل الأول نبذة جغرافية وتاريخية مختصرة عن الإقليم، كما يستعرض الأعمال السابقة التي تعرضت إلى إنتاج زيت الزيتون/النبيذ خلال العصر الروماني، بدءًا من الرحالة الأوائل إلى أحدث الدراسات حول هذا الموضوع. أما الفصل الثاني فيقدم أسئلة البحث والطرق التي أُتُبعت في المسح الميداني الأثري، في حين يبحث الفصل الثالث تصنيف أنواع دواليب وأحواض جرش الزيتون في الأقليم، يليه الفصل الرابع الذي يغطي عنصر كبس عجينة الزيتون، يتبع ذلك الفصل الخامس الذي تُعرض فيه معلومات عن خصائص عنصري الجرش والكبس اللذين تم مناقشتهما في الفصلين السابقين، ثم يأتي الفصل السادس بتلخيص عن تصنيف المواقع الأثرية في الإقليم وأنماط توزيعها، بينما يبحث الفصل السابع في إنتاج زيت الزيتون في الإقليم، ويُقدم تقديرًا لعدد سكانه لتقييم حجم الطلب المحلي لهذه السلعة، ويتيح هذا المقارنة بين إنتاج زيت في كيرينايكي وإقليم المدن الثلاث Tripolitania ومناطق البحر المتوسط الأخرى، ويستعرض الفصل الثامن أدلة الإنتاج المحلي للأمفورات (جرار نقل زيت الزيتون) والتجارة الخارجية، حيث يحدد هذا الفصل بُنية الطينة والأنواع المحلية المعروفة للأمفورات وتوزيع انتشارها داخل الإقليم وخارجه، إلى جانب التطرق للجرار الأخرى المستوردة، ثم يأتي في الختام الفصل التاسع الذي يستعرض أهم النتائج التي خلصت إليها الدراسة مع تقديم عدد من الاقتراحات لمزيد من البحث المستقبلي في اقتصاد ريف كيرينايكي واستيطانه. أما الجزء الثاني من الكتاب فيشتمل على بيانات إضافية ويقع في ملحقين، يحتوي الأول على جداول قياسات وأشكال توضيحية، بينما يعرض الثاني فهرس المواقع التي تم زيارتها.

إجمالًا، توضح الأدلة الجديدة المقدمة في هذا الكتاب إنتاج زراعي متزايد وفقًا لما تشير إليه بقايا المزارع المتخصصة في إنتاج زيت الزيتون، مما يعد إشارة إلى أن كلا من مراكز الحضر ومناطق الريف في الإقليم كانت مكتظة بالسكان بعد فترة طويلة من زمن سينيسيوس، لكن ذلك لم يواكبه إلا ازدهارًا اقتصاديًا متواضعًا. إن الاستنتاج الأساسي الذي تخلص إليه هذه الدراسة هو أن إنتاج زيت الزيتون قد اقتصر على الأسواق المحلية، على الرغم من أنه ربما كان هناك في بعض السنوات أنتاجًا فائضًا صُدر للأسواق الخارجية، وختامًا يمكن القول أن هذه الدراسة قد أدت بشكل كبير إلى إثراء معلوماتنا حول إنتاج زيت الزيتون في كيرينايكي.